Max L. Stackhouse

Creeds, Society, and Human Rights

A STUDY IN THREE CULTURES

WILLIAM B. EERDMANS PUBLISHING COMPANY

GRAND RAPIDS, MICHIGAN

This book is
dedicated to
the Seminarians
of
Andover Newton Theological School,
Das Sprachenkonvikt, and
United Theological College.
They taught me more than they know.

Library of Congress Cataloging in Publication Data
Stackhouse, Max L.
Creeds, society, and human rights.

1. Civil rights. 2. Social justice. 3. Social
ethics. 4. Ethics, Comparative. I. Title.
JC571.S775   1984   320'.01'1   84-10186

ISBN 0-8028-3599-6

Contents

Preface

"HUMAN RIGHTS" is such a small phrase to demand such a large book. But the full title of this work suggests the reason for its length. It is also a study in comparative religious ethics. I realize that many people do not think of human rights in the context of religion or on a cross-cultural basis. Many people think of human rights only when they feel that they want something or have a claim to something they are not getting. As Father Theo Steeman recently pointed out to me, most people are not aware that the struggle for human rights involves a program of reform for a great number of human structures in the direction of a humane global society. For this reason, human rights thinking demands of most of us a kind of conversion, a redefinition of basic perspectives. He is correct. It is for this reason that I have found it necessary to attach this discussion of human rights to some of the basic issues in religious ethics and to cross-cultural concerns. The issues are all the more important in the present American political context, for as I was working on this manuscript a more "nationalist" president—backed in part by newly vocal "evangelical" religious voices who show little sensitivity to historical, comparative, and social-structural issues in the formation of their moralism—reduced American accents on human rights in both domestic and foreign policy.

Indeed, some contemporary scholars are arguing that the directions of the present administration are threatening both the idea and the practices that could sustain human rights. Henry Shue, for example, has put the matter in very strong terms:

> The bizarre notion has been promulgated by the Reagan administration that each government should be allowed to pick and choose among established human rights its own favorites and attend exclusively to those favored rights. This attempt at selective enforcement of human rights is authorized by a formal policy memorandum adopted by the Department of State on Oct. 27, 1981, which states: " 'Human Rights'—meaning political . rights and civil liberties—conveys what is ultimately at issue in a contest with the Soviet bloc. The fundamental distinction is our respective attitudes toward freedom.

... We should move away from 'human rights' as a term, and begin to speak of 'individual rights,' 'political rights,' and 'civil liberties.' "

Such a narrowing of human rights to political rights and civil liberties would omit rights to physical security like the rights against torture and "disappearance" that are explicitly listed in the laws controlling U.S. foreign assistance. It also dismisses the third general category of internationally recognized human rights, the right to fulfillment of vital needs such as food, shelter, health care and education. The supposition seems to be that a nation can simply focus on the rights that are "at issue in a contest". . . . Human rights [in this view] . . . seem to be used as a means toward other ends.*

It may be that the present administration and many of those who are attracted to it for its apparent reliance on "religious values" have not recognized that such a treatment of human rights in fact undercuts both the deeper meanings of the term and, more dangerously, the most profour ᶫ religious fundaments on which they rest. If for no other reason than this, we must attend to the intimate relationship of human rights to religious creeds and the world's societies.

Human rights implies a universal conception of what is human and what is right. At present, human rights are not universal in either the sense that everyone believes in them or the sense that they are everywhere observed in social practice. Nevertheless, the phrase "human rights" implies a universal ethic which claims that they *ought* to be believed and observed everywhere by everyone. The central questions of this volume are these: What are the conceptual and social conditions which make such a universalistic ethic viable? What kinds of "creeds" and what kinds of social patterns support belief in and action upon universalistic values? What kinds of metaphysical-moral visions allow people to respond to human problems in economic, political, educational, familial, and other relations by cultivating a social order conducive to human rights? Such questions are, I found, especially difficult in an age of relativism. They forced me to take up the question of whether it is possible at all to remove the psychological, social, and cultural blinders we all wear.

In one way or another, these are the questions that have preoccupied me for more than a decade. For me, the problems were acute at the time of the Viet Nam crisis as they bore on war and peace. They also appeared in a different form as I became aware of the problems of urbanization—indeed, of the metropolitanization of the world. In both *The Ethics of Necropolis* and the more personally satisfying *Ethics and the Urban Ethos,* I tried to wrestle with these issues, as I also was forced to do while editing materials by Walter Rauschenbusch and James Luther Adams. In those studies and in this one, I became more and more convinced that certain theological-ethical categories could simultaneously open the door to universalistic ethical guidelines and assist historians, sociologists, and anthropologists in understanding the character and

*Henry Shue, "Playing Hardball with Human Rights," *Philosophy and Public Policy* (Nov. 1983), p. 9.

structure of complex social systems. My decision to spend three study leaves in India and to accept an ecumenical church assignment which would take me to the German Democratic Republic on three occasions was based in part upon a concern to find out whether theological-ethical categories could in fact do what I think they can do when confronted with deeply religious but nontheologically oriented societies. Readers, of course, will have to decide whether that concern has borne fruit.

It is a persistent conviction of mine that we must find appropriate tools to deal with complex social-ethical issues in a world that seems to get more complicated week by week. Most people don't think about large-scale social problems very much—not even as much as they speak of human rights. Many teachers of ethics and religious and political leaders seem to prefer to focus on more manageable issues such as premarital intercourse, conflicts of interests, or the cultivation of personal virtues. These are not false or trivial issues, but behavior on these significant moral issues is, I think, as much influenced by the general belief patterns and the characteristic modes of social practice in a civilization as it is by anything else. Unless the governing beliefs and dominant social-institutional fabric of a society are identified and assessed, we are unlikely either to understand what is going on around us or to be able to alter it. "Ethics" tends to become less a grasping and an implementation of universal values than a convenient adjustment to the cultural drifts in the society in which one lives, with "responsibility" defined by the current fads of the generation. In my view this is most irresponsible. The modern world is in the midst of a great Kulturkampf, a great struggle as to what principles and which groups will shape the future. Much, much hangs in the balance. Thus I am concerned that all who are called to leadership in ethical matters should attend to large-scale social problems in complex societies, even if this requires working through unfamiliar ways of thinking. Specifically, I am concerned that church leadership, those in principle committed to concerns beyond the practicalities of their own life, family, or society, should take up such questions as I am trying to address.

To aid the reader in digesting a book of this scope, I have made several decisions. In the first chapter I have tried to lay out in relatively brief compass the basic presuppositions and definitions which I found useful in treating three distinctive cultures over long periods of time and with reference to a number of sectors of these complex societies. Further, in presenting the materials from these several cultures in a limited study, I found that I had to make choices about how to interpret this or that aspect of one of the three societies, or this or that phase of cultural history. Specialists often have highly disputed readings of these matters. Rather than attempt to give every reason why I have chosen one interpretation of these things over another, I decided to use the footnotes as a kind of annotated bibliography. If a reader has serious doubts about my understanding of one thing or another, I think he or she would be able to find the arguments as to why I have chosen what I have in these texts.

I am indebted to many for help in preparing this book. Parts of this book were delivered as lectures at Andover Newton Theological School, Weston School of Theology, Illinois Wesleyan University, Vancouver School of Theology, the Society of Christian Ethics, the Society for the Scientific Study of Religion, and the American Academy of Religion. The United Church Board for World Ministries has generously supported my work and provided opportunities for me to do research in India and East Germany. Drs. Jane Cary Peck, Eleanor Mc-Laughlin, and Brian Hehir were helpful critics in regard to the Western sections of the manuscript. Christoph Schmauch and Robert Goeckel, as well as two G.D.R. scholars who prefer to remain unnamed, made several suggestions for revision of the section on East Germany and Marxism-Leninism. Drs. Somen Das, Christopher Duraisingh, Richard Taylor, and John Carman were of invaluable assistance in working through Indian materials. And Dr. Russell Chandran of Bangalore, India, Dr. Edmund Leites of the International Society for the Comparative Studies of Civilizations, Dr. James Luther Adams of Harvard, and Dr. Walter Muelder of Boston University read the entire manuscript in various stages of drafting, gave continual and sustaining support, and made innumerable useful suggestions. My inability to include all the rich suggestions they have made does not detract from the gratitude I feel.

In regard to the actual preparation of the manuscript, Deborah Perkins and Martha Rahte-Winchell typed drafts of particular chapters, and Kay Coughlin, the ever-dependable and pleasant faculty secretary of Andover Newton Theological School, exercised her usual patience in deciphering some of the manuscript revisions given to her. Mary Hietbrink, Roland Gunn, Douglas L. Clark, Chester R. Dziczek, William J. Fitzgerald, and Douglas Kries all gave invaluable help in final preparation of this material for publication. Every book, these people have demonstrated, is a team project. I am very grateful.

Max L. Stackhouse
Newton, Massachusetts
May 1983

CHAPTER ONE

Introduction:
Perspectives, Focus, and Methods

A. HUMAN RIGHTS AND DOCTRINE

IN the current debates about human rights, the Judeo-Christian traditions of the West confront one of the greatest challenges of the modern age. Appeals to human rights appear on all sides, with claims and counterclaims debated in congresses and caucuses, in voluntary associations and international arenas, in law schools and union halls, in doctor-patient relations and in liberation movements.

In all these settings we find an emerging, if still ambiguous, metaphysical-moral vision of what is sacred, inviolable, and absolute in human affairs. The ambiguity entails numerous debates about the true nature of freedom, justice, and democracy; about what demands persons may properly make on other persons or on society; about what claims groups may make on persons or on society as a whole; and about what claims societies may make on persons or groups. In brief, the current surge of concern for human rights represents the potential development of a universal "doctrine" about humanity in community, implying a social ethic. Contained in this doctrine is the implicit assertion that certain principles are true and valid for all peoples, in all societies, under all conditions of economic, political, ethnic, and cultural life. Further, human rights implies that these principles are somehow present in the very fact of our common humanity, properly understood.

The rise of this doctrine—still fragile and obscure on many points—represents a modest revolution against much of the treasured wisdom of modernity. It entails a set of ideas that do not easily lend themselves to ordinary divisions of "liberal" and "conservative." It is at once seriously reactive against many modern trends toward relativism and profoundly progressive in its demand to care for the weak and the oppressed. It directly opposes ideas of morality derived from the calculation of social utility. It is in conflict with "social contract" theories which view morality as a construction of parties joining together for mutually rewarding ends. The emerging notions of human rights go against the

1

grain of evolutionary theories which accent the changing character of norms for behavior, with the view that different norms must be devised for each stage of development. And human rights inject doubt into those views of natural law which presume an inevitable hierarchy of some people over others.

Little consensus yet exists as to the basis of this emerging doctrine. In some circles, widespread skepticism abounds regarding its nature, its roots, and its specific content. More cynical observers see human rights as an ideological weapon by which they can win rhetorical battles in international diplomacy for political advantage. Some skeptics see the "Western" calls for human rights as a shrewd move by which one group can impose ideas emerging out of its history onto other cultures—a new kind of ethnocentrism. Frequently these critics note how selectively human rights concerns are applied—often giving way to geopolitical interests. No one can deny that these elements are present in much of the public debate.

But these views, I believe, are wrong in the final analysis. At the core of contemporary appeals to human rights is a very fundamental religious, philosophical, and sociopolitical assertion which transcends these distorted and limited uses of it. Human rights implies, above all, that there is a universal moral order under which all peoples and societies live. Here is a doctrine of a very high order.

The question is whether this *doctrine* should become a *creed*. A *doctrine* is a teaching, claim, or assertion; a *creed* is a doctrine held to be true, embraced with commitment, celebrated in concert with others, and used as a fundamental guide for action.

Among philosophical and political thinkers and in society generally, doctrines rise and fall with amazing rapidity. Those doctrines which make universal claims, which become adopted as creed, and which become institutionalized, however, more frequently develop slowly. They are modified and refined in multiple debates and under multiple social pressures. When they do become pervasive, they are called "religious." They shape civilizations in a fundamental way. The shift from doctrine to creed is not always dramatic; it happens when the presuppositions of a doctrine become a part of the deeply believed assumptions of a people and become built into the fabric of a society's institutions.[1] If human rights become a pervasive creed, a matter of religion, they will threaten much of what many ordinarily understand as religion.

Specifically this emerging doctrine of human rights presents challenges to some aspects of conventional Christian tradition. In the first place, human rights represents a belief about what is sacred in human relations and the pattern of civilization. The doctrine of human rights did not emerge in a mystical experience or a single dramatic revelation. This doctrine has emerged partially from within and partially from outside the beliefs of the biblically rooted orientations. The language of discourse about "human rights" is foreign to many religious groups. In many respects it is a postbiblical development. Many parts of the Western religious traditions are very ambiguous as to what they think about the religious import of certain political, economic, social, and cultural "rights."[2]

Particularly those Christian groups which have denied the authority of any post-biblical traditions find human rights claims to be a great problem. Yet over the course of several centuries the vocabulary of rights has become a chief vehicle for religious and ethical discourse in specific minority traditions. If the biblically based religious communities of the West are to maintain the kind of social-ethical leadership and prophetic witness which they have, at their best, demonstrated in the past, they must undertake a clear assessment of rights. In order to do that, they need a renewed appreciation of "tradition."

In the second place, the current discussions about human rights are not at all clear about the meaning of the term "human." Implied in all the debates about human rights are underlying assumptions regarding what being human actually entails. On this point the Judeo-Christian traditions have, to varying degrees, been clear, consistent, and ecumenical.

The Judeo-Christian traditions, whatever their manifold disagreements on many other points, have held that humans are creatures, made in the image of God, who have betrayed that dignity, sinners in need of salvation, recipients of God's loving care and mercy, a combination of *both* body and spirit who live in history, capable with God's help of making moral choices, and called to responsible living in community. This understanding of humanity, with all its elaborations, implications, and nuances, is clearly one of the most profound understandings of humanity ever developed. It has become pervasive in the West, even among those who are not overtly Christian.

It is precisely this view of humanity that is under attack in the twentieth century from both within and beyond the West. Indeed, the Kulturkampf on this point is of major proportions. On the one hand, "holistic," "spiritualistic," and "gnostic" understandings of humanity which focus on the finding, cultivation, and release of inner transcendental powers as the clue to true humanity are challenging the Judeo-Christian understandings of humanity from the standpoints of both Eastern religious and some modern psychologies. On the other hand, the materialist, rationalistic, anti-transcendental perspectives on humanity of Marxism-Leninism (as well as much secular Western philosophy and social science) challenge major assumptions of the Judeo-Christian perspective from another side. Both of these perspectives have very powerful understandings of humanity and human nature. Each of these contains elements which commend them to our minds and hearts. They are not nonsense or empty of moral worth. Yet each of these—when worked out as creed in society—directly threatens Christian views of both human nature and human rights. If we are to embrace a *fundamental* understanding of humanity and thereby give a rooted content to human rights that is genuinely universal, we must work out our creeds fully aware of the strongest alternatives to our own positions.

B. HUMAN RIGHTS AND MEMBERSHIP

The third way in which the emerging social ethic of human rights presents a challenge to the Judeo-Christian traditions is institutional. With regard to the definition of rights and the understanding of what is basically human, we are dealing with those aspects of *credo* that have to do with deep convictions and beliefs. Persons demand beliefs; societies need convictions; and civilizations require a basic social-ethical vision by which to guide behavior. A creed is an indispensable part of human existence. Just as surely each creed is sustained and implemented accordingly as it is lived out by groups of people who take it as a basis for structuring their life together. Not all doctrines or creeds make a social difference. People have believed all sorts of things about rights and humanity, but these beliefs have been socially and historically important only when they have become the basis for social bonding and action, forming a sustained movement and affecting surrounding social institutions.

In the West the most important movement bonding around a creed has been the church. Empires, kings, nations, tribes, clans, and dynasties have come and gone. Political powers and economic structures and family patterns—each of which has been held to be the absolute center of civilization—have risen to dominance and have decayed or been overthrown. But the church, forever claiming indisputable and God-given rights to its own existence, and perennially reasserting its basic understandings of what it means to be human—even with all the dress and colorings of various epochs and seasons—has been a continuing center for social bonding around its creed. This has had a tremendous impact on the shape of Western civilizations, for it has meant (among other things) that a distinctive kind of "social space"[3] has been created in Western societies: a social arena partially dependent on, but also partially independent of, political and familial authority or specific economic structure. There exists, in the West, an institutionalized "space" for human solidarity and bonding that allows in principle a *credo* to develop and be critiqued, revised, and lived out (more or less) in the midst of history. Whatever its frailties, however much it has failed to provide moral leadership in this or that crisis, however frequent the stupidity of church leadership, the tenacious existence of the church has had a major structural impact on human rights.

The social space defended by the church over the centuries has now broadened to allow a wider range of "voluntary associations," interest groups, dissent committees, experimental associations, opposition parties, and "private assemblies." This is of considerable importance in human rights discussions, for it is precisely in these organizations that the competing doctrines of human rights are hammered out, and it is from these centers that governmental policies, economic structures, and familial and personal understandings are influenced. Where the space for these organizations is constricted, torture, political imprisonment, economic deprivation, intellectual and cultural constraint, and religious repression dominate and dehumanize life.

The importance of this social space will become more apparent later in this volume when we undertake a comparative analysis of an Eastern society and a Marxist society. For in one we shall see the overwhelming institutional power of an elaborately extended family and kinship pattern as the decisive basis for social bonding, according to "caste," rooted in an Eastern belief about what rights are and what it means to be human. And in the other we will encounter a political party, with a monopoly on government, as the guardian of a creed which officially defines both "humanity" and "rights." In these societies, to live outside a prescribed family pattern or beyond the prescriptions of the political party is to live a very precarious existence. There is little "social space" for membership and communal life beyond kinship and *polis*.

It seems to me that the primary importance of this institutional dimension of human rights is missing in much of the current literature on human rights. Such an omission has led many authors to accent the ideals and principles of human rights without giving attention to their institutional underpinnings. It has also led many observers to hold that the decisive disputes about human rights are between the Western "individualist" views and the more "collectivist" definitions of socialist ideologies.[4] Substantive issues are sometimes involved in such distinctions. It makes a considerable difference whether we view the whole (the species) as the sum of the parts and thus reducible to the parts, or whether we hold the whole to be more than the sum of the parts and thus able to destroy a part for the sake of the whole (or demand the absorption of a part in the whole without remainder). At the institutional level, however, no social system is simply individualistic or purely collectivistic. At this level the question is not one of individualism versus collectivism but one of *membership*. To be a member is to be an individual in a social relationship, in a kind of solidarity with others. On what basis are persons to be included or excluded from community? How extensive should particular communities be, so that they can displace, influence, or control other memberships? What kinds of solidarity are to be permitted or denied? What are the legitimate patterns of participation, of living together, of belonging? What *social* relationships are constitutive of *individual* dignity?

At the institutional level, human rights have to do with the basic and universal questions of membership—and the social spaces which allow varieties of membership and participation, each with a distinctive view of individuation to be expressed. In both "bourgeois" and "anti-bourgeois" societies, human rights have to do with the groups to which one may belong, with whom one may associate for concerted action, with what organizations may form, with how groups may influence individuals or the whole society (or defend them against other groups and social forces), with what social behaviors are to be judged reprehensible or criminal, and with what categories are used to assess human privileges and responsibilities. At present, widely believed theories of human rights directly challenge Christian views of membership at the institutional level. We shall treat this matter at some length as we proceed.

In any case, the starting point for this study may be clear by now. I begin with the assumption that human rights discussions and human rights action must proceed at two levels. The first is at the basic level of doctrine in the quest for definition of "rights" and "human" to which we may become creedally committed; the second is at the level of social structure—specifically regarding the social space that is available for human membership, and the concrete practices of inclusion and exclusion. Between creed and the structure of social membership, human rights as a living norm is hammered out.

C. HUMAN RIGHTS AS RELIGIOUS ETHICS

Because human rights involves both a question of creed and a question of social membership, human rights is essentially a matter of religious ethics. Religion, after all, has to do with commitments to ultimate meanings *and* with the concrete formation of ritual behaviors, loyalties, solidarities, and relationships. Various religious ethics identify certain ultimate meanings and certain relationships as holy, or sacred. These may not be violated under penalty of the loss of meaning and the breaking of membership. When that happens, life becomes dehumanized by chaos, isolation, and tyranny. On the basis of ultimate meanings and concrete relationships, all religions set forth a social ethic—a more or less coherent set of moral guides about what is right and wrong, good and evil, fitting and unfitting—to prevent chaos, alienation, and tyranny. All this is rooted in a fundamental sense of what is holy, in a metaphysical-moral vision of what is "really real."

Claims about human rights are religious in this sense: each view of human rights entails an ultimate metaphysical-moral vision about what is meaningful, about what relationships or memberships are sacrosanct, and what social ethic should be followed in order to prevent chaos, social alienation, and tyranny from destroying essential humanity. Because human rights claims and movements are religious in this sense, and exist both within and without the major world faiths, it is important for the world's religions to come to terms with human rights. Human rights as a religious-ethical orientation claims to have universal implications. How can, how ought *this* religious ethic be assessed by the world's religions?

It could be argued, of course, that the modern ideas of human rights are not related to religion at all, but are a product of quite different forces. It has become common today to attribute human rights concerns to "postreligious" philosophy and/or the necessities of power politics.[5] Is it not the case that nonreligious philosophers and political activists struggle with human rights issues while millions of religious people seem unconcerned? There is no doubt that philosophers and politicians have treated human rights in a number of ways.[6] Nevertheless, their proposals have gained historic importance only when one of two conditions has existed: when the ethos in which they live has accepted as a matter of creed that their concerns are valid; or when their ideas have been selectively included in religion, taken up by religion, or organized into a religious system—that is, made a matter of public creed and given an institutional form. The reason for this is quite simple: philosophy has an elaborate and articulate body of thought—indispensable in dealing with any doctrine—but it distrusts commitment beyond intellectual certitude. However, nothing is absolutely certain at any given moment; philosophy demands doubt. It thus can develop no committed constituency or institutional form. Politics lives by commitments and organized constituencies to structure its power, but has no inherent body of belief. In the final analysis, coercive power, not thought, is a medium of purely political activity. Only religion can transform doctrine into creed and evoke committed membership without coercion in a fundamental way.[7] The matter can be put another way. Philosophy can help refine definitions of what is human and what is right, but philosophy is concerned with conceptual understanding and knowledge, not with institutionalization. Politics is concerned with institutionalization, but politics institutionalizes *civil* rights which change as the political system changes. Politics focuses on what is to be granted in a regime. Human rights are broader than politics in reach; they stand beyond and legitimate or critique any definition of civil rights. Religious ethics grasps this transcendent element and makes it present in social life.

Others, of course, see human rights as a matter of law.[8] Much of what already has developed and much of what will develop from human rights discussions is directly related to the institutionalized patterns of law—in constitutions, in treaties, in procedures, and in jurisprudence—and is properly discussed in legal terms. But two prior questions are more important. One is, what doctrines of human rights ought to be so institutionalized? And the other is, what are the limits of law itself? It is human rights as religious ethics, defined by the interaction of creed and bonded membership, which will determine what areas of life must be protected *by* law and which ones are such that they must be protected *from* law, if human rights are to be secured.

In recent intellectual history it has been argued that *basic* human rights are not rooted in religion, philosophy, politics, or law at all. Instead, they are rooted in very empirical biophysical needs.[9] In this view human rights talk is actually an elaborate cultural and idealistic way of speaking of what is necessary for biophysical survival—at least food, shelter, and sex. The struggle for survival is a natural drive which cannot be denied. Indeed, one could say that material needs are holy—they are what makes humans whole and they are inviolable; they are awesome in their power and to them we must be obedient. Whatever denies them must be altered.

Such ideas seem so obvious to so many today that we forget how rare such views have been in human history, how rooted in debatable assumptions, and how close they are in character to religious assertions (even when held in opposition to most traditional religions). It is so manifestly clear that everyone who is hungry or shelterless knows such urgent needs that the biophysical arguments seem immediately compelling as clues to what it means to be human and what human rights might be. And social survival lasts but one generation without sex. But that these needs *ought* to be met; that they should be met *as a matter of social duty*; and that they should be met *for all*, whatever the condition of age, strength, health, or status, entail a range of ideas that has been not at all obvious to philosophy, politics, law, natural law theory, or, for that matter, the biological sciences themselves. Notions of biophysical drives and needs for survival have given rise more often to doctrines of competition, of the "law of bloody tooth and claw," of destruction of the weak, of exclusive meeting of these needs for "our" kind, than to doctrines of human rights. Such notions also neglect certain needs which humans have as civilized beings. Seldom do biological perspectives speak of needs for education, legal procedures, art, or even medical care.

The idea that material needs ought to be met for all humans becomes powerful only when "survival" is taken up by a religious movement. Then survival is put in the context of wider needs for civilization and meaning. Only some religions take up such questions. Only in those societies informed by a creed where such questions are central do we find a focus on hunger, shelter, and sexuality as matters of urgent concern among those not suffering directly from their absence. Then such questions are placed in a context of the quality of life, not only the quantity of life. Only some religions affirm moral meaning beyond the competition for survival and yet see the meeting of biophysical needs as a matter of spiritual duty for all humanity.[10]

Over the long history of Western ethics, numerous authors have attempted to combine a concern for law and a concern for nature through a series of concepts of "natural law." This long tradition resists efforts to treat basic matters of ethics, such as justice, equity, or human rights, as "religious." Reason, it is argued, is a sufficient basis for knowing the natural law, which in turn informs politics, jurisprudence, and the way we understand the moral meaning of the biophysical order. In this view religion is "transrational," a "privileged" special and particular orientation known only to the recipients of a specific tradition or a special revelation. By definition it is not universal in import, whereas reason is a universally distinguishing feature of humankind which allows all to know what is right for humans.[11]

The theory of natural law has come under increased criticism in modern thought. Whole libraries have been written on this concept. We shall return to these ideas in the course of this study; at this juncture the point I want to make is a simple one, but, I believe, telling: *All natural-law theories rest on a faith assumption.* Natural law presupposes that there is a normative, objective, moral order in the universe and that it can be known by unaided (not revealed) human reason. This presumption is, I think, religious in character—profoundly so. Where this religious assumption is not maintained, natural-law theory fades and reason does not lead us to universal moral principles such as those taken up by human rights concerns. The ironic fact, however, is that where natural law is taken up as a religious concern, reason also is seen as integral to "true" religion. The divorce between ethics and rationality on one side and religion and commitment on the other is overcome. Faith and reason are both seen as guides to what is universally and distinctively human, the proper basis of rights.

Without question, however, any discussion of human rights as a feature of religious ethics will have to accent those fundamental presuppositions which are taken up by philosophy, politics, law, the biophysical sciences, and natural-law theory—as well as by other aspects of social life—for it is precisely as fundamental notions about what is holy become incorporated in the so-called secular areas of life that they become decisive for the social system. It is often through these areas of life that we can see the social-ethical outworking of religion.

Not all religion is relevant to human rights. Some religion resists any overt connection with philosophy, politics, law, material needs, and natural law. For purposes of this study of human rights, such religions are irrelevant. Further, some religions have openly violated human rights by identifying something as holy and inviolable which induces chaos or promotes tyranny. When that happens, various movements bearing the flag of philosophy or politics or law or science or natural law have surfaced—reasserting human values, demanding recognition of basic needs, and forming specific groupings dedicated to living out a doctrine more universal than that of the religion they reject. They in effect insist that something holy is being violated and that only by recovery of a profound social ethic in thought and social fabric can dehumanization be avoided. Advocacy of human rights in this fashion is in fact a religious attempt to go beyond specific religions. It transforms an "antidoctrine" into a new creed. Properly understood, it is not, however, the denial of religion as such, but a respecification of what is holy. It says, in effect, not *that* but *this* is what is holy and must become the basis of philosophy, politics, law, and the rest. The new doctrine is held with religious zeal as a religious creed.

All of the positions to be discussed in this book are, in this broad sense, religious. We shall look first and most extensively at human rights in the West, where specific strands of the Christian traditions can be shown to be foundational for American understandings of human rights. We shall do so in some detail, for it is precisely in the West where the loss of awareness of the religious heritage that shaped human rights threatens the foundations of a viable social ethic. The blindness of much of the world to the religious roots of human rights in the West also means that claims from the West are often misperceived. We shall then compare and contrast these Western views with those of the German Democratic Republic, perhaps (with the Soviet Union) the most orthodox Marxist-Leninist country in the world. And, finally, we shall turn to India—the world's largest democracy, with socialism as a part of its constitution, and with its deepest spiritual roots in Hinduism, mother of many Asian religions.

It may seem strange to some that I treat Marxism as a religious ethic, but it should not. Communism is a world faith, having a very articulate definition of the "human," of "rights," and a concrete bonding of groups in societies to carry out its moral vision and its understanding of what is holy and inviolable. It is a doctrine that has become a creed, sustained by a remarkable body of believers. Even in its origins it was religious in this broad and fundamental sense. Robert Tucker recognized this some time ago when he wrote:

> In general, [those] . . . who create myths or religious conceptions of reality are moralists in the sense in which this term has been used here. They may in fact be obsessed with a moral vision of reality, a vision of the world as an arena of conflict between good and evil forces. . . . They are passionately committed persons. . . . It is to this class of minds . . . that Karl Marx's belong[s].

> The religious essence of Marxism is superficially obscured by Marx's rejection of the traditional religions. This took the form of a repudiation of 'religion' as such and an espousal of 'atheism'. . . . [But] denial of the transmundane God was merely a negative way of asserting that 'man' should be regarded as the supreme being or object of ultimate concern. Thus his atheism was a positive religious proposition.[12]

In any case, to focus on human rights in terms of religion is not, given the dominant forms of modern academic study and public discourse, a conventional way of dealing with the whole matter. Yet a primary purpose of this book will be to show that such an unconventional approach in fact grasps the many dimensions and implications of human rights more accurately than most current treatments.

D. THREE RELIGIONS

As already indicated, this book will look at questions of human rights in terms of three world religions: Christianity, Marxism, and Hinduism. There are several reasons for these choices—beyond the facts of personal interest and opportunity.

One reason for choosing these three relates to the recent history of human rights in the public sphere. The modern political discussion of human rights got its greatest impetus from the reaction to Hitler and his allies. The Fascist movement in Europe and Asia threatened all that those concerned about human rights held to be most dear. The war against Fascism was a religious war. The Nazis denied the fundamental tenets of the dominant faiths in the world; they denied that humanity was one. Hitler's special target in the West, the Jews, claimed in an explicitly religious way that there is one holy and ethical reality under which all peoples and nations stand and by which they are to be judged. Their claim symbolized the problem for all humanity. Hitler denied that claim with guns, tanks, and gas chambers.

In West Berlin a statue of Wagner that was built during the Nazi period still stands opposite the ruins of Axis buildings. Wagner sits on a throne surrounded by symbolic representations of the genius of the Germanic spirit, a spirit he immortalized in music. At the foot of the statue stands a boy with a slingshot and a harp, pointing up to Wagner—clearly indicating that the spirit of a particular people had displaced the more universal, religious Spirit of the psalmist. World War II was about this displacement of the Spirit. The three great world faiths that had universal visions for humanity—Christianity, Marxism, and Hinduism—rallied to defeat that demonic spirit. Whatever the complicity of the Christian churches in the rise of Fascism, whatever the travesties of the Hitler-Stalin pact, whatever the racism of Aryan Hindus, the struggle against "National Socialism" was a religious and inevitable one in which these three cultures cooperated.

After the war the United Nations was formed to develop a basis from which to prevent such travesties from ever happening again, and an extensive process was begun to set forth a basic declaration on human rights. That United Nations and that process were dominated by Christian, Marxist, and Hindu representatives who had to rely on the first principles of their creeds in the tough negotiations. The result is the opening of a new chapter of human rights discussion.

Very quickly, however, the apparent agreement began to dissipate. The world became divided into three camps: the "free world," led by the United States, which claimed Judeo-Christian values as the basis for its democratic creed; the Warsaw Pact countries, led by the Soviet Union and followed by the German Democratic Republic, which adhered most closely to Marxist-Leninist doctrine; and the developing countries, led for decades by India in the international arena, which often chided both the first two groups for abandoning spiritual principles. In all areas, however, questions of human rights were not settled.

In 1970 the World Alliance of Reformed Churches met in Nairobi, Kenya, and issued a mandate for a study of the theological basis of human rights.[13] Andrew Young, a young minister who was a disciple of Martin Luther King, Jr., was drawn into this study. And when he became a chief advocate of an overtly Christian candidate for the U.S. presidency, Jimmy Carter, the language of human rights became a part of lively political rhetoric.

In 1973, while I was first in India, the debates erupted there which eventually led to the "Emergency" declared by Prime Minister Indira Gandhi. The debates took the form of a struggle between the judiciary and political leadership. Mrs. Gandhi tried to amend the constitution so that the judiciary would be under the control of political authorities, and thereby amenable to political priorities. I was drawn into several discussions with religious, political, and philosophical leaders as to whether the provisions for rights in the Indian constitution, defended vigorously by some "strict constructionists" in the judiciary, were a matter of basic human rights or merely a reflection of a non-Indian import. Did they meet the growing needs of the burgeoning population? This power struggle involved questions of political ideology and expediency; it also involved questions of the feasibility of borrowing certain concepts of human rights from Western and socialist models. Had India imported something that was intrinsically incompatible with and basically irrelevant to the Indian setting? Were social and political ideas of human rights pertinent to a developing nation facing poverty and want? I traveled to India a second time, during the Emergency. This time I was also drawn into the discussion of human rights—

in concern for political prisoners, censorship of the press, limitations on unions, and so forth. In these discussions Christian theologians connected with the Christian Institute for the Study of Religion and Society and several Marxists attached to the *Marxist Review* (Calcutta) were among the most articulate and outspoken interpreters of the situation. During both excursions the depth and power of Hindu thought—even among those who were non-Hindu and those who were Hindu in background but not necessarily religious in terms of daily practice—forced me to reconsider the fundamental possibilities for human rights in this religiosocial tradition. How were the possibilities different from those in the Western and socialist traditions?

I also traveled three times to the German Democratic Republic as a participant in an ecumenical church exchange. East Germany has been, of course, the scene of two great revolutions in world history: the Lutheran Reformation that shaped much of European history, and the orthodox Marxist-Leninist revolution under the influence of the Soviet occupation. My first visit took place soon after the Helsinki Accords were completed. These agreements finalized a series of border disputes left over from World War II, and called for greater economic, social, and cultural exchange between North Atlantic and Eastern European nations. At the insistence of some Western negotiators, these agreements also included "Basket Three"—dealing with human rights.[14] Everywhere I went in the G.D.R. I was bombarded with questions about what Americans, what Christians in the West, what scholars and politicians were thinking about human rights. In church circles the questions were even more intense, for notable religious leaders there had also undertaken study projects focusing on the theological foundations of human rights, comparing and finding compatible Lutheran and Marxist understandings,[15] both apparently at odds with some principles of Helsinki.

My most recent visit (1983) occurred during the sharp international debates about the installation of new nuclear rockets in NATO countries. The fear and hostility were pervasive, especially in official circles. But unofficial peace groups, most frequently connected with or taking form under the protective shelter of the churches, and meeting in a semi-clandestine way, were raising new questions about human rights. The young people gathered in the three peace groups whose meetings I attended see the increased tensions between East and West as the ultimate threat to their human rights; but they repeatedly expressed most intense and persistent hostility toward the lesser and more proximate threats. That is, however strong their commitment to peace and to forming a moral consensus against the NATO rockets, they were more frustrated by the fact that they could not form their own peace groups openly, could not propagate their views in public, and were harassed or arrested if they attempted to wear badges or insignias bearing the symbols of "Swords into Ploughshares." They felt their human rights to be doubly threatened.[16]

In brief, comparing Western notions of human rights to the ones of these two societies may also provide somewhat representative and fascinating points of reference. India—as mother of both Hinduism and Buddhism, and as the civilization socially embodying a religious, philosophical, and social world-view that has existed longer, with fewer dramatic changes, than any other great civilization—represents a major option for a social creed. Through the influence of the Hindu Renaissance, that movement of great consequence in the late nineteenth and twentieth century sparked by the Indians' contact with Western Christian, Liberal, and Marxist ideas (which we will discuss later), India began renewing itself precisely when major social shifts were occurring in the United States and Eastern Europe.

East Germany, so close to the West in many ways yet more deeply affected by the Lutheran and Marxist revolutions than perhaps any other Western country, is also a viable touchstone for comparative analysis. The profound poverty and destruction East Germany suffered during World War I, compounded by World War II and its aftermath, has been followed by a dynamic vigor in economic, political, and cultural life. East Germany is a model of a relatively complete and relatively successful attempt to reorganize life and thought on orthodox socialist principles.

By comparing Western notions of human rights and their social forms to one of the oldest and most complex civilizations in the developing world and to one of the newest and most vigorous Marxist societies, we will have a fair test of how such ideas relate to the so-called "first," "second," and "third" worlds.

I also have another motivation for making these comparisons. I teach in a Christian seminary, and in the last two decades my students have felt deeply ambiguous about several features of Western religion, ethics, and society. Part of their ambiguity derives from ignorance of what presuppositions have in fact shaped their world. They have been taught in universities by secular professors who have seldom been concerned with the influence of religion in history. Consequently the students don't have a firm basis for interpreting what they experience and believe. They ask what other, non-Western perspectives have to offer. Students have at times turned to Eastern religions and to Marxism to find the leverage for a moral and spiritual perspective on their own traditions. On a given day certain candidates for the clergy may practice Transcendental Meditation or yoga and participate in a demonstration to support liberation movements around the world. In their studies they may pore over both the *Bhagavad Gita* and *Das Kapital,* as well as Calvin's *Institutes* and Thomas's *Summa.* Even when they do not become so intentional in their work, they often hold ideas that are spiritualistic or "gnostic" about religion, as is Hinduism, and historicist or materialistic about society, as is Marxism. In their work as ministers, people who believe in the transmigration of the soul (one aspect of Hinduism) or in the determination of societal development by technological and economic development (one version of Marxism) are confronted with great frequency. Many laypeople also have numerous questions about the "evangelical" forms of Hinduism, such as Hare Krishna, and the new discussions among some theologians of "Liberation," which contains heavy doses of Marxism. By these comparative excursions I hope to prepare myself and them for a discerning look at cross-cultural values.

E. THE METHODS OF STUDY

If, then, we intend to look at human rights as a matter of religious ethics shaped on one side by doctrine and creed and on the other by questions of the social structures of membership, how shall we pursue the comparative study of the world faiths which give human rights different contours and accents?[17] I propose to use three related methods: the longitudinal, the cross-sectional, and the evaluational.

1. The *longitudinal* method is primarily historical. That is, it traces the development of our subject matter through its influences from the past. Longitudinal study as developed here is not necessarily what historians do, although it is fundamentally dependent on what historians have done. A longitudinal study in the sense used here attempts to trace the development of major themes by selecting those particular "deep trajectories" of thought and social movement which have become institutionalized in subsequent intellectual and social life so that they form a stratum of human presupposition and habit of which people are not always fully conscious.

Historians, as I understand their craft, attempt to understand the movements and ideas of a period on its own terms and in terms of the previous forces and contemporary influences which caused them. A longitudinal study is less concerned with the intentions of various authors or the various causes that produced certain trends and is more interested in what consequences ideas and social patterns had—often quite beyond the intentions of the authors or the origins of various movements. A historian might ask about Abraham Lincoln, for example, what the facts of his life were, what currents of thought and what sociocultural factors influenced him, what he himself intended, and how he is to be understood in the context of his times. A longitudinalist, on the other hand, might ask what the consequences of his life and thought were for the modern condition of Black-White relationships in America. A longitudinalist keeps contemporary questions in the foreground and *uses* the results of historians' work for overtly contemporary purposes. Questions that may well have been of paramount importance for understanding Lincoln's own self-conception or the epoch in which Lincoln lived and worked may not be of much significance at all in a longitudinal treatment, except as they shape the trajectories of historical development which have determined deeply embedded traditions which have direct importance today.

Longitudinal analysis is as much like depth psychiatry, in one respect, as it is like history. When a person confronts a conflict, problem, or crisis that prevents healthy living in the present and constructive steps toward the future, it is often necessary to return to those creative, or destructive, emotionally laden moments of the past which have brought about the immediate contradictions.

Not everything from the past, however true, is pertinent. An in-depth psychological analysis is not a historical biography; it is highly selective. So, too, is a longitudinal analysis in large-scale civilizational conflicts, such as the ones about human rights. Drawing upon the memories kept alive by careful historians, a longitudinal effort attempts to identify those decisive moments of crisis and creativity from the past which have so shaped the deep trajectories of social-ethical life that they are still present, even if in unrecognized forms. We can deal creatively with the present and future only by recalling these moments, lifting them into consciousness, identifying analogies, tensions, and conflicts, and wrestling with them once more.[18]

Because of the nature of the human rights questions, much of our longitudinal analysis will be religious. If religion is the clue to human rights, as I have already suggested, then failures in the areas of human rights may be religious failures. And if we are to construct today a viable vision of and program for the realization of human rights, we are likely to have to wrestle once more with some of the fundamental religious questions from divergent traditions of the past that leave us divided in our creeds and in our societies about the nature, meaning, and structures of human rights.

To deal with religious matters longitudinally is not a characteristically Protestant way of addressing social issues—at least not one consciously employed. Many Protestants, and many others influenced by Protestant traditions, hold that only two points of reference count in dealing with moral and social issues: namely, the immediate problem and the immediately authoritative religious teaching. Karl Barth once announced that the resources for preaching could be found by having the newspaper in one hand and the Bible in the other. The methods employed in this volume are quite distinct from those he suggests. Indeed, the work of Barth is far more dependent on tradition, both in theology and social analysis, than his own image admits. Specifically, the longitudinal concerns developed here will suggest that both the understanding of society and the understanding of authoritative teaching are rooted in long-term developments decisive for contemporary life, which can be accurately perceived only if we are aware of those perennial options that confront humanity and the specific social and intellectual contexts by which we, often unwittingly, perceive both religions and civilizational structures. In the grinding confrontation of perennial options, the glasses by which we view ideas and societies are polished. Only by seeing how our glasses are ground can we correct our own myopias. Investigation of the comparative spectacles of cultures requires awareness of tradition. Thus this effort is, in part, a corrective to the constitutional blindness of modern, Western thought to tradition—a blindness brought about by some Protestant and Enlightenment influence.

2. Beyond the longitudinal analysis, although interlocked with it at many points, is the *cross-sectional* method. Cross-sectional analysis attempts to identify the dominant structures in a given culture. It takes a slice out of time, as it were, and looks at it sideways. As a longitudinal analysis is like theater or film,

cross-sectional study is like still photography or portraiture: it attempts to concentrate on the chief contours of enduringly significant patterns as they are present in a specific time.[19]

Cross-sectional interpretations of society present a major problem when comparative materials are under scrutiny. Each culture understands itself in its own terms, and each feels itself misunderstood if the categories from another culture are used to portray it. Western societies, Marxist countries, and Eastern civilizations have their own ways of interpreting doctrines and creeds, membership, the decisive institutions, social forces and social spaces, and human rights. These grow out of the deep trajectories of their past. To develop a single set of categories to treat these various traditions runs the risk of an insidious cultural imperialism. Yet merely to present each on its own terms prevents us from making clear, normative comparisons and contrasts. We gain very little fundamental understanding of what is universal about human rights by merely pointing out that every culture does things differently. The question is whether some set of categories can be developed for cross-sectional analysis which is sufficiently comprehensive, not unduly biased toward one arbitrary set of values yet open to comparative normative judgment.

Surely it is not nonsense to quest for such general categories. Study of or travel in other cultures immediately reveals a simple but profound fact: whether German or Indian, whether Marxist or Hindu, people are human. Everywhere they fall in love, suffer, rear children, work, eat, try to stay out of trouble, worry about their health, seek some control over their environments, sing, play, weep, organize social systems, participate in various rites and festivals, and face death. It is hardly remarkable that when I, an American WASP professor, conversed through a translator with a Hindu outcaste, a leper who was poverty-stricken and illiterate, the conversation made sense. The word "humanity" conveys something real. The question is how to chart out both descriptively and normatively the decisive contours of what that means.

I had been fretting about this problem for some time before beginning this particular study. I found that most of the great social theorists agreed that *every* people had to address certain unavoidable social needs. These *social* needs represent simultaneously the expression of human relatedness, the functional requirements of civilization, an indication of common features of the human spirit, and a way of shaping social mechanisms to define and meet the most important aspects of human nature. Each civilization, of course, meets these needs differently. Each civilization is affected by its peculiar religious and sociopolitical commitments, and by its particular sociohistorical background. But even with these differences, certain *constant* features of human societies can be identified cross-culturally which point to major elements, at least, of human nature. In exploring these constancies on theoretical grounds, I developed a "map" for the analysis of complex civilizations.[20] I have used this analytical map in my teaching for the past several years, and it has helped my students clarify the social implications of the ethical claims of various religious-philosophical traditions. I had it in mind as I encountered these other traditions and societies, and I began to use it as a tool for sorting out experiences in cross-cultural analysis. I have subsequently found that the main contours of this theoretical work have also been confirmed by independent empirical work in comparative anthropology.[21]

Although it may take some readers onto ground where they would rather not tread, I think it important to explain at the outset the tools which I am using to shape my cross-sectional analysis of these three cultures.

How is the map formed? First, because every society is formed within the interaction of its biophysical environment and its mythological or creedal assumptions, the north end of the map is tagged "Mythos Boundary," and the south end "Biophysical Boundary." Second, each society is shaped by its relationship to other societies beyond its boundaries. Social interactions with other groups give a society a sense of where it belongs in relation to the rest of humanity. They also require specific collective institutions (trade agreements, territorial limitations, defense structures, treaties, and the like) of a more or less formal nature to deal with this wider range of humanity. Every social system must also have a way of dealing with particular individuals in relationship to the social system. Every individual modifies the whole society in some modest measure, and every individual is socialized and acculturated by the society. If an individual cannot adjust to the society, or the society cannot adjust to the individual's capacities, they separate; one or the other is damaged, diminished, or destroyed. Every society must establish ways of dealing with humanity at large and with particular persons. In every society, in every culture, biophysical and mythic dimensions intersect, and both interact with the lateral, crosscutting divisions on a spectrum from intersocietal to individual; thus the west side of the map is marked by an "Intersocietal Boundary," the east side by an "Individual Boundary." Every society operates within these general boundaries. The history and the direction of every societal development could be written in terms of the interaction, predominance, or neglect of these variables.

Within a society various functions, roles, and institutions are established to deal with fundamental social needs. They are structurally similar in every society; on this map three levels are represented—the material, the associational, and the ideational—and three types of structure are identified: interpersonal, civilizational, and collective. By identifying these various institutional arenas, we can also identify what must be recognized as basic to human nature for civilized living. Further, we can arrange these according to their proximity to the various external boundaries, and thereby gain a basic transcultural set of concepts that render a map of basic institutional sectors or social spaces of all societies. Each sector meets a distinct social need and reflects a dimension of our natures. Any complex society without one of these sectors is defective; it is headed for change or collapse. Such a map gives us, I suggest, a basic grid by which we can compare and contrast cross-sections of our three societies as they bear on human rights. Societies may arrange these institutional sectors differ-

Figure 1.

A Map of Institutional Sectors of Society Based on Universal Human Needs

MYTHOS BOUNDARY

INDIVIDUAL BOUNDARY

	Interpersonal Structures	Civilizational Structures	Collective Structures
Ideational Level	Educational (Science & Philosophy	Cultural/ Expressive (Arts & Recreation)	Legal (Constitution & Judiciary)
Associational Level	Familial (Sexuality & Kinship)	Voluntary (Ecclesia)	Political (Regime & Military)
Material Level	Medical (Health care & Therapy)	Technical (Tools & Skills)	Economic (Industry & Market)

INTERSOCIETAL BOUNDARY

BIOPHYSICAL BOUNDARY

ently, and by seeing the differences, we can grasp the basic religion, the operating creed and social bonding, which is present. Social form reveals content. In one society, because of its trajectories from the past, its creed, and its arrangement of these institutional sectors, the rights pertaining to membership in economic (collective-material) institutions may be seen as decisive; in another, academic freedom (ideational and interpersonal) may seem more important. A wide variety of arrangements is possible.

This map is not a map of any particular society; it is a map of certain necessary institutions in all societies. In any given social system the relations between the various institutional sectors of the society may be drawn in different proportion. In some societies parts of this map would be undeveloped and indistinct. The legal institutions provide an example: some other sector or combination of sectors might carry out (something like) the legal functions. The medicine man or the scholar may legitimate judgments, render decisions about punishment, and resolve disputes about claims to goods or services. Further, institutions, once formed, are not fixed and static. In every living society constant changes in the boundary conditions—changing weather patterns, encounters with other cultures, poetic genius which reinterprets mythologies, new individuals in the social system—affect the internal relationships between the institutional sectors. The system is simultaneously altered by the dynamic changes which constantly occur within each sector. Also within each sector are "leaders" and "followers" in some pattern of superordination and subordination. These too can change dramatically, affecting the whole society. Nevertheless, predom inant patterns are very persistent. Structure often remains stable even as generation after generation experience change. The point is that the flow of change moves in channels, and the experience of change is interpreted through the spectacles of constancy. Thus form not only reveals content; it also delimits change.

The map may appear to be directly concerned not with human beings but only with formal, objective structures. This is not the case. Humans are social creatures who live in societies according to the various memberships available. The various sectors of society are expressions of human needs and decisive memberships as well as mechanisms that provide for those needs and memberships in concrete ways. The map portrays the institutional arenas in which basic human needs are shaped by creed and social bonding. It also identifies universal structures of human needs and thus is a concrete test of whether the creeds which are developed are in fact pertinent to empirical humanity in community.

Empirical cross-cultural studies show that religion is one area of society that is universally present, even if in diverse forms and proportions. Yet I have not specifically included it on the map for a simple reason: religious organization has been variously identified with each of these institutional sectors of society.

How, then, could religion be drawn on the map? Perhaps as a circle encompassing the whole. For religion in the broad "metaphysical-moral vision" sense in which I am using the term includes the cosmos and the mythos, the individual and social dimensions. Religion affects all the various boundaries and each of the sectors. Education mediates a sacred element in wisdom; artistic creativity has a divine dimension; legal argument and judgment hold a sacred trust; familiar intimacies of friendship and kinship are mediated through grace; political power embraces godlike majesty; the healing and care of the suffering embrace a universal ethic. Technology makes humans Promethean gods, and economics makes some lords. Religion, in the broad sense already indicated, gives meaning, conviction, and social bonding to all aspects of life.

Christianity, Marxism, and Hinduism agree about this comprehensive character of religion (or ideology, as the Marxists say). The fundamental metaphysical-moral vision, the existential "knowledge" of the "really real" touches every aspect of life. They disagree, however, about precisely what the "really real" actually is and about where and how it appears particularly in society. Hence they disagree about what, in the final analysis, it means to be human. The West has developed "covenantal" institutions at the center of society to sustain what it believes to be most human, while caste (closely tied to family) is central in

Hinduism, and party (focused on political-economic power) occupies that "voluntary" space in Marxism-Leninism. These are institutional-structural facts of tremendous importance for human rights. I call these three core-organizational centers "ecclesia." Each is understood to be a "redemptive," "liberating," "truly humanizing" community, called into solidarity by the ultimate forces of the universe and given moral responsibilities for shaping the whole society.[22]

If human rights is developing as a religious-ethical doctrine, then surely both the creedal commitments and the "sacred" institutions of the society will differently influence the shape of that doctrine as a basis for human action in different cultures.

3. The third method for this study will be *evaluational.* The longitudinal and cross-sectional analyses will allow us to compare and contrast the three cultures under consideration. By these means we shall see the fundamental value decisions, of a religious and metaphysical-moral sort and of a social organizational sort, that have been made by these three civilizations. Value questions thus enter in at three points. First, in the selection of a topic, such as human rights, we suggest that we will be looking for universal values as we conduct our longitudinal and cross-sectional research. Second, in the treatment of each culture, the inner logic of the values which give cohesion to the society must be identified. No serious analysis of societies can be value-neutral in this respect; values must be taken into account. It is the task of all comparative studies, however, to be value-neutral in the sense that one does not attribute to the inner logic of societies values which are not present. A Christian analyzing a Communist or a Hindu society must be value-neutral in one way. A Communist or a Hindu must be able to say: "I might not put it just that way, but what you have presented is a viable way of perceiving what we are, believe, and do."

As we shall see, however, it is not possible to remain at this value-neutral level. A third set of value questions immediately confronts us. Because the ultimate presuppositions of a Christian, Marxist, or Hindu society are in principle accessible to all people (otherwise we could not understand what one of the others is about in the first place), we have to discern which in fact more accurately grasps the fundamental structures of human life. In brief, we have to decide among the options which we can, in some measure, comprehend.

By focusing on human rights, which by definition are universal in scope, we are forced to wrestle with the question of universal normative principles that transcend any particular historical-cultural context. Questions of value at this level demand comparative evaluation. We cannot be value-neutral. We must take the next precarious step. On what basis shall we do so? Is it possible to say which, if any, of these basic metaphysical-moral visions is better?

As soon as we pose this question, of course, it becomes clear that this entire book is not primarily about the historical trajectories of doctrine or creed, or centrally about comparative societies. It is fundamentally about religious ethics. The issue, the decisive issue, is which fundamental vision is most true and most fully meets the widest range of basic human needs and thus *ought* to be adopted

universally as creed and institutionalized in every society. If we arrive at anything less than that, we are not dealing with universal human rights, with
genuinely human rights, but only with the creeds and social patterns of this or
that idiosyncratic culture. What view of human rights is right?

The clue to evaluation is "holiness." I have already stressed that human
rights is a religious matter because of its claim about what is sacred, inviolable,
and absolute in human affairs. In a very real sense, comparative evaluation
forces us to ask which definitions of the sacred are truly holy.

Where is it possible to get the tools to deal with such matters? Such questions
seem to stand beyond most of modern thinking. There is, however, a resource
to which we can turn: theological ethics. It is a resource which we must use
with great care, for it is highly confused in its present state, and in ill repute
among many. Yet theological ethics provides precisely the tools that are necessary. The term itself is a compound of three elements. *Theos* has to do with that
mystery which is ultimately true and holy, and is the governing force in the
universe. *Logos* conveys the notion of rational and scientific analysis of the
decisive structures and processes of that mystery. It remains a mystery, for no
one knows it wholly; we can speak about it in some measure because it is
accessible to human experience and reason. And *ethics* focuses our attention
on the norms for human behavior in an *ethos*. By linking these terms together,
we define a field of study which has to do with the science of the holy as it bears
on social morality. This is the queen of the sciences.[23]

It should also be noted that in the term "theological ethics," "ethics" is the
noun and "theological" is the adjective. This suggests that the subject matter of
ethics defines the focus and thus can leave aside, or correct, theology when it
becomes unethical or anti-ethical. But the adjective must be preserved precisely
because only that which can give focus and comprehensiveness to ethics is that
which is, in the final analysis, rooted in the truly holy and accessible to reason.[24]
Otherwise, we are speaking only of opinion (or ideology)—either that, or we
are not communicating sense at all, in which case we must remain silent. To
include the term "theological" means that we may reasonably know and speak
about the ultimate and universal norms that are so sacred that they are to guide
all human behavior in every *ethos*. That is precisely what is at stake in human
rights debates.

A brief word must also be said about the relationship of "theology" and
"religion" as they relate to ethics. They are often thought of as the same, but I
see them as quite different things. Religious ethics has to do with what people
actually hold as creed and what people actually bond themselves to in "memberships," thereby affecting the arrangements of the social spaces in a society.
Theological ethics has to do with the critical analysis of religions, the evaluative
assessment of which ones are valid, and the investigation of the grounds on
which such evaluations can be made. We may live by religious ethics, but we
must think by theological ethics. Theological ethics can tell us whether our
religious ethics is true or false, and therefore whether we ought to demand

agreement to or transformation of our religious ethics. Theology is the critical science for religious phenomena.

I fully recognize the ways in which theological ethics has distorted its own character. Many religious thinkers have spoken of theological ethics in highly parochial terms. Some have used the term "theological" in a merely confessional manner, as a way of rationalizing their own (personal, traditional, or cultural) creeds about God. Nonreligious thinkers often have severed *Theos* from *Logos* in order to protect reason and science from the dogmatic interference of such confessionalism, but in the process have often divested themselves of any serious tools for comparative evaluation. And both religious and nonreligious thinkers have sometimes separated ethics from theology on the one hand and from the social analysis of *ethos* on the other—making ethics a matter of individual morality only. But these betrayals of theological ethics have only led to the predictable consequences that theological ethics as a discipline is rendered incapable of dealing with fundamental large-scale issues such as human rights, and is relegated to the sidelines of serious discussion. If there is one scholarly purpose governing my own efforts of the last two decades—of which this study is a part—it is to rehabilitate theological ethics as a discipline, one pertinent to the analysis and guidance of human existence in society. At many junctures in tracing the longitudinal trajectories and in portraying the cross-sectional analysis, theological-ethical evaluation will enter in. In the concluding chapter I will offer some explicit theological-ethical reflections.

F. THE OUTLINE OF THE BOOK

With these perspectives and foci in mind, we will attempt in what follows to wrestle with the multiple variables involved in human rights. The next chapter will trace some of the decisive moments in the background of the human rights debates as this background has had an effect on all modern discussions. This background is essentially European and serves obviously as a prologue to both Marxist and modern Western motifs. The European background is also analogous to as well as obviously different from Indian history at certain points in the distant past. It is also the case that this Western background came to impinge on modern Indian history in decisive ways, as we shall see. It should not disturb us that something discovered or developed in one cultural history is pertinent to other cultures. Few civilizations have ever lived in isolation, and all sorts of things worked out in a particular setting are pertinent for all settings. Human rights may be one of these. Particularity of origin does not prevent universality of significance.

After this general background, we shall turn to three sets of two chapters each. The first set (Chapters Three and Four) will deal with the longitudinal and cross-sectional analysis of Anglo-American understandings of human rights. In these chapters I will show how Western understandings were decisively shaped by a "Liberal-Puritan" synthesis which has become "ecumenical Christian" and institutionalized in a "pluralist society"—presently informed by a rather ill-defined Judeo-Christian creed. Because I am writing primarily for an American audience, and because there is enormous religious confusion today, these chapters will be the longest of the study.

We will turn next to explicitly comparative studies. Chapters Five and Six focus on the German Democratic Republic as a key example of an institutionalized Marxist-Leninist creed, in a context profoundly shaped by an "evangelical" (especially Lutheran) piety. I will show how these have produced a "conformed society." One chapter will be more cross-sectional, the other more longitudinal in emphasis. Of particular interest throughout this section will be, of course, the relation between the "evangelical" and Marxist elements of the dominant creed, and the interaction between their organizational bases. In the interplay between institutional Christianity and Party, some of the important disputes on human rights are revealed—especially those having to do with the arrangements of the "social spaces" for formulation of doctrine and memberships. Then we shall turn to India (Chapters Seven and Eight), where comparisons and contrasts with both the Western and Marxist societies can be drawn, and the influences of Judeo-Christian, Liberal, and Socialist ideas and organization can be set forth as they affect the fabric of the culture generally and human rights specifically. Again, one chapter will be cross-sectional, the other longitudinal. The deep traditions of Hinduism, amazingly powerful and resilient in a nation struggling to modernize, remain decisive in this "neo-traditional," "hierarchic," spiritualistic society. In the treatments of both East Germany and India, I have decided to present the cross-sectional analysis prior to the longitudinal interpretation, reversing the order I use in discussing the West. The reason for this is that I cannot presume a familiarity with those societies and creeds as I do in regard to the United States. American readers, on the other hand, are likely to see how the depth trajectories of the Western past turn out to shape the present.

Finally, in a concluding chapter (Chapter Nine) I shall summarize what has been presented in brief form and offer concluding comparative evaluations in an overtly theological-ethical vocabulary. If I am successful, the reader will not only gain in understanding but will also feel called to commitment and action for humanity on theological-ethical grounds. He or she will recognize human rights as a proper *credo*.

---

1. On the social and historical importance of *credo*, see my *Ethics and the Urban Ethos* (Boston: Beacon Press, 1973), especially Chapter VI.

2. See, for example, the highly divergent interpretations in "European Responses to Human Rights" (New York: I.D.O.C., 1978).

3. I draw the term from James Luther Adams, *On Being Human Religiously* (Boston: Beacon Press, 1976), especially Chapter 5.

4. See, for example, V. Ikonitskii, "The Crisis of Bourgeois Democracy and Violations of

Human Rights in the Capitalist World," *Soviet Studies in Philosophy*, 16 (Winter 1978 – 79), 69 – 77.

5. A. H. Robertson, *Human Rights in Europe* (Manchester, G. B.: Manchester University Press, 1977).

6. See the "Bibliography on Human Rights" (New York: I.D.O.C., 1977).

7. Peggy Billings, *Paradox and Promise in Human Rights* (New York: Friendship Press, 1979); George Forell and William H. Lazareth, *Human Rights: Rhetoric or Reality* (Philadelphia: Fortress Press, 1978).

8. Ronald Dworkin, *Taking Rights Seriously* (Cambridge, Mass.: Harvard University Press, 1977).

9. Edward O. Wilson, *On Human Nature* (Cambridge, Mass.: Harvard University Press, 1978), pp. 198f.

10. Interreligious Taskforce on U. S. Food Policy, "Identifying a Food Policy Agenda for the 1980s," *Impact*, 1979.

11. Leo Strauss, *Natural Rights and History* (Chicago: University of Chicago Press, 1953).

12. Robert Tucker, *Philosophy and Myth in Karl Marx* (New York: Cambridge University Press, 1961), pp. 21f.

13. See Allen O. Miller, ed., *A Christian Declaration on Human Rights* (Grand Rapids, Mich.: Eerdmans, 1977), especially Chapter 1.

14. The "Final Act," Conference on Security and Cooperation in Europe, signed on Aug. 1, 1975.

15. J. Lissner and A. Sovik, "A Lutheran Reader on Human Rights," *LWF* Report, 1 (Sept. 1978); see especially pp. 29 – 31, 107 – 38, and 170 – 76.

16. See John Sandford, *The Sword and the Ploughshare: Autonomous Peace Initiatives in East Germany* (London: Merlin Press, 1983).

17. Three very significant efforts at comparative ethics have influenced the content and methods of my own efforts, although I have settled on an approach quite different from all of them. It is not the purpose of this book to show what I believe to be the weaknesses of the alternative approaches, but the reader may want to consult John H. Barnsley, *The Social Reality of Ethics: The Comparative Analysis of Moral Codes* (Boston: Routledge & Kegan Paul, 1972); Ronald Green, *Religious Reason* (New York: Oxford University Press, 1978); and David Little and Sumner B. Twiss, *Comparative Religious Ethics* (San Francisco: Harper & Row, 1978).

18. One could speak, here, of the importance of "story," as has been accented by several important contemporary ethicists. See, for example, Stanley Hauerwas, *Vision and Virtue* (Notre Dame, Ind.: Fides Press, 1974). In dealing with large-scale social questions, however, the methods developed by American ethicists influenced by Ernst Troeltsch in his *The Social Teachings of the Christian Churches* (trans. O. Wyon [New York: Harper & Row, 1931]) tend to focus less on personal narrative than on social and intellectual story. It is this tradition of scholarship to which I am indebted more than any other.

19. The most important single influence on my work in this regard derives from the work of Max Weber, especially in his treatments of the religions of India and China and of Judaism and Protestantism. He clearly draws constantly from longitudinal methods, but is essentially concerned to portray distinctive structures of divergent civilizations.

20. In fact, I had developed the map in several versions, sometimes focusing on universally necessary social institutions and sometimes on the philosophical-religious variables by which normative positions have been and can be justified. See "Ethics: Social and Christian," *Andover Newton Quarterly*, 13 (Jan. 1973), especially 182 – 86; and "The Location of the Holy," *Journal of Religious Ethics*, 4 (Spring 1976), 63 – 104. Related essays include "Technology and the 'Supra-natural,'" *Zygon*, 10 (March 1975), 59 – 85; "Social Ethics: Some Basic Elements East and West," in *A Vision for Man*, ed. S. Amirtham (Madras: CSI Press, 1978), pp. 326 – 38; and "Gesellschaftstheorie und Sozialethik," *Zeitschrift für evangelische Ethik*, 32/4 (Oct. 1978), 275 – 95

21. An interdisciplinary team, under the direction of George P. Murdock, studied several hundred societies to identify the decisive institutions of civilized society. The results correspond in nearly every detail to my theoretically derived "map." There are three exceptions. First, "religion" is treated differently, as I will shortly discuss. Second, Murdock makes no distinction between political and legal sectors, speaking only of "government." The cross-

cultural data, however, suggest that most cultures have a distinction not fully recognized by the Yale team. Third, Murdock does not include a "voluntary" sector. The reason for this is simply that it does not exist in all cultures. These institutional distinctions, however, turn out to be of critical importance for human rights, as we shall see. See G. P. Murdock et al., *Outline of Cultural Materials* (New Haven, Conn.: Human Relations Area Files, Inc., 1942); and F. E. Merrill and H. W. Eldredge, *Culture and Society* (Englewood Cliffs, N.J.: Prentice-Hall, 1952).

22. See F. L. K. Hsu, *Caste, Club, and Clan* (Princeton, N.J.: Van Nostrand, 1963). In this comparative study of India, the United States, and pre-revolutionary China, Hsu points out that the most distinctive social feature of America is the "club." His analysis, in my judgment, is basically accurate, although he does not seem to understand the religious roots of this phenomenon as he does in regard to India and China.

23. See my "The Location of the Holy," pp. 63 – 104.

24. In my judgment, this is the most important contribution of Ronald Green's *Religious Reason*.

CHAPTER TWO

The Roots of Human Rights:
Ancient and Medieval

A. A CONTEMPORARY INCIDENT: WHERE DID IT COME FROM?

SOON after the 1976 presidential election, several organs of the National Council of Churches, the Jesuit Office of Social Ministries, the social outreach officers of the Church of the Brethren, and the Americans for Democratic Action, with several other groups, sent a joint letter concerning human rights to President-elect Jimmy Carter.[1] The letter supported his campaign advocacy of human rights and called for him to stress human rights in international relations (see Appendix I). The authors urged that all foreign policy, as well as domestic programs of the United States, reflect the civil liberties guaranteed by the Bill of Rights of the United States Constitution, and the aspirations stated in the United Nations' Universal Declaration of Human Rights. America's born-again president and his nominee for ambassador to the United Nations, the Reverend Andrew Young, had already been advocating human rights as a cornerstone of their philosophy of international relations. Within months that policy became official,[2] creating among some politically vocal groups consternation about such injections of "morality" into political life.

In many respects the joint letter was not particularly remarkable. In fact, such expressions of concern are quite ordinary on the part of American churches and various voluntary associations. Yet its very ordinariness offers a glimpse of some of the more remarkable features of the contemporary understandings of human rights in the American context.

The National Council of Churches is the coalition of Protestant and Ortho-dox denominations, related to many international Christian organizations. It operates under a specifically Trinitarian theology, and it coordinates the work of various denominations on worship, educational, ecumenical, social-service, and social-action projects. It grew out of the Federal Council of Churches, which was founded in 1908 and which had set forth, as its first public document, the "Social Creed" (see Appendix III), which advocates human rights and the pro-

26

tection of minorities, children, organized labor, and dissenting political parties. The National Council of Churches has, throughout its history, spoken with vigor and reforming zeal on the moral aspects of social issues. It has been most vigorously supported by those denominations rooted in the Reformed traditions, and most heartedly opposed by certain evangelical and spiritual religious groups, and ignored or criticized by a wide range of political organizations, both of the left and the right.

The Jesuit Office of Social Ministries is the social-action arm of the Society of Jesus, one of the most influential orders of the Roman Catholic Church, historically linked to papal authority. It has consistently advocated intellectual excellence in law, politics, and the sciences as well as theology. The Jesuits have traditionally been in conflict with Protestants and political "liberals" on matter of papal authority and church-state relationships. Their contemporary solidarity with Protestants and Liberals on the issues of human rights is a significant historical recovery of an aspect of Catholic teaching sometimes obscured by post-Reformation Catholic developments, but significantly reasserted by two contemporary Popes in particular: John XXIII and John Paul II.

The Church of the Brethren is a representative of the sectarian movements of the so-called Radical Reformation, which has historically been in conflict with many Catholic and Protestant groups. This church is one of the cluster of Protestant churches which never became established in a formal sense in any country. In style, churches of this kind are often theologically conservative and Bible-centered. The churches of the Radical Reformation constitute a third stream of religious history in the West. It has often been considered heretical, but it has survived ideological and physical warfare inside Christian circles and in the face of political power. This sectarian tradition is distinct from "the Church" thinking of Catholics and from the denominational thinking of most Reformed Protestant movements in America. It has included militant conversionist perspectives and passive, utopian communitarian experiments. However, on the question of human rights, especially as it reflects freedom of religion, the group in this stream have expressed themselves clearly and affirmatively over the centuries. Their participation with Catholics, main-line Protestants, and secular groups shows how this element of doctrine unites even though other elements continue to divide.

Americans for Democratic Action is a group composed of "progressive" activists from Jewish, Christian, and humanist orientations. Founded by Eleanor Roosevelt, it finds its unity in advocacy of practical political action. It operates in effect as a secular, political "denomination" or "sect" dedicated to humanistic and democratic values under a sense of universal law, specifically as reflected in the American constitution. Many members see themselves as "social democrats" and are intrigued by West European "socialist" policies in areas such as medical care and control of undue corporate power and profit. Resistant to both Marxist-Leninist doctrine and to "old-liberal" notions of laissez-faire capitalism, the ADA represents a particular modern philosophy of popular government which traces its roots from—at least—John Locke, Thomas Jefferson, Woodrow Wilson, and F. D. Roosevelt to philosophical stances represented by such modern thinkers as economist John Kenneth Galbraith and philosopher John Rawls.

The social concerns espoused in the joint letter mentioned came from a coalition of groups that, at first glance, seem to have little in common with each other and with the one to whom it was addressed. Indeed, on many issues, tensions and disagreements remain intense. Different members of these groups would, on the conventional spectrum identifying one as a "liberal" or a "conservative," ally themselves in highly diverse ways. On the issue of human rights, however, they find themselves in fundamental agreement. And they do so precisely at a moment when the conventional distinctions between liberal and conservative are breaking down—both theologically and politically. The breakdown is troubling to many. It is marked by single-issue politics, by new alliances, by de facto ecumenism, and by numerous doubts about the nature and character of leadership. Yet, in the area of human rights, Jimmy Carter, the National Council of Churches, the Jesuits, recent popes, the churches of the Radical Reformation, and secular "progressive" activists have found common cause, whatever their other intramural disputes. Why is this so; how did it come to be; and what does it mean?

To answer these questions, we shall turn shortly to a "longitudinal analysis" of the deep trajectory of thought and social history which has shaped them all. We will see that they share certain basic perceptions of creed and society which have rendered a remarkably unified view of what it means to be human and what, therefore, may be claimed as a human right. At base, we shall see that all hold to a distinctive "public theology" that has become obscured from even those who hold it, but that is being painfully and slowly rearticulated because it is presently under attack, both religiously and politically, from both the right and the left. More dangerously, the groups which advocated these ideas often seem confused about their source and their character. None of these groups is, at present, clear about the basic foundations of its convictions. Often they seem to be without intellectual rootage and direction, and are justly criticized as being merely "knee-jerk liberals," in favor of more government in political life and more freedom and tolerance in personal lifestyles. The experiences of Viet Nam and Watergate on one side and a widespread perception of the breakdown of the family and personal character on the other, however, have forced doubt about the morality of these tendencies. The recovery of an emphasis on human rights reflects a contemporary attempt to reclaim a firm foundation for social ethics. More, however, is implied in the turn to human rights than many suspect. Thus our first task is to expose the historically rooted presuppositions which stand behind the joint letter, for they represent in principle the distinctive beliefs of Western society on human rights, struggling at present for survival amid confusion.

Second, this joint letter presumes that nongovernmental groups may properly influence government. The idea that churches and voluntary associations may participate in the shaping of public policy is common in American society, yet we sometimes fail to note how unusual it is in the history of world civilizations, or how precariously the structures which sustain the possibility are presently balanced. In some measure these groups have presumed an *ethos* that reserves a social space for groups which are not, in the governmental sense, official. A distinctive institutional arena is established and protected which creates a space wherein independent groups may form. Such groups are assumed to be able to raise money, to elect officers, to meet and form coalitions without interference, to extend membership to persons of all ethnic, class, and personal backgrounds, to have ideological foundations distinct from those of the government, to formulate a moral consensus, and to be able to shape official policy by direct communication and indirect influence of public opinion through propaganda. The implications of this are vast. For one thing, it means that the political order is, to a significant degree, presumed to be the servant or instrument of other organizations in society, or of the people they represent. Whether these particular groups are or are not the most influential on this or some other question is not, at the moment, the important issue. Wherever social space for other groups is assumed in a *polis,* governments are in principle subject to the influence and the ethical concerns formulated by those institutions which are outside governmental control. The political community is *not* the comprehensive community of loyalty. Rulers are to rule over *some* and *not all* features of life; through religious and voluntary groups, people may call upon these rulers to obey a moral duty that stands above them. Yet today, precisely those groups that signed the joint letter embrace policies which, in the long run, could undercut all they presume and stand for. On the one hand, many leaders of these groups are anti-institutional, impatient with any serious social analysis. On the other hand, many are purely "instrumentalist," that is, they view an organization only in terms of its ability to accomplish specific political objectives. The irony is that the human rights principles to which they appealed involve institutional guards for pluralist, voluntary organizations which are not, and are not to be made, subject to coercive political authority.

Third, the joint letter calls for an effort to bring the foreign policy of the United States into line with civil liberties of the Constitution, and with the ideals of the United Nations. Several things are fascinating about this aspect of the appeal. The letter does not deal with what are ordinarily thought to be "church" or "voluntary associational" matters. For much of the population and, indeed, for many social scientists and politicians, the question of the enforcement of rights is a secular, political responsibility having little to do with religion. The Bill of Rights attached to the United States Constitution is not, at least in the ordinary sense, a religious document. However, these religious groups suggest that this particular political legal document contains a set of values or principles that is proper to religion and is basically valid from a religious perspective. In a profound way the authors of this letter claim that they have the authority and knowledge to instruct political authority regarding first principles. The basic

29

principles of human rights are seen to transcend any and every political or civil order and are understood to be a guide as to what ought to govern the political behavior in all contexts and systems. The authors of this letter hold that what is embedded in the American Bill of Rights is not only civil but human and universally ethical in character. They ask that these rights be more fully implemented within the civil order, and that they be expanded to become the basis for international affairs. They call upon this government to live up to its historic commitments and to see these commitments as guidelines for peoples with other historical commitments.

They appeal also to the ideals of the United Nations' Declaration of Human Rights. After its organization in 1946, the United Nations composed the Universal Declaration of Human Rights as one of its first major actions. In 1948 the Assembly passed that declaration by unanimous vote. It consists of thirty articles, including the following:

—the right to life, liberty, and security of persons
—the right to recognition as a person before the law
—the right to be presumed innocent until proved guilty
—freedom from arbitrary interference with privacy, family, home, or correspondence
—the right to own property
—freedom of opinion and expression
—the right of association and of assembly
—the right to social security
—the right to work
—the right to rest and leisure
—the right to education
—the right to a standard of living adequate for health and well-being
—the right to participate in the cultural life of the community

This declaration was a remarkable achievement. Later (in Chapter Four, Section D), we will return to an analysis of these provisions. For the moment we need only note that in appealing to these principles, the coalition of religious and "progressive" voluntary-associational groups which petitioned the president about human rights affirmed a set of values upon which they had found common agreement beyond all other disagreements. They presumed a social situation wherein independent groups could influence limited government, and they were appealing to a set of ideas which they held to be normative for all cultures and societies everywhere. In short, the authors of this joint letter claimed to know a *primary moral law* to which all persons, political authorities, and institutions ought to be held accountable. They claimed that this *primary moral law* is partially institutionalized now in some areas of life, and needs to be expanded and implemented.

This cluster of assumptions is not "natural" to civilizations. It is not something which automatically occurs when a certain level of social development is reached. Indeed, on the heels of the United Nations' declaration, a series of conventions has been worked out to translate the provisions of the declaration into legally enforceable provisions. Key among these have been the Covenant on Economic, Social and Cultural Rights, the Convention on the Elimination of All Forms of Racial Discrimination, and the Covenant on Civil and Political Rights. No nation has signed all of these documents[3]; indeed, several highly developed societies put people in prison for advocating and organizing groups committed to human rights in these terms. Such a cluster of assumptions appears only where the possibilities of social development are given a specific direction by fundamental beliefs powerful enough to shape persons, attitudes, social habits, and institutions. Concern for universal human rights occurs only when a social system is informed by a specific creed and is successfully maintained by an effectively organized constituency.

B. THE ANCIENT ROOTS OF HUMAN RIGHTS IDEAS

Does this cluster of assumptions derive from the American Constitution and the United Nations? Clearly not. These are but latter-day formulations. The sources are much deeper, and failure to see the roots is to live in a myopic world of immediacy. If this were the case, human rights could be altered by holding a new constitutional convention or by calling for a new vote in the United Nations. If we are to speak of human rights, we need to seek the foundations on which they rest. In this chapter we shall see that the roots of human rights as understood by the West and represented in the joint letter discussed above derive from nowhere else than from one stream of Christian thought as this thought has interacted with certain other themes in Western thought and social experience. (Aspects of this background also have informed the basic understandings of Eastern European definitions of human rights and are analogous to Indian ones, as we shall see later in this study.)

The deepest roots of human rights are found in the biblical conception of life. The words "human rights" do not, to be sure, appear in the Bible, but the themes that provide the basis of human rights do. It is important for our purposes to attempt to grasp certain of these themes in their most general terms. Decisive for all human rights thinking and action is the notion that there is a pattern of righteousness which can be known by humans in empirical life but which is not the same as empirical life. A reality, directly related to daily living, to human meaning, and to social relationship, is nevertheless not the same as what can be found at all points in life. This reality, which we call "God," is not in the biblical view a figment of our imagination, a projection of our needs, or a product of human creativity. Nor is it an eternal part of ourselves. It is "other" than we are; we live *under* it. It is the source and the norm of all that is, a living reality in itself, yet not identical with the sum total of everything that we can find as we look around in the world. Humans stand, and must stand, under this reality whether we want to or not, whether we are aware of it or not.

31

According to the biblical view, humans are free in the sense that we can and must make choices, but we are not free to do whatever we wish. We have the most profound aspects of human identity *conferred* upon us in love by a reality beyond us.[4] To that we *must* be faithful—not in the sense that we are, as puppets, manipulated to, but that we ought to, if we are to be truly human. There is an "otherness" about this reality which is more real than our own desires and fulfillments, or even our souls. Yet the otherness is not entirely removed from us. Humans—all humans—are made in the image of this otherness. That which is beyond is also present; it can be known and seen in decisive aspects of creation and in human historical experience, providing hints, clues, directions, and guidelines as to how the otherness is simultaneously "present," giving guidance to freedom without destroying the capacity for or necessity of choice. Failure to attend to these present aspects of otherness induces chaos, pretense, oppression, and destruction. The distance between God and humanity is commonly called "sin"; the presence is commonly called "revelation" or, simply, "grace." Those who know the difference are called into "covenants" to discern, celebrate, enact, bear witness to, and live out the ethical implications of the difference. Indeed, the first marks of those who know the difference is that they live under a sense of moral law grounded in God's righteousness, not their own. They are liberated by the vision of God's righteousness to reform themselves and the society around them, but in their liberation they are called into a new voluntary discipline and responsibility to God and neighbor. They are a "covenanted people." In the ancient Hebraic encounters with the presence of this otherness, moral law and expectant hope, religious depth and social renewal are thus intimately tied together.[5]

For ancient Israel, such a perspective had immediate consequences. Because the Hebrew people were the first to clearly articulate this perspective, they had a dramatic sense of its specialty. It was not the perspective of the groups they encountered around them, many of which had similar or superior experiences of the environment, of techniques for social organization, and of changing fortunes amid contending empires. Yet the Hebrews felt that they had somehow come in contact with that which was in fact really real. They subjected their social, political, and economic experiences, and even their view of nature and its laws, to the scrutiny of this decisive perspective. It altered their way of life. It forced them to reassess their social structure and to develop basic principles for social life which assured, relative to the other peoples they knew, a sense of universal justice and historical expectancy which influenced every aspect of life. Richard Deats put it this way:

> The universal implications of this faith in the righteous God, creator of the earth and of all living things, continued to permeate the life of Israel, expanding their faith to widening horizons of inclusiveness and compassion. "Am I my brother's keeper?" and "Who is my neighbor?" are questions that never ceased to stir the conscience of the people of God. . . . Isaiah especially

caught the universality of this faith that is a "light for all the peoples;" "all flesh" will see the glory of the Lord.[6]

The Hebrews saw that the perspective which developed in their midst had implications for all humans everywhere—even for those who thought such notions strange. Hence they were able to draw from surrounding cultures those features of societal law and those tendencies toward the new future which were compatible with their basic sense of what was really real.

At times, however, the special character of their perspective made them close in upon themselves, to see this fresh perspective as leading not to a special obligation to be "a light to the nations" but to special privilege. "Covenant" became an attempt to gain superiority, not an occasion to be a servant of the deepest vision. The Hebrews attempted to organize all of life in one structure under this decisive perspective. In spite of the constant resistance to Baal worship with its accent on sexual fertility, and in spite of the deep memories of the dangers of the sacred kingship of Pharaoh in the "flesh pots of Egypt," religion became identified on the one hand with family-based ethnicity, and on the other hand with political authority. The "otherness" was obscured by the attempts to totally institutionalize, even domesticate, the "presence." Familial loyalties or political interests prevented closest adherence to the deepest insights they had received. In the cities taken over from the Canaanites, the loss of perspective seemed acute, but in these same cities a pluralism and a complexity allowed the thinking of new thoughts and the re-examination of old ones. Wherever the social situation opened up to provide space for the recovery of the central perspectives, prophets rose up to call the people once more to their basic perspective and to rearticulate, in view of new and changing conditions, what the moral law and the expectant hope meant. In these prophets we can see the reaffirmation of covenantal concerns, the ancient creedal foundations of human rights: there is a universal moral order, rooted in the righteousness of God, which is other than ordinary experience yet directly pertinent to ordinary experience; and human responsibility involves action toward the future which can reconcile the contradictions without dissolving the difference between the otherness of God and human reality. Further, in cities which witnessed the rise of prophets, we find the first glimmerings of a "social space" from which they were able to oppose false loyalties to both familial-ethnic solidarities and political-economic opportunism. They critiqued efforts to unite ethnicity, covenantal religion, and political power into a single web; they demanded that the people distinguish among them. Nathan critiqued the sexual and military actions of David; Amos attacked the political arrogance of Israel and Judah; Hosea adapted antifamilial images to speak of God's faithfulness in covenant. The most important natural human associations, familial and political, were placed *under* a higher law and seen as subject to change in view of the covenantal commitments. A godly future, a truly humane future, depended on it.

In the short run, the prophets were not often successful. The loyalties to family and political community obscured the people's capacity to read the hints of God and to keep the universal notions of law and hope at the forefront, especially in periods of economic success. In time the society began to crack from within and succumb to asssault from without. On several occasions the people were driven into exile and diaspora or placed under the occupation of foreign invaders. Ancient Israel was destroyed as an ethnic, theocratic regime. Yet the power of the originating perspective did not collapse under these pressures, even if family institutions and political life were radically altered. The religious-moral dimensions of the tradition were renewed in a fresh way with the creation of Judaism.

The organizational base of Judaism was the synagogue, not the family or the nation or the ethnic state. It could not be the nation (political authority was in the hands of others), although the memory of the kingship and its closeness to the old temple kept nationalistic dreams alive—so much so that restoration of these became a part of the expectant hope. Nor could the organizational base be the family. Intermarriage was a problem, and a single family, even if entirely Jewish, could scarcely withstand the impact of alien cultures. The synagogue, ambiguously divorced from the family by the subordination and exclusion of women yet encouraging ritual laws to guide all family practice, formed the substructural matrix for keeping alive the vision of law and the expectant hope. In the synagogue it was clear that the witnesses to a covenantal, moral law of universal import and those expecting a new order of mercy and love were of a kingdom that was "other" as well as "present."

It is in this context that Christianity arose. In Christianity many of the Hebraic perspectives were radicalized. Not a jot or a tittle of the fundamental moral law was to be compromised; indeed, the demands were intensified (Matt. 5ff.). In Jesus Christ, Christians saw fulfilled the promise of overcoming the tension between "otherness" *and* "presence." Ordinary life could be lived in terms of the ultimate source of righteousness. The hope for the future was confirmed by its first fruits. Both the law and hope were seen as manifestations of a love that surpassed ordinary comprehension. In Jesus Christ a new dignity was confirmed for all humans, a dignity which was not innately present or earned or constructed by human action, but sacrificially given. Grace overcame sin concretely in time and space. Henceforth all dimensions of spirituality, ideals, and universal moral principles must be discussed, discerned, and acted out in the context of historical interpretation and lived response. When Jesus said that God could raise up children of Abraham out of the very stones of the earth (Matt. 3:9), the connection between political and familial identity and the community of redemption was broken. Jesus went further: he relativized both familial and political power. When he said, "For I have come to set a man against his father, and a daughter against her mother. . . . He who loves father or mother more than me is not worthy of me . . ." (Matt. 10:35ff.), the power of familial and ethnic absolutism was compromised in a radical fashion. And when he told the people to "render therefore to Caesar the things that are Caesar's, and to God the things that are God's" (Matt. 22:21), distinction between nationalism and religious tradition was, in principle, secured. From these moments on, Christians thought, people had to live in the midst of pluralistic centers of identity and loyalty, constantly discerning where the core of divine presence was to be found. Family life and sexuality were affirmed, but not as central (1 Cor. 7); political power was validated, but not as the central matter (Rom. 13). Reconciliation with God meant structural diversities and distinctions in history that overturned simple visions of organic social consolidation. No family, no ethnic identity, no regime, and no political-economic order could serve as the fundamental basis for universal integration. The radical overcoming of sin by grace meant the denial of ultimate meaning in the sexual-genetic continuities of family, clan, and ethnic group on the one hand and in the power, responsibility, and glory of political governance on the other.

Because reconciliation was believed to have been accomplished for all, believers were driven by the very nature of their belief to take the Hebraic message to all peoples, to universalize the covenant to all who would live by its terms. The Jewish sense of being "special," of being a people "called out," was broadened to embrace all nations and families who would accept the new vision. Especially receptive were those who lived in the developing cities of the ancient world, those who, in terms of their own traditional cultures, were anything but special. The outcaste, the marginal, the dispossessed, those skeptical of the moral and metaphysical foundations of their own societies, those for whom the parochial loyalties to political deities and familial cults made no sense in the cosmopolitan Mediterranean world—these were the members of the renewed covenant, bearing the witness to and for all humanity.

Much has been written about the many aspects of early Christian development. It is clearly a mixed history marked by moments of confusion, falsehood, arbitrary authority, foolishness, failure, and irrelevance. Yet out of this ambiguity came several significant developments that were of historic importance for human rights. For our purposes, five points are the most important. First, Christianity held firmly to the Hebraic notion of a universal moral law rooted in the righteousness of God. Indeed, it radicalized the idea by claiming that it was no longer merely an objective, "other" law but was in principle written on the hearts of all people. Hence no one had an excuse, by claim of ignorance, when laws of justice were violated. Second, Christianity radicalized the sense of hope, for it felt that the future was already breaking in. Thus a certain kind of change in all areas of life, a change that did not violate the universal law but brought it to fruition, was to be the focus of discernment and activity in history. Change meant freedom from the unnecessary burdens of the past which kept people in bondage, but change also meant recovery and reaffirmation of what was of perennial weight from the past now lost to the present. In Jesus Christ the ancient hopes were reinvigorated; one could face the future with courage and find new meaning in the past. Tradition, when it portrays the law and the hope, must be preserved, but the present patterns of life which do

35

not contain these two things have no legitimate power over us. Therefore, we may expect a recreated future.

Third, the great Hebraic themes of law and hope were radicalized in a personal direction. Not only were peoples and classes, nations and families to be brought under the protection of a universal just law and into the courage of hope, but individuals were to have a place of dignity and respect. Because all are loved by God, each is a member of the human community under God. All other memberships are secondary. Each can claim from the neighbor a recognition, and each must render care for the other person—not only as a matter of law but because all are members of the same community. To violate the neighbor is to violate God's love for that neighbor and the basic community of life—whatever the status, gender, race, social worth, capacities, or idiosyncrasies of that person.

Fourth, the early Christians formed the church, based upon commitments of law, hope, and love. At first almost indistinguishable from the synagogues, the early churches were even more independent of political authority and familial-ethnic loyalties than the organizations of their Jewish brothers and sisters. Christians moved into the cities of the Mediterranean basin with the view that, through Jesus Christ, they were citizens of a universal community not yet recognized by the world. Under God they had a right to create new social bondings *not* based on family, ethnicity, or national power—bondings which preserved the moral law, renewed the hope, and expressed the delicate tissues of love more immediately than did all surrounding institutions. From the beginning, Christians believed in a community life which was to occupy and expand an inviolable social space for true freedom obtained in rigorous discipleship and discipline. These communities were the very "body of Christ," the place where a new spirit could manifest itself between master and slave, male and female, rich and poor, Jew and non-Jew. They had no small difficulty with such claims. They were misunderstood as licentious by outsiders who felt that if social conventions were broken, nothing would hold together, and they were tempted by licentiousness from within by those who felt that the new freedom and the atmosphere of love meant that all of the ancient moral law was passé. Others thought them so rigorous that they feared all the joy would be squeezed out of life if these people became numerous.

Over time this movement developed more articulate perspectives, and expressed a firm belief that neither familial (tribal-clan-ethnic) attachments nor political (city-state, national, or empire) memberships were or could be the *basis* for fundamental meaning or righteousness. Instead, they drew a circle at the very center of civilization and said that this "covenanted group,"[7] different from the ways of the world, was the group who knew what was decisive for everyone else. In doing this, the church de-absolutized, relativized all other aspects and sectors and perspectives of society. It thereby developed a particular affinity for cosmopolitan life which appeared again and again in the growing cities of the Mediterranean world.[8]

In the relativizing of surrounding institutions and perspectives, however, the alternatives were not negated. The family was maintained, and regular prayers for political authority were offered. Christians were enjoined to be obedient to the just demands of spouses, and to care for offspring and the unattached. They were instructed to be obedient to just political authority. Nevertheless, they pushed back and redefined the boundaries of family life, seeing the community of faith as the *genuine* and truly primary fellowship of brotherhood and sisterhood. While introducing a new level of mutuality and responsibility within the marital relationship, they challenged the cultural definitions of the absolute sacredness of family life and of primal responsibility to kith and kin.[9] Early Christians asserted what was viewed as scandalous then (and still is by many) when they suggested that virginity, celibacy, and continence were more holy than marriage. Sexuality is, surely, a natural law of human life. It also keeps alive the family tree and provides for future devotion to sacred genealogy. But early Christians saw it otherwise. It is always a temptation to particularist loyalty. They saw marriage, when it did occur, as an estate given by God (for those called to it) and legitimated not by the needs of the state or the family elders but by primary human needs, and approved by the more primary community, the church. In this subordinated position it was subject to universal principles. It was to be pursued with a sense of sacred responsibility, care-full responsiveness, and discipline; but it was not the center of meaning or the means of salvation, identity, or fulfillment. Children were not initiated into the family cultus or dedicated to the gods of the state, but were baptized into the church, the true community of identity. Symbolically, God was the father, the church was the mother, and Jesus was the brother; the true family was not the sexual family. As this worked out, especially in the later monastic ideals when patriarchal structures threatened to swallow the church and the family, the social power of the empirical family was reduced and relativized further. Yet from these early Christian days onward, the family is affirmed and is to be constantly reformed *under* a notion of universal moral principles.

While this community of faith was displacing those social patterns which put the family at the center of life's meanings for most of the people, it also began a long and arduous struggle with political authority. The Creator, not the emperor, was the true lawgiver. Christ was king, and the Holy Spirit truly ruled. Christians were labeled subversive because they would not pledge primary loyalty to the political powers. Regime was not the center of meaning; *polis* was not the primary community; the lords of the realm could offer no fundamental security or salvation. Christians suffered martyrdom and persecution for their independence, gained a precarious toleration within a few centuries, but only belatedly obtained freedom from political domination.[10] For them the true kingdom was not of this world. Again, to those then and now who see all meaning and historical significance in political terms, the early Christian assertion was, and remains, a scandal. But it was and is the comprehensiveness and the moral-spiritual competence of politics as a force able to produce a truly universal human life that are challenged.

C. THE INCLUSION OF GRECO-ROMAN THOUGHT

The church interacted with its environment in other well. The early Christians relativized, but did not negate, their surroundings by adopting and adapting the most important thought forms from ancient, non-Hebraic cultures. The biblical peoples had done the same thing, as can be seen in many parts of Scripture. In the early centuries of the faith, Christians encountered the highly sophisticated wisdom of the Greek and Roman philosophers, wisdom intimately related to problems of *polis,* of urban and cosmopolitan values. Christians were sorely tempted to preserve without modification the biblical modes of thinking and to condemn all "worldly" wisdom as irrelevant. At the same time, other religious cults were speaking of their own special religious knowledge. It is very difficult to speak of the universal significance of one way of thinking and living if one does not use universal categories, even if many things universal in significance are particular in reference or source. Christianity appeared to be merely another of the esoteric, particular cults flourishing in the Greco-Roman world.[11]

Christianity gradually modified its use of biblical categories alone in favor of the inclusion of categories from Plato, Aristotle, and the Stoics. They gained thereby a capacity to set forth their universalistic views about, especially, moral law and human nature in more universalistic terms. On the anvil of debates about these issues, the basic contours of all Western thinking about human rights were hammered out. This is the fifth, and in some ways a culminating, contribution of ancient Christianity to human rights. Theology as a science was created; a systematic, rational, and faithful set of methods was developed to guide the selection, ordering, and application of insights from the past, to connect piety with reason, and to refine symbols and concepts so that they made sense in guiding thought and action toward the future. The wedding of Hebraic and Greco-Roman thought provided the theoretical foundation for a cosmopolitan, theological ethic.[12]

Theology was not created merely as a matter of convenience. Hebraic thought and Greek thought have certain similarities, whatever their sharp contrasts in other areas. As Jews and Christians believed in an "otherness" that was also "present," the Greeks had discovered "theory." There is, they held, a "realm of ideas" where one can grasp matters of universal importance, where one can learn about the form of justice, even if the situation in which one empirically lives is not just. Both traditions understood all humans both as having a unique individuality—an "image of God" for Jews and Christians, a "soul" for Greeks—and as being social creatures. In both traditions humanity has a capacity to know and discern an "other" world, and to attempt to enact it in this life, in both private and public life. Further, neither this capacity for knowledge nor the accessibility of that which is known is determined by the family or political institution into which one is born. The philosopher stands in, but he is not finally of, the empirical order.

These two traditions were also marked by sharp differences. Whereas the Greeks accented the human capacities to attain the universal "higher order" by energetic thought or effort, Jews and Christians believed that it was given to humanity by God by a gift of grace or revelation. Hence the Greeks thought it arrogant to speak of "inherent human abilities." Whereas Greeks thought in organic and hierarchical terms, Christian concern for the marginalized people modified the aristocratic bias toward greater inclusion. And whereas the Greeks often oscillated between a conception of life as constant and somewhat static and a conception of life as radical flux, the Hebraic-Christian hope for radical transformation in the future that would be in concert with the law of God sustained a dynamic expectance that had, nevertheless, a constant normative shape. Still, in the wedding of these motifs, in the formation of a new alliance between revelation and reason, Christianity had established by the time of Athanasius (and still more firmly by the time of Ambrose and Augustine) a "public theology," a creed held to be philosophically viable and capable of giving moral shape to complex civilization.

The community of faith, living under a covenant of law, hope, and love, was seen by its members as possessing a vision of life that established a genuinely human right for all peoples, one which reached from the very foundations of creation to the highest wisdom of philosophy. It contained, in principle, the clue to the core meaning and dignity of each self, and extended that meaning to the whole of humanity. Thus the church was the "soul of civilization," claiming a divine and natural right to a social space, in but not of the world, distinct from family-ethnicity and from political power, and capable, from that space, of informing and reforming both.[13]

Rome collapsed, as had the Hebraic and Greek political orders before it. The ancient family-clan and ethnic lines became jumbled, although a widespread paternalistic, hierarchical, familial authority-pattern survived that has influenced the West deeply. More decisively, the church remained, preserving the universalistic values of both Greco-Roman and Hebraic belief, without which modern discussions of human rights would have been impossible. It is true that the church in its middle millennium baptized more authoritarian familial and political structures than its early experience and subsequent developments could have approved. More importantly, it preserved a distinction between family, state, and church, sustained by an organized constituency that manifests a continuing universal concern for all members of humanity, guided by a powerful sense of duty to a universal moral law.

The implications were legion. In the doctrine of the Trinity which emerged, the very character of God, and therefore the character of all that is really real, is understood as persons in covenanted relationship under a more ultimate integrating principle.[14] In Augustine's *City of God* we find an interpretation of human history with a profound sense of the relationship of "otherness" and "presence," of sin and grace, of Greek and Roman thought and Hebraic law and hope, unified in love. And in the moral teachings of the early medieval church, often codified in law, we find a Stoic-Christian perception of universalistic duty and claim which both de-absolutizes and supports familial and political order.[15]

D. THE MEDIEVAL RESPONSE TO CRISIS

During the Middle Ages these decisive roots of all modern discussions of human rights were deeply planted in the church: there is a universal moral law governing all human relations known by faith and reason. Thus there must be space, social space, for a universalistically oriented community to exist, to form a base from which to challenge all natural loyalties to one's own kind and from which to transcend the particular loyalties to family and power. These themes supported the growth and influence of monasticism and the power of the clergy in general. In the church one was a member of the most universal community conceivable. In taking vows of poverty, chastity, and obedience, one voluntarily assumed a discipline, in accord with the laws of this community. Material interests were declared to be subordinate to a higher order, and the two social institutions which catered to material interests, the family and the regime, were seen only as secondary institutions. In the Middle Ages, however, these ideas were only partially effective beyond the church, and they were refined and extended only in response to severe challenges.

The first challenge was an exterior one, an overtly religious one: Islam swept much of the Mediterranean world. Like Judaism and Christianity, Islam claimed one God and a universal moral law by which nations and persons were to be judged. But its message was in certain ways strikingly different from the Christian message. For one thing, it did not develop "theology." It developed jurisprudence in a highly sophisticated way, and at certain stages it developed subtle modes of philosophical reflection—surpassing the West—under the influence of the Greeks. But its doctrine of revelation, fully and finally contained in the literal words of the Koran, gave rise to a biblicism which has always been judged to be a fundamentalist heresy in the West. It led also to quite different social and political forms. It had no *ecclesia*. Its religion was, in its social base, entirely familial and political, united by an absolute legalism. Its law was organized and enforced by dynasty and paramilitary political brotherhoods, by tribes and Caliphates. It has had, to be sure, internal divisions of an intensive sort, but even the tensions between the two major sects are rooted in the question of whether familial lineage or political authority shall be the dominant force in determining the succession of religious leadership. In both forms Islam conceived of a holistic society where family and political power are fully Islamicized and integrated into a single undifferentiated social and legal fabric.[16]

The response to the challenge of Islam was twofold. From 732, when Charles Martel slowed the tide of Muslim advance, the church tended to depend upon political protection, to utilize military force for its own purposes, and to use its theology to legitimate specific political and military powers. These tendencies issued soon in the imperial power of Charlemagne. Three centuries later they influenced the Crusades.[17] In a variety of ways, developments in these three centuries tied the church to feudal authority, especially as represented by the knights. Over time the church nearly lost its organizational autonomy, becoming merely the domesticated chaplain to those established familial and political authorities who could repel the infidels. Of this period Roland Bainton writes, "The bishops and abbots resembled the counts and dukes in their status, function, and behavior."[18] Yet, because of the deep and abiding distrust between church and imperial power, the church refused to submit entirely or easily. During these three centuries, intense and complicated conflicts between *regnum* and *sacerdotum* were in principle mitigated by the papal claim of the right to crown emperors. The autonomy of the church, and its guardianship of moral principles which limited the absolute authority of political power, had been stated in principle since the "Ordinance of 817" was drafted by clergy. That document set forth a formal procedure for penalizing a tyrannical king. The majesty of political power, which in ancient life was often sanctified by the incantations of subservient priestcrafts, was here relativized, subordinated in worth and power, reduced in holiness, and yet affirmed. It was dignified and recognized as necessary for human life *under* a higher law. Some feudal practices regarding the limits of authority fit well with these principles and allowed their partial acceptance in practice. These developments reinstituted the idea of limited, but legitimate, political authority. The viability of political life was not undercut. Yet the root insight of the Judeo-Christian understanding of politics as secondary, not primary, was preserved. There is a majesty in political power which is to be honored and obeyed. No civilization can exist without political power. The Hebrews in one way and the Greeks in another had already seen, however, that the majesty of political power resides not in the fact of power itself but in its quality. *Just* power alone is majestic, and power evaluated for the quality of justice is power placed under a higher principle. The idea is clear, but it was not until Christianity formed a differentiated substructure wherein the church could evaluate political authority, not simply serve it, that the idea became a powerful force in the operating history of the West. Whatever we may attribute to the influence of the great prophets of ancient biblical times, who indeed anticipated this development, and whatever we may grant to the Greek philosophers who defined justice above and beyond conventional practices of the *polis*, it is through these often-forgotten struggles of the pope and the emperor (or the king) that the social-intellectual foundations were laid to bring about a universalistic community which could be a witness for justice and righteousness without being crushed. The Germanic emperors who were the heirs of the ancient views of "priest-kings" opposed these notions. They presumed a more absolute authority for political governance. They assumed the power to appoint bishops. Yet their piety restrained their tendency to subordinate the church utterly.

As Professor Fritz Kern has shown, it was during this period that a new alliance was formed between ancient claims.[19] On the one hand, the Germanic peoples, who had brought about the fall of Rome, claimed that injured tribes could take up arms against pretentious power. On the other hand, some Christians set forth ecclesiastical claims that all authority was held as a trust, to be exercised only so long as God's justice was upheld. The interaction of these claims formed a moral "right of resistance" to tyrannical authority *as a basic human principle,* ideally to be enforced by the church, representing the whole of humanity, with the freedom of the church defended by political authority.

Ironically, however, in resisting Islam and in struggling with internal regional divisions, the Western Christian Church as represented by papal authority became more like its opponents, sometimes losing its relative independence of political power and thereby its capacity to criticize existing institutions. At many points it was unable to maintain any critical distance from the predominant structures of culture and society.

A second set of developments was just as fateful. New movements among the monastics, typified by Saint Francis, sought to renew piety and learning among the people. These gave rise to groups of itinerant preachers, deeply concerned with the souls, convictions, and needs of the peasants and the townsmen. They addressed the people in the idioms of the day, infusing their ordinary commitments with a religious zeal. These developments brought about a new self-consciousness among the peoples of Europe. A spirit of regionalism which had long been present was reinvigorated—a deep sense that the Germans, the French, the English, the Italians, and the Spaniards each had their own cultural memories and traditions, their own quests for prominence and power, which were threatened equally by the Muslims and by the imperial church which fought them. The bishops and priests of these areas were dependent on local practice and trust, and often baptized what they knew best. The new "people's spirituality" did the same thing now for simple folk: it created a new, vigorous piety from the ground up. Joachim of Fiore, a monk who in some ways anticipated the pre-reformers Wycliffe and Huss, foresaw a new age of "spiritual democracy" in the church. He expected a new period of life in which all orders of sacrament, law, and hierarchy would be overcome. His ideas encouraged the spiritual populism that became influential among many who never read his works, often becoming the vocabulary of proto-nationalism.

Collective national identity arose slowly, and came to full realization only in the modern nation-state. But from the tenth and eleventh centuries onward, it contributed to a growing sense of lay spirituality, regional identity, cultural-political pluralism, and particularity. The principles and vision of the universality of God's reign were intensified, yet the "imposed" ecclesiastical order, represented on earth by a unified church, was compromised. Linguistic and regional groupings backed different parties in the church. For several centuries the church was able to contain these developments and preserve unity. Eventually, however, the multiple pressures broke the containment, giving rise to numerous sectarian groups and, at some points, to the enthronement of more than one pope. Each religious faction was tempted to become an instrument of political influence in international intrigue. The universality which was claimed against the Muslims was fragmented from within. In another way than in those tendencies which issued in the Crusades, the relative independence of the church from political interest was compromised.

Still another threat to the conventional views of religion and society paralleled the encounter with another world religion and the internal struggles. In the midst of Western feudal society, the "free cities" were growing, especially during and after the eleventh century. The people of these cities elected city councils to manage their business. They were influenced by both biblical motifs and civil concepts from the Greco-Roman period. These cities passed new laws, developed new theories of property, and established civil rights for the burghers. Membership in the city was by election, and participation in the Mass served as the centerpoint for common identity. In many instances the Mass became the religious celebration of particular, individual membership in a system of meaning which served as a reminder of universal participation in a universal church, and the sign of civil solidarity (hence Jews were excluded). Furthermore, the development in the cities of relatively autonomous "corporations," first in the guilds and eventually in the university centers, gave form to a kind of membership partially independent of political and familial authority. Against the feudal alliances of family, miter, and crown, these cities and their "corporations" developed notions of participation, claim, "pluralism," and "rights" which were to be of enormous consequence later on, although at the time they were quite localistic and exclusive, opportunistically allied with whichever prince or bishop, emperor or pope granted the most freedom. Yet again, as in the ancient experiences of Israel and Greece, these particular circumstances pressed toward a recognition of the critical role of a normative order, of universal implication, and the need for both a vision of a cosmopolitan future and a fresh definition of "membership."[20]

In the midst of these threats, one of the most significant church responses is represented by the Gregorian Reforms. When he was elected pope (1073–1085), Hildebrand, himself deeply influenced by the monastic centers which had resisted feudal political practices and the passing of church offices to heirs, tried to establish a unified, universal vision of spiritual truth and of moral society beyond these emerging divisions. He took the name Gregory VII, thereby affirming solidarity with a previous Gregory who had been forced out of office by political authority, and with Gregory the First, who is noted as the interpreter of Augustine to the masses of Christians and the consolidator of the early medieval church. He preached a fiery "right of resistance" to unjust political rule. He established a centralized ecclesiastical government *to which every person had the right of appeal beyond feudal authority, regional ruler, disobedient clergy, and civic order.* As J. W. Maitland has shown, in the medieval period there was no "public" law[21]; all rights were private and direct. The feudal oaths between persons on behalf of families determined both duty and claim. In contrast to this tradition, the new development by Gregory VII meant that persons had a point of appeal beyond the particular, personal, political-familial-economic network of obligations in local and national society.[22] They had a "membership" beyond the particular dictates of family, city, and nation. This decisive move in church law was paralleled by other moves that were equally important. Gregory VII supported monastic communities which operated transnationally, recognizing the viability of at least an ecclesial international corporation. Religion at its purest is *not* to be a national affair or a family matter. He called for celibacy among the clergy, which further removed the representatives of the church from entangling feudal responsibilities and privileges by reason of traditional familial obligations. In brief, he reasserted the priority of universal thinking and of an ecumenical community of faith over the accouterments of social, familial, and political power. The attempt to challenge the established structures of authority and to make effective his universalistic efforts, however, proved too much for the times. He was exiled by the emperor, and his efforts at reform were less than fully effective. Nevertheless, they stood then and they stand even today as symbols, more than as actual signs, of the efforts of organized religion to encounter the questions of universalism of claim, pluralism of fact, and localism of experience in religion and society. The gains were of such import that the noted commentator E. Rosenstock-Huessy can write, with only slight exaggeration, "In western civilization, at least since Gregory VII, two sovereign powers have always balanced each other. This, and this alone, has created European freedom."[23]

E. UNIVERSALITY AND CONCILIARISM

The impact of Islam, the threat of national and city autonomy, the entanglements of the feudal family, and the attempt to control political power were made more difficult by a major intellectual crisis, reflected in a far-reaching theological debate over "universals." The debate was simultaneously metaphysical, epistemological, ethical, and sociopolitical. It pitted the realists against the nominalists. The realists held that general or generic terms, such as "humanity," refer to universal realities of which individuals are an instance. The nominalists held that only individuals had real existence and that general conceptions exist only as constructs of the human mind. Ideas and concepts do not refer to any extramental reality. The realist-nominalist debate was conducted primarily in theological terms. Questions of whether the "real presence" of Christ was in the elements of the Mass, whether the three "persons" of the Trinity had an ultimate, transcendent unity, and whether the corporate unity of the church had a reality beyond the sum of particular members were the critical issues.

Even the much-maligned question "How many angels can dance on the head of a pin?" takes on deep significance in this context. Not only was this a rather primitive way of asking a quite modern question (does all energy—

including all spiritual energy—have mass?), but it was a profound way of inquiring as to whether several objects of loyalty can belong to the same geographical space. Must one authority reign, or may several overlap in a given area?

All these issues pointed to the fundamental question: Is there a universal moral reality for all humanity? If there is, what is its relationship to particular persons and groups? If there is not, are we not plunged into an anarchy of individuals and particular groupings? The question of "universals" had been anticipated in philosophy from the time of the Greek philosophers, and the ancient Hebrew prophets had struggled against varieties of localistic piety and politics in the face of the Jahwistic claim for a single and universal center of loyalty and moral law. At the time of the creation of theology as a science by such figures as Athanasius, Ambrose, and Augustine, the question of universals had again been given vital articulation. It had surfaced again, at the time of the Gregorian Reforms, in the works of Anselm, Peter Abelard, Peter Lombard, and John of Salisbury, scholars who anticipated the issues of Conciliar Catholicism, which was to challenge absolute papal authority. But here once more the very viability of a genuinely universal public theology was challenged.

The questions were debated in great detail, and some of the greatest names in the history of thought are connected with the struggle. Every question—moral, epistemological, ontological, and social-organizational—was affected by it. The church in time rejected both the extreme realist position and the extreme nominalist position. Instead, it moved toward the moderate nominalism of Ockham (Occam) and the moderate realism of Thomas Aquinas. At the least this meant, with Ockham, that universals stand for real qualities that can be abstracted from individual things. This view had great importance for metaphysics and for the eventual development of modern science, as well as for ethics. In ecclesiology Ockham pressed toward an inclusion of the laity and the rights of the laity in determining the fundamental truth of the whole. In his *Dialogue* (1342?) he put forth the argument that, indeed, pope and cardinals might perish and still a general council including women and children could arrive at a truly universal understanding of faith and morals. The Holy Spirit, through the instrument of reasoning in charity, could bring the people of God to truth. At most it meant, with Thomas, that in God there is an eternal law which sustains a natural law governing the relationship of all particulars, a law confirmed to our knowledge by divine law in revelation. Ockham's view pressed toward democratization of authority; Thomas's preserved a vision of spiritual hierarchy; both saw the prospect of theological discernment of a universal ethic.

For a time the mediating positions seemed to work, supported by the traditional authority of the church and by the relative stability of feudalism. The "public theology" persisted and was temporarily able to comprehend within itself the concreteness of particular private experience, the awareness of group identity, and a religion for the common life. But the integration was fragile, and the acids of interior and exterior challenge began to consume the tissues of integration. Public theology began to deteriorate. Public meanings seemed less convincing, and traditional solidarities began to decay. Dante, whose thought had some affinities with that of Thomas, argued that there were two realms, and that, properly ordered in complementary hierarchy, each confirmed the other. In *On Monarchy* he stated that exterior, temporal peace could best be secured by the emperor, while the best guide to inward, eternal blessedness was the pope. Neither should interfere with the other; both represented the authoritative, normative orders of life. Although they were complementary in the whole, organic order of the cosmos, they had to be distinct in ordinary life. A contrary view, closer to that of Ockham, was set forth by Marsilius of Padua. In *Defensor Pacis* he argued that *all* authority derives from the general discernment of the people, and that all persons, not just those in authority, had rights. The true church is the whole body of the people. Thus it determines, through common meeting in a council, what should govern both *imperium* and *ecclesia*. Insofar as the emperor and the pope were symbols of separate institutional realms, the distinction was to be maintained. But what they propagated as truth was subject to debate. The people had to be sufficiently convinced to agree with them in conciliar decisions. The earlier notions of truth and justice derived from biblical and Greco-Roman sources were here supplemented by a profound sense of inclusive procedural patterns developed within feudalism to assure universality in the discernment and articulation of the substantive concerns. These notions were generally condemned by officials, both political and ecclesiastical. Within but a few centuries, however, they were the common currency of intellectual life. By the late fourteenth century they were invoked repeatedly in attempts to reformulate a public theology. The issue between these two representative postures is an issue which haunts all discussions of human rights: are claims about universals fundamentally to be decided by an appeal to an objective order of things, which presumably only some can know with clarity, or are they to be derived from a consensus formed in dialogue? The former stresses the question of truth, whether all agree or not; the latter stresses procedures whereby people can come to agreement about the truth.[24] One asks, "What is?"; the other asks, "Who says?"

Nothing represents the fruition of this crisis more than the Council of Constance in 1415. It was, in a very direct sense, the last great effort (until the twentieth century) of a truly "catholic" church to establish a public theology for "all" the "civilized world." A central dispute was about the real presence of Christ in the particular elements of the sacrament. In this dispute, so apparently esoteric to moderns, all the questions of the realist-nominalist debates and the questions of authority were present—with all their metaphysical, moral, and sociopolitical overtones. More visible was the scandal of multiple popes, but the same issues of authority were present. John N. Figgis indicates how important these disputes were when he claims that "the most revolutionary official document in the history of the world is the decree of the Council of Constance."[25] That decree asserted the superiority of the council to the pope. It appeared that

Marsilius had won. Further, that council also burned at the stake John Huss, a forceful, even violent representative of popular religious, sectarian church order and nationalistic sentiment—a hero and forerunner of the Reformation. Burning Huss was made the more dramatic because Huss had been given a "safe conduct" guarantee by the Holy Roman Emperor. Thus, in an indirect way, the council asserted church authority above political authority as well. In a series of swift moves, the council thereby claimed that the "ecumenical" religious community was the true custodian of moral discernment and judgment, above and beyond the papacy, any particular ethnic or national authority, sectarian groups, and the sovereignty of political power.

Pope John XXIII, who was deposed by the council, was reigning when the council was called. (Note the intended irony when, in the twentieth century, the most celebrated innovator in modern Catholicism took the name Pope John XXIII, called a new council, Vatican II, and published *Pacem in Terris*.) Schismatics such as Huss and Wycliffe were the forerunners of the Reformation and of the Radical Reformation (which much influenced later Protestant and Marxist thought), men who claimed religion to be intended for the simple people. The Bible was taken from the hands of clerical experts and given to the laity. Moreover, religion was taken as the key to national freedom. The Holy Roman Emperor found his power eroding at the hands both of the new national enthusiasm and of the trading populations in the cities. Significantly, the delegates to Constance were appointed by region, and for the first time formed "caucuses" around "national" interests. All the ideational and social forces of the late Middle Ages seemed to converge in this council. People date the turn to modernity differently. If I had to choose a moment of turning as it bears on the question of human rights, this would be it.

The remarkable thing about this council is that it failed—Figgis says that "it failed utterly."[26] It did not fail in expressing the modulation of feudalism in the West, but it failed to bring about a new vision of universal meaning and a viable organization committed to universal values to sustain the vision against the power of familial and political authority. The failure meant that the vision of a normative moral order that could comprehend persons, groups, and collectivities broke down. The pieces and parts went in several directions. Thereafter, faith became increasingly disconnected from outward reasoning in community. Laity became increasingly separated from overarching ecclesiastical authority; the universal church broke into regional bodies. Multiple sects and "churches" began to emerge, established on spiritual, confessional, nationalistic, or ethnic bases. Catholicism suppressed its own conciliarists and became militantly reactionary for centuries. Religion became, in the minds of many, distinct from political philosophy and from universal claims. Philosophy and science went one way, religion and ethics another. As we shall see in the subsequent chapters, the way was paved for Luther and Machiavelli, for Calvin and the counter-Reformation, and eventually for Hobbes, Locke, Hume, Rousseau, and Marx. The way was also open to new encounter with the non-Western religions and societies, eventually culminating in the twentieth-century formation of a secular conciliar effort in the form of the United Nations.

The eclipse of a "public theology" with a universalistic ethic moved religion toward private confession with fresh emphasis on the inward individual, toward group consciousness of particular solidarity groups, and toward "civil religion,"[27] with its historical confidence in nonchurch, political salvation. The failure of the Roman Catholic Church to be truly catholic in this time, yet its having nearly achieved the ideal, caused a sharp reaction against Roman faith and morals, even if its relative accomplishment has served subsequently as a constant model to both its defenders and its critics. Only one cluster of traditions, one that was a minority, kept alive the universalistic orientation, sustained by an ecclesial community, remaining distinct from familial and political authority by linking the gains of the medieval church with a renewed dedication to recovered biblical motifs and a renewal of theology.

Between the time of Constance and the twentieth century, these fragments of basic religious orientations have combined in different and intriguing ways. From then until now, no single trajectory can convey the whole story. Instead, a minority Christian tradition became heir to the ecumenical Conciliar Catholic effort. Another preserved the hierarchical spiritual influence of sacramentalized feudalism with its sanctification of traditional, hierarchic authority and metaphysics, and still a third turned to political power as the means of salvation. These different paths to the present can, I think, be typified by the three societies under scrutiny in this book. In ways that we shall trace, we shall note both the convergence and divergence of Conciliar Christian, Marxist-political, and traditional hierarchic perspectives on religion, family, politics, and human rights as they influence all sectors of the society. In the following chapters we shall see how, in East Germany, there is a particular link and a tension between religion as a matter of private confession and the powerful development of a civil religion, very like the trends that can be seen in the realist-nominalist debates. And in the discussion of modern India we will see how notions of practical utility derived from one branch of Western liberalism have become linked to a particular hierarchical, organic, feudal order very much like that of the medieval period of the West (but in this case organized around caste). We shall trace these developments longitudinally and by cross-sectional analysis. Each of these developments has a specific view of human nature and moral order, and therefore of human rights, quite different from that of the modern West.

But before we proceed to examine these non-Western perspectives, we turn to those developments in religion and society which shaped the United States and which provide the context for such events as the sending of the joint letter to President Carter with which I began this chapter. This too will be traced longitudinally and cross-sectionally. The Western tradition drew from biblical, Greco-Roman, urban, corporative, and conciliar foundations, but moved them in a specific "free church" direction. It is no accident that the recipient of the letter is a sectarian, puritan, "liberal," born-again Baptist; that he appointed

Andrew Young, a minister of a denomination founded by a Puritan and a follower of Martin Luther King, Jr., to be the chief ambassador to the United Nations; or that their public rhetoric and international policy have been focused more on human rights than on any other moral issue. Whatever their failures as political leaders, they represent a profound aspect of the Western tradition on human rights questions which successors cannot ignore. Even more significant is the joining together of groups, representing the divergent social ideologies and social interests which Constance could not hold together, to petition political authority to maintain universal human rights as a cornerstone of international relations. The traditions they represent are deeply rooted ones still struggling for recognition and implementation. Only in some societies are such groups vigorous and influential. We turn next to the analysis of the minority reports of Western thought and society, which turn out to have been of major consequence for American life.

---

1. "An Open Letter to President Carter on Human Rights," National Council of Churches Press Release, Jan. 20, 1977. See Appendix I.

2. President Jimmy Carter, "Address to the United Nations General Assembly," March 17, 1977.

3. See Stanley Stuber, *Human Rights and Fundamental Freedoms in Your Community* (New York: Association Press, 1968); and the U. S. Department of State, *Selected Documents*, No. 5, revised (Nov. 1978).

4. Hugh A. Koops, "Pressing the Claims, Interpreting the Cries," in A. O. Miller, ed., *A Christian Declaration on Human Rights* (Grand Rapids, Mich.: Eerdmans, 1977), pp. 55ff. See also Walter Harrelson, *The Ten Commandments and Human Rights* (Philadelphia: Fortress Press, 1979).

5. See my "Reaffirmations," *Journal of Ecumenical Studies*, 15 (Fall 1978), 662ff.

6. Richard L. Deats, "Human Rights: An Historical and Theological Perspective," *Engage/Social Action Forum*, No. 38 (March 1978), pp. 10f.

7. At the time of the writing of the New Testament, the formation of independent groups outside family, political authority, or traditional ethnic groupings was illegal. Hence, so numerous biblical scholars tell us, the explicit references to "covenant theory" in the New Testament are muted, but the implicit references abound.

8. Max Weber is surely correct in his claim that early Christianity was of the "congregational type of religion [and] has been intimately connected with the urban middle classes of both the upper and lower levels." It is related to "the recession in the importance of blood groupings," and the loss of confidence in imperial political power (*Economy and Society*, II, ed. G. Roth and C. Wittich [New York: Bedminster Press, 1968], 482f.).

9. Fustel de Coulanges, *The Ancient City* (Garden City, N.Y.: Doubleday, n.d.).

10. C. M. Cochrane, *Christianity and Classical Culture* (New York: Oxford University Press, 1944).

11. Rudolf Bultmann, *Primitive Christianity* (New York: Meridian Books, 1956).

12. See my *Ethics and the Urban Ethos* (Boston: Beacon Press, 1973). This view, of course, is in sharp tension with both "liberal" theological ones such as that represented by Harnack, and "conservative" biblicist ones. Both see the engagement with philosophy and with Greco-Roman culture as a "fall."

13. See J. C. Brauer, *The Impact of the Church upon its Culture*: Essays in Divinity Series, II (Chicago: University of Chicago Press, 1968).

14. See *Ethics and the Urban Ethos*, especially Chapter VI.

15. Ernst Troeltsch, "Stoic-Christian Natural Law and the Modern-Secular Natural Law," from *Gesammelte Schriften*, II, 515ff. Forthcoming.

16. See W. M. Watt, *Islam and the Integration of Society* (London: Routledge, 1961); W. M. Watt, *The Influence of Islam on Medieval Europe* (Edinburgh: Edinburgh University Press, 1972); and W. C. Smith, *Islam in Modern History* (Princeton, N.J.: Princeton University Press, 1957). See also my "Democracy and the World's Religions," *This World* (1982), 108—20.

17. See Edward Powers, ed., *Christian Society and the Crusades* (Philadelphia: University of Pennsylvania Press, 1971); and Hans E. Mayer, *The Crusades* (London: Oxford University Press, 1972).

18. Roland Bainton, *Christendom*, I (New York: Harper & Row, 1966), p. 149.

19. F. Kern, *Kingship, Law and Constitution in the Middle Ages* (New York: Harper & Row, 1956).

20. See Weber, *Economy and Society*, Vol. III, Chapter XVI, especially "The City," 1241ff. I am very concerned at these turning points of the historical development of human rights to show, at least by reference and brief synopsis, that there is, as the Marxists claim, a connection between theology and "bourgeois" rights, but that the sense of rights did not grow entirely out of substructural economic conditions so much as reflect a particular, theologically rooted, ecclesiological response to social conditions. The theological issues involved in this period are cogently set forth in Colin Morris, *The Discovery of the Individual, 1050—1200* (London: S.P.C.K., 1972).

21. J. W. Maitland, Introduction to Otto Gierke's *Political Theories of the Middle Ages* (Boston: Beacon Press, 1959). See also, on this period, Walter Ullman, *A Short History of the Papacy in the Middle Ages* (London: Methuen, 1972).

22. The networks of particular obligations characteristic of this period are, in many ways, comparable to what we shall find in India (Chapters Seven and Eight).

23. E. Rosenstock-Huessy, *Out of Revolution* (New York: Morrow, 1938), p. 543. See also Ronald Stone, *Realism and Hope* (Washington, D.C.: University Press of America, 1977), Chapter 3.

24. See especially Gierke's *Political Theories of the Middle Ages.*

25. J. N. Figgis, *Studies of Political Thought from Gerson to Grotius, 1414—1625* (1907; rpt. New York: Harper, 1960), p. 41.

26. Ibid.

27. The term finds its current usage in the work of Robert Bellah especially. See his "Civil Religion in America," *Daedalus* (Winter 1967); "American Civil Religion in the 1970s," *Anglican Theological Review*, Supplementary Series, No. 1 (July 1973); and *The Broken Covenant* (New York: Seabury Press, 1975). Historically, the term derives from Rousseau, as we shall see (Chapter Six), who in turn adapted it from some of the Stoic philosophers who defended the Roman Empire against such critics of it as Augustine.

CHAPTER THREE

The Western Revolutionary Tradition: A Longitudinal Interpretation

A. THE CORE OF AMERICAN SOCIETY

ONE of the most distinctive features of American society is the power, extent, and character of "intermediary" institutions. Whether called "mesostructures," "mediating organizations," "voluntary associations," "interest groups," or the "third sector," a cluster of nongovernmental and nonprofit organizations occupies a distinctive and protected social space in the societal organization of the United States.[1] Nearly six million organizations represent grassroots, regional, national, international, vocational, artistic, advocative, ethical, and charitable concerns. One out of every ten service workers and one out of every six professional workers in the United States is employed by these organizations—more than are employed by the government and far more than are employed in any industry.[2] However powerful the government, however influential the industrial and commercial sectors of American life,[3] and however much everyone is shaped by familial and ethnic identity, the presence and vitality of these groups have given the social fabric of America a peculiar form that is especially remarkable in any comparative analysis.[4] Indeed, as we shall see, political life and industrial life in America are themselves decisively shaped by the pluralistic, multiform ethos which these groups have produced.

These organizations derive from the impact of religious groups on Western social life as they have extracted key motifs of the ancient, medieval, and conciliar traditions and applied them in revolutionary ways. A particular branch of the Christian tradition, the Free-Church tradition, although now expanded beyond specific Christian confession, created a distinct arena for community organization, a social space for participation and membership in voluntary associations, that is prior to and inviolable by public authority.[5] The churches prepared the way, demanding a guaranteed autonomy from exterior control. The autonomy was, at first, to ensure the freedom of worship and the congregation's right to govern its own affairs. But as the implications of the message and the polity were translated into habit and public behavior, the patterns inev-

51

itably spilled over into the reform of professional, political, economical, and familial institutions. The church in effect produced socially active efforts to transform all of society according to a powerful sense of a moral law and godly purpose which could shape a commonwealth and judge its legitimacy. The social space that this effort secured has been expanded so that now all sorts of "nonofficial" and "nonreligious" organizations populate the free social spaces of American life once reserved for the churches. Many feel the kinds of commitment and loyalty to these groups also once reserved for the church. Every call for a new social orientation, for a new public policy, for a change in or the preservation of present corporate practice, for a new kind of solidarity or family lifestyle, for the pursuit of intellectual, spiritual, or material interests, borrows from this Free-Church heritage—even if the new orientation is antiecclesiastical.

The "rights" of these intermediary institutions and nongovernmental organizations are rooted in the fundamental claim that the social space occupied by the church is not to be violated because it is sacred. The church is the body of Christ, who is King; hence no one else can be sovereign. Under the biblically rooted notion that we are to obey godly and not human authority, those gathered together to discern and act out God's law and purpose for humanity form inviolable groupings. These groups gained the right to organize, assemble, publish, analyze, criticize, collect contributions or dues, own property, evangelize, demonstrate, propagandize, and lobby, boycott, influence, or oppose any other group or policy, official or unofficial. Individual rights in the American tradition, articulated under the impact of these groups, is most profoundly understood to mean the right of the person to participate in such groups.[6] It is precisely such groups which articulate the source and norm of human dignity, practically empower persons to care for the neighbor, and act to defend the rights of individuals when they are thought to be compromised by governmental or corporate or ethnic discriminations—claiming that they are "members" with equal standing in a more universal community. It is presupposed by the American Constitution and in the social ethos that neither any private person nor the government as the chief organ of coercive power may intervene in the free operation of these groups so long as they do not infringe on the rights of others or resort to violence. This, I intend to argue, is the decisive root of American civil liberties and civil rights. These group rights reflect the basic understanding of what it means to be human, and thus what human rights should be at their deepest.[7]

The formation of these groups and the establishment of this privileged social space are decisive for understanding not only civil rights but also human rights in the American context. Indeed, the development of these groups, and both the social creed and the social support systems which sustain them, is the story of the Western revolutionary tradition—indelibly a religious one, one that if not understood in religious terms makes America incomprehensible.

B. THE REFORMATION SOURCES OF THE AMERICAN ETHOS

To understand this tradition, we must remember the effort, and the failure, of the Council of Constance a century before the Reformation. Constance did not stop growing nationalism, proliferation of sectarian groups, or the changing alliances of religious and political authority; nor did Constance resolve the realist-nominalist tensions. Actually, each increased, and alliances were formed between the bearers of power and the bearers of legitimacy. An old existential question was eventually renewed: What happens when political authority does not consider itself under the constraints of higher law? Who is to guard the guardians?

The Catholics had spoken of the "right of resistance." They spoke of this cautiously, guardedly, and in a highly circumscribed manner. Usually passive disobedience was recommended; other times, as in such remarkable writings as *Policraticus* by John of Salisbury, friend of Thomas à Becket, more active possibilities of tyrannicide were discussed.[8] Canon lawyers and moral philosophers took up these questions and attempted to put them into legal form.[9] The idea that social and political authority had limitations, and that it was morally permissible to organize and struggle against it, became a part of popular lore and scholarly argument, perhaps provoking, but certainly contradicting, the emerging doctrine of "the divine right of kings." Every group which has power knows that it does not possess all the power and that there are practical limits to its use before a reaction sets in. But drawing on deep, but often obscure, theological arguments, numerous authors established *moral* limits in principle. It was morally legitimate to constrain power. Supported by traditional authorities and by biblical texts, as well as by popular distrust of particular rulers, the idea of inviolable rights beyond those rights granted by political authority or gained by personal contracts or oaths entered into the mainstream of much scholarly ethical, ecclesiastical, and judicial thinking. In the Magna Carta of 1215, much celebrated by later Protestants from the 1560's on, these motifs are evident.

It would be wrong to suggest that these developments represented the most widespread discussions of piety or learning in the pre-Reformation period. The Renaissance, with its recovery of Greek and Roman sources and its new celebrations of human capacity, had profound influence among the literate elites, including many biblical scholars and theologians. Most people, however, seemed to be preoccupied with a wide range of other issues. The Conciliar Catholics, among the late-medieval scholars who worked on such notions, were not in the majority. Yet these thinkers began a new synthesis, with a reconstruction of philosophical reflection, a vision of representative participation, and a profound religious loyalty that laid the basis for subsequent developments in the area of natural rights and human rights. The heirs of these Conciliar Catholics, often driven into defensive postures by increasing disputes between conservative Catholics and Lutherans, turned more and more to secular "humanist" learning. Erasmus in Holland, Colet and More in England, and Lefèvre in France transmitted an intellectual heritage which could have been lost in the crossfire of the times.

Early Protestants often moved in the same world of thought as these Conciliar Catholics and their heirs.[10] Many Protestants were concerned specifically with the questions of belief with intellectual integrity, the reform of church authority, and political and social rights as well as manifestations of false piety and specific abuses of church power. They often tried to work through conciliar means to rectify matters they thought were wrong, appealing to arguments made by the Conciliar Catholics.

Protestantism, of course, is inconceivable without Martin Luther. Luther challenged the authority of the Catholic Church, particularly in its most pretentious efforts to determine by earthly acts (especially indulgences) the salvation of the soul, and to use the wealth of the people to establish social privilege for church authorities. Luther wanted to recover the deeper spirituality of Christianity which he felt had been compromised by long entanglements with political and legal questions, and which had led to an unqualifiedly aristocratic authority-system within the church. His spiritual attack was everywhere understood to have direct social and political implications. Certainly Rome saw it that way, and many of the urban workers and rural peasants who were under severe economic and political pressure saw it that way as well. For nearly half a century, the rumblings of the Radical Reformation—or, as it is sometimes called when viewed from a political perspective only, the Peasants' Revolt—had been on the horizon. The leaders of these movements, most often disenchanted priests who not only were deeply engaged pastorally with their increasingly dispossessed congregations but also had been exposed to the ideas of such pre-reformers as Wycliffe and Huss, turned to Luther's teachings enthusiastically.

But by 1525, barely a decade after Luther made his break with Rome, it was clear that he was primarily engaged in a spiritual and narrowly conceived ecclesiastical revolution. He was quite unsympathetic to the political and social movements advanced by the priests, radical peasants, and craftsmen who at first responded to him. It is true that under Lutheran influence thousands of people gained a new sense of the independence of the church from Roman politics and of the decisions of the soul from institutional control. Lutheranism further restored to each person the personal sense of a God-given right to obey his or her own conscience when that conscience is informed by "the Word of God." And occasionally Lutherans took public stands on the issues that had fretted the Conciliar Catholics. The Magdeburg Confession of 1550 claimed "the natural right of resistance of the lower ranks of government" against imperial injustice. But this Lutheran formulation was soon taken to be a defense of the power of the German princes against the Holy Roman Emperor, backed by the Roman church, and not a limitation on political power itself under a fundamental moral law. Lutheran traditions did not finally follow the channels which had been developed by the Conciliar Catholics. Furthermore, Lutheranism did not develop a genuinely urban base which would allow appropriation of notions of civil rights, corporate independences, or cosmopolitan values. Its social doctrines remained attached to more authoritarian, medieval conceptions of social hierarchy, even as it advocated spiritual equality for all. Luther held rather closely to the "concession" theory of political life which had dominated some medieval Catholic thinking. In this view the right to organize groups for any purpose beyond family, church, and government was seen as something requiring the king's permission. Indeed, Luther called upon political authority, and the public at large, to "kill, stab and slaughter" those who wanted to apply notions of religious freedom to a social-political revolution.[11] (We shall return to a more extended discussion of the implications of Luther's theological efforts for ethical, social, and political life on the Continent in Chapter Five.)

In terms of basic impact on America, it was the "Reformed" part of Protestantism that made the greater difference. Those Protestants who were informed by John Calvin linked certain of Luther's religious motifs directly to sociopolitical concerns. They simultaneously recovered some ancient biblical, Greco-Roman, and late-medieval notions of law and covenant, and some humanist notions.[12] This new mix of ideas, developed self-consciously in the developing cities, empowered the movement charted in the early church and restated by the Conciliar Catholics. Meanwhile, Conservative Catholics, with pronounced organic, hierarchical, and authoritarian theology and social theory, came increasingly to dominate Roman ecclesiastical authority—in part as a reaction against the Reformation. They allied—again and again—a highly restrictive family and sexual ethic and increasingly constrained aspects of intellectual life with the privilege of social elites and with reactionary political regimes, attempting to protect doctrine and church authority from the acids of modernity. At the level of popular piety, they held the loyalty of traditional peasantry by infusing their simple (sometimes almost magical) credulity with Christian symbols. Not until the late nineteenth and early twentieth century did Catholicism re-enter the mainstream of Christian history as it bears on questions of human rights.[13] Luther stands as the great heroic and symbolic leader of the ecclesiastical conflict with conservative Roman views and practices on spiritual matters; the entire "evangelical" wing of Protestantism derives from his dynamic influence and profound intellectual and spiritual achievements. Nevertheless, he continued to share many of the conservative Roman attitudes on social and political organization; much more consequential for American concepts of religion and human rights was that wing of Protestantism deriving from John Calvin and the Reformed traditions he set in motion.

The Reformed movement is a pluralistic one. It is not all of one piece; historians of the movement have shown its tremendous diversity. Still, it is possible to identify the three major branches of the Reformed tradition that have had dominant influence in intellectual and social life:

1. The first can be called the Evangelical Calvinism. This continental school

of Reformed thought finds its distinctive relationships in continuing discussion with Lutherans and in controversy with Renaissance humanism, Catholicism generally, and the Radical Reformation. It is dogmatic in focus, heavily accenting the theological importance of revelation and, especially, the radical freedom of God. It is suspicious of humanistic ideology and of human efforts at social and political reform. Yet its tough-minded doctrinal base gives it a vertebrate position from which to speak against the pretensions of political efforts to bring salvation to the human community by forcefully attempting to establish the Kingdom of God on earth. This is the tradition that most recently produced Karl Barth, one of the great theologians of the twentieth century, as well as Jacques Ellul, the contemporary French lay-theologian who has written so extensively and critically of the perils of modern technology and urbanization. In academic theological circles this branch of Reformed thought has been among the most influential. The clarity and intensity of its work in biblical studies, its development of doctrine, and its polemical outworkings of the Calvinist tradition have had dramatic influence. Further, this tradition is politically and socially involved, although usually in a negative way. It calls for critique of the structures of community life from the standpoint of the fundamental meanings of the gospel and theological doctrine. The Barmen Declaration in the twentieth century (to be considered later) is a hallmark of this branch of Calvinism.

2. The second Reformed tradition could be called Imperial Calvinism. This branch replaced some of the late-medieval imperialistic ecclesiasticism with a Protestant one. Calvin's Geneva had moments of pronounced Imperialism; so did Puritan Massachusetts in colonial America. It appears today in the hardline heretical Calvinism of South Africa,[14] but it has from time to time gained temporary ascendancy in a wide variety of locales in Britain, America, and Holland. Doctrinally this branch is deeply suspicious of the use of modern philosophical, social, and psychological sciences. It wants to work out all moral issues solely on the basis of the propositions of revelation. In its language it often appears to be close to what I have called Evangelical Calvinism, but in reaction against progressive social and intellectual movements it has hardened frequently into a dogmatic fundamentalism. This is due in part to its doctrine of God. It is not the freedom of the sovereign God that is accented in this view; it is the *order* of God. This branch holds that what God intends for human life can be seen in the inevitable ascendancy of some over others. Such dominance of the "ungodly" by the "godly" is part of the given order of righteous life according to the plan of God. Men shall rule over women, the industrious over the improvident, the pious over the unconverted. Hence Imperial Calvinism is often constrictive and fearful of spontaneity, openness, equalities, and diversities. Socially and politically, this branch has tended to identify the "elect" as the successful political and economic leaders—an identification which has led, functionally, to theories of the racial, cultural, and religious superiority of North European, capitalistic (male) entrepreneurs. Both Evangelical Calvinism and Imperial Calvinism have tended to become "established" churches—that is, the

official church in a nation-state or territory, closely tied to and supported by the political regime.

3. The third group could be called the Free-Church Calvinists, or Puritans. This group was deeply influenced by Swiss and Dutch motifs, and in England became associated with the roots of the Radical Reformation. There they tended to break with state authority but to develop explicit theories of political respon sibilities.[15] In its early days it was influenced by Renaissance scholars such as Erasmus, More, and Lefèvre. Subsequently it was influenced by the "Liberal" philosophical traditions of British and American political theory. Free-Church Calvinism is characterized by an emphasis on the right ordering of the community of faith according to the ancient concept of "covenant." Its theology is often influenced by practical questions of church polity and by its emphasis on lay initiative and responsibility, which it derived from late-medieval conciliar movements.

The churches in this tradition are not known by doctrinal formula so much as by organizational principle or practice, indicated by names: "Presbyterians," "Congregationalists," "Separatists," "Baptists," "Friends," and even "Episcopalians" in the American tradition (as distinct from Anglicans in the Church of England). Methodists and Christian Unitarians, groups which developed a century later than the earlier Puritans, also belong in this cluster, as do a number of denominations of the nineteenth century, such as the Disciples and the Reformed churches. These movements often differ sharply among themselves on critical matters of doctrine and ecclesiology.[16] The sometimes bitter intramural struggles among these groups should not, however, obscure the fact that they belong together with respect to our questions.

The common theme in this cluster of movements is the motif of freedom under moral law—a liberation to new duty given by the grace of God, which leads to voluntary community, disciplined personal life, lay intellectuality, and social outreach. Individuals, to be faithful to Christ and to conscience and reason clarified in community, must be free to organize self-governing associations to determine their own destinies under a profound sense of God's universal moral law and a vision of God's coming Kingdom. The basic, primordial freedom of the church to order its own life is taken as the basis for the organization of political, economic, educational, familial, and other aspects of life. Political authority does not grant "concessions"; it does not have the authority to allow or disallow these groups to be formed, or to give or to withdraw permission[17]— quite the contrary. This branch openly drew on the social models of independent organizations that had been developed in the cities, guilds, and universities, and claimed them as "divine rights," on the analogy of the right of the church.[18] Intellectually they drew on Greco-Roman and Renaissance philosophical motifs (and, later, on the philosophical motifs of the Enlightenment) to express the universal character of their creeds.[19] Recently they have taken secular, social, and scientific theories as necessary, supplementary parts of the formation of theology. The use of secular social and intellectual motifs, however, is governed by an affirmation of biblically rooted categories. In such modern representative thinkers as Abraham Kuyper, William Temple, Walter Rauschenbusch, H. Richard Niebuhr, Reinhold Niebuhr, John Bennett, Martin Luther King, Jr., and James Luther Adams, sociopolitical and intellectual values of a cosmopolitan sort are dealt with in a fundamentally theological way. These heirs of the Free-Church Calvinist tradition see "common grace" in ordinary experience. The knowledge of the universal laws of justice is intimately related to the special insights of the Bible as discerned, interpreted, and applied by reason and spirit to form and reform tradition. This tradition tends to call participatory assemblies, conventions, synods, and councils to make decisions, and these decisions are often intensely focused on public issues, theologically interpreted. This branch thus recapitulates the social-organizational heritage as well as the intellectual heritage of the minority movement of Conciliar Catholics.

C. THE THEOLOGICAL FOUNDATIONS OF HUMAN RIGHTS

The three branches of the Reformed tradition interacted at many points. The three directions are all possible to find in Calvin's own life and work. The theology of Calvin is, at points, overwhelmingly evangelical in its thrust, deeply marked by Luther's imprint, and strongly dogmatic. Calvin also had "Imperial" moments, such as those during the trial and burning of Servetus.[20] But large sections of Calvin's work also focused on covenant and ecclesiastical polity, governed by God's law, purpose, and love, and seen as normative for separate political authority—the Puritan themes. Yet each accent implied a somewhat different understanding of "rights" because each possible direction of Calvinism had somewhat variant views of what is genuinely "human."

Evangelical Calvinists share with Luther an understanding of "justification by faith alone." This type of Calvinism sees the radical corruption of the Fall so profoundly that claims about human rights border on arrogant pride. Humanity is so irremediably sinful that to assert a claim on the basis of innate worth, because one is human, is nothing but pretense. In the face of the sovereign freedom, holiness, and righteousness of God, everyone is recognized as wicked and undeserving of rights or mercy. However, through the unmerited grace and unfathomable love of God, sin is forgiven and humans are called to become obedient, temporal servants of the Lord in worldly vocations.

In this theological perspective, social and political authorities, which are the "principalities and powers of the world," must provide for a certain freedom from constraint. For Luther "freedom" meant, essentially, to preach "the Word of God" and to believe it in one's heart. Evangelical Calvinists significantly broke with Lutheran tradition on this point. They affirmed what Luther affirmed, but they demanded more: the right to organize. That "more" gave all of the Reformed branch of Protestantism a socially dynamic base. From the time of Luther, the Lutheran tradition has generally held that the organization of life and work was given in the very "orders for creation."[21] As women are to be mothers and men fathers, so some are to be farmers, some soldiers, and some rulers. In this, Lutheran tradition is closely allied with Conservative Catholic theories of the Middle Ages (and similar to hierarchical, organic spiritualities of many cultures, including Hinduism). Organizational life and the structures of work are rooted in a pregiven "cosmos of vocations," a hierarchical, natural fabric of social roles into which each individual fits, and to which each is to bring an inner dedication.[22] As Max Weber argued in his seminal treatment of the Protestant ethic,[23] both Lutherans and Calvinists perceive the secular calling as a decisive arena in which to work out one's God-given duty. Evangelical Calvinists, however, do not necessarily affirm that the structure of social roles is pregiven by God in creation. God's will is dynamic, and new roles may be required as God works out his purposes through recalcitrant humanity. And, while humans are viewed as essentially sinners, the power and grace of God is such that *we can become what we are not.*[24] The Calvinists affirm the possibility of *transformation*—not only of the inner heart but of the outer organization of life. Because of the Fall, sin is rampant in human hearts. Only divine initiative can "justify" human existence. Yet beyond justification there is the obligation, bestowed on us in God's call to duty, to "sanctify," to make holy and righteous, both the person *and* the social world in which persons live. To carry out this "sanctification," people may rearrange social roles; they may "reform" social, economic, and political institutions in accord with God's law, purpose, and love. Indeed, anyone may be *called* by God to do precisely that in any area of life, whether he or she is of royal or peasant stock, owner or worker, rich or poor, clever or dull, strong or weak. Thus the Calvinists affirmed the possibility to claim, on the basis of vocation, a right to change things, to do things in a new way, without loss of membership in the basic community, for membership does not depend on these social variables.[25] Although at the highest theological level, before God, human rights may *not* be claimed, a secondary principle of vocation affirms a necessary freedom for persons in society to reform pregiven patterns of social role, to give social space for the working out of godly duty.

The logic and social psychology of this argument were vital to the developing life of the cities of the West. Peasants and freemen who became artisans, tradesmen, merchants, manufacturers, and—above all—citizens with self-governing responsibilities found in this way of thinking a convincing justification for innovative social change. It brought the prospect of radical reorganization into line with a powerful sense of moral duty. Under God's righteousness, life was governed by a moral law that was severe; it was also, by God's grace, dynamic and liberating. Individual rights were given a firm foundation—indeed, a divine foundation—in the membership of God's *humanum.*

The second type of Calvinist thinking, that represented by the Imperial branch, applied these rights only to the "visible saints," to the "elect" who demonstrated by their rectitude and success in life that they had been favored by God and were living in accord with universal moral law. Again and again visible success obscured for some Calvinists the radicality of their own doctrine of sin, and they uncritically identified their race or class or civilization with God's will, believing that they were predestined to rule. The Calvinist notion of predestination, which was intended to emphasize the fact that God and only God ultimately rules the universe, was here taken to entail a kind of predetermination of historical events and civilizational order which could not be altered, only endured. As already mentioned, Imperial Calvinism gained temporary ascendancy in Holland, England, Scotland, and New England in times past, and reigns still in parts of Northern Ireland and South Africa. Wherever it has taken hold, it has tended to be elitist, dogmatic, repressive, rigid, and theocratic. Its doctrine of Scripture makes it closer to Islam than to orthodox Christianity; its view of providence produces a militant theory of "manifest destiny" in history comparable only to Leninism; and its view of election renders a caste-like ethnocentrism. Yet the arguments from this strand of Calvinism (and from all hierarchic parallels) on one point have often served as a corrective to radical social-change movements from within and beyond Christianity—namely, the threat to universal truth, to moral law, and to human rights. This threat comes not only from the dangers of obsequious obedience to pregiven order, nor only from tyranny; it comes also from the perils of chaos when humans believe they can change anything they want to change and make up their own rules. Not only humanist thought is viewed as dangerous in this regard. Some Christian thought (especially in its Pelagian or Arminian forms) has so accented the freedom and grace of God, and the reality of will, that it too, in the eyes of this group, has lost its sense of a *God-given* moral structure. The danger is antinomianism, seeing all forms and standards as a legalism to be overthrown. The Imperial Calvinists recognize that even the innovative, dynamic change introduced by fellow Calvinists can become an occasion for libertine permissiveness. Although they have often become the agents of constricting oppression, the Imperial Calvinists have demanded that others acknowledge that chaos is a perennial peril to human souls and societies. Change can be degenerative as well as regenerative. Undisciplined liberty leads to license. Without some secure modicum of obedience to duty and order, talk of human rights is empty. All becomes arbitrary; the lower urges become indistinguishable from higher principles.[26]

The third Reformed branch, the Free-Church Calvinists, found itself in agreement with the theological emphasis of its allies. Sin is powerful and real, and only God's liberating grace can lead to the dynamic prospect of social change. Also, chaos is acknowledged as a perennial danger. But the Free-Church Calvinists were less individualistic than the Evangelical Calvinists, and less willing to coercively enforce conformity than the imperialist Calvinists. More emphatically than either of the two parallel branches, Free-Church Calvinism accented the idea of covenant, and by its successful advocacy of this concept it overwhelmingly influenced the entire Puritan movement whereby all branches of Calvinism shaped the ethos of America.

A "covenant" is a community of persons voluntarily bonded together by a common perception of truth and a dedication to earnest attempts to live out the universal moral law. A covenantal people live under the law of God, dedicate their lives to the purposes of God, and find themselves empowered to live together by the love of God. This, they hold, is the clue to universal human meaning.[27] The covenant is voluntary in the sense that it is not a community given by birth in a family, class, or nation. People must choose to be active members. This is so even if, in another sense, it is not voluntary at all. God initiates the covenant; humans only receive it, as signified by baptism. The members of this community, as adults, join together to "own" the covenant, to worship the source of this truth. They become bonded together to discern the meanings and implications of this truth and its attendant law. They agree that truth and its moral law is prior to their discernment of it. It is not something to be read out of the present structures of life. It is not something they make up. No one may know it fully; but because all may know it in part, all members become participants in its discernment and active in attempting to live out its mandates. Hence it is a bonded pluralism and inevitably a community of discourse—an active "standing under," or "under-standing," of what is universally true and right.

In more recent thought the idea of the covenant is often confused with the ideas of "contract," a humanly constructed agreement of mutual responsibility and accountability.[28] There may be commercial contracts, marriage contracts, or, indeed, as one finds in Hobbes and Rousseau, a general "social contract" wherein people forfeit some of their primordial freedoms for common benefit, to control evil and to construct good. As we saw earlier, however, in origin the covenantal notion rooted in biblical sources is quite different. In covenantal theory an element of individual choice is preserved for people to enter into social agreements, but the *finding* of the true base for sociality is the centerpoint. The essential base of a covenant is in the religious truth and the moral law within it as given by God. It is to be tested by mutual edification in rational discourse. The religious and ethical fabric governing a covenanted community is *not constructed* by agreement of the parties, as in contract theory, but *discerned*. It thus contains a realist element that would have satisfied the late-medieval realists. Convinced persons "own" or confess this spiritual and moral reality and construct their communities, as best they can, as relative approximations of it. Common discernment by reliance on particular experience could have satisfied the nominalists. In this view, people are under a universal moral reality whether they know it or not, and when they fail to live up to it, they finds themselves constricted by oppression or driven to chaos, unable to find the liberation of covenantal order.[29]

Reason plays a role in covenantal thought which is different from that of many other Christian thought-patterns. Free-Church Calvinists give a particular interpretation to the general Christian view of mankind which stresses the creation of humanity "in the image of God." All persons, in principle, can give witness to the reality of God, and to the moral law, because of this primordial image which is an unmerited gift from God. Because of the fall, this image is tainted; but guided by God's grace, by careful religious instruction, and by the objective standard of Scripture, it can serve as a foundation for conscience. Conscience is understood as "co-science" or "common knowledge." In principle, everyone can in some measure participate in the discernment of what is true and morally right because of this *imago dei* and conscience. Hence no one is exempted from general participation in the moral community. All must cultivate the conscience and testify to its leadings in public discourse. All are responsible. Reason thus becomes a formidable element of common spiritual and ethical discussion. Reason is not something totally different from revelation, for it too is a gift of God. God does not demand that we believe nonsense. Reason cannot displace or replace the special awareness of Jesus Christ, but reason can criticize any faith claim that leads to the denial of the *imago* present in all persons or to moral and social absurdity. Reason operates in the inner light of prayerful dialogue, which is at the core of community. This must be protected in any social arrangement, for it is conscience that makes it possible for people to discern valid covenants and to commit themselves in an inner, and not only exterior, way to the moral law of public life. Yet conscience and its reason are not esoteric.[30] Religious claims of the heart must be reasonable in a public sense if they are to be heeded. All are called to "testify," to give explicit utterance to conscience, an utterance that requires "edifying discourse." Not only is this a personal requirement of church membership, but it requires being responsible in a way that is convincing in community. As David Little puts it, "Only in voluntary consent can true order be achieved. Consent is the glue of the Body."[31] Because of this feature of Free-Church Calvinism, the movement was almost suspicious of "priestcrafts" who claimed access to esoteric knowledge and mysteries beyond comprehension, grasped only by the spiritually elite. They constantly got into trouble by teaching and preaching to unlettered people, and by giving them voice and vote in church matters. Not to do so, however, seemed to this branch of Christianity a violation of reason, conscience, and genuine community. Indeed, it violated the very image of God, given by grace in creation. It denied true "membership."

A fascinating development took place as Free-Church Calvinism shaped the entire Puritan tradition so decisive for American social life and American understanding of human rights. Calvin, in a tiny section of his *Institutes,* had very cautiously admitted the possibility that "middle magistrates" in a body politic could restore order in the face of abuse by "higher magistrates."[32] Like the Conciliar Catholics, he was quite careful to restrict this right to those who were clearly in official positions of authority. But as Calvinism began to interact with other developments of the Radical Reformation to form the Puritan, Free-Church legacy, the question arose as to how far this right extended. What if the middle magistrates and higher magistrates conspired to gain power and advantage? What if they betrayed their offices by violating the universal moral law, oppressing the weak and the poor? Is it not the responsibility of the "lower" magistrates to reform the whole hierarchy?

At this point the claim among Free-Church Calvinists that laity could rightly speak and vote in church spilled over into the political sphere. The lay member is also citizen, and as citizen has certain inalienable rights based on the image of God and the capacity to discern truth and moral law. In fact, laity is "the lowest magistrate," the guardian against higher magisterial distortion. Hence, in the body politic, as in the ecclesial community, members acting together have the right—indeed, the duty under God—to establish a moral regime and to hold political authority accountable to a just, higher law.[33] The church itself may not exercise coercive power. The church is the covenant community for worship and for moral discernment by faith and reason whereby all members are schooled, and school their neighbors, in ethical and spiritual matters. From this inviolable base the legitimacy of political authority is to be evaluated. Other groups, by analogy with the principle of church membership, have the right to form "civil covenants" to secure public order and righteousness. The legal-political vision of such a pluralist order had already been worked out by Althusius and Grotius, the internationally read Dutch Calvinists.[34] On these bases, parliamentary, pluralist democracy was given a firm justification in an articulate public theology, with an organizational substructure among the people.[35]

Nowhere is this more dramatically illustrated than in the Cromwellian Revolution. In England the traditions of the Magna Carta and of the English church's break with Rome had already given a flexibility, even an instability, to the traditional regime. There also John Wycliffe and his followers, the Lollards, had already developed a taste for lay involvement in church membership and leadership.[36] When Calvinism in its several branches reached into England through Scotland, Holland, and France, and when the established church sided with the Crown to repress the independent clergy and congregations and to claim the necessity of obedience by authority and not by reason, the tinderbox of revolution was lit.

The revolutionary army, led by Cromwell and demanding a new and genuinely representative parliament as a matter of natural and divine justice, organized itself on a "New Model."[37] The army adopted the free-church structure of covenantal groups. Soldiers elected their own chaplains who would present their beliefs and moral reasonings in formulating military and political policy. Further, the soldiers demanded recognition of fundamental rights for all citizens. Eventually, an "Agreement of the People" was reached, a moment in history, according to A.S.P. Woodhouse, that

> marked the apotheosis of the covenant idea and its complete and triumphant translation to the civil sphere. In the 'Agreements,' the covenant's every principle is represented: the recognition of a fundamental law . . . , which the terms of the [agreement] must embody and by which alone they are conditioned; the ideas of voluntary association and government by consent; the preservation of the individual's inalienable rights, implicit in the church cov-

enant and safeguarded by the power of withdrawal, but necessarily explicit in the Agreements [since the power of withdrawal is virtually nonexistent in the civil state]; the delegation of power, under due safeguards, to those who must act for the community; the elaboration of an 'order,' or the necessary machinery of administration and of popular expression; and the whole thing extended and raised to a national scope and level, . . . and [recognizing] . . . a basis for discussion . . . to serve as explorations leading to truth and consent. Behind the Agreements lies the belief in free and equal discussion which . . . dominates the proceedings of the General Council of the Army.[38]

Under the flag of this newly articulated public theology, the "saintly revolutionaries" beheaded the king and made the possibilities of Western societal life begun in early Judeo-Christian history and extended by the Conciliar Catholics a living, world-historical force.

Similarly, the Puritans claimed that they had a right to form other covenantal institutions for different purposes. Indeed, the very meaning of human rights involved, in their view, the inalienable right to form intentional communities of mutual support and discipline, to reconstruct earthly memberships on the basis of a divine one. The precarious traditions of the independent city, the university, and the charitable corporations (hospitals, for example) were given an ultimate theological legitimacy based on the analogy of a free church.[39] The freedoms demanded were not individualistic nor were they laissez-faire "contractual," although they accented the dignity of the person and the necessity of agreements. They entailed, first of all, a freedom to establish a social space distinct from regime and paternalistic authority wherein they could find and fulfill vocation in community under God's moral law. Calvinists claimed what Kuyper calls a "sphere sovereignty" for the decisive institutions in society.[40] The covenants of the independent Free Churches became, in the Anglo-American traditions, the paradigms of political parties for shaping governments, of corporations for shaping the market, of unions for influencing corporations, of lawyers for shaping jurisprudence, of doctors for shaping the practice of medicine, and of scholars for shaping the sciences. Even the family was transformed, for it was to become the "little congregation." In the eighteenth century John Wesley carried these themes, set forth in a new key, into the communities of the dispossessed in British coal fields. Baptists and Methodists carried them forth on the American frontier and then into other lands by missions. In the nineteenth and twentieth centuries, this same pluralistic, covenantal model became the basis of mass movements for abolition of slavery, reform of women's status, prohibition of alcohol abuse, control of child labor, defense of consumer rights, and dozens of other movements.[41] Without the public theology and social space carved out by the Puritan tradition, modern American society would be very different indeed. This is the tradition which carried out in revolutionary practice ideas suggested by ancient Scripture and philosophy and developed by the Conciliar Catholics before the Reformation.

Protestantism was, at the outset, essentially "protest." It did not have a positive social philosophy. In these developments, however, a fundamental creed, a public theology, was engendered and refined by what was clearly a minority tradition—with enormous consequences.

Christopher Dawson, the noted Catholic scholar, describes the importance of this tradition when he writes.

> . . . [in the sixteenth and seventeenth centuries] the Calvinist tradition was united with that of the independent sects to produce a new movement which was political as well as religious and which marks the first appearance of genuine democracy in the modern world. And in this revolutionary [event] . . . the Calvinist conception of the democratic aristocracy of the saints provided the inspiration and the driving force.
>
> The translation of the conception of the Holy Community from an ecclesiastical ideal to a principle of revolutionary action was . . . accepted by the leading Independent divines . . . and in fact it does mark the beginning of a new world. . . . [It] opened the way for a new type of civilization based on the freedom of the person and of conscience as rights conferred absolutely by God and Nature. This connection . . . leads us directly to the assertion of the Rights of Man. . . .
>
> The modern Western beliefs in progress, in the rights of man, and the duty of conforming political action to moral ideals, whatever they may owe to other influences, derive ultimately from the moral ideals of Puritanism and its faith in the possibility of the realization of the Holy Community on earth by the [obedient and engraced] efforts of the elect.[42]

D. THE LIBERAL CRITIQUES OF THEOLOGY

The Puritans' zeal to establish democratic procedures and human rights reestablished what had been lost since the Council of Constance. They founded for modernity a social space from which they pressed every sector of society toward transformation. But they also encountered many of the same problems that the Council of Constance had faced. Their confidence and their audacity, which often bordered on arrogance, called for a righteous society, consisting of a community of communities, in which each could fulfill his or her vocation in disciplined and godly freedom. The pluralism, however, led to contentiousness and conflict both among the Puritans themselves and between them and those who gave primary loyalty to nation. While England burned with the flames of contending lights, while Calvinist parties were snuffed out in France or rekindled in Holland and New England, philosophers became skeptical. They attempted to return to the issues of the ancient Greeks and Romans. They tried to avoid or bypass or refute theology and recover the fruits of natural reason. Liberal schools of thought became predominant, but they were no more unified than the Christians. Like the Reformed tradition, Liberalism came in several varieties; three branches are most important.

Thomas Hobbes, in some ways an heir of the Renaissance author Machiavelli, wrote that the agitations which produced such unrest were primarily due to the "seditious ministers of Puritanism. It would have been better that they had been killed rather than allowed to preach."[43] At the end of the Cromwellian Revolution he wrote his famous work *Leviathan*. He described all those sects and enthusiastic preachers as "worms in the entrails of Leviathan." He perceived no covenant community as the center or sign of God-given human dignity or mutuality. He saw only two realities: the free Individual, who was by nature nasty, brutish, and mean; and the State, which had to overcome that misery by asserting total political authority. He not only wrote this as a tract for the times, but he was well aware of the fact that he was attacking the whole ecclesiological tradition of the church. He challenged a world view that had been held by many, from the early church to the Conciliar Catholics and the Puritans. Not ecclesia but coercive political government and authority were the center of majesty, power, and meaning. People had to give up their freedoms and their contentious groupings. Authority must establish a social compact and enforce peace by threat of the sword. He shared the notion of human depravity with the Calvinists, but he had no doctrines of *imago dei,* grace, vocation, or church by which to overcome natural depravity. In his view freedom is simply vicious lawlessness. Pluralism only encourages war. Giving up freedom means becoming bound to an "absolutist social contract." In *that* we find peace.[44]

Hobbes's views do not sound "liberal" to modern ears, yet he argued his points for a very liberal reason. He did not think that in social and political matters humans were *under* moral law not of their own making. Whatever authoritarian consequences Conservative Catholicism and Imperial Calvinism led to, they both believed that the regime was under the judgment of a higher law. Hobbes was a liberal in that he did not believe this to be the case. He insisted that there are no moral absolutes standing over sociopolitical matters which require human understanding. Humanity, in the person of the sovereign who forms the social contract, defines its own meanings. Law is an act of human fiat, an act of political creativity. Humanity is free to forge its own destiny. There may well be natural laws, such as those known to mechanics or geometry, but they are ethically neutral; they render no definitions of right or wrong, no fundamental view of justice, no claim or duty. All definitions of that sort are human constructs, he pointed out: "It belongs to the sovereign power to set forth and make known the common measure by which every man is to know what is his, and what is another's; what is good and what is bad; and what he ought to do, and what not. . . ."[45] All human rights are, in fact, civil rights constructed by human will for the benefit of the body politic. Hobbes's liberalism is rooted in his emancipation of humanity and politics from theological norms and his reliance on human initiative. It is a voluntaristic liberalism which recovers nominalist accents opposed by the Catholics at Constance and by all branches of Reformed Protestantism.

Thus Hobbes's position is based on a denial of the twin pillars of the Christian heritage which supported the Puritan Revolution. First, he did not think that there is—or, at any rate, that one could know—a universal moral law which could govern political life. Such claims seemed to him highly arbitrary, as the contending interpretations of that presumed law by Christians seemed to confirm. In particular, claims about the rights of conscience seemed to lead to an individual absolutism that allowed each person to do as he or she wished. He did not see all this as providing the conceptual base for the common life; it only reflected the natural state of things, where each is in contention with the other. Second, he did not think that there is a community—covenantal, ecclesial, or otherwise—which is prior to, or even distinct from, political solidarity. Writing at the time of restoration of kingly rule after the Puritan Revolution, he saw the re-establishment of a unified political sovereignty as a parable of universal social realism. The natural divisiveness of humans demanded a chosen, willed, artificial integration, not differentiation or pluralism. E. D. Baltzell rightly points out that "Hobbes recognized the decline of the [traditional] vision of reality. . . . [He] laid bare the need for any and all defacto establishments in the tradition of Machiavelli. . . . With no faith in the sacred himself, Hobbes, as well as many materialists after him, saw life as a perpetual and restless desire for power."[46]

John Locke was the Liberal philosopher who tried to answer these objections on the basis of natural human reason. Locke, the son of a member of Cromwell's army, was a Protestant deeply influenced by the dissenting Puritan tradition, but he too had grown weary of their unending contentiousness and theological quarrels. He was also shocked by the Imperialist tendency in some Calvinism, a tendency as dangerous in his view as Conservative Catholicism and Hobbesian political absolutism. His "principled liberalism" was forged out of a desire to state the case for tolerance and pluralism *with* order and coherence, and to do so in a way that was compelling to the human mind without need of claims about revelation. He wanted to show that, indeed, there is a natural basis for knowing a moral law, that there is a valid reason for toleration of pluralism, and that turning to arbitrary political authority is no better than turning to arbitrary religious authority. Only if we have some secure basis of moral knowledge can we find something to link us together beyond private interests or contending factions yet short of absolutistic solidarity. The right of dissent and the inviolability of the individual conscience must be preserved, yet a basis for community must be discovered.

Locke argues that some things, such as the value of life, liberty, and property, are "self-evident."[47] But *how* are they self-evident? They are self-evident to *experience*. Truths come to us through experience, which has two aspects: Perception and Reflection. Locke assumes that there is an order in the universe. This natural order is filled with many objects with qualities which are perceived by our senses. The mind, having no innate idea, is basically blank. But though it receives impressions, it is not utterly passive. It observes its own operations and contents, and it combines things that are impressed on it, a process triggered by the reception of impressions. As the mind works with these impressions and reflections, ideas are generated. Some ideas are mostly "pictures" of the data, but some are generated because of the way the mind processes the data. For instance, we may see objects which resemble an isosceles triangle, a right triangle, and an obtuse triangle. We can abstract and generalize about these and thus get an *idea* of "triangle." Even if no "pure triangle" exists, there are objective, natural laws of triangles. The greater the complexity of the generalization, the less close it is to sensation, but both the perceptions and the reflections are experience. Both lead to ideas. Thus we find "self-evident truths," a particular kind of natural law.

According to Locke, this natural knowledge applies also to morals and public ethics. Generalizations (such as an idea of natural rights) are both a *product* of experience, as idea, and a *reference* to something objective—much like a natural law. Generalizations do not exist only in the mind; they correspond in some measure to the way things are. What we know is a mental image, but it refers to real structures beyond our minds, to the natural structure of things.[48]

The possibility that there are self-evident truths, given in natural law and known by experience, meant, of course, that a foundation for moral discourse and for community was available to humans prior to the formation of a religious covenant under a sovereign God and prior to the formation of a Hobbesian compact under a political sovereign. Like the Calvinists, Locke believed that moral society was prior to political regime, and could judge it, control it, alter it. But that moral society was "naturally" based on a philosophy informed by Christian values. Like Hobbes, Locke thought that humanity had the capacity to form governments, but they were not so much creations of human will alone as they were reasonable reflections of natural rights and duties knowable (in principle) to all.

Locke also had a theory of "opinions." Opinions, he argued, cannot be fully tested by experience. They are abstract generalizations that the active mind generates, or which are believed by those simple minds who, without leisure and learning, take things on authority without any scientific surety of correlation to the natural order of things. Opinions can only be believed and held in the affections, not known. They are uncertain in a scientific sense, although they may be held with great intensity and may even determine a person's basic orientation toward life. Because they are uncertain, however, they may not be imposed on others. Some opinions, such as those of Christianity, are marvelously close to what can be known scientifically, Locke believed. Yet religious doctrines remain opinion and are often interpreted in a wide variety of ways. Since no one can ever be certain about opinion, we must have toleration in things religious.

Locke's two kinds of ideas—those that are self-evident and those that are opinion—implied two realms which must be kept distinct. One is called "state," the other "church." Thus Locke the Liberal was opposed to those Imperalist Calvinists attempting to establish a Christian commonwealth, imposing *opinions* as self-evident *truths*; and he was opposed to the Conservative Catholics (including the Anglo-Catholics of the establishment), as he was opposed to Hobbes, who wanted the state to govern religious and all other opinion. According to Locke, crimes must be distinct from sins, and punishment distinct from repentance. Faith is distinct from knowledge and religious membership from citizenship, although the public side of faith and membership is governed by self-evident truths.[49] Locke removed confessional religion from public matters. Human society, as the arena of accessible "natural rights" and thus under moral principles, is the central reality; both the specific confessions of a particular church and the specific arrangements of a particular state are secondary. Theology, understood as confessionalism, and political theory, understood as party preference, are subordinated; natural philosophy is the reliable human guide.[50]

The utilitarians, espousers of a third variety of Liberalism, emerged at a later date. Like Hobbes, this group was skeptical of anything metaphysical or traditional. They did not believe in self-evident truths of a natural-law sort. Thus philosophy returned to the view of Hobbes: there is no "right," there are no "rights," except what humans construct. But instead of turning to an absolutist state to find a solution, utilitarian liberals turned to the absolute individual.[51] John Stuart Mill, more than any other single author, represents the utilitarian-liberal critique of theology and the concern for human rights.

Mill is famous for his vigorous plea for individual freedom. Society, with all its compromises, laws, regulations, and rationalizations, was a threat to human spontaneity and feeling. Drawing on the work of David Hume, Jeremy Bentham, and Adam Smith, Mill turned to a psychological theory to ground his ethics: good can be known by pleasure, wrong by pain. There is no knowable *law* separate or apart from these direct experiences. All laws are to be judged according to their capacity to render more pleasure and inhibit or reduce pain, which, in fact, can be known only by the individual. In this view reason becomes the rational calculation of probable pleasure or pain and the instrumental means by which to produce those conditions which would produce the better state of affairs.

As we shall see, utilitarian liberalism became increasingly important in the West. It aided the Industrial Revolution, produced a consumer society, and demanded a higher use of technical reason. It combined with the ascendancy of economic institutions and of psychological theories of human nature, and with the decline of religious and political institutions (as we shall see in the next chapter). However, in the formative stages of those social and intellectual developments which gave structure to American life and to Western concepts of human rights, this perspective was not originally decisive. Hence there is often a disjunction between the basic and historic structures of American life and the way it is presently conceived. Thus the term "liberal" is variously used today: if used in political discourse, the term takes on Hobbesian overtones, suggesting a need to strengthen the sovereign state; if used to describe one's personal life, it means permissive attitudes toward action based on individual feelings and idiosyncrasies. But if we wish to understand the theoretical and social background of America's public theology, so decisive for human rights, we must turn to the "principled liberalism" of John Locke as it interacted with Christian ideas.

E. THE LIBERAL-PURITAN SYNTHESIS

The legacy of Free-Church Calvinism and the logic of Locke converged at a number of points. In England it became the Whig tradition of political life. In America the religious side of the synthesis has predominated. What the Puritan claimed as a right out of deep conviction, the principled liberal protected out of uncertainty. The principled liberal was not convinced that the leadings of conscience and the claims of religion were more than opinion, somehow loosely, but unprovably, connected with personal experience. Puritans gave "reasonable faith" and "covenanted community" a priority that was beyond the competence of politics to manage. Indeed, it could and should shape the state. Liberals, too, demanded free social space for "opinion" beyond the reach of political power, even if their focus was essentially political. The Liberals demanded an institutional arena for the church and for other organizations—the press, associations, professional societies, and the like—for the free sharing of opinions; but they were motivated to do so out of doubt, not confidence. Nevertheless, the Liberals protected the social space which the Puritans occupied.

The Puritans and the Liberals also shared the view that the state and public institutions were to be governed by self-evident truths. For the Puritans these were the laws of God tested by reasonable discussion in community. For the Liberals these were experience-based ideas of natural rights. Both held the conviction that "agreement" had to be reached before public action could be taken, and that all action was to be under law. Law was to be given a relative autonomy from political authority. Constitutions, and bills of rights specifying the limits of the rulers and limiting even the will of the majority, had to be drawn up to embody and make explicit the inviolable moral laws which can be known.

In economics, too, the two groups shared a view, but for different reasons. The Liberals saw property as a self-evident natural right for private persons. Each person had a claim over material goods, much as each person's body was inviolable. If the product of one's labor was taken away arbitrarily, one's humanity was violated. The Puritans were also interested in property, but not as a "natural" right. They believed that some people were "called" to be stewards of material things. They viewed economic success as a visible mark of one's responsibility in carrying out an invisible duty. Property was but a means whereby one could work out one's vocation to serve the common life under the watchful eye of the living God. Everything belongs to God; some are temporal trustees of his assets. Thus wealth is not to be loved or enjoyed but used for God and the common good. Society ought, therefore, to be so arranged that those who were appointed by God as trustees over things could carry out their appointment without undue interference. Puritans saw a direct analogy: as people must be free to form churches, so they must be free to form communities of economic responsibility, corporations, to fulfill their trusteeship of temporal goods.[52] The Puritans advocated a work ethic, with a high doctrine of social responsibility and ascetic behavior, as well as an "independent church" model, which became adapted for independent joint stock companies.[53]

The "freedom" entailed in religion, law, and economics was paralleled in other areas. The family is and must be independent and free; so must the university.[54] Puritans held that freedom of discussion is necessary for the true discernment of faith. The earliest arguments for the freedom of the press were made on this basis. By 1646 John Saltmarsh and John Lilburne had made some of the earliest Puritan efforts to establish the principle of the free press—fifteen years before Milton's powerful and better-known defense of liberty, and a half-century before Locke's *Treatises on Civil Government*. John Saltmarsh wrote:

> Let there be liberty of the press for printing, to those that are not allowed pulpits for preaching. Let that light come in at the window which cannot come in at the door, that all may speak and write one way, that cannot another. . . . Let there be free debates and open conferences and communication, for all and of all sorts that will, concerning difference in spirituals; . . . Where doors are not shut, there will be no breaking them open. So where debates are free there is a way of vent and evacuation, the stopping of which hath caused more troubles in states than anything; for where there is much new wine in old bottles the working will be such as the parable speaks on.[55]

This idea of freedom of discussion was also institutionalized in education. Long before the Puritan Revolution, the Conciliar Catholics had worked out a pattern of relative autonomy for the leading educational institutions. The University of Paris, in a long and complex ideological and social struggle, had established the rights of "masters" of the university to arrange curriculum, do research, teach, and govern their own affairs independent of bishop, Crown, and feudal patron. That model was adopted in Oxford and Cambridge, and early notions of academic freedom were established. But the Evangelical-Calvinist Huguenots in France and the Puritans in England felt ambivalent about such matters. Calvin had established a college and insisted on learned clergy in Geneva. Yet in France and England these centers seemed to foster idleness among the sons of the rich. Pompous ritual and esoteric speculation were associated with the university; both smacked of popery. Nevertheless, formal education was not rejected. Indeed, the need to read the Scriptures and to understand doctrinal preaching prompted Puritans to provide education for the poor in the "suburban slums" surrounding the cities by forming "academies" as well as attempting to set Cambridge on a different course than Oxford. When Cromwell had gained power, a concerted effort was made to provide public education, something that was not to come to general fruition for more than a century.[56] Notions of the "learned clergy" and "learned laity" gradually became predominant, and Calvinism developed an alliance with science in a new way, as Robert Merton and others have demonstrated.[57]

The Liberals, too, fostered learning. The Hobbesians focused on the arts of political rule clearly influenced by the "mechanics" of the new science; the principled liberals on the sciences, mathematics, logic, and astronomy; and the utilitarians on technology and economics. All doubted the importance of "mystical speculations" and called for a public discourse which was, in doctrinal terms, "value free." Educational systems now accomplished what the Renaissance and parts of the Reformation had already attempted on the Continent: they dethroned the "queen of the sciences" and reintroduced a cleavage between religion and philosophy, between faith and reason which had been overcome in theology as created by the Christian encounter with Greco-Roman thought.

In popular thought, however, the cleavage was not great. The Lockean tradition had a profound place for religion, and the Puritan divines who were most influential had a profound place for reason. Further, both Liberals in this mold and Puritans believed in "equality." Local school and local church advocated egalitarian moral virtues that were both philosophically and religiously rooted. For Liberals, knowledge derived from experience led to the understanding of the laws of life. All people can experience and all have access to the immediate knowledge of those principles which are to govern public behavior. Calvinists saw sin as the great equalizer. Some people are smarter, stronger, or more advantaged socially than others; but we are not to put our trust in brains, brawn, or status. What dignity we have is conferred by God, and in this, too, all humans are equal—equally dependent on the sovereign God. Differences in talents, resources, and responsibilities are secondary to primal equality; they are occasions for particular duties, not sources for special pride or privilege. The equal rights that humans have are the equal right of opportunity to carry out these unequal duties under God's watchful eye.

For the Liberals, equality was rooted differently. Knowledge, after all, is derived from experience, which can lead to self-evident truths. The equal dignity of persons is rooted in the individual capacity to know the laws of life. Locke held that the leisured philosopher could work these out in a scientific way, but for the masses, faith, based on religious experience, could supply much of the same content in mythical, sentimental, "opinion" form. The basis of equality for Liberals was not rooted in sin and dependence on God but in the innate human capacity to learn from experience.

These Liberal ideas had an enormous impact on American Protestantism. American history is peppered with a series of enthusiastic revivals, awakenings, and mass movements designed to induce religious experience. The source of much populism in America is precisely in the "Lockean Calvinism" of Jonathan Edwards and the "Liberal neo-Puritanism" of Baptist and Methodist revivalists. Subsequent attempts to seek and save every individual by evoking that kind of experience—in which one would be given religious assurance, be brought to moral rectitude, join in the covenanted community, witness to the universal moral law, and become a responsible citizen—have permanently shaped the American ethos. The impact of the principled liberal's natural arguments for much that the Calvinists held made it possible for non-Calvinists to find a place in the Puritan world. The earlier "public theology" of a few became the common vision of many. Puritans supplied the conviction that true law is rooted in the righteousness of the one true God, the zeal to make that a reality in historical life, and the organizational matrix, the church. They strived to convince the people and school them in the ways of righteousness. Liberals supplied the philosophical formulas that seemed convincing to unbelievers. Together they preserved the possibility for theology as a science; together they developed a constituency which gave the theology a social base. They did for modernity what the church fathers long ago, and the Conciliar Catholics, had also done.

F. THE INSTITUTIONALIZATION OF THE LIBERAL-PURITAN SYNTHESIS

Nowhere are the branches of Calvinist thought and philosophical thought more overtly joined, outside the church itself, than in the constitutions of America.[58] This deep trajectory of intellectual and social history has influenced every aspect of American life; it is constitutive of all social life in the United States. But in the constitutions the institutionalization of these themes can be most clearly traced. America is unlike the countries in Europe and Asia in this regard: it was discovered, settled, and organized as a nation when these ideas were most hotly debated. Furthermore, America had no history or tradition in the European and Asian senses. The history and tradition the settlers brought with them was a biblical history and a Reformed ecclesial tradition, both of which they feared were being repressed at home. The people who settled the early colonies felt compelled to state in clear, written form the covenantal fundamentals by which life was to be governed in a way understandable by all and universal in scope.

In 1616 a group of Puritans had addressed a petition to James I, claiming that they had formed a society with a "right" to exercise "spiritual administration and government in itself and over itself by common and free consent of the people, independently and immediately under Christ." Principles of individualism had been enunciated by Greco-Roman philosophers and by Renaissance thinkers. Independent congregations had appeared before, most notably in the early Jewish synagogues and Christian churches, and later in the pre-Reformation sectarian movements. But in this "modern" document the explicit claim appears for the first time that a society, based on a freely chosen covenant, is a "right," a human and legal right which must be *recognized* by all authority, although this right is not *granted* by earthly power. This right, therefore, is not to be restrained by any earthly power—including any established church.[59] The logic is quite simple. If Christ is the Lord, no one else can be. In Christ the church finds its conscience, its covenant, its vocation, its moral law. Nothing can alter this. In this act, points out G. Jellinek, "what had until then slumbered in . . . dust-covered manuscripts . . . [of ancient and medieval texts] became a powerful, life-determining movement."[60] The petition was ignored, but the movement grew. In England rights were claimed and often granted in practice, but they remained civil rights, capable of being revoked by civil authority. In America the Liberal-Puritan synthesis went beyond civil convention or concession and demanded universal and eternal recognition of inherent rights for communities of persons *prior* to legal, civil, and political life.

In 1620, the exiled Pilgrims signed the Mayflower Compact before settling in Plymouth. A decade later John Winthrop established a similar structure for the Massachusetts Bay Colony. With these documents began a series of "plantation covenants" which were to set the pattern for the new land. In 1631 Roger Williams, a minister in Salem, called for a compact which would separate church and state in the new land, and allow religious liberty. Such a compact, he held, would allow the free development of conscience. He was driven from Salem by a new burst of Imperial Calvinist zeal. He founded another colony in what is now Rhode Island.[61]

His migration was followed by others, and in 1639 the "Fundamental Orders of Connecticut" were drafted; thus the first written constitution of modernity was set forth. The stated purpose of this constitution was to provide a civil order which would allow "the liberty of the Gospel and the Church," and all to be "ruled by law." These views found their way back to England, where they were eagerly reprinted and devoutly read. In 1647 a proposed new constitution was delivered to the general council of the New Model Army and to Parliament. It claimed the "inherent human right" of "religious liberty" in faith and practice.[62] These rights gained fuller recognition in 1663 in the charter of Rhode Island. Meanwhile, John Locke had been asked to draft a constitution for North Carolina. His constitution called for religious toleration and strictly prohibited all violence against religious assembly. Only atheists could be excluded from the community, he reasoned, because they did not see themselves as under a higher order and were not trustworthy. New Jersey in 1664 and New York in 1665 made similar provisions. William Penn developed these principles in the Pennsylvania Constitution of 1701 by adding a new element. These rights, he promised, "should remain forever inviolable," and should "not be changed in any particular." Massachusetts remained more closed to dissent for another generation, although the rights of life, liberty, property, education, equal remedy before the law, and due process in trial were claimed as inherent rights. Maryland, populated by those Catholics fleeing persecution by the Imperial Calvinists in Europe, took up the tradition of the Conciliar Catholics of long ago, and granted religious freedom to all who believed in Christ.

All of these rights, plus those pertaining to the freedom of the press, the right to bear arms to protect against tyranny, and freedom of assembly and free movement, which had been already institutionalized in British practice, were incorporated in the constitution of Virginia in 1776, in which the phrasing of Locke and Montesquieu is liberally used. That constitution, like the earlier charters and covenants, begins with an assumption of inalienable and eternal human rights based on a moral law given by God and known by reason. The civil law and the political authority which these constitutions establish are themselves subject to these principles. The Virginia Constitution became, at the hands of "liberal" Thomas Jefferson, the model for the national Constitution in the Revolutionary War, as is well known. But it was the Puritan James Madison who fought for and finally won the inclusion of the Bill of Rights to embody these primary principles. The revolution which produced these documents was a conservative revolution—conservative in two senses. First, it conserved the ancient Christian perspectives on community, moral law, and "membership" which had been reinvigorated by the recovery of a "public theology" based on biblical notions of covenant.[63] Second, it did not put into effect the heritage it represented. To find unity, the founding father had to bow to special interest. The states were less than universal in their application of the term "human." Slave states said "freeman" instead of "man," all meant "males" instead of "humans," a few meant "property owners" instead of "inhabitants." Hence the incorporation of these themes into the American Constitution and subsequently into the Bill of Rights did not end the story. The struggles of the Jacksonian era,[64] of the Civil War, against Jim Crow laws and the broadening of the franchise to women still lay in the future. But even these struggles, to be won with sweat and blood, were but extensions of the deep trajectory and the logic of the Liberal-Puritan synthesis and the public theology it recovered and reshaped. These struggles were won in large part because people believed the causes were just under God. The public theology legitimated the sacrifice.

It is this tradition that forms the deepest ethic of American life and provides, consciously or preconsciously, the framework by which Americans view human rights. The Liberal-Puritan creed lives in the fabric and structure of our ethos even where it is forgotten or distorted. The two sides of this synthesis live in an uncomfortable alliance. Yet each side needs the other. Without the living, righteous God of Puritanism, Liberalism tends toward Deism and toward an elitist, experiential humanism not unlike that of Locke (as one can see in many liberal university circles where Lockean views have become pervasive and where religion plays a highly subordinated role, and in the debates about "civil religion" recently identified by Robert Bellah).[65] Without the vibrant church-life of Christianity, Liberalism loses its sense of self-evident truths and tends toward more and more comprehensive political control, not unlike that of Hobbes, or toward more utilitarian, pleasure-oriented individualism, as we saw anticipated in Mill. Thus "liberalism" in politics has come to mean greater and greater reliance on governmental institutions to determine all areas of public life, and in personal lifestyle to mean permissive sexuality and consumption. But without Liberalism, Puritanism tends to assert its Imperial dimensions, which happened in old Massachusetts, or to break up into combative, sectarian factions, which happened in the Cromwellian Revolution. Intellectually, without Liberalism—that is, without the inclusion of philosophy to form a genuine theology, conceived as a "science"—Calvinism has been threatened from within by a tendency to move its evangelical concern toward "revivalist fideism," a view that faith involves a private decision utterly beyond the capacity of reason to grasp, and beyond any concern for social structure.[66]

Nevertheless, for all its potential pathologies, the Liberal-Puritan synthesis has brought about a pluralistic society centered in ecclesial and voluntary associations. This society presumes that Judeo-Christian traditions are central sources of meaning, needing understanding by human reason. "Freedom," "equality of opportunity," "multiple political parties," "the limited state," "separation of powers," "government under law," and the "relative autonomy of 'corporations' "—all legitimated by the "agreement of the people"—emerge from these foundations. The freedom of religion and the right of religions to influence persons and the body politic from an inviolable social space are the basis of these developments. The hallmarks of "human rights" are rooted in these fundamental presumptions.

These are the deep trajectories and the fundamental creed that have shaped American piety, public discourse, polity, and policies throughout its history. Sidney Mead captured the core of American history when he wrote:

> Our foundations were quarried not only from legal ideas, but also from the political, social, philosophical, and theological learnings of the 18th century. . . . all these were dominated by a belief in the 'laws of nature and of nature's God.' Faith in a 'higher law' which had achieved a venerable place in the history of ideas through the speculations of jurists, monks, and scholars, burst forth toward the end of the 18th century into a 'fanatical' creed. . . .[67]

Indeed, it was on the basis of this creed that Americans fought the Civil War in 1865, fought Spain in 1898, fought Germany "to make the world safe for democracy" in World War I, imposed new constitutions on West Germany and Japan after World War II, pressed for the United Nations' Universal Declaration of Human Rights thereafter, and demanded "Basket Three" in the Helsinki Accords in 1976.

But these developments take us into the twentieth century, where the Liberal-Puritan synthesis has undergone considerable strain and where the lived experience of the heritage has been altered. That is the subject of the next chapter.

---

1. Peter Berger and Richard John Neuhaus, *To Empower People* (Washington, D.C.: American Enterprise Institute, 1977). See also the discussions of this book by T. Kerrine, J. Mechling, and D. Price in *Soundings*, 62 (Winter 1979), 331 – 416.

2. J. H. Filer et al., *Giving in America: Report of the Commission on Private Philanthropy and Public Needs* (Washington, D.C., 1975).

3. Theodore Levitt, *The Third Sector* (New York: Amacom, 1973).

4. See D. B. Robertson, ed., *Voluntary Association* (Richmond, Va.: John Knox Press, 1966).

5. See James L. Adams, *On Being Human Religiously*, ed. Max L. Stackhouse (Boston: Beacon Press, 1976).

6. Robert Bellah is surely correct when he argues that American individualism has always been seen in the context of an inner personal conviction which brings the self to an acceptance of relationship to God and to solidarity with others, in community. See *The Broken Covenant* (New York: Seabury Press, 1975), especially pp. 16 — 21.

7. Here, and throughout the discussion, I take issue with the conventional "post-theological" view of the history of human rights in the West, recently articulated by James Sellers in "Human Rights and the American Tradition of Justice," *Soundings*, 62 (Fall 1979), 226ff. Sellers tries to show the influence of the Enlightenment (especially Hobbes and Montesquieu), and utilizes Nietzsche and Scheler to explain why these ideas were received. Then he argues that human rights grows out of American experience and that calling for *universal* human rights on this model runs the risk of exporting "American" individualism. If there is merit in his hypothesis, his fear of the risk would be justified, for human rights would have no universalistic basis.

8. See also *The Letters of John of Salisbury*, II (London: Oxford University Press, 1979).

9. Specifically, Gerson, D'Ailly, Zabarella, and Dietrich of Niem.

10. See J. T. McNeill, "Natural Law in the Teaching of the Reformers" *Journal of Religion*, 26 (July 1946), 171f.; Robin Lovin, "Natural Law and Popular Sovereignty," paper delivered to the American Society of Christian Ethics (mimeo), 1979; and R. Somerville and K. Pennington, eds., *Law, Church, and Society* (Philadelphia: University of Pennsylvania Press, 1979).

11. The theological treatments of these motifs in Luther are too numerous to mention. The following treatments by political theorists, however, are very helpful: S. A. Lakoff, *Equality in Political Philosophy* (Boston: Beacon Press, 1964), especially Chapter II; and Sheldon Wolin, *Politics and Vision* (Boston: Little, Brown, 1960), especially Chapter Five.

12. Ralph B. Perry is, I think, correct when he argues that Calvinism, in the main, is the heir of medieval Christianity. See *Puritanism and Democracy* (New York: Vanguard Press, 1944).

13. I am convinced that James Hastings Nichols, *Democracy and the Churches* (Philadelphia: Westminster Press, 1951), is essentially correct in his argument on this point. It seems to be confirmed by the fact that David Hollenbach, in the best work about Roman Catholic understandings of human rights, takes up his narrative at the point of the "social encyclicals" of the late nineteenth century. See *Claims in Conflict* (New York: Paulist Press, 1979). See Chapter Five, Section C, for a partial explanation of this.

14. See J. D. Van der Vyer, *Seven Lectures on Human Rights* (Capetown: Juta & Co., 1976). In *Puritans, Indians, and Manifest Destiny* (New York: Capricorn Books, 1978), C. Segal and D. Stineback argue that comparable notions were part of early New England.

15. Center for the Study of Federalism, *Conference Papers on Federal Theology and Politics* (Philadelphia, Feb. 27 — 29, 1980). See especially the papers by J. Wayne Baker, James D. Bratt, and James W. Skillen. See also R. T. Kendall, *Calvin and English Calvinism to 1649* (London: Oxford University Press, 1980).

16. See E. D. Baltzell, *Puritan Boston and Quaker Philadelphia* (New York: Macmillan, 1979). This very significant recent study displays some of the social consequences of this spectrum of belief. He contrasts the character and legacy of Massachusetts Puritanism (which was closest to the Imperial type, as I have sorted them, among the American Free-Church traditions) with the Quakerism of Philadelphia. The former accented justice, order, and rigorous duty; the latter, having pious doubts about any exercise of authority, led to a renunciation of political responsibility. It left politics open to purely practical arrangements by those without a "public theology" and turned its zeal entirely to "doing well while doing good" commercially. These Massachusetts Puritans took a stand much like that of the Lutherans.

17. See J. H. Nichols, *Democracy and the Churches*; John T. McNeill, *The History and Character of Calvinism* (London: Oxford University Press, 1954); and Abraham Kuyper, *Lectures on Calvinism* (Grand Rapids, Mich.: Eerdmans, 1931).

18. Introduction to A. S. P. Woodhouse, *Puritanism and Liberty* (London: J. M. Dent, 1938).

19. James K. McConica, *English Humanists and Reformation Politics* (London: Oxford University Press, 1965).

20. Roland Bainton, *The Travail of Religious Liberty* (Philadelphia: Westminster Press, 1961), pp. 72 — 98.

21. Interestingly, Luther echoes a theme from Dante, as well as from one interpretation of Augustine and Paul.

22. Whatever the limitations of Ernst Troeltsch's treatment of Luther, he is surely correct in this aspect of his critique ("Stoic-Christian Natural Law and the Modern-Secular Natural Law," in *Gesammelte Schriften*, II, 515ff. Forthcoming).

23. Max Weber, *The Protestant Ethic and the Spirit of Capitalism*, trans. T. Parsons (New York: Harper & Row, 1958).

24. This phrase from Calvin's *Institutes* appears in various forms in literally hundreds of Calvinist sermons and theological texts.

25. This is one of the decisive characteristics which marks the difference between Western understandings of humanity and both Communist and Hindu perspectives. The definitive role of class for Marxism, and of caste for Hinduism, means that persons are always to be understood in terms of the group from which they came. Calvinism, with the exception of some aspects of its Imperial form, makes categories of social origin irrelevant to the understanding of who people are as persons.

26. See Jan. J. Loubser, "Calvinism, Equality, and Inclusion: The Case of Afrikaner Calvinism," in *The Protestant Ethic and Modernization*, ed. S. N. Eisenstadt (New York: Basic Books 1968), pp. 367ff.; and T. Dunbar Moodie, *The Rise of Afrikanerdom* (Berkeley: University of California Press, 1975).

27. See my "Democracy and the World's Religions," *This World* (1982), pp. 108 – 20. See also W. Walker, *Creeds and Platforms of Congregationalism* (Boston: Pilgrim Press, 1960); Champlin Burrage, *The Church Covenant Idea* (Philadelphia: American Baptist Society, 1904); William Haller, *The Rise of Puritanism* (New York: Columbia University Press, 1938); Perry Miller, *The New England Mind: The 17th Century* (Boston: Beacon Press, 1961); Edmund Morgan, ed., *Puritan Political Ideas* (New York: Bobbs-Merrill, 1965); and Peter DeJong, *The Covenant Idea in New England Theology* (Grand Rapids, Mich.: Eerdmans, 1945).

28. D. Sturm, "Corporations, Constitutions and Covenants," *Journal of the American Academy of Religion*, 61 (Sept. 1973), 331ff.

29. J. F. A. Taylor, *The Masks of Society: An Inquiry into the Covenants of Civilization* (New York: Appleton-Century-Crofts, 1966).

30. Max Savelle, *Seeds of Liberty: The Genesis of the American Mind* (Seattle, Wash.: University of Washington Press, 1965).

31. David Little, *Religious Conflict, Law and Order* (New York: Harper & Row, 1969), p. 222.

32. Calvin, *Institutes*, Book VI, Chapters 19 – 20.

33. This group of themes first emerged when John Knox asked Calvin whether there was a right of rebellion if a Catholic ruler suppressed Protestant worship. It was radicalized in the Cromwellian Revolution by the Independents. See Woodhouse, *Puritanism and Liberty*, especially Part I; and Michael Walzer, *The Revolution of the Saints* (New York: Atheneum, 1968), especially pp. 100ff.

34. See the edition of Althusius' *Politica Methodice Digesta* ed. by C. J. Friedrich (Cambridge, Mass.: Harvard University Press, 1932). Compare J. W. Gough, *The Social Contract*, 2nd ed. (New York: Oxford University Press, 1957), especially Chapters 6 and 7.

35. Woodhouse, *Puritanism and Liberty*, Part III.

36. T. C. Hall, *The Religious Background of American Culture* (Boston: Little, Brown, 1930).

37. See the Introduction to Woodhouse, *Puritanism and Liberty*; Walzer, *The Revolution of the Saints*, pp. 265ff.; Christopher Hill, *Puritanism and Revolution* (London: Oxford, 1959); and Robert Paul, *The Lord Protector* (London: Oxford, 1955).

38. Woodhouse, *Puritanism and Liberty*, p. 76.

39. John P. Davis, *Corporations* (New York: Revell, 1908).

40. Woodhouse, *Puritanism and Liberty*, especially pp. 78 – 109.

41. See G. H. Barnes, *The Anti-Slavery Impulse* (New York: Harcourt, Brace & World, 1933); and S. E. Ahlstrom, *A Religious History of the American People* (New Haven, Conn.: Yale University Press, 1973), especially Chapter 26 and Parts IV and V.

42. Christopher Dawson, "Religious Origins of European Disunity," *Dublin Review* (Oct. 1940), pp. 157ff.

43. Thomas Hobbes, *De Cive*, iii.

44. In my judgment, the treatment of the Liberals given by Sheldon Wolin in *Politics*

and Vision, Chapters 8 and 9 especially, is among the most compelling available. I am particularly indebted to Wolin for my understanding of Hobbes and Locke.

45. Thomas Hobbes, *Leviathan,* V, 26.

46. Baltzell, *Puritan Boston and Quaker Philadelphia,* p. 74.

47. All Americans are familiar with these terms from the Declaration of Independence: "We hold these truths to be self-evident, that all men are created equal, that they are endowed by their Creator with certain unalienable rights, that among these are Life, Liberty and the pursuit of Happiness." Note that the term "property" of Locke's phrase is dropped and "pursuit of happiness" is substituted. The substitution represents a concession to those not willing to see property rights, in a day of chattel slavery, as self-evident. "Pursuit of happiness" is also a phrase open to Aristotelian and to utilitarian-liberal interpretation. It is fascinating to note that in the United Nations' Declaration of Human Rights, both are dropped, and "security" is added—possibly taken from one aspect of the French Declaration of the Rights of Man.

48. John Locke, *An Essay Concerning Human Understanding,* passim. Locke is obviously influenced by Newton. Indeed, Montesquieu and Voltaire, who became the Anglophile interpreters of Locke to the Continent—and, indeed, the medium through which many of these ideas influenced American authors at the time of the American Revolution—viewed Newton as the physicist and Locke as the metaphysician of the most important developments since Plato and Aristotle. See C. Dawson, *The Gods of Revolution* (New York: Minerva Press, 1975), pp. 25ff.

49. John Locke, *A Letter Concerning Toleration* (1689; New York: Liberal Arts Press, 1950), pp. 14f.

50. At least for those who have the leisure for learning, faith may accomplish the same thing for those who are Christians but who do not have the leisure or learning to work through the presuppositions and logic of nature (Locke, *An Essay Concerning Human Understanding*).

51. S. A. Lakoff is correct, however, about Mill and the utilitarians when he argues that it can also go in a socialist direction (*Equality in Political Philosophy,* pp. 128ff.).

52. This is one of the most important features of American capitalism, which is seldom understood and which leads to so many silly errors in attempts to reform American capitalism. What drives many in positions of corporate leadership is not "greed" but "duty." It may well be a duty tainted with greed, but the energy derives from an often forgotten set of religious motivations that operate in our collective life. See Max Weber, *The Protestant Ethic and the Spirit of Capitalism.*

53. See Davis, *Corporations.*

54. See Chapter Six of this book.

55. See John Saltmarsh, "Smoke in the Temple," in Woodhouse, *Puritanism and Liberty,* pp. 179 − 85.

56. Richard Greaves, *The Puritan Revolution and Educational Thought* (New Brunswick, N.J.: Rutgers University Press, 1969), especially Chapters 1 and 3.

57. Robert Merton, "Puritanism, Pietism and Science," in *Social Theory & Social Structure* (London: Collier, 1959), pp. 574ff. See also Greaves, *The Puritan Revolution and Educational Thought,* Chapter 4.

58. See the paper by Daniel Elazar in *Conference Papers on Federal Theology and Politics.*

59. G. Jellinek, *Die Erklärung der Menschen und Bergerrechte,* 2nd ed. (Leipzig: Dunsker und Humbolt, 1904).

60. Ibid., p. 24.

61. See Richard Quinney, *Providence* (New York: Longman, 1980), who sees in these events the anticipations of a contemporary reconstruction of social order rooted in theology and moving toward a new form of democratic, pluralistic socialism.

62. Woodhouse, *Puritanism and Liberty,* pp. 266f.

63. See McLoughlin's essay in J. P. Greene and W. G. McLoughlin, *Preachers and Politicians* (Worcester, Mass.: American Antiquarian Society, 1977).

64. J. F. Berens, *Providence and Patriotism in Early America, 1640 − 1815* (Charlottesville, Va.: University Press of Virginia, 1978).

65. Bellah, *The Broken Covenant.*

66. The tension between fideism of a personalist, decisional sort and a kind of theology

that was to include reason and social witness appeared early in American Puritanism. It was most pronounced in New England, where the tension split churches into the Congregational and Unitarian parishes. Subsequently, of course, Unitarianism has become increasingly relativist and romantic in character. See Ann Douglas, *The Feminization of America* (New York: Knopf, 1978).

67. Sidney Mead, *The Nation with the Soul of a Church* (New York: Harper & Row, 1975), p. 57.

CHAPTER FOUR

Human Rights and Society
in Modern America:
Cross-Sectional Encounters

A. THE GREAT TRANSITION

FROM the Mayflower Compact and the Great Awakening until World War I, America was decisively influenced by the Liberal-Puritan synthesis. What had emerged as a fragile minority report in the churches of Europe became the public theology for a new nation. The critical battles of these years, both social and ideological, were all understood by the contenders as rooted in one or another school of Liberal or Puritan definitions of human nature in its relations to God, society, and creation. The formation of a constitutional polity, at first for the colonies and then for the nation, was dominated by Liberal and Puritan presuppositions. The debates and curriculum of the institutions of higher learning were conducted in these terms even as economic, technological, and medical sciences were formed by these presuppositions. The relative success of this synthesis, however, served as a catalyst for an expansive dynamic that tested the capacity of the creed and the society to contain and channel its own potential.

The first fundamental test came during the Civil War. Puritans and Liberals had compromised their understandings of human nature to gain a union with the slave-holding states. Further, the northern versions of the synthesis had produced a burgeoning commercial and manufacturing economy threatened by collusion between southern plantation-owners and European industry. Ideological, political, and economic interests conspired to propel the nation into bloody conflict. Liberal-Puritan understandings of human rights undercut earlier compromises on the question of chattel slavery and induced fervent agitation for emancipation.[1] The war economy, in turn, stimulated America's late entry into the Industrial Revolution. Rapid economic and technological development burst the bonds of old Puritanical discipline. The corporation as an institution became less a covenanted fellowship of those called to be responsible stewards for the glory of God than a legal fiction by which to gain wealth. The factories went

81

up as rumors of jobs invited disadvantaged waves of immigrants from Europe.[2] This influx in turn forced westward expansion. What had been a trickle of settlers beyond the Mississippi became a flood.[3] The slaves were freed, legally if not economically and educationally, but the Indians became objects of more intense scorn. The open frontiers of industrial and geographic expansion, unrestrained by Puritan probity or Liberal civility, evoked a competitive individualism in piety, economics, and lifestyle that is not yet tamed. And when, in 1892, the Homestead Act was repealed, the western agricultural expansion was ended. Henceforth the United States would grow by urbanization and industrialization.[4]

The massive influx of Catholic populations brought a distrust of both Protestant hegemony and Enlightenment Liberalism. The Puritan heritage itself split into new divisions. One branch focused on the intensely inward, personal, and trans-rational character of faith, and gave rise to both transcendentalist Unitarianism and, ironically, to its opponent, American frontier evangelism. The other accented the rational and social aspects of theology, and became, eventually, "progressive" and ecumenical.[5] The Liberal component of the synthesis also split, with one branch rooting itself in American Transcendentalism, while the other became increasingly utilitarian and pragmatic—even opportunistic—with a weakened perception of "self-evident" principles.[6] These shifts in creed shaped and were shaped by social transformations in every sector of society.

Expansion and transformation characterized every aspect of life during the time between the Civil War and World War I. Transportation, communications, and education became large-scale. The United States, motivated by a new burst of Imperial Calvinism and a commercial need to control international trade routes, defeated Spain in 1898 and itself became a world power. Under the slogan of "manifest destiny" the United States intervened in Asia and Latin America for the first time to save the Philippines and Cuba from popery and from dictatorial governments. Military development became irrevocably linked with industrial contracting as A. T. Mahan, Elihu Root, and Leonard Wood forged a new ideology of "international responsibilities" using the newer forms of laissez-faire liberal economic theory with national zeal.[7] Many of the most powerful corporations and great family fortunes of today trace their roots back to the tycoons of this time.

The Blacks of America began a drive for equality. The emancipation was subverted during the Reconstruction by Jim Crow laws and economic dependency. Yet the Black churches, themselves formed around a fresh and African-influenced appropriation of Liberal and Puritan values, became centers of hope, identity, and organization.[8] At the periphery of the churches, the elitist visions of Booker T. Washington and the socialist sympathies of W. E. B. Du Bois carried the drive for equality into the areas of education and economics.[9] Meanwhile, white racists linked evangelical zeal to biblical fundamentalism and social Darwinism to "prove" their right to rule.[10]

The women's suffrage movement emerged from various Protestant "missionary associations" and Liberal "literary societies." Through their efforts,

Non-Profit Organization
U.S. Postage Paid
Permit #3
Pender, NE 68089

The United Church of Pender
RR #1, Box 160A
Pender, Nebraska 68047

MARCH USHERS

Michael McQuistan   Eric Fendrick
Brin Beza   Jeff Cooper
Joey Larson

MARCH NURSERY WORKERS

5 & 12   Edwina Christiansen
            Erin Svoboda
19 & 26   Angela Paeper
            Megan Minert

MARCH CANDLE LIGHTERS

Megan Minert & Jessica Cooper

ATTENDANCE

Feb.	
5	108
12	78
19	88
26	78

Prayer Concerns

PRAYER CONCERNS

Merlin Christiansen, surgery recovering at home; Susan Strahm, loss of her grandmother; Hattie Mutz family; Harold Lake, was hospitalized; Margaret McQuistan, was hospitalized.

ALTER FLOWERS

Cleone Kelly is working on an alter flower schedule for the year. If you wish to place flowers on the alter to celebrate a certain occasion, or for a memorial, please

Alter Fl

The Church Council met on February 8, 1995. Pastor Ben welcomed all the new Council members--Art Cline, Ron Smith, Tami Svoboda, Joy Whitfield, and Cleone Kelly.

The Council voted to ask Janice Schmitz to serve as Clerk with pay for her time at the meetings. This was in consideration that the Clerk's job time commitment was beyond what any of the Council could give.

On the request of Margaret McQuistan, Pastor Ben suggested to the Council that the church purchase a new United Church record book. This book will record all members as well as baptisms, marriages, deaths, confirmations, etc. The record books of both the Methodist and Presbyterian churches would be closed. The new book will track all United members from the merger in 1990.

We are encouraging youth to go to camp this summer. The church office is collecting information about opportunities. It was thought that we should spend our energies and resources to encourage youth to have a camp experience in lieu of Vacation Bible School. This was thought as our youth and parents are so busy that such would be a good alternative.

The Council voted to have a representative from the Worship and Education committees meet with the Care of Property Committee to develop a job description for our janitor.

The Finance Committee reported that estimates of giving have reached $36,000. This shows good work from the congregation. We thank all members, committee members, and workers.

The next Council meeting will be March 8th at 7:00 p.m.

GOD GAVE HIS SON SO THAT OUR SINS MAY BE FORGIVEN

MARCH 1995

SUNDAY	MONDAY	TUESDAY	WEDNESDAY	THURSDAY	FRIDAY	SATURDAY

FEBRUARY 1995
S M T W T F S
     1 2 3 4
 5 6 7 8 9 10 11
12 13 14 15 16 17 18
19 20 21 22 23 24 25
26 27 28
 	
APRIL 1995
S M T W T F S
                1
 2 3 4 5 6 7 8
 9 10 11 12 13 14 15
16 17 18 19 20 21 22
23 24 25 26 27 28 29
30
 	
NEW MOON 1
FIRST QUARTER 9
FULL MOON 17
LAST QUARTER 23
NEW MOON 31
			1
			6:45 am Lent. Breakfast
			4:00 Confirmation
			7:00 p.m. Outreach/ Mission Committee
			7:30 p.m. Ash Wed. Service
			Ash Wednesday
				2	**3**
					World Day of Prayer, Cornerstone Church 9:30 a.m.
						4

5 Youth Brunch 9:15 S. School 10:30 Worship	**6**	**7** 10:30 Newsletter Committee	**8** 6:45 Lent Breakfast 2:00 United Women 4:00 Confirmation 7:00 Council	**9**	**10**	**11**
12 9:15 Adult Parenting Class 10:30 Worship	**13**	**14**	**15** 6:45 Lent Breakfast 4:00 Confirmation	**16**	**17** Deadline for Newsletter Articles ST. PATRICK'S DAY	**18**
19	**20** Parenting Hospice Training, ...an, 6:00-9:00	**21**	**22** 6:45 Lent Breakfast 4:00 Confirmation 7:45 Christ. Ed. Committee	**23** 6:00 Hospice Training, Emerson	**24**	**25**
26 r Parenting Hospice Training, ...an, 6:00-9:00	**27**	**28** SPRING BEGINS	**29** 6:45 Lent. Breakfast ...firmation Training, Emerson	**30** 6:00 Hospice Training, Emerson	**31**	

women gained the right to vote and secured educational and employment opportunities. New laws protected women and working children.[11] New educational structures and employment patterns broadened the gap between childhood and adulthood—a trend institutionally recognized and supported by the formation of Liberal-Puritan voluntary organizations outside church and political authority: Boy Scouts, Campfire Girls, the YMCA and YWCA, and a host of similar organizations.[12]

Independent labor organizations emerged, singing hymns on the picket lines and surviving harsh reprisals at the hands of company-employed goons, police, and militia who wanted the covenantal rights for corporations but only individual rights for workers. The notion that workers too could form solidarities and have identity through "independent congregations" recapitulated earlier "established" and "disestablished" church arguments in the economic sphere. This time the heirs of the Puritans played establishment roles.[13]

Under the influence of Jane Addams, Henry George, Edward Bellamy, and others, the "welfare" phrase of the Constitution was redefined, bringing about a new phase of public responsibility for the poor, disabled, and handicapped under the flag of "practical Christianity."[14] Ecological concerns were reflected in landscape architecture that advocated "park laws" and "green belt" urban planning.[15] President Teddy Roosevelt symbolized the ambiguity of American economic ideology by prescribing the Liberal-Puritan theory of pluralism in a peculiar combination of "trust-busting" and a celebration of "the free-enterprise system," by advocating both rapid industrial growth and the preservation of wilderness reserves.[16]

In religious groups, which have always been decisive indicators of the pulse of life in America, missionary movements evolved into an ecumenical movement. Church groups had spawned missionary outreach to the former slaves and to the settlers of the American frontier. They sent evangelists and teachers around the world who brought home accounts of other societies and cultures while exporting the biases of America to other lands. New modes of social involvement on the part of the churches were heralded by the Social Creed of 1908, and the study of "Christian sociology," the forerunner of modern Christian social ethics, and several American schools of sociology.[17] But by now the Liberal-Puritan synthesis had once more been nearly reduced to a minority report—surely an echo of earlier hopes, perhaps a vision of future possibilities. At the moment the voices uttering the creed were nearly drowned out by the furious noise of national expansion and by the increased identification of Protestantism with revivalistic evangelicalism.[18] The concern to shape the ethos of the nation through a "public theology" was again present, but the means became indirect and pluralistic. The pluralism was reinforced by the religiocultural consciousness of multiple ethnic groups and several classes—each forming a "denomination."[19] New American denominations such as the Mormons and the Christian Scientists were engendered, and Jews were viewed more and more as but another denomination. The "Social Gospel" perhaps best represents the attempted restatement of the Liberal-Puritan synthesis in a new key appropriate to industrializing America. It became the dominant orientation of the growing ecumenical movement.[20] Its successors, "Christian Realism" and "Liberation Theology," denote the dominant stream of official ecumenical church policy derived from earlier Liberal-Puritan themes. Just as important, however, has been the personalistic version of Liberal psychology and Protestant revivalistic zeal, closely allied with pragmatic thought on public issues.[21] The evangelistic revivalism of frontier religion brought in its wake a new populism. Only fractions of each denomination saw the need for a fundamental public theology to give affirmative shape to social institutions and to combat the "superpersonal forces of evil."[22]

These accents were no longer confined to the Puritan traditions; they became a part of the Protestant experience, generally, in America. Most American Protestants in effect became Liberal-Puritans, the majority heading in an "evangelical" direction, the minority in a "progressive" one. Both in fact influenced public policy, even though some focused their attention on the evils of drinking, Sunday baseball, dancing, and the theater, while others focused on socioeconomic justice for the poor and disadvantaged.[23]

Intellectual currents, mostly from Europe, also shaped the religious and social situation during this period. New techniques of historical analysis were applied to Scripture, producing a new literature of "higher criticism." For the most part such techniques were resisted by the evangelicals and the Catholics, affirmed by the progressive heirs of the Liberal-Puritan synthesis.[24] The natural sciences, especially theories of biological evolution stemming from Darwin's theory, suffered a similar fate. Psychology and psychiatry as aids to understanding humanity's inner life were more ambiguously received, but gradually the writings of Freud and Jung became standard fare in the progressive seminaries and were viewed with distant suspicion in evangelical ones, where William James's pragmatic and individualist conversionism was more widely accepted.[25] Sociology as a discipline in America was founded by progressive clerics, while evangelicals and Catholics of the period doubted its validity and utility.[26] And at the fringes of these developments, some progressives toyed with Christian socialism, trying to link it with the burgeoning labor movement.[27] At the same time, some Evangelical and Imperialist Calvinists became entwined with fundamentalist doctrines, forming organizations which occasionally erupted into anti-Black, anti-Jew, anti-Catholic, anti-Socialist, anti-Darwin, anti-psychology movements.[28] At more "respectable levels," business and political leaders sought a prayer-centered spirituality which could transcend such disputes and provide "peace of mind."[29]

Since the dramatic developments of this period from the Civil War to World War I, the social structure of America has been relatively constant. Neither World War I itself nor the Depression, World War II, the Cold War, the Korean War, the Black Revolution, the Viet Nam War, or Watergate and contemporary "crises" have brought about fundamental structural, social change. Nor has the *basic* creed been altered, although it is increasingly attenuated and neglected. In each of these previous challenges, indeed, it is the values of one or another version of the Liberal-Puritan public theology which have been invoked to justify America's institutions, world view, conception of that which is genuinely human, and definition of rights. In addition, each challenge has brought adjustment and modification—sometimes in the direction of greater individualism, some times in the direction of greater equality and solidarity, sometimes in the "isolationist" direction which would withdraw from international responsibilities, and sometimes in an expansionist direction which would export American values to the world. But these variations have not brought basic change in institutional fabric, class structure, or public creed. Twentieth-century America, for all its drama and experience of flux, is living in a relatively constant framework of creed and social form rooted in the ancient Liberal-Puritan synthesis, intact but stretched to the limits by the internal social and ideological pressures of the great transition of the late nineteenth and early twentieth centuries. Today these pressures are such in each sector of society that both active church people and the general population are confused. Flights to private spirituality on one side and new stirrings of nationalism (Socialist and anti-Communist) on the other are heralded as the clues to salvation. Neither provides an adequate account of our contemporary stress. Both could destroy the deeper legacy of human rights. A better account is needed.

B. THE EXPERIENCE OF CONTEMPORARY STRESS

The framework established by the Liberal-Puritan synthesis proved to be tremendously powerful in fueling the engines of modern industrial society. It also created a social system which was attractive to those who did not share its religious presuppositions. Waves of immigrants came to America with dreams of getting a new economic chance in the land where "streets were paved with gold." Utilitarian and pragmatic liberal ideology began to displace the Liberal-Puritan synthesis in public discourse, and "democracy" became the religion of folk piety—often with a loss of the first principles upon which it rested. Yet the framework provided by the deeper heritage remained basically intact in the institutions of society if not in the popular consciousness, even as new issues of social change put increasing pressure on the framework itself. We shall examine this structure, and the stresses upon it, in terms of the "cross-sectional method" outlined in Chapter One. The "longitudinal analysis" has dominated the presentation thus far, although the cross-sectional concerns have been implicit. Now the cross-sectional method will guide the presentation of material, although connections with the longitudinal motifs will be drawn.

Three great shifts are especially notable in twentieth-century America. As these shifts have occurred, the institutions formed by the Liberal-Puritan synthesis have been stretched to their limits. The people most involved in these shifts have often had the least acquaintance with or loyalty to the synthesis. The three movements are the massive technological concentration to form modern cities, the intense development of the professions, and the pervasive influence of the mass media. These developments in technology, culture, education, law, and medicine represent the institutional results of the Liberal-Puritan synthesis, but seldom do they reveal their roots or their theoretical connections with basic understandings of what it means to be human—theologically understood. We must look at these sectors of society one by one, identifying by our cross-sectional analysis something of the lived experience of American life effected by the modifications of the Liberal-Puritan synthesis brought by the "great transition."

1. Technology and Urbanization

Figure 2.

Focus on Technology and the Social System. The comments will indicate the implications of technology for the other sectors of the society. (See the base figure for this cross-sectional analysis, p. 18.)

Educational	Cultural/ Expressive	Legal
Familial	Voluntary	Political
Medical	Technical	Economic

With the closing of the frontier in the late nineteenth century, the die was cast: America would grow in an urban direction. The specific values of the Liberal-Puritan synthesis fomented a love for inventiveness, tinkering, and the quest for new techniques as part of an urbane life—as we see in the life of Benjamin Franklin. In turn, the technology of building construction, communication, transportation, industry, and exchange allowed and demanded increased urbanization and eventually metropolitanization. The percentage of people living on farms has steadily declined since the turn of the century. Only 3.4 percent of the American population today remains primarily engaged in agriculture, supplying the food and fiber for the rest of the nation and nearly 40 percent of the food grains sold on the world market. And even the farms are technological outposts deeply linked with the urban-centered suppliers, markets, and communication systems, and the administration of law, education, medical care, and transportation.[30]

Massive technological urbanization has many implications. For a discussion of religion and human rights, one dimension is most remarkable. In an urban environment, whole and multileveled relationships between persons called for by religion are less and less prominent. The persons with whom one conducts business or from whom one obtains medical care may not be the persons with whom one worships or socializes. The people to whom one turns to educate children or to handle a lawsuit are as likely as not to be of a different political, cultural, or religious background. Each relationship, including the religious one, is reduced to its own functional particularity.

We know one another only in segmental roles. Each person may participate in the voluntary relations of religious, familial, commercial, political, and cultural life in a combination that is unique to him or her.

Urbanization, based on complex technology that makes high-density living possible, and a value system that celebrates freedom thus create a context for increased individuation, with all the perils of anomie and isolation as well as the promise of liberation from inherited ascriptions and enforced stereotypes. In such a context the question of "membership" is increasingly personal and voluntary. We may join, or resign from, just about any group in any sector of society. The dignity, responsibility, and just claims of each self can no longer be defined by a particular relation to political participation, to contribution to the culture, to level of education, to legally enforced status, to function in a family, or to religious preference or affiliation—even if a specific variety of religious orientation and polity was historically and sociologically decisive for the rise of the urban *ethos* which made the individuation pervasive. The capacity to live in the "freedom" of the city may in fact be deeply influenced by health and economic factors, and by the level of technical skill that is available to one or one's class, but in the city the chances of overcoming disabilities of this sort are higher. That is why the sick, the poor, and the unskilled go to the cities.

In the urban environment, relationships are experienced as contractual and utilitarian. In fact, these relationships are possible because of a deep and pervasive set of shared values which make the relationships possible, but we experience our relations to one another on a short-term, *ad hoc* basis. Each party is presumed to gain something useful in an exchange of goods, services, or views. If a specific relationship does not render discernible and useful benefit, the relationship is broken. Visitors to the United States often see the easy friendships of Americans as superficial, short, and unreliable. It is more rare than regular that students attend the schools or colleges of their parents. Corporations spend billions trying to hold the fickle loyalties of stockholders and customers. And, at least within Protestantism, believers go "church shopping" among a number of acceptable denominations when they move to a new city.

The individualistic, contract-based, utilitarian character of urban society reinforces those possibilities within the Liberal-Puritan synthesis which press toward fragmentation. There is freedom for persons in the urban areas un-dreamed of by those forerunners of the modern metropolis who said, "City air makes one free."[31] No longer are persons victims of the old fixed roles. As Calvin had once announced: "We can become what we are not." Immigrants from the peasant populations of Europe, the Blacks freed from slavery, the youth of the twentieth century, and the minorities of Latin American, Asian, and American-Indian background have fled to the cities, leaving behind much of their tradi-tional culture and adapting to the apparent demands of a Liberal-Puritan syn-thesis by making pragmatic, personal adjustments.

Personal crisis is also present in the cities. Shorn of traditional support systems, networks of established connection, and pertinent skills for urban com-plexity, the naked self is often alone, lonely, and overwhelmed. Lacking a sense of "vocation" or "covenant," unsure about self-evident truths, the newcomer experiences the system as a soulless machine against which one must assert selected features of traditional cultural and religious identity. In such a setting, individuals have new freedoms and new rights simply as members of the human community, but few resources by which to claim the rights and transform the freedom into constructive participation. Yet in the city people find more complex interdependencies and possibilities than in any alternative society. The city presses all who come in contact with it to define anew the purposes of their lives, to order their worlds from within (since the exterior possibilities are so manifold), to synthesize the old and the new, to seek more universal standards by which contraries may be integrated, to work out their ethical stances and lifestyles by *electing* uncoerced standards and communities of trust among the myriads of possible associations. Everyone is forced to decide for himself or herself. The primal right, in this context, becomes the right to decide one's primary com-munity of identity. The city unwittingly invites all inhabitants to religious re-newal.[32] It breaks particular "brotherhoods" and opens the prospect to universal "otherhood."[33]

In the deeper roots of Christian theology and the Liberal-Puritan synthesis, one can find a rich variety of theological, ethical, and sociopolitical resources to guide the city and to guide persons in the city—resources which are sup-portive of human rights and which give shape to these decisions.[34] In the period of the great transition, a variety of scholars, pastors, theologians, and social scientists began the reclamation of those resources in both practical and the-oretical ways. The "Social Gospel," as it was called, identified most of the prom-ise and many of the perils of rapid and pervasive urbanization. And again in the 1960s and 1970s a new burst of interest in the city issued in a flurry of urban publications and social projects.[35] Yet Americans do not love their cities. The vision to found a "city set upon a hill," to be a light to the nations for the glory of God, is transformed into a mechanical instrument for self-advancement. Insofar as the cities survive, they do so on a legacy of covenanted duty, civic responsibility, and institutional structures generated out of the Liberal-Puritan synthesis. For many if not most Americans, the cultivation of a public theology to sustain an urban civilization capable of making human rights a living option has become a matter of individual choice embraced only when it is contractually useful. The modern technological city is using up its ideological capital.[36]

2. *The Professions*

Figure 3.
The Professions Today

Educational	Cultural/ Expressive	Legal
Familial	Voluntary	Political
Medical	Technical	Economic

Another major shift in America since the great transition has been the growth of the professions. Academic or scholarly societies, such as the American Philosophical Society, the American Historical Society, and the American Academy of Science, had been in existence for more than a century, but in the "period of transition," new professional organizations came into being. The American Economic Association was founded in 1885, followed soon by the American Sociological Association. Nonacademic professionals followed these models. In 1907 the American Medical Association was formed—one of the first and most powerful professional associations. Shortly thereafter the lawyers followed suit, forming the American Bar Association. By 1927 some thirty professional groups had been formed. Today more than two hundred such associations operate nationwide.[37] The deep historical roots of the professions are found in specifically Christian doctrines of vocation and covenant, but increasingly the sense of divinely given responsibility for service and the "professing" of values in, among, and for all the people have been displaced by utilitarian, Liberal conceptions of expertise and economic advantage.[38]

In 1893 Emile Durkheim published his justly famous *The Division of Labor in Society.* He saw in the period of the great transition that an increasingly complex society would require professional and vocational grouping with shared value systems which would serve as communities of identity, especially if tra-

89

ditional religious groupings failed. He recognized that intermediary associations between the isolated person and the general society were absolutely critical to prevent anomie and totalitarianism. His analysis seems to have been proved correct in modern American experience. Those in medicine, law, and higher education represent the most visible and privileged professional experts in the country, but engineers, business managers, schoolteachers, psychologists, nurses, social workers, real-estate dealers, hairdressers, etc., are today imitating these classical vocations and are increasingly professionalized. Indeed, for many the professional association has become *the* center of moral consensus and loyalty beyond the family and the state. The university has become, in the West, the training ground for professionals, the "secular church" for intellectuals. These groups often influence legislation and public values. The values dominating these groups are often a utilitarian version of the Liberal-Puritan synthesis. Hard work, care for the common good, a sense of living under standards of excellence, a process for guaranteeing "qualified" membership, as well as a sense of privileged "election," are all values that motivate these groups. At the same time, increasing complexity in the society means that knowledge is power, and specialized knowledge has come to be seen as a right to privilege instead of an obligation to service. The fact that lawyers, doctors, and other professionals have recently been implicated in some of the greatest scandals of public life (such as Watergate), and the tendency of some professionals to see their expertise as an occasion for entrepreneurial activity with exorbitant financial gain are forcing many professionals to re-examine the interior foundations of their professions. Journals, courses, special workshops, and institutes on medical ethics, ethics and law, business ethics, and similar topics appear on all sides.[39] Like the cities, professionals have been drawing on a repository of "public theology" which they have neither inculcated as creed nor replenished by open "professing" of basic vocational or covenantal presuppositions and humanitarian purpose. The public suspicion of the "experts" and of the professional is growing, even though more and more parents want their children to gain the advantages of professional training.

The professionalization of society has brought about two somewhat contradictory developments in the understanding of human rights. The reaction against professionalization has brought with it additional controversies. Let us note these briefly. First, the professionals have removed persons from primary communities of church, family, neighborhood, and national background to treat them. Children are bussed to schools; youth go away to college; sick people go to hospitals or clinics; academics fly to professional meetings; and the testimony of family is disallowed in many court proceedings. In principle, although less often in fact, professionals work with their clients best the more they are abstracted from the concrete matrices of life. Persons are treated as cases. At the same time, it means, in principle, that whatever one's background, each is to be treated equally. And this is the second point. Professionals are supposed to apply, equitably, universal standards of judgment and to maintain those standards for all. This aspect of professionalism is profoundly compatible with human rights. The derelict is *entitled* to medical treatment, the disadvantaged to education and social service, the ex-convict to competent legal defense with a presumption of innocence before the bar of justice. In principle, professionalism means that concrete social conditions which might disable persons do not count.

In fact, they do, and everybody knows it. The reaction against the professions tends to focus on the fact that certain groups in society—definable by categories of race, sex, and class—neither get the benefits of professional service nor the opportunity to become professionals themselves. Numerous efforts are afoot to form voluntary associations outside the professions, or "caucuses" within them, to force by political action greater equity and to reduce the "monopolies" or "old-boy networks" of professionals. At the same time, some groups have given up on professionals altogether and are trying to form alternative, reintegrative communities. Less radically, new clusters of professionals are forming alternative institutions for health, educational, and legal services. These groups accent the human right to choose professional associations (on the model of the parochial schools), and are working very hard to provide real alternatives which deal "holistically" with each person. Few realize how closely their efforts are modeled after the Free-Church traditions and how analogous they are to "free market" theories of the corporation. In this context human rights mean freedom of professional association and freedom of professional-client relationships—freedom to choose them, freedom to restructure them.

3. Mass Media

Figure 4.

The Contemporary Arts: Mass Media

Educational	Cultural/ Expressive	Legal
Familial	Voluntary	Political
Medical	Technical	Economic

The third major development in twentieth-century America which has built on, but not often helped to sustain, its own foundations is the mass media. Rooted in the complexities of urban technology and related to the differentiation and professionalization of the arts, journalism, film, and television have become the decisive forms of mass expression in modern America.

The rights of freedom of expression and of the press had been hard won by dissenting Puritans of long ago. These rights had also been defended by subsequent Liberals, and we must briefly bring the trajectory from the past up to date to understand our present context in this sector of society. Certainly the kinds of materials which were to be freely expressed were rather restricted by modern standards. The Puritans were very suspicious of the theater, out of which emerged many of the patterns for film and television programming. They saw the theater as the pastime of courtesan cavaliers and their attendants. Theater symbolized the love of indolent leisure, it catered to the less seemly forms of human intercourse, and it promoted profligate living. Puritans, and many of the classical Liberals, never understood theatrical drama. They saw it as much related to papist pageantry, as a studied insincerity, as an artificial creation of an image of what one was not, as a celebration of pretense and illusion. For the Puritan, *the* drama was the drama of human salvation, played with ultimate seriousness on the worldly stage and under the direction of the living God; not the interplay and artificial repartee of public personage. *The* drama required engaged commitment, not passive observation. It was Milton's *Paradise Lost* and Bunyan's *Pilgrim's Progress,* not Shakespeare's theatrical imagination, that best portrayed the true drama of life.[40] For generations, pious Americans never set foot in a theater.

This is not to say that Puritans had no place for the arts; they focused on music.[41] Hymnody, with congregational singing, was its primary vehicle. Over time music became the mass art of the Puritan traditions. Music was designed to do for the heart what the sermon did for the mind: to provide the basis for participation of the affections in the freedom and order of God.[42] Every major subsequent movement in the Liberal-Puritan synthesis has accented singing. It is not possible to imagine the power of that late-Puritan movement, Methodism, without the hymnody of John and Charles Wesley. The frontier religion of Puritan Baptists in America was characterized by the hymnody of the *Ira D. Sankey Songbooks.* The zeal of these older movements carried over into the twentieth-century efforts toward Liberal-Puritan renewal at the grassroots level. The Black religious experience in America is expressed more poignantly in "spiritual" and "gospel" music than in any other single mode. The mark of whether one was really on the inside of the labor movement in the early days, or a part of the civil rights struggle or the counterculture in the 1960s, was whether one knew the songs.[43] This musical tradition is distinct from theater and the graphic arts; America has remained somewhat philistine in these areas.

One striking development, however, has challenged the Puritan doubt about drama. Television crushed the Puritan resistance by penetrating people's homes

92

with irresistible force, shaping images and values in still unpredictable ways. For millions, the TV has become the primary locus of interpreting the nature and character of public symbol, myth, and drama.

In the age of the great transition, the mass-circulation magazine, the telegraph, and the "wireless" anticipated the modern media. Throughout most of the twentieth century, radio, film, records, paperbacks, and television have brought a new immediacy to world events and multiple opinion. Exposure to drama made available to all what was once the privilege of the few and under suspicion by the many. On the foundation of "freedom of expression" developed by the Puritans, the United States kept the media free from governmental control. The freedom of the pulpit has translated into freedom of the press. As the media developed—especially the electronic media, which communicate drama easily and sustained argument badly—they increasingly came under the control of people little interested in Puritan values. Puritans abandoned drama, and the media abandoned Puritan values; still, they shared the principle of the "free press." That relative autonomy is also responsible for the media's exposure of public corruption by government or corporation in every decade of the twentieth century. Without them the civil rights movement and the anti–Viet Nam mobilization could not have occurred in the way they did.

Electronic media give wide circulation to ideas and perspectives, yet television has focused on the dramatic interplay of personality as the clue to reality. Television programming has developed an understanding of life that focuses on individuals, in episodic conflict and resolution, without a social fabric, without a history or a destiny, without overarching moral, religious, or intellectual concerns. Religious, political, and intellectual issues are presented in terms of an emphasis on "personality." Debates over who has rights of access to this media, and how the media shall treat moral matters, are unresolved.[44]

The city—with all its complex structures, skills, interactions, and technological sophistication—the professions, and the mass media have all pluralized and modified the Liberal-Puritan synthesis in the twentieth century. All have drawn on resources from the tradition; each has brought about the ambiguous actualization of some aspects of human rights from the tradition. Yet none of these areas or sectors of society has found a way to replenish the store of moral conviction which sustains them. All wobble without the rudder of a basic creed, and most consider it bad form to appeal overtly to religion. All try to improve well-being while pragmatically doing well. Most involve vast networks of interdependences and employ elaborate techniques to find out what the people they serve want and need. Still, a vision of the truly human is lacking. Moreover, the impact of these developments has been most sharply felt in the other sectors of society which must be treated in a cross-sectional analysis. In the *family* (Section C), in *political life* (Section D), in the structures of the *economy* (Section E), and in the *ecclesial and voluntary* sectors of society (Section F), the impact of the Liberal-Puritan heritage as modified by urbanization, professionalization, and the expansive role of the mass media on the heels of the great transition has had major consequences. We shall look at these four sectors of society in turn.

C. THE FAMILIAL APPROPRIATION OF HUMAN RIGHTS

Figure 5.

The Familial Sector

Educational	Cultural/ Expressive	Legal
Familial	Voluntary	Political
Medical	Technical	Economic

In the twentieth century and particularly in recent years, Americans are experiencing a widespread redefinition of family structures and sexual roles. Even monogamous, heterosexual, nuclear families are witnessing new definitions of what it means to be male and female, and what the terms of relationship are to be. Ambiguity and confusion dominate issues of sexual morality and right.[45] The birthrate shows significant decline, and debates rage about contraception, abortion, homosexuality, and a growing divorce rate (some nineteen percent of all schoolchildren live in single-parent families). Furthermore, we have seen a dramatic transformation of adolescence in the past three generations. Between puberty and adulthood, a six- to ten-year span of life has produced a new stage in human development with imprecise guidelines as to what it means to "grow up."[46] Unanswered questions about the rights of youth vis-à-vis parents, members of the opposite sex, schools, and the body politic appear in legislatures and parent-teacher-student-associations as well as in the home and the popular advice columns with enormous readerships. A clear revision, if not a revolution, of human sexuality and family is occurring in our consciousness and in our most intimate relationships.

This revision is partly a product of the general social shifts taking place in twentieth-century America and in most industrialized countries. Urbanization and its accompanying technological leaps make obsolete many of the traditional role definitions by sex. There is a greatly reduced dependence on differences between averages of gross muscle weight to define man's work and woman's work. The sterilized bottles and infant food formulas on the market make baby-feeding a task transferable to men. The increased professionalization of function in society, with its increased pressure to find identity in specialized training, has had two effects. It has brought many women to a point where they can find a fulfilled identity only if they too become professionals, developing and using their talents in the professional world or the world of work. At the same time, the need for increased specialized training has made it more and more difficult for youth to enter the job market directly. More education, which entails a longer dependency on parents or educational institutions, delays the time when young people can make their own way in the world. The changing technological needs of the society mean that youth can depend less and less upon parental skills as models for themselves; at the same time, they are economically dependent far beyond adolescence.

Not all of the changes in family life can be attributed to these very real pressures, however. Part of the change derives from changing attitudes toward sexuality, toward the family, and toward young people. For one thing, basic attitudes toward these matters have been deeply influenced by psychological and psychiatric findings. The giants of these sciences—Freud, Jung, Piaget, and the rest—did much of their creative work precisely during the great transition. Their ideas have been imported from Europe and have become a part of the ordinary vocabulary of daily conversation and the mass media. "Neurosis," "repression," "subconscious," "animus," "therapy," "reaction," "transference," and dozens of other highly technical terms have become common parlance. Intrapsychic relations and many interpersonal relations are often understood in these terms. Especially significant is the view that sexuality is a major and pervasive human drive which must find expression. Denial of the fact that humans are sexual beings leads to disaster. Still, as Russell Jacoby has argued in a very important and far too neglected book, *Social Amnesia: A Critique of Conformist Psychology from Adler to Laing*, it is likely that much of the American appropriation of these terms and understandings has not addressed the fundamental issues of either self, intimacy, or society.[47] Indeed, it may well be that, in America, the popular appropriation of the ideas of these figures is merely another product of our industrializing, urbanizing, professionalizing environment, where pressures toward individualism and contractualism are pervasive.

The real shift is deeper, I think. It is deeper historically and conceptually; and it is rooted in the Puritan and Liberal developments of several centuries ago. If we take a close look, we shall see in the conventional understandings of the Puritans that the common accusations against them—that they were individualistic, against sensuality, and joyless—are simply not true. I shall argue that the seventeenth century saw the beginnings of a revolution in understanding of sexuality and the family that is with us still. It has been mediated to the present by hundreds of pious families, from parent to child, who believed that "the family which prays together, stays together." I believe that the full impact of this shift could not be seen until the twentieth century, because the ideological and social conditions that would allow this revolutionary conception to break fully into practice were not at hand. The fact that until the twentieth century most people depended on an agricultural economy which supported age- and sex-specific divisions of labor, the fact that Liberal-Puritan understandings of sexuality and the family in the nineteenth century were almost overwhelmed by immigrants and southern slave-holders with views contrary to their own, and the fact of the rise of Victorian prudery (often adopted as "biblical" by the frontier-evangelical branch of Protestantism) meant that the interior logic of Liberal-Puritan understandings of marriage has only recently come into fuller vision. The more basic views reappear—it must be said—under the impress of a sharp challenge from individualistic, utilitarian, and contractual perspectives which derive from laissez-faire economics and pressures against the extended family in the modern city.

The ideas of "covenant" are decisive for Puritan views of sexuality and marriage. They stand in opposition to the "spiritual," hierarchical view of sexuality and marriage that was held by the majority in the church for centuries before the Reformation, which we must briefly review longitudinally. Secular philosophers, such as Cicero, and major classical theologians, such as Augustine, shared a conservative perspective, as did many of the Anglo-Catholics who were in contention with the Puritans and Liberals. This traditional view made a brief, but vigorous, reappearance during the reign of Queen Victoria, and almost captured the center of religious and moral reflection before being dramatically displaced once more in the twentieth century. The view was simply this: the spiritual intercourse of the soul with God and of the mind with other minds was the purer, superior relationship for humanity. Physical and passionate relationships were lower, impure, and less worthy of genuine and virtuous humanity. Carnal intercourse might be necessary for reproduction, and thus there must be a moral concession toward that necessity (and toward women in general) under controlled conditions, but it was primarily a "natural" and not a "spiritual" matter—thus it was not central to redemption or, finally, to the understanding of what it means to be human. Virginity and celibacy were superior states, for in these the soul (including one of a woman) might be wedded to God without carnal distractions. A married woman was also to avoid carnal interests as much as possible. Friendship, a good thing, was basically the "Platonic" meeting of minds. This was the form of intercourse which was higher in the life of virtue. Sexuality, of course, was necessary for the propagation of the species, and in some cases it could lead to the friendship of spiritual exchange. When sacramentalized—that is, when infused with the blessing of supernatural grace—it could lead to an unbreakably permanent spiritual status which allowed proper control over material possessions and over the bodily and animalistic passions.[48]

This was not the whole of Catholic teaching. The Conciliar Catholics of the late-medieval period had argued otherwise, and the break between the Anglican

Church and Rome over sexual matters had already opened the door to a moderated view in England before the Puritans became a force. Celibacy had already been rejected as necessary for ordination. Edmund Leites, in his helpful treatment of these issues, points out that there were countervailing tendencies even in some teaching of Saint Thomas Aquinas, who in many other respects held hierarchic, spiritual views. Drawing from Aristotle's notions on "friendship," Thomas argued that marriage is a special kind of friendship and that equality is a condition of true friendship. At the same time, his view of "ensoulment"— that it was later for females than males—implied an inferior status for women. This view has seemed more compelling to many disciples of Thomas.[49] More importantly, some Conciliar Catholic voices, such as John Major, argued that "whatever men say, it is difficult to prove that a man sins in knowing his own wife for the sake of having pleasure." Such views were vigorously attacked by the Conservative Catholics, who fought to retain a more traditional view, but the views of Major had begun to take hold in England.[50]

These are the views that the Puritans shared. They too attacked the Conservative Catholic view. According to the Puritans, the latter implied that being alone, in a celibate state, was superior to being together, that the body with all its sensuousness was something that tended to taint the spirit, and that sexuality was essentially to be granted a grudging concession of permission only for purposes of procreation. It also implied that women, who are necessary for reproduction, were understood as existing primarily for that inferior function. Typical of the Puritan critique of these views is the pronouncement in the wedding sermon of John Cotton: "They are a sort of Blasphemers then who dispise [sic] and decry them [women], and call them a necessary Evil, for they are a 'necessary Good;' such as it is not good that man should be without."[51]

Leites points out that the Puritans often argued for the universal excellence of marriage by pointing out that in the book of Genesis, the marriage of Adam and Eve took place *before* the Fall. Thus the covenant of marriage was not essentially formed after the recognition of temptation and wickedness, to control them. Sexuality and marriage are part of the reality of Paradise. Further, against those who believed that celibacy, with its implied individual spirituality, was the superior state of affairs, the Puritans pointed out that God himself had said, "It is not good that man should be alone" (Gen. 2:18). All of creation is good, but solitude is not as good as it can be. Thus a partner was created for companionship—long before the injunction to be fruitful and multiply was given. One of the Puritan authors put it this way: "Though he (Adam) was truly happy, yet he was not fully happy; though he had enough for his board, yet he had not enough for his bed. . . . he must be completed by conjunction. . . ."[52]

The covenant of marriage is given in the very process of sensual exercise of companionship. Persons alone are made in the image of God, but something material and earthy serves as the spiritual occasion for more genuine fulfillment of what it means to be human. Sensual togetherness is, from the foundations of creation, spiritual. Physical mutuality is necessary for full humanity. Indeed, "desire" becomes a "duty," as Leites puts it. Humans require another bodily to be spiritually whole. It is a very incarnational view of spirituality.

James Johnson's detailed study of Puritan attitudes confirms this view: the Puritans universalized the covenant view of sex and the family by making it part of the very foundations of creation. Companionship, mutuality, and a certain equality of the sexes are signs of God's grace. Further, this grace sometimes issues in procreation—itself a gift of God. Parents are called to participate in the very act of creation with God. When this happens, God confers the vocational duties of fathering and mothering on persons, adding these duties to church, political, and economic responsibilities. Neither male nor female has these duties "by nature," even in marriage. They are conferred by grace. However, society must be so arranged that these duties can be fulfilled when they are given. The Puritans also recognized that sexuality and marriage and children do not always remain in such an idyllic state. Because of the Fall, unruly children may need strong discipline, and marriage is also a remedy for sin and lust; it can sometimes become a living hell. When that happens, a careful discernment must be made as to whether a genuine covenant is present. If not, the relationship must end. Thus divorce was a live option, although only for a very few reasons. By the time of John Milton's Puritan writings on the topic, a false covenant of marriage could be declared to have been no covenant at all. A second, true covenant could be made. Divorce and remarriage were not such total scandals as more hierarchic views would have it, for marriage was not rooted in an eternal natural order nor blessed by an eternally valid sacrament.[53] However, the breaking of a covenant by infidelity while one was still within it, and "playing covenant" for fun before such an agreement was present, remained horrible scandals in this view—as all who have read Hawthorne's *Scarlet Letter* can see. These motifs are still current in American life, although few are aware of their point of origin. Divorce is widely accepted, but infidelity or sex without formal commitment is viewed with embarrassment unless one is intentionally flaunting opposition to Puritan values or drawing one's normative values from sectors of life least affected by Puritan influence—the media, aspects of psychology, and economic individualism and contractualism.

After the Fall, according to the Puritans, chaos tended to break into the covenantal relationship, with two consequences. First, humanity has to earn its bread by the sweat of its brow. In this the Puritans made it very clear that woman was to be a co-partner in the world of work. The people were enjoined, as Baxter said, not only to "keep up your conjugal love in a constant heat and vigor" to preserve the vision of paradise, but to "choose a mate who can be a co-partner" in the world of work.[54] Gataker put it this way: woman is to be a "yoake-fellow, a fellow labourer in the managing of affairs."[55] Passion and labor, however, do not always contain chaos. Hence an order of governance is required in the family. The family must have an order based on the analogy of the church covenant, where the "priesthood of all believers" preserves the vision of fundamental equality but where clergy are assigned special responsibilities of guidance and leadership, and on the analogy of the civil covenant, where all citizens are under the common law but where some are set aside for magisterial functions. The father is to be head of the household.

The fact that paternalistic authority is required to prevent chaos, in the Puritan view, did not compromise the deeper principle of coarchy and coequality in theory. It did compromise it in practice. The Imperial Calvinist strain, which has been a part of the whole Reformed tradition to one degree or another, particularly accented these notions and was especially powerful wherever Protestantism moved into places where civil government was not well established— such as the American frontier and South Africa. Still, the view that both husband and wife were to live under a covenanted order as equally subject to a moral law meant that the wife could criticize the husband. Husbands and wives were urged to pray together in private where each could openly appeal to God to remedy some defect in the other. And, if some husband did not fulfill his husbandly duties of passion, work, and governance in a godly way, the matter could be taken before God's community. If the husband did not heed such spiritual warnings, the wife could take him before the elders of the congregation.[56] The elders could, in the case of flagrant and persistent violation of duty, take the matter before the civil authorities. At this point, however, caution had to be exercised. The family as instituted by God, like the church, was prior to the state. It occupied a privileged social space which was inviolable by the state. Civil authority could not create covenants; it could only correct flagrant violations of family rights and duties, reminding the "governor" of the family of the godly duties of passion and responsibility in the exercise of a husbandly calling.

Even today, because of this heritage, the laws governing family life are limited. Progressive groups fight to keep the courts and the police out of all private actions between consenting adults. Laws passed in the Victorian period are fought in contemporary legislatures. Even in documented cases of child abuse or husband-wife violence, state authorities are cautious about intervening in family matters;—not, as some critics of this hesitance say, because wife and children are viewed as private property, but because of a deeply rooted conviction that home and family ought to be inviolable vis-à-vis the state.

The key Puritan notions, briefly sketched here, find their parallels in Liberal thought, with one major exception. For liberals, the foundation for marriage is not a God-given covenant but a voluntary contract. That is to say, marriage is an agreement of autonomous individuals, meeting as rational equals, to live together, sharing bed and labor, and providing for the care of children, according to their mutual inclinations and interests. The Liberal view shares with Puritan practice a paternalistic preference and, even more clearly, a wider door to divorce. As Leites has shown, their view also opposes the classical views of the Conservative Catholic and Anglo-Catholic traditions, but Liberalism does not develop the deep concern for the earthy and sensual side of marriage, nor does it presume that mutuality and fellowship are required to be more wholly human. It does develop a theory of property in marriage, and often sees husband-wife relationships in terms of a "commercial contract" and of "rights" to "possess" the other's body by mutual consent. Although never celebrating celibacy, Liberalism is much more individualist and calculating in its view of the human institution of marriage.[57]

In any case, through a long and complicated history, the Puritans and the Liberals formed a working consensus on the nature and character of sexuality and marriage, at least in contrast with competing views. The new synthesis, comprising both covenantal and contractual elements, was worked out in the various marriage ceremonies used in Protestant churches in America by some sixty percent of the couples being married. The results of these developments in our day are very clear. Sexuality is part of what it means to be human, and all persons must have the rights to form unions uninhibited by state or hierocratic metaphysical-moral assumption. Male and female are to be seen as theological equals; institutions may not morally deny that equality in the public sphere, although freedom of religion requires tolerance, by law, of those who advocate inequality (such as the Mormons). Procreation is *a* proper end of intercourse, but not its central purpose. When children come, however, the fidelity of the couple is to be expanded to care for them until they can reach their own independence, which means to form their own marriage and household economy. Divorce is a genuine possibility. The family and sexual practice are basically independent of the authority of the state, although many Victorian laws remain on the books.

In one sense the urban, technological, and professional world of modernity as well as the power of media perspectives on sexuality has undercut the more traditional economic, social, and cultural pressure to hold the family together. More than one third of all marriages end in divorce; among urban populations, the rate is higher. Families are thrown back to questions of first principles. Families stay together only if the marriage is a fundamental covenant and is perceived as a gift of grace—otherwise it reverts to a contract of convenience which may be freely negated by the consenting wills which formed it. The covenantal view of marriage has not been mediated into the present. If it were, the Equal Rights Amendment to the Constitution, recently proposed, would have been quickly passed, and many marriages would have a firmer base.[58] In the present confusion, however, many under the influence of Victorian and pre-Reformation views see only the threat of pure contractualism in this proposal. On another aspect of the present perspective on the family, Liberals increasingly view the present instability of the family as a function of increased economic pressures, and call for centralized governmental policy changes to provide increased educational, medical, and housing support systems for families.

A more dramatic crisis, however, is evident in the debate about abortion. The classical Calvinists and the principled liberals have always held that elective abortion without clear indication of severe threat to the mother is wrong. In this they were in substantial agreement with the whole testimony of the Catholic

100

tradition. Human life, even in the fetal stage, is inviolable because it is a gift of God. Basic human rights are to be extended to the unborn child simply because it is a creature of God, a member of the human community, and is in "fellowship" with the mother.[59] At the same time, the Puritans and Liberals held that sexual matters and all issues having to do with decisions about intercourse and procreation are matters to be dealt with by the family and in the context of church teaching. They are not ordinarily matters for legal and political coercive intervention. The Conservative Catholic tradition holds that the church may so influence the state that coercive power may be used to demand or prohibit sinful behaviors in the family—or in any other sector of society. The family (and the medical profession, in this case) is not a communal sphere with moral and spiritual autonomy but part of the whole *polis* which comprehends and guides behavior in all its subordinate units.

The Liberal-Puritan creed is caught in the middle, both believing in the human right of the fetus not to be destroyed arbitrarily, and deeply committed to the limits of law and to the independency of conscience and sexuality from coercive political controls. Yet women in the middle- and upper-income brackets have the resources to pay for abortion, to make a choice. Should not the government pay the costs of abortions for those who already get government welfare payments for other medical needs? To do so would seem to bring political policy to the point of using coercively collected tax money for a morally ambiguous purpose. Several Supreme Court decisions have ruled on this matter, but the issue of human rights as they apply to abortion is unsettled at the moment. The key question remains: Is the fetus a member of the human community—and if so, at what stage of development, and how shall its rights be weighed in the face of the freedom of the mother and the medical professional to decide against it? Must political and legal authority support the fetus or the mother?[60]

D. THE POLITICAL APPROPRIATION OF HUMAN RIGHTS

It is not only in views of sexuality and the family that the idea of covenant has had a major and lasting import, now modified by contractual notions. This is also true of the vision of civil government.

The Puritan vision influenced the formation of civil liberties and civil rights in the American colonies and in the United States Constitution. Protestantism in its early days was essentially protest, as already mentioned. It attempted reform within the given church, familial, and political systems. But when the Pilgrims came to America, they had no basic governmental system within which to work, so a new one had to be created. The Mayflower Compact was a famous first effort. It was created on the basis of an understanding of covenant renewal and the fresh application of the universal principles which the Pilgrims thought they had recovered. A decade later, in John Winthrop's sermon on the occasion of the founding of the Massachusetts Bay Colony, we can also see this to be the case:

Figure 6.

The Political Sector

Educational	Cultural/ Expressive	Legal
Familial	Voluntary	Political
Medical	· Technical	Economic

Thus stands the cause between God and us. We are entered into covenant with him for this worke. . . . Now if the Lord shall please to hear us, and bring us in peace to the place we desire, then hathe he ratified this covenant . . . but if we shall neglect the observation of these articles . . . , the Lord will surely break out in wrath against us. . . .[61]

The core of this new system was the church. The covenanted congregation contained the principles of and for all governance and was to be the model for the state. These principles could be stated as a series of articles which were to govern the "limited state," a governmental system which was subject to a primal moral law. While government was an eternal feature of human communities, as God decreed, any particular regime was revocable by God or capable of being reformed by those who knew the moral law if the regime transgressed such principles. As later, Liberal ideas also entered the modes of public discourse, comparable motifs in less pious language were accented.

Out of the Liberal-Puritan synthesis, a passion for the limited state was engendered. It was to be limited first by the fact that other organizations, especially the church, had a prior or privileged social space that was inviolable. This was the organization that was to protect the *imago dei,* the sacredness of marriage, and the necessity of fellowship. Also, this was the group called to confront persons with the reality of sin, to aid in the discernment of vocation, to articulate the moral law in reasonable discourse, and to do all these in the context of a covenant founded of God's grace and righteousness. The state was also to be limited by law, law embodying first principles in regard to the state's treatment of persons. On this basis the constitutional heritage of the West has included stipulations regarding civil liberties and civil rights as a part of its internal political structure. Throughout American history it has been believed that this particular heritage had discovered something of universal significance. Indeed, the nation's foreign policy against the Crown in the eighteenth century, against the French and Spanish in the nineteenth century, and against Fascism and Communism in the twentieth century, and its suspicion of the Vatican throughout, seemed arrayed against the absolutist state.

At this point we must also briefly remind ourselves that the entire Reformed tradition presses toward principled civic participation. Here is no retiring religious modesty. Saintliness in this tradition meant accepting the vocation, given by God, to transform public life into a model of justice and righteousness for the glory of God. The exercise of power, under God's law, was a positive religious duty of universal reach. Vigorous political activity, no less than sexual activity, was a divine duty. The result (as we traced in Chapter Three, Section F) was constitutional democracy with specified bills of rights.

It was not, however, until well after the great transition that America had the occasion to articulate in a fresh way its universalistic creed. As the Western leader of the Allies who defeated Hitler, America took the initiative in defining its understanding of human rights when it pressed for a United Nations' declaration on the subject. The pressure to have this statement adopted was both political and ideological. Politically it was an attempt to form a bloc of nations who would all agree on the principle of the limited state—so that National Socialism, with its tendency toward totalitarianism, would not and could not happen again. Ideologically it was an attempt to gain assent to a set of first principles historically developed in one sociocultural context but believed to be universal in import. But these principles could not be articulated in the particular language of Christian piety which had shaped both the Christian and the "secular" Liberal philosophers who had first developed them. Representatives from many cultures and religions would have resisted overt theological formulations in christological or deist terms. The principles had to be stated in "confessionally neutral" terms. But even at this point we see the triumph of the basic assumptions of the Liberal-Puritan synthesis. The state itself should not be "religious." In this view the theologically and morally valid state is one limited by righteous principles and one that allows other organizations to define what is religiously valid. In brief, the "godly state" is a secular state.

Not all the parties to the discussion of the U.N. declaration were sympathetic. The Warsaw Pact nations had strong reservations. In fact, they did not become party to any full agreement to the U.N. principles until thirty years later. It was only when the U.S. negotiators of the Helsinki Accords insisted on "Basket Three," entailing agreement on human rights as a condition of final agreement on World War II boundary lines and on economic and diplomatic cooperation, that the U.N. principles were accepted by the Eastern European powers.

The developing nations of the day were more sympathetic. Led by India, the key model of the "non-aligned" countries and the world's largest democracy, those nations not clearly in the circle of U. S. or Soviet influence were deeply concerned with finding the principles for a lasting peace and for developing a rationale for the "secular" indigenous state which could both resist colonialism and overcome internal religious (which means, in most non-Western contexts, tribal or caste) strife. To grasp the significance of this high moment in the political appropriation of human rights as a creed, it is important to take a close look at some of its most fascinating provisions. Not since the pre-Reformation councils had such an assemblage of national representatives attempted to define what is universally valid as a creed for all.

The first paragraph of the preamble begins with a statement heavily laden with basic assumptions: "Whereas recognition of the inherent dignity and of the equal and inalienable rights of all members of the human family is the foundation of freedom, justice and peace in the world. . . ."[62] In this statement an act of consciousness, "recognition," is seen as the foundation of all civility. But "recognition" is a nicely ambiguous word. It may mean the acknowledgment that something is true, it may mean confessing to an unavoidable conviction, or it may mean the renewed identification of something that was known before. In any case, the echoes of a Liberal-Puritan assumption resound here—a "mental action" that identifies essential truths about humanity as valid is the basis of all else in basic social ethics.

That which is taken to be valid is the "inherent dignity" and the "equal and inalienable rights." Immediately we confront another nicety. The word "inherent" can mean something that is conferred (as a privilege or duty that is vested with an office) or it can mean something indigenously present. The latter would have satisfied the Liberals and the Indians; the former is closer to Marxist and Puritan views. Later, when the document restates this motif in another way, the authors nod in both directions. In Article 1 we read, "All human beings are born free and equal in dignity and rights," a formula which would delight Locke and perhaps even Rousseau. But the next sentence nods to the other side of the synthesis: "They are endowed with reason and conscience and should act towards one another in a spirit of brotherhood." There is no hint in this political document of Who did the endowing, but Conciliar Catholics and Calvinists of all stripes know what is at stake here; Marxists get nervous. This two-sided beginning finds its convergence in the assertion of human "dignity." All—even the most terrible sinner, the most reactionary scoundrel, and the most ignorant fool—are worthy of respect. Further, all have "equal" rights. People may not be equal in brains, brawn, position, moral rectitude, or in many other respects, but the fact of equality overrides these differences. Nor may that dignity or equality or claim to worth be removed by any human agency interior or exterior to the society, personal or organized. These qualities are "inalienable." They may not be changed by or in history.

At this point the preamble comes to its first reference to whom it is that "equality" and "rights" pertain. It is to "members," to "members of the human family." Persons are not, in this political statement of principles, understood in the first instance to be isolated individuals. Persons are first of all "members"; they are related and relational beings. In Article 22 the matter is quite clear: "Every*one, as a member* of society, has the right to social security. . . ." And again, in Article 29, the relational character of personhood is accented: "Everyone has duties to the community in which alone the free and full development of personality is possible."

It should be noted, however, that community and society are themselves seen in a larger relationship. The primary relationship is universal in scope: it extends to the whole human race, which is understood in familial terms (see also "brotherhood" in Article 1). As we shall see at several later points, the uses of family metaphors in this way are quite significant. Human membership is not to be identified with the particular social and genetic group into which one is born. Article 2 specifically forbids genetic factors in determining rights, and Articles 13 through 15 deal specifically with the right to leave a group of origin without loss of rights. What is significant about our humanity is not the genetic character of our being nor the kinship structure of our family or origin by which genes are transmitted. In this view we may not derive our own sense of dignity or right, nor assess that of others, from our parental, sibling, clan, tribe, caste, ethnic, class, or national particularity. Specific "gene pools" are not the basis for human solidarity, identity, and "membership"; voluntary bonding is.[63]

A slight digression is in order here. Family is taken very seriously in the declaration. In Article 16 (3) the family is stated to be "the natural and fundamental group unit of society." That statement is made in a context already altered from either the racial theories of the Nazis or the traditional power of family identity in clan, tribal, or caste societies where family membership is a matter of religious identity also. The family is understood to be a sphere of relative sovereignty, "entitled to protection by society and the state." Family structure may not be prescribed or proscribed by the society or the state. (See also Article 26 [3].) The family is an independent and autonomous unit, engendered by intentional and equitable covenant. Thus the character of the family presumed to have rights is one in which men and women "without any limitation due to race, nationality, or religion, have the right to marry and to found a family." The family is not ontologically, genetically, socially, religiously, or traditionally determined; it has to be founded, and it may be dissolved (16 [1]). Family is created or founded in marriage, which is to take place "only with the free and full consent of the intending spouses" (16 [2]).

A universalistic brotherhood and sisterhood is seen as the basis for "freedom, justice and peace." Here are the declaration's understandings of the political virtues. Political instrumentalities, nation-states and conciliar assemblages of nation-states, are here seen to be themselves under a mandate more ultimate than they. According to these opening words, the violations of freedom, justice, and peace are due essentially to the failure to acknowledge a public creed, which now is recognized.

The "disregard and contempt for human rights" brought about two things in the minds of this document's authors (see paragraph 2 of the preamble). First, they brought about "barbarous acts which have outraged the conscience of mankind." But a second result has followed, evidently emerging out of that outrage: "the advent of a world in which human beings shall enjoy freedom of speech and belief and freedom from fear and want . . . as the highest aspiration of the common people." In these phrases we see a covert reference to Hitler's racist genocide, for barbarism is understood to mean a militant policy which is racially or ethnically founded but not universally founded.[64] We see also a covert reference to Franklin Roosevelt. It was his "Four Freedoms" speech as much as any other single statement which roused the United States to join Churchill's Britain in the struggle against the Nazis. He touched something deep in the American character when he spoke first of the freedom "from fear" and then of the freedom "from want." The order is significant. The Liberal-Puritan synthesis had founded its alliance essentially on those freedoms which permitted open, fearless discourse and discernment, group formation and free association, and unhampered practice and organization in matters moral, spiritual, familial, and political. These motifs are taken up as explicit provisions again in Articles 18 through 21 in terms which echo, almost without alteration of wording, profound convictions held as early as the 1640s by the Puritans and the 1680s by Liberals.[65] It has never been a part of this tradition that freedom from want—material resources—comes first. People experience want, sometimes severely. More oppressive than the want itself is the denial of the right to give utterance to the need, to be unable to turn to the neighbor and to God and cry out in the despair of suffering, to name the oppressor, to teach the reasons for suffering, and to receive guidance and courage, consensus and orientation, solidarity and empowerment to remedy the ills. The power of words, resting ultimately in a belief in the power and freedom of "The Word," allows want to be addressed. It is on this basis, the tradition held, that we find the models by which to establish a kind of civil government wherein we need not fear speaking out, one that is democratic and covenantal, open to free association and assembly. In turn, as open discussion and genuine religion lead to democratic government, so then the groundwork is laid to deal with want. On *this* basis, Articles 22 to 25 deal with the question of work, remuneration, social security, health, food, clothing, and shelter in the context of the rights of workers to organize and claim, from governments, support to meet these needs. It is also the case that just before rearticulating the rights of thought, religion, and expression on the basis just identified, Article 17 introduces the "right to own property alone as well as in association with others."

It is this sequence of priority that has been deeply troubling to Marxist (and other) critics of the Liberal-Puritan tradition and of the United Nations' declaration. As we shall see in Chapters Five and Six, the Marxist-Leninists are convinced that priorities must be exactly the other way around. Material needs for work, security, health care, food, clothing, and shelter are the fundamental ones for humanity. Society and governments are erected to provide these. These

106

are the need-based or "positive" rights which humanity must have first, to be human. The freedom-oriented or "negative" rights viewed as primary by the Liberal-Puritan synthesis are secondary or derivative, mere ideological froth to hide the egoistic concern to preserve private property and a feudal or a capitalistic system of privilege for the few. At stake is the matter of historical facts about social history and, behind that, the fundamental question of what it is that is basic to being human. While Western (and U. N.) and Marxist perspectives have a place for both "negative" and "positive" rights, the priorities are heavily weighted one way in each. No passing comment that both are important solves the problem, for much of the central strategy of divergent civilizations rests on these differences. What is true about humanity doctrinally and socially? Is it true that the associations and ideas of human life are constructed by human praxis out of and for the purpose of meeting biophysical, material needs *and nothing else?* Or is it true that the shape of human associations and technological-economic structures is constructed on the basis of and for the purpose of nonmaterial, "ideal" potentialities? What is present in the U. N. declaration is a central conviction of the Western religious traditions: at the core of human social reality is the fact that we live under a moral order *not* constructed by human praxis, and that foundation is the basis of associational bonding that includes respect for persons as "members" with rights. On *this* basis, persons are presumed to be free to meet positive material needs (such as the needs to work and eat) guarded by negative rights that prevent interference with freedom of speech and voluntary association. The defense of freedom of speech and association is thus the *prior* condition for pursuit by the people of those activities which will meet material needs.

What is clear is that the United Nations' declaration is a "creedal" articulation, religious in root and branch. The use of the terms "advent" and "highest aspiration" in this connection and the call in paragraph five for the nations to reaffirm their "*faith* in fundamental human rights" confirm the kind of universalistic, covenantal public theology that is just below the surface of this document.

On the basis of this *credo,* the preamble turns to the very difficult matter of the relation of such a creed to the law. The third paragraph of the preamble points out that if humanity is not to have to resort to violence every time these ideals are threatened by tyranny and oppression, a rule of law is required. In this, we find an even more genuine appropriation of the Liberal-Puritan heritage: the governments not only have placed themselves under a vision of high ideals held to be universal, but they have limited themselves from interfering with speech, religious and other assemblage, democratic processes, and the rights of workers. The governments party to the declaration now see themselves as also properly limited by law.

This is an awkward matter. Governments make law, and yet here governments are subjecting themselves to law.[61] How can we subordinate ourselves to our own creations without lapsing into one or another form of idolatry or fetishism, or without having our interests so bias our formation of law that not justice but the egoism of the ruling power reigns? The presumed answer in this declaration is that some laws are embodiments not only of the will of their makers but of a universal moral law that is often inconvenient to lawmakers. Not dealt with in the declaration are the essentially religious and philosophical *grounds* by which we know that moral law. The entire statement in this regard is dependent on sources beyond itself. This is a document enacted in a political process which hopes to move toward law, but the provisions of the U. N. declaration are not themselves law. They are statements that point toward a transcendent moral law and thus serve as plumb lines for the law to be enacted. They are "common standards" which Conciliar Catholics would know by "graced reason," Calvinists by "common grace," and Liberals by "self-evident truths." They may not exist very completely in any legal or social arrangement. They cannot be derived only from the empirical examination of what the historical, social, and legal situation actually is.

Articles 4 through 12 focus on legal treatment of persons. The basic conceptual framework already exposed is applied as a standard for all legal systems. Slavery, torture, denial of legal standing, the negation of equality before the bar of justice, an absence of effective tribunals for remedy, arbitrary arrest, detention or exile, disallowance of an independent and fair judiciary, presumption of guilt, unequal application of punishments, and interference with privacy of correspondence, domicile, reputation, or free movement—all are forbidden. These are all viewed as wrong, as violations of what is basically human. The view that emerges from these provisions is fascinating. *Each person* is to be protected from these violations. This would appear to be "individualistic" at first reading; however, each person is understood to live in extension and relationship. It is the relationships, memberships, and associations which protect personhood that are the center of attention. Not only the biophysical life of a person is to be protected, but the kinds of relations one has to others are essential to personhood. Indeed, Article 29 bears repetition: it speaks of "duties to the community," for it is "community in which alone the free and full development of . . . personality is possible." Slavery may, in some instances, preserve life, but it is a noncommunal, dehumanizing relationship. Not only is the person to exist as an individual, but "free" social memberships and relations are to be officially defined as having a claim and place in public institutions, whatever the merits of any particular individual case or personal character.

The governments that subscribed to this document also seem to recognize the importance of the public conduct of public business. Law enforcement, if carried out secretly, is likely to become corrupt (Articles 10 and 11). If done only at the behest of political power and in accord with arbitrary political policy, law enforcement tends to become an instrument of oppression (Article 12). Hence formal barriers in procedure and presumption have to be enacted by governments to prevent state powers from exceeding their own limits. At one point, secrecy is demanded—in secret balloting where individuals may judge against the state. Governments derive their ability to make law from the "consent of the people" (see Article 21). This provision is remarkable precisely because it implies that the people could, acting privately but in concert, legitimately revoke the right of a government to rule. The regime is in principle replaceable; the moral law protecting human relationships is not.

Finally, the declaration calls for the public propagation of these ideas.[67] Hence all are called upon to promote these rights by teaching and "progressive promotion." Education, which is to include indoctrination on human rights, is to be "free," "compulsory," and "equally accessible," at least in its earlier levels (Article 26). Education is not confined to formal academic or vocational training but extends into the arenas of cultural life, into the arts and the sciences (Article 27).

In the thirty years since this statement was adopted, a number of efforts have been made to translate the ideals into law. A series of "covenants" have been developed on these terms, often with sharper focus on the "positive rights," and incorporated into international law through treaty agreements. Many political powers, including the United States, have resisted full ratification of these covenants because they feared that the "negative rights" most precious to the Western tradition would be subordinated and that the principle of national sovereignty would be compromised, and because the "liberal" forces in the society have resisted some of the social-economic provisions of the covenants which challenge property rights.[68] These would, in fact, be the case. Not only would the law of a nation be subject to evaluation in terms of compatibility with the basic principles of the nation's constitution, but political, social, and economic structures would be subject to international review. The principles of the Liberal-Puritan tradition are not empirically realized; their validity is.

This summary treatment of the U. N. declaration points to a powerful and comprehensive creed. If my analysis is correct, it is the latest and most widely acknowledged statement of motifs which have had a long nurturance in ancient Judeo-Christian history, which via a Liberal bias have burst beyond the specific Conciliar Catholic and Free-Church Calvinist developments processes which brought them to maturity, and which now stand as relatively autonomous standards, appropriated and promulgated by the modern world's most prestigious conciliar political authority.

The irony of the situation, however, is that precisely as we have moved toward such an articulation of creed in the twentieth century, we also have been engaged in several battles against tyranny and against economic dislocations brought about by the ways in which the Liberal-Puritan tradition effected the development of modern capitalism. The massive mobilization of the Allied nations to defeat the Depression and then the Nazis—as well as to defend the values later to be embodied in the U. N. declaration—brought about more and more centralization of authority in the state. As I have shown elsewhere,[69] the structural linkages forged between government and corporation in the period of the great transition were elaborately developed during World War II into the present "military-industrial complex." The Liberal-Puritan synthesis also gave license to the development of corporations that are relatively independent of political control—so much so that under conditions of modern technology and communication they have become "multinational," beyond the control of any nation. Thus Western societies are faced with simultaneous and contradictory developments: the universal acceptance of its core creed, which challenges nationalism and economic exploitation on moral grounds; the increased national centralization of economic and political power through the "complex"; and the formation of nearly sovereign economic corporations, apparently beyond the reach of either moral influence or any national sovereignty.[70] These developments are taking place precisely as the values of the economic order—those of utilitarian liberalism—begin to pervade an increasing number of our public institutions. It is to economics that we must now turn.

E. HUMAN RIGHTS AND THE ECONOMIC ORDER

Figure 7.
The Economic Order

Educational	Cultural/ Expressive	Legal
Familial	Voluntary	Political
Medical	Technical	Economic

The covenantal traditions of the Puritans decisively shaped the public theology of American consciousness. As modified by Liberal thought, they became the essential contours of American institutions and social creed, with profound implications for the shape of familial and political as well as religious life in America. Under the specific impact of twentieth-century social conditions which this synthesis helped create, the definition of "human" has become refined in terms of religious, sexual, and political-legal principles and extended to education, the professions, and, in some aspects, the arts.

The ways in which this tradition has influenced economic life are no less profound. It is in this area that the critique is often the most harsh; it is in this

110

sector (and the arts) of American society that the Liberal-Puritan tradition has been most ambiguous in its impact; and it is in the economic arena that the American public theology has been most ambivalent regarding human rights.

The concepts of covenant and vocation, which were so decisive in working out the Free-Church tradition and subsequent dominant visions of human rights for educational, familial, and political institutions, were differently accented in the economic sphere. In the church, in the area of sexuality, and in the legal and moral guidelines for regimes, "covenant" was given an importance equal to that of "vocation." A personal "calling" to serve the Lord in covenanted worship became the basis for vigorous family affection as well as political responsibility. In economics the associative, communal, covenantal notion was radically subordinated to a more individual, more "private" notion of vocation. Further, the concept of vocation had deeply influenced the rise of the "professions"—especially ministry, law, medicine, and teaching—but professionalism as a profound sense of developing expertise in both theory and practice for service of the common good never developed comparable patterns in economics or business.

The massive scholarship deriving from Max Weber's seminal work *The Protestant Ethic and the Spirit of Capitalism,* written early in this century, shows that the Reformed tradition (in "selective affinity" with a series of material forces) unleashed an era of economic transformation that is of enormous import.[71] In analyzing the economic implications of this tradition, Weber shows the structural consequence of a view in which each person is called by God to work in the world in one or another trade or profession to the greater glory of God. The world of work, of labor, of production, is a decisive arena in which the individual "shows forth" that he or she lives a godly life. Weber is probably in error insofar as he does not see the covenantal notions as of equal importance in church, family, or political life, or the ways in which these affect economic developments; but he is surely correct in identifying the power of the Puritan heritage as a major catalyst in economic life more narrowly construed. As R. H. Tawney has suggested, it is also quite possible that some people became Protestant in this tradition because it gave considerable license to economic opportunity,[72] but Weber's accents on the spiritual redefinition of disciplined work are surely more significant.

I presume basic familiarity with the concept "work ethic" as a behavior-orienting understanding of life in which people find decisive elements of ultimate meaning, of holiness, in industrious, worldly, rational, productive activity. It may take "capitalist" or "socialist" form—that is not the central issue at this point.[73] In all its forms, people see such activity as holy, as a mark of vocation to true humanity, as a law of psychological as well as financial security, and as an indication of moral and spiritual worth. Those who cannot or, even worse, those who will not engage in regular, disciplined, productive work as a matter of inner conviction (and not only exterior performance) are judged to be morally inferior.[74]

The power of this work ethic has had at least four major consequences for the West. First, it aided in breaking the power of the hierarchical feudal system of the late Middle Ages. Classical Catholicism, Lutheranism, and Anglicanism shared a metaphysical-moral conception of the social world in which all was arranged, by nature, in a series of interdependent levels of social function according to a "great chain of being."[75] Some were born to be peasants, some cobblers, some kings. Each must infuse his or her natural role, as given in the orders of creation, with a firm sense of particular duty and the gentling spirit of charity within a liturgically sanctified "ortho-praxis." The Reformed tradition challenged the pregiven character of "natural role" in the name of "orthodoxy." Each person has his or her own calling from God, and not from the pregiven orders of nature or society. Indeed, in challenging the metaphysical vision of cosmic hierarchy which lay behind this vision, the Puritans desacralized and demystified nature. Metaphysical and sacramental defenses of social rank may be ignored, altered, or overturned if they block the capacity of the person to live out the mandates of God, which may call us to labor not sanctioned by the presumed "cosmic order." (The impetus of this orientation also allowed the Puritans to establish a domination over all nature. That orientation is once more being challenged by the "ecology movement," which has recovered the sense of the great chain of being.)

Second, the work ethic plunged a whole population into vigorous economic activity. People worked hard, not merely for survival. True, that was an issue for some, but most earned more than was necessary for minimal subsistence. The drive to work hard, however, was essentially based on the simple conviction that in work well done—as in worship, speech, sex, and politics when these are rightly ordered—one lived out what it meant to be human in the service of God. The gain that resulted from this intense application of mind and body to worldly tasks was not to be squandered, or wastefully consumed, or even really enjoyed. Greed was not the motivation; gain was not the end. Any profit was but a by-product which itself was to be redeployed in further activity. Frugality, prudent investment, and careful stewardship of the gain would themselves become occasions for renewed economic diligence. It would mark, but not bring, the fulfillment of genuine humanity under God's watchful eye. The consequences of such attitudes transformed the stagnant traditional economies of the West into a vibrant, continuously growing dynamic, and confirmed, in the eyes of believers at least, that God was shedding his blessing on the vigor of disciplined, godly economic activity.

Third, the sense of discipline in work gave tremendous impetus to practical preparation for work. Each person was to spend his or her early life in preparation for a "vocation," learning the disciplines and the skills to be applied in order to be a productive member of society. The modern sense of "vocational training" derives from this root. Such a view released and brought focus to enormous reservoirs of psychic energy among working people. It also gave impetus to the "professions," as already mentioned. The optimism and buoyancy which derive from what otherwise seems to be Calvinistic pessimism are surely rooted in such factors. Closely related, of course, is the fourth consequence of this view: economic independency is seen as a critical mark of maturity. The independence of the church, of the family, of political party, is paralleled by relative economic autonomy—although here independency is essentially individual. One is not fully human in the eyes of the community unless one has land, income, a craft or trade by which one can pay one's own way. Without fiscal independence one's convictions can be too easily coerced by pulling the purse strings. Indeed, in some of the early theories, only one who had become independently wealthy could be an officer in the church. More widely, the right to marry and the right of franchise in civil government were sometimes activated only for those who had achieved economic independency by completing one or another kind of training and entering into the world of work as a "freeman." The fact that the universalistic principles of freedom, equality, and mutual rationality came to be applied only gradually to women, "servants," "apprentices," "alms-takers," students, and children is rooted in this perspective.

This notion of economic independency also made the alliance with the Liberals possible. Locke had accented the "self-evident truth" that "property" was a natural right. Property was not only a claim which an individual has over some worldly goods, established by the energetic application of mind and body to nature so as to make its fruits his or her own; property was also, once possessed, the foundation by which enough security was gained to apply the mind to higher things. The propertied person gained a modicum of leisure—not for indulgence but for higher duty. The leisured person could become a thinking person, free to apply the intensities of the mind to problems of politics, science, and morality. This leisure the common laborer did not possess.[76] It was not even clear that working parents had the leisure to train their children properly in most areas; hence educational institutions needed to be established at public expense, led by those who could cultivate and inculcate proper morals, proper political attitudes, and the practical arts so that the next generation could itself be economically independent and properly responsible. On this basis the Western social creed, which had so jealously guarded the relative autonomy of church, family, university, and press from the control of the state, put the public schools directly under governmental supervision, thoroughly infused with liberal economic presuppositions. (The Evangelical Calvinists and Episcopalians who founded the academies and "private" schools of old New England, and subsequently the Catholics, Lutherans, and Seventh Day Adventists—to mention a few—who founded "parochial schools," all recognized this. So also did those who, in the 1960s and 1970s, attempted to establish a variety of "experimental" or "alternative" school programs on "radical" principles.) But for the most part, the Puritans and the Liberals cooperated in attempting to spread economic liberalism and the work ethic through political control of the public schools. It became illegal not to attend school and prepare for economic independency.[77]

In the area of the economy proper, the Liberal-Puritan synthesis also sanctioned the corporation. Having established the right of the church, the family, and the political party to form without consent of the political regime, the drive to allow the free formation of the economic corporation was mounted. The Puritans were not sure. They saw in the joint-stock company a kind of "trusteeship" of the commonwealth which was compatible with their understanding of vocation. And they saw the wisdom of a sphere of independence between economy and regime. The distrust of unfettered political power made them open to the counterbalancing influence of economic power not beholding entirely to regime. It would be surprising if self-interest did not play a role. Yet their profound sense of sin made them equally suspicious of unfettered economic power. Economic accumulation seemed to be a matter of personal, or perhaps family, diligence. Also, because of temptations to sin, the state had to regulate trade to prevent unscrupulous behavior. Thus craftsmen, shopkeepers, and corporations were to be licensed by governments.

The Liberals were less ambiguous. They had already relegated nearly all matters of faith and matters of sexuality, and most matters of political association and opinion, to the realm of "the private." So also the corporation was to be a private matter. A joint-stock company is in the "private sector." The corporation, in fact, was conceived of as a "person," drawing on ancient juridical views of the *persona ficta*. [78] Thus a corporation was a "person" in the sense that it had standing before the law, could sue or be sued; it could hold private property, buy, sell, manufacture, distribute, and accumulate profits. But a corporation, while having all the "rights" of private human persons, had no soul. Thus it was not accountable before God, and it had no duty to enter into covenantal relationships with others to be whole. The church, the family, and the political order were, or could be, godly; the corporation could be self-sufficient. Indeed, its owners, employees, trading partners, customers, and suppliers could all be upright persons and deeply responsible in church, family, and political life, and they would sooner or later have to come to a reckoning before the Almighty; but the corporation was a "person" which had no such day of reckoning. It could, in principle, live forever and never have to face heaven or hell. The Ten Commandments or the Sermon on the Mount was the model for religious groups; Adam and Eve's covenantal bliss in the Garden was the model for human sexuality; and the covenant of Israel and the words of the prophets against unrighteous political authority, with parallels to modern constitutional laws or universal declarations of human rights, was the model for political institutions; but there was no revealed standard of justice and righteousness for economic institutions.

For most of Western history since the Reformation, the questions of the systemic morality of the economic sector of society did not seem to be decisive. The virtues of Liberal civility or Puritan duty seemed sufficient to guide the gigantic economic machine the West was developing. There were difficulties in the industrializing periods: the hazards and the inhumanity of sweatshop factories cut life short for many. Yet people flocked to the industrializing centers.

In part they were driven there by the "enclosures" of land and the end of peasantry. But they were also drawn there because they saw better chances, circumstances less bleak than those from which they fled. After all, there was always America, where the frontiers were open to all who had a strong back and a willing mind. The work ethic and the desire for privacy of control in economic matters fitted well the objective conditions at hand.

New logics were also at hand to explain how things worked. The "new science" of economics "proved" that humanity was really a calculating creature, and that the social order found cohesion in the providential "hidden hand" of the free market, where each made a private decision.

Robert Heilbroner speaks of the new dicta which were to become a part of American life:

> "Every man is naturally covetous of lucre."
> "No laws are prevalent against gaine."
> "Gaine is the centre of the Circle of Commerce."[79]

As he points out, "A new idea has come into being: economic man—a pale wraith of a creature who follows his adding machine brain wherever it leads him."[80]

It has never seemed accidental that Adam Smith published his *Inquiry into the Nature and Causes of the Wealth of Nations* in 1776. Utilitarian liberalism had been given its grounding already in the thought of David Hume (1711–1776). He doubted Lockean notions of self-evident truths, and was even more suspicious of theology. The laws of morality and justice, he argued, were based neither on divine nor natural law but simply on the principle of utility, that is, on what was useful in bringing happiness. One of his disciples, Jeremy Bentham (1748–1832), was soon to argue that happiness really meant the gaining of pleasure and the avoidance of pain, and that by the simple calculations of these, we could set all personal and social policy. But it was Smith who spelled out the utilitarian logic specifically in connection with an account of how a market economy worked. It was, he argued, not useful to attempt to control the market, which had its own autonomous internal principles. The laws of supply and demand, coupled with business acumen, would lead to the greatest number and quality of goods at the lowest price for the greatest number of people. It would make available the greatest number of jobs and bring the greatest reward to the most industrious and deserving people. Hence monopoly—by cartel or by government—was a danger to be avoided. The world of Adam Smith passed quickly in England, but the logic of *homo economicus* was resurrected in the public theology of America, where it became an addendum to the Liberal-Puritan synthesis.

It fit well with some features of the synthesis. Smith did not approve of accumulation as a function of greed. He shared the Puritans' approval of hard work and care for detail in the ways of the world, as well as their conviction that accumulated capital was to be responsibly used to multiply the capacities of production. He embodied the Liberal's "professional" view that a person of leisure should occupy himself or herself with scientific, political, and moral investigations (which others could not attain) for the sake of all. But, from Smith on, the Liberal vision of America has been split into principled and utilitarian factions, with the former most closely attached to familial, artistic, educational, and political matters, and the latter tied to economics and the corporation (as well as the mass media). Thousands now work, and work hard, with little inner conviction except for gain. In this view the laws of the market and the principles of contract make all theological talk of covenant or moral law unnecessary, except as a purely personal matter.

The echoes of unexamined theological presumption are deeply hidden in these views. The "hidden hand" of which Smith speaks gives the market its coherence. The idea is actually a secular and little-examined version of "providence." The laws by which the market operates are presumed to be rational and self-evident "natural laws." American economics has struggled so hard to separate itself from the moral theology and philosophy which gave it birth that it has cut itself off from its own roots and blinded itself to its own presuppositions.[81] In doing so, it has also cut itself off from examining its own understanding of what is human and what is entailed in human rights in the economic sphere. Only when the presumptions are directly challenged does the creedal character of "scientific" economics reappear. When the work ethic, the sense of privacy, or the corporate structure is questioned, the response indicates how closely commitment on these points is related to specifically religious passions and presumptions about self-evident truths. All the negative features of creedalism appear in full force: irrationality, dogmatism, absolutist appeal to fundamentalist principle, jeremiads of doom in oracular form, and suspicions that the critics are in league with demonic forces (usually labeled "medieval moralism" or "godless communism"). The failure to see, critically examine, and constantly reconstruct the theological and ethical dimensions of American public theology in this area has led to a systemic disjunction and constant tensions between the basic principles of the West and how we actually live our economic lives. However, the frequency and range of theft from corporations—from shoplifting to white-collar crime to industrial espionage—betray both a breakdown of economic morality and a contempt for the present success and wealth of the corporation.[82]

As pointed out earlier, it was in the period of the great transition that industrialization with its great corporate structures and personal fortunes was given a new and powerful stimulus. That was also the period when new linkages between the corporations and the military aspects of political authority were forged, and precisely when both the urban expansion was made necessary due to the closing of the frontier, and the massive waves of immigration brought a heterogeneous population to these shores. It was also in this period that social Darwinism, with its views of competition in the struggle for survival and the triumph of the "fittest," gave "modern scientific" sanction to the economic doctrine that the laws of competition are beyond moral critique. They were applied to the market.

In the twentieth century the economic engine formed out of this history has outproduced and outemployed all competing economic systems, and it claims still the intense loyalty of most Americans. But it is a loyalty which has lost its sense of godliness and holiness, and it is governed by little sense of confidence in self-evident truths. It has become, for many, merely pragmatic. No one doubts that industry and commerce are good and necessary. No one doubts that many persons in business are of high moral character. But people within and beyond the predominant economic institutions seem to have lost confidence in the system and do not know how to correct its inner emptiness. That is not to say that Americans do not support the present system; it means that it does not have the moral and spiritual stature which freedom of religion, constitutional democracy, and the voluntarily covenanted family have. These matters they know to be matters of basic and universal principles. Regarding economics, they know only that the alternative systems on the world scene—traditional communal economics in the developing nations and single-party socialisms in Eastern Europe—are less attractive and less successful. Hence Americans hold to the system with the zeal of successful fanatics, fighting the growing suspicion that they may be wrong.

The consequences of this powerful but ungoverned economic reality are several. Every other sector of society feels its impact. The mass media are controlled by commercial interests; the schools train for the corporate world; technological development depends on business decisions. Government is deeply influenced by the power of the corporations. Domestically it is the linkages with the military which are decisive for the economic health of many communities. Corporate lobbyists have more direct political influence than any other group of citizenry. In several areas corporations have so outstripped many branches of government in size, sophistication, and expertise that many regulations can only be ineffectively applied, and many other regulations are so outdated that they are irrelevant to the problems faced by corporations. In foreign affairs we have two sets of American policy—one set by the official government, the second by the multinational corporations, which have outgrown the capacity of any nation-state to regulate. On some occasions, such as that of the reactions to Alliende's election in Chile, agencies of the government (in this case the C.I.A.) become instruments of corporate policy. Other nations around the world that are intrigued or even attracted by American freedoms and constitutional forms and declarations of human rights wonder whether it is necessary also to unleash the corporations to make those gains, and whether it is too high a price to pay.

It is extremely difficult to implement policies for the actualization of human rights without access to economic support systems. While women gained the rights to education and to suffrage in the early part of the century, economic discrimination remains a powerful force. When the New Deal introduced governmental responsibility for labor and the poor during the Depression, the corporate world reacted with a resistance that pervades all economic and political debates. When the American Black community brought about a fuller implementation of educational, political, and legal rights during the 1960s and 1970s, the problems of economic exclusion and disability continued to haunt them.

The impact of the economic system on the professions is pronounced. Over sixty percent of all legal litigation is focused on corporate, property, and contractual law. In the criminal justice system, study after study shows that poor people are treated differently in arrest, indictment, processing, prosecution, and sentencing. And in medicine some thirty percent of American families stand one medical disaster away from poverty as medical costs skyrocket and doctors resist "socialized medicine."[83]

It is not too much to say that the achievements of the Liberal-Puritan synthesis in propounding human rights in religion, family, politics, and expression are today threatened by the failure of the religious traditions to develop a viable ethic for corporate economic life, the complicity of the Liberals in fomenting a kind of individualistic utilitarianism which produces economic associations without any community save the mutually calculated benefits of contract, and the compulsion of many economic leaders to resist all value questions which challenge the system. Again, the capital of our public theology is being used up, and in this area it was never coherently constructed in the first place.

F. THE CHURCH AND HUMAN RIGHTS

There is one group throughout most of the twentieth century which has seen these problems and which has spoken out frequently about them. I refer, of course, to the ecumenical churches. To be sure, they did not always use the

Figure 8.

The Church and Voluntary Associations

Educational	Cultural/ Expressive	Legal
Familial	Voluntary	Political
Medical	Technical	Economic

language of contemporary human rights in their teaching, but the fundamental themes are present. Frequently their accents are as much from liberalism as from covenantal-theological roots. Yet from the time of the great transition, ecumenical Christianity has been the most sustained movement pressing these questions.

At the forefront of this movement, the Social Gospel was formed out of the nineteenth-century residues of the old Liberal-Puritan synthesis. Washington Gladden, a Congregationalist, Walter Rauschenbusch, a Baptist, and W. D. P. Bliss, an Episcopalian, initiated the modern theological discussion of godliness as it related to economic matters in an industrial, urbanized society at the turn of the century. Rauschenbusch, perhaps the most representative of this movement, had begun his public writing in the 1890s. Summarizing his moral assessment of the most important institutions of society as he saw them in 1912, he treated the core institutions of society in turn.[84]

The despotic, patriarchal family, he argued, was the dominant structure of human history, often marked by concubinage, polygamy, and adultery—all allowed for the master, with servanthood and exploitation the appointed role of the mistress and children. But through the influence of Christianity, the family had undergone an ethical transformation:

> The despotism of the man, fortified by law, custom, and economic possession, has passed into approximate equality between husband and wife. The children have become the free companions of their parents, and selfish parental authority has come under the law of unselfish service. Economic exploitation by the head of the family has been superseded by economic cooperation and a satisfactory communism of family equipment. Based on equal rights, bound together by love and respect for individuality, governed under the law of mutual helpfulness, the family today furnishes the natural habituation for Christian life and fellowship.[85]

The church, a great influence on the family, had undergone a similarly great transition:

> At the beginning of the modern era the church was a despotic and exploiting organization. . . . Though founded on the principles of love and freedom, it coerced belief and terrorized men into uniformity by physical constraint. . . . [In contrast, today] some protestant churches have entirely democratized their organization; others . . . have at least been steeped in the democratic spirit.[86]

A third sector of society which had undergone dramatic transformation was education. For most of the world over most of human history, education was available only to the elite and the privileged. If there was education for the majority of people, it was a separate and inferior grade, punctuated by passivity in the face of the teacher and not a small amount of corporal punishment for the slow and the unruly—or the original. The development of democratic educational systems with respect for the rights of all students was the result of nothing less than "a regenerating process."[87]

And, finally, political life had been transformed. This was the most fragile transformation, Rauschenbusch held, yet it was enormously significant that we got terribly upset about things in political life that were common practice in most societies:

> When the rich and the poor have justice meted to them in our courts with an uneven hand, . . . it is felt to be an outrage and a betrayal of the spirit of our institutions. . . . When the property of the rich is partly exempted from taxation by unequal methods of assessment, and the burden of public expenditure is thrown on the poorer classes, we feel free to protest against it as a departure from the clear intent of our fundamental laws. In short, inequality and oppression, the denial of equal rights and of the equal humanity of all is felt to be a backsliding and disgrace.[88]

However, wrote Rauschenbusch, one sector of our life was not yet transformed, and it tempted all the other institutions to retreat and corruption. For one thing, "the collective intelligence of the Christian Church has not really come to any clearness about the fundamental moral relations involved in modern economic life." For another, the world of business had adopted the "law of tooth and claw" as its operating ideology. Winning, gaining, and competitive selfishness were the goals, and often the only rules, of the game.

Rauschenbusch, as well as many of his contemporaries, was well aware of the fact that all industry depended on fundamental "fiduciary relationships" that provided more moral guidance than frequently admitted in economic theory and action. He was also clear that reward for work well done, regard for the integrity of one's work, and the significance of concern for human relations were necessary and present in business; still, the economic arena seemed to be "the last intrenchment of autocracy."[89]

The voice of the Social Gospel was a minority report at that time. It was an echo, a recovery of the social-ethical meanings, if not always the doctrinal meanings, of the old Liberal-Puritan alliance, almost obscured by the newer liberal philosophies and the power of Christian fundamentalism (both in the frontier form of "evangelicalism" among Protestants and in the Conservativism of Catholic immigrants), as well as by the overwhelming social changes of the period of transition.

The Social Gospel was not to go without doctrinal correction for long, however, nor was it to remain but an echo of the deeper past. Instead, it served as a forecast of some of the most dramatic, if yet unfulfilled, religious developments of this century, both as it led to new ecumenical cooperation on social issues and as it became more profound in theological concept.

In the 1920s and 1930s Reinhold Niebuhr became the chief American advocate of "neo-orthodox" theology, leveling his considerable polemical skills against both "liberalism" and "fundamentalism" (his term for this was usually "obscurantist"). By "liberalism" Niebuhr meant especially the pragmatic optimism and utilitarian individualism of modernity. Indeed, he thought that a false liberalism had infected the Social Gospel movement. The idea that each person pursuing his or her own enlightened self-interest would produce a "natural harmony" and "inevitable progress" was a bourgeois fantasy. The idea that mutual calculation of contractual interest could build or sustain community was an idealistic chimera. And the notion that humanity was *essentially* rational was a lopsided distortion. This heir of the Social Gospel refined his heritage by making a theological shift to the right as the basis of his socioeconomic shift to the left. He utilized Marxist categories to expose the interest and class conflict which much of the liberal prattle obscured—even as he attacked the Marxist understanding of human nature and society as equally distorting in another direction.[90] And, in his most significant effort, *The Nature and Destiny of Man*—truly one of the most important works of the twentieth century—he systematically evaluated the main alternative conceptions of the human, the secular, and the theological, and argued that only revitalized Christian perspective could carry the promise of serious reform and the weight of serious human analysis.[91] Thus he attempted to link the Anglo-American traditions with more continental ones for a more cosmopolitan vision; "A new synthesis is therefore called for."[92] This involved a rejoining of the insights of Reformation Christianity with those primal forms of principled liberalism which he identified with the core of the Renaissance.

As he spelled out the implications of this fundamental synthesis for today, he explained that it means a constant striving for truth, wherein intellectual honesty demands acknowledgment of the significance of faith, modified by the demand for tolerance. Second, the synthesis requires awareness that life is governed by the Law of Love which covenantally binds communities together. The social form of Love is institutionalized by democratic structures of justice. And third, the synthesis demands a vision of hope for freedom and liberation, constrained only by the realistic recognition that true fulfillment is finally beyond, and not within, human history.[93]

The directions charted by the Social Gospel and by "Christian Realism," under Niebuhr's leadership, were not to remain solely a conviction of these two. They were taken up by the Federal Council of Churches, which represented most Protestant denominations. Harold DeWolf and Walter Muelder among the Methodists, James Luther Adams from the Unitarians, Paul Tillich, a Reformed Evangelical, John Bennett, a Congregationalist, and Charles West and Paul Lehmann among the Presbyterians—to name only some of the most noted figures—trained literally hundreds of religious leaders in directions parallel to these, whatever their intramural disputes. And, most significantly, Martin Luther King, Jr., nurtured in the Black church and trained in the thought of these figures, offered a new public vision of the implications for the American scene. The ideas forged by these scholars and groups, and transformed into reforming action by King, gave breadth and depth to the new synthesis and made it a pervasive, ecumenical creed once more.

Nor were these directions confined to the Protestant community. The American Jewish community had found relative freedom from traditional Christian persecution in social contexts influenced by the Liberal-Puritan synthesis. Ever since Cromwell opened the door to Jews during the period of the Puritan revolution and Locke had argued for tolerance, the Jewish communities have turned to the West and embraced democratic principles, often with a passionate concern for the equalities of economic opportunity long closed to them in most of Europe. In these contexts they found freedom to practice religion, access to public education, a social space for Jewish families, open possibilities for civil liberty and political participation, and opportunities to hold property and engage in economic life which had been denied them elsewhere. The underlying metaphysical-moral vision of a moral God who gave dignity to persons demanded living under a covenantal law, and called particular peoples to live in bonded communities as a light to all nations was shared by Jews and Puritans in a way that has never been quite extinguished by even the most irreligious, nonpracticing, secularized heirs of these traditions. In such organizations as the Civil Liberties Union, Americans United for the Separation of Church and State, Americans for Democratic Action, and numerous reform and labor organizations, Protestant clergy from the Social Gospel and Christian Realist schools of thought joined with Jewish scholars, lawyers, and concerned lay people to define the principles given modern historical power in the Liberal-Puritan synthesis.

In the early decades of this century, culminating in the political-economic programs under Franklin D. Roosevelt, the concerns of the Social Gospel were debated, repudiated, embraced, and gradually institutionalized. The responses to the Depression of the 1930s could have gone in any number of directions, the causes of our ills could have been interpreted in a number of ways; but the influence of preachers of the Social Gospel, liberalism, and Christian Realism in local community after local community led the nation to move toward some and not other policies. The American economic system gradually took on a new shape. Laissez-faire capitalism was modified toward what is variously called a "mixed economy," "welfare capitalism," or "progressive capitalism." In this situation, which remains basically unchanged today, government regulations and social programs—both voluntary and tax-supported—have attempted to reduce the exploitation, inequality, and manipulation of labor which had attended earlier forms of capitalism. Welfare programs, social security, minimum-wage laws, wage and price guidelines, unemployment insurance, health programs for the needy and the elderly, official recognition of unions, industrial health and safety regulations, food-stamp programs, subsidized housing, government employment as a possibility in last-resort situations, and vast expansions of community-based services—all have served to put an economic floor under that section of the population which was least advantaged economically. It was an extension of one version of "covenantal responsibility for all" put into actual operation. In one of his early messages as president, Roosevelt spoke of the one-third of the nation that was ill-fed, ill-housed, and on the brink of abject poverty. Through these programs that number has been reduced to about ten percent, and they are kept within the edges of the social fabric by institutionalized Social Gospel programs.

What these groups and programs did not institutionalize was a ceiling for those who had much and gained more. In spite of higher rates of taxation on a progressive scale, there are few significant regulations of income or property for those above the floor. The principle of maximum freedom for people to act together commercially was preserved. Equality was defined as equality of opportunity, not of results. Hence the relative discrepancies based on economic resources remain pronounced—and in all sectors of society, health care, education, housing, etc. Compared to most of the world, America has largely defeated absolute poverty. Compared to the middle and upper classes in America, roughly ten percent of the American population live in scandalously poor conditions.

American Catholicism has also undergone major changes. Near the end of the American Civil War, Pope Pius IV had promulgated his "Syllabus of Errors," condemning the separation of church and state. Archbishop Spaulding of Baltimore felt free to criticize this edict as not pertinent to the United States, for freedom of religion was, in his view, a proper rendering of the truth of God. The reaction of the Vatican was harsh: by 1899 it had condemned "Americanism." But the main contours of development within Catholicism were to move in other directions. After centuries of relative silence on human rights issues in the modern sense, Pope Leo XIII (1878–1903) issued a fundamental defense of human dignity and equality in the encyclical *Rerum Novarum.* Just as significant, it claimed, is the recognition that such dignity demands the right of people to form associations—specifically, workers have the right to form unions. This part of Catholic teaching drew immediate and warm response from the leaders of the Social Gospel, who saw in this move an extension of the covenantal model into a new segment of modern society. And in the twentieth century, Father John A. Ryan in the 1920s and 1930s, and Father John Courtney Murray later on, began to develop theologically rooted concepts of human rights and social pluralism.[94] Fresh concern for economic rights and political pluralism based on fresh readings of Catholic tradition and the "Social Encyclicals" eventually began to appear as a central concern of the church. These motifs were more fully developed in official Catholic circles, and by 1942, Pius XII offered in his Christmas message—obviously directed against the new terrors of fascism—a list of rights of membership which could have been embraced by most Calvinist Christians and most principled liberals during any time since the Reformation:

> . . . the right to maintain and develop one's corporal, intellectual and moral life and especially the right to religious formation and education; the right to worship God in private and public and to carry on religious works of Charity; the right to marry and to achieve the aim of married life; the right

to conjugal and domestic society; the right to work, as the indispensable means toward maintenance of family life. . . .[95]

Meanwhile, in France, where the Calvinistic Huguenots had long been suppressed, long-forgotten or repressed notions were taken up again by leading Catholic intellectuals. Jacques Maritain offered a careful reinterpretation of Catholic philosophy which accented again motifs from the Catholic Conciliar tradition.[96] His work was widely read, and his ideas became influential in the formation of the U. N. Declaration of Human Rights. Eventually the concern for a conciliar church triumphed in Pope John XXIII (the Second), who took the name of the pope deposed at Constance so long ago, and called a new council with Protestant observers. The upheavals brought about by this council, Vatican II, have been very difficult for Conservative Catholics to take; but from a longer historical perspective, it has meant that something of the Conciliar Catholic positions of long ago has been preserved and made historically powerful. Key motifs kept alive by the Liberal-Puritan synthesis re-entered the Catholic mainstream by highly indirect routes. The way was opened for common social witness to both Protestants and Jews. (The Vatican took the office that deals with the Jews out of the office focused on world religions and relocated it in the division that works on ecumenical relations.) It has also meant that as American Protestants were growing increasingly nervous about their alliances with utilitarian and individualist commercial liberalisms, many were finding solidarity on human rights issues with the Catholics and Jews after centuries of mutual suspicion. In the pioneering Catholic research on these matters undertaken by the Woodstock Center at Georgetown University, a profound and compelling basis for Catholic commitment is shown to have always been present but too often obscured by other Catholic accents.[97] The primary divisions are less and less Protestant, Catholic, and Jew; instead they are ecumenical and social religion against obscurantist fundamentalism on the one side and humanist utilitarianism on the other.

Several obstacles to genuine ecumenicity remain. With regard to the relationship between Protestants and Catholics, two points are most critical—one concerns "covenant," the other "vocation." The internal structure of the Catholic Church is not reformed in principle or in operation. The hierarchical control system of church authority remains monarchical, with only a few concessions to limited government. At the time of the Second Vatican Council, major strides toward reform were made on this front. Principles of "collegiality" and "subsidiarity" moved official teaching closer to democratic participation. But the hierarchic principles remain basically intact, and are invoked against movements that become too populist. On this front Catholics seem closer to the Imperial Calvinist tradition than to any other. Both resist and fear, especially, democracies in the tradition of the French Revolution or the Marxist People's Democracy, even with regard to the inclusion of women in church leadership.

Catholicism also continues to hold fast to a vision of vocation haunted still by the monastic ideal. The ancient vows of "poverty," "chastity," and "obedience" (to one's spiritual director) pointed toward an assumption that vigorous economic participation, sexuality and marriage, and the assumption of coercive authority in the common life were spiritually perilous. These three vows recognized the power and significance of economics, the family, and politics, but assessed these powers negatively. For Protestants, especially those under the influence of the Liberal-Puritan traditions, the creation and responsible employment of wealth, sexual unity in a covenanted family, and political action (with all the latter entails in terms of the possible exercise of coercion) are spiritual duties to be performed for the sake of righteous community.

Nevertheless, Protestants and Catholics increasingly cooperate on human rights issues. More and more, groups of evangelicals are joining this ecumenical interchange. There are some strong signs that groups which previously were fundamentalist are giving rise to a new generation of Protestant Evangelicals who are recovering a more orthodox position. The "Chicago Declaration" of 1973 brought about a confession of sin on the part of a number of leading evangelicals. They repudiated fundamentalism and its attachments to right-wing political and economic forces. They called for a new engagement in renewing the church, preserving human rights, securing the stability of the family, and resisting the temptations of Mammon.[98] Books, journals, and conferences are appearing all over the country as these groups recover the deeper roots of their tradition and begin tentative cooperation with ecumenical Christians and "progressive" voluntary associations.

Ecumenical Protestants, Conciliar Catholics, Reformed Jews, some neo-evangelicals, and principled liberals find themselves allied against both doctrinaire fundamentalism and utilitarian liberal analyses of values and the social situation. Fresh theological efforts quote from each other with ease.[99] Such efforts represent a new awareness of a public theology that could easily be lost. Indeed, there is some evidence that both ecumenical leadership and many local pastors have lost confidence in the capacity of theology and the churches to make any difference in contemporary life.[100] Many turn to Marxism or to Eastern spiritualities to find again the meanings they feel they have lost. We too shall turn to an examination of these options shortly. But in the West the longitudinal and cross-sectional analysis reveals that the Western view of what it means to be human and to have rights rests on a public theology, rooted in the biblical tradition, developed by Conciliar Catholics and the Liberal-Puritan synthesis, presently sustained by a growing Christian ecumenicity, and partially institutionalized in some sectors of American society. The most significant forces in the West still derive from these roots.[101] This is not the case elsewhere. Creed and social bonding are decisively influenced by other forces in Eastern Europe and the developing countries. It is to examples of these that we turn next.

1. G.H. Barnes, *The Anti-Slavery Impulse* (New York: Harcourt, Brace & World, 1933; reissued in 1964 with a new Introduction by W.G. McLoughlin).

2. See James Dombrowski, *The Early Days of Christian Socialism in America* (New York: Octagon, 1936); J.Weinstein, *The Decline of Socialism in America, 1912 – 1925* (New York: Monthly Review Press, 1967); Robert Hunter, *Poverty* (1904; New York: Harper & Row, 1965), especially the Introduction by P.Jones; and B.McKelvey, *The Urbanization of America* (New Brunswick, N.J.: Rutgers University Press, 1963).

3. See O.Handlin, *The Uprooted* (New York: Grosset & Dunlap, 1951); and Marcus L. Hansen, *The Immigrant in American History* (New York: Harper & Row, 1940).

4. Aaron Abell, *The Urban Impact on American Protestantism, 1865 – 1900* (Cambridge, Mass.: Harvard University Press, 1943); and Henry F. May, *Protestant Churches and Industrial America* (New York: Harper, 1949).

5. See Ann Douglas, *The Feminization of America* (New York: Knopf, 1978).

6. A.L. Jamison points out that these were often connected in a host of American "gnostic" cults, in J.W. Smith and Jamison, eds., *The Shaping of American Religion* (Princeton, N.J.: Princeton University Press, 1961), pp. 219ff.

7. See my *The Ethics of Necropolis* (Boston: Beacon Press, 1971), Chapter 3; and Martin Marty, *Righteous Empire* (New York: Dial Press, 1970), p. 198.

8. See E. F. Frazier, *The Negro Church in America* (New York: Schocken, 1967); C. G. Woodson, *The History of the Negro Church* (Washington, D.C.: Associated Publishers, 1921); and J.Washington, *Black Religion: The Negro and Christianity in the United States* (Boston: Beacon Press, 1964).

9. A. Meier, *Negro Thought in America* (Ann Arbor, Mich.: University of Michigan Press, 1963); J.H. Clarke et al., eds., *Black Titan* (Boston: Beacon Press, 1970); and G.Myrdal, *An American Dilemma*, 2 vols. (New York: Harper & Row, 1944).

10. T. F. Gossett, *Race: The History of an Idea in America* (New York: Schocken, 1965), pp. 62ff. et passim.

11. A. Kraditor, *The Ideas of the Women's Suffrage Movement* (New York: Columbus University Press, 1965). See also C. N. Degler, *At Odds* (New York: Oxford University Press, 1980).

12. S. E. Ahlstrom, *A Religious History of the American People* (New Haven, Conn.: Yale University Press, 1973), especially Chapter VII; and Robert Handy, *A Christian America* (New York: Oxford University Press, 1971), especially Chapters IV and V.

13. This was the case partly because much of the labor force in the industrializing cities was Catholic, Lutheran, or Jewish, and they brought with them quite different conceptions of piety and community; and partly because much of Puritanism had gone through a transition toward individualistic revivalism. See H. R. Niebuhr, *The Kingdom of God in America* (New York: Harper & Row, 1937); and Jamison and Smith, eds., *The Shaping of American Religion*, especially the chapters on "Catholicism" by H. J. Browne, "Judaism" by O.Handlin, and "Revival" by P.Miller.

14. See C.N. Degler, *Out of Our Past* (New York: Harper & Row, 1959), especially Chapter XII; and C. H. Hopkins, *The Rise of the Social Gospel in America* (New Haven, Conn.: Yale University Press, 1940).

15. See McKelvey, *The Urbanization of America*; and H. J. Schmandt and W.Bloomberg, Jr., eds., *The Quality of Urban Life* (Beverly Hills, Calif.: Sage, 1969), especially Chapters 2 and 4.

16. R. Hofstadter, *The American Political Tradition* (New York: Knopf, 1948), pp. 206ff.

17. See A. Dudley Ward, *The Social Creed* (Nashville, Tenn.: Abingdon, 1961); and my Introduction to Walter Rauschenbusch, *The Righteousness of the Kingdom* (Nashville, Tenn.: Abingdon, 1968).

18. See P.Miller, "Revival," in *The Shaping of American Religion*; and T. L. Smith, *Revivalism and Social Reform* (New York: Harper & Row, 1957).

19. H. R. Niebuhr, *The Social Sources of Denominationalism* (New York: Harper & Row, 1929).

20. This is the origin of the "Social Creed" discussed in Chapter One (see note 17 above). The "Social Creed" remains a part of the *United Methodist Discipline*.

21. Wm. G. McLoughlin, ed., *The American Evangelicals* (New York: Harper & Row, 1968).

22. I use the phrase of Walter Rauschenbusch, *A Theology for the Social Gospel* (1917; Nashville, Tenn.: Abingdon Press, 1978).

23. See Hopkins, *The Rise of the Social Gospel in America*; Abell, *The Urban Impact on American Protestantism, 1865 – 1900*; and especially R. M. Miller, *American Protestantism and Social Issues* (Chapel Hill, N.C.: University of North Carolina Press, 1958), Part I.

24. J. L. Altholz, *The Churches in the Nineteenth Century* (New York: Bobbs-Merrill, 1967).

25. A. L. Adams and S. Hiltner, eds., *Pastoral Care in the Liberal Churches* (Nashville, Tenn.: Abingdon Press, 1970).

26. V. K. Dibble, *The Legacy of Albion Small* (Chicago: University of Chicago Press, 1975).

27. James Dombrowski, *The Early Days of Christian Socialism in America*; and "Richard T. Ely" in Robert Handy, *The Social Gospel in America* (New York: Oxford, 1966).

28. S. G. Cole, *A History of Fundamentalism* (New York: Harper & Row, 1931); and R. Hofstadter, *The Age of Reform* (New York: Knopf, 1956), pp. 293ff.

29. See T. L. Smith, *Revivalism and Social Reform*, especially Chapter IV; and D. Meyer, *The Positive Thinkers* (Garden City, N.Y.: Doubleday, 1965).

30. The foundations and meaning of urbanization are what I focus on in my *Ethics and the Urban Ethos* (Boston: Beacon Press, 1973). Documentation for these observations can be found there.

31. A slogan, reported by Max Weber, widely used in the late-medieval cities of Italy and the Hanseatic League. See "The City" in *Economy and Society*, III, ed. G. Roth and C. Wittich (New York: Bedminster Press, 1968).

32. Peter Berger is undoubtedly correct in arguing that modern society forces us to choose and that the guidelines for choice are not clear. See *The Heretical Imperative* (Garden City, N.Y.: Doubleday, 1979). What he does not attempt in this work is to set forth the basis for a reasonable choice. In this regard he remains thoroughly "evangelical," although in the sense of Schleiermacher.

33. This refers to the subtitle of Benjamin Nelson's groundbreaking work on the transition to modernity, *The Idea of Usury: From Tribal Brotherhood to Universal Otherhood*, 2nd ed. (Chicago: Chicago University Press, 1969).

34. See my *Ethics and the Urban Ethos*, especially Chapter 5.

35. "The Most Significant Minority" (Washington, D.C.: Institute for the Development of Educational Activities, Charles Kettering Foundation, 1980).

36. Robert Cross, *The Church and the City: 1865 – 1910* (Indianapolis: Bobbs-Merrill, 1967); Harvey Cox, *The Secular City* (New York: Macmillan, 1965); and Gibson Winter, *The New Creation as Metropolis* (New York: Macmillan, 1963).

37. This is the central message of E. D. Baltzell, *Puritan Boston and Quaker Philadelphia* (New York: Macmillan, 1979); Jacques Ellul, *The Meaning of the City* (Grand Rapids, Mich.: Eerdmans, 1970); and K. A. Ostrom and D. W. Shriver, Jr., *Is There Hope for the City?* (Philadelphia: Westminster Press, 1977).

38. This does not include such organizations as the National Association of Manufacturers, for it has not developed the sense of professional standards and focus on values present in the professions. The American Management Association, a much more recent phenomenon, is attempting to develop standards for management as a true profession. The reasons that the Liberal-Puritan synthesis failed to be carried over into the economic arena will be discussed in Section E of this chapter.

39. See The Hastings Center Report: "Special Supplement on Ethics and the Professions," 7 (Dec. 1979).

40. The feeling of dislike was evidently mutual. See Harold Fisch's treatment of the "covenant" motif by Shakespeare in *Hamlet and the Word: Covenant Pattern in Shakespeare* (New York: Ungar, 1971).

41. Calvin was almost thrown out of Geneva when he introduced congregational singing of the psalms in parts. See T. H. L. Parker, *John Calvin: A Biography* (Philadelphia: Westminster Press, 1975), pp. 87ff.

42. Max Savelle, *Seeds of Liberty: The Genesis of the American Mind* (Seattle, Wash.: University of Washington Press, 1965), Chapter IX.

43. Indeed, many of the tunes are the same. See *The Workers' Songbook* (Cleveland: n.p., 1904).

44. As I write this, the National Council of Churches is planning a major conference

on the "electronic church" in response to the growing influence of the Christian Broadcasting Corporation and a number of "radio preachers." The signal role of the United Church Office of Communication in attempting to "democratize" access to the media is an example of deep church concern in this area.

45. In the last decade some twenty-seven books, by my count, have been published with the title *Human Sexuality.*

46. E. Z. Friedenberg, *Coming of Age in America* (New York: Vintage, 1965).

47. Russell Jacoby, *Social Amnesia* (Boston: Beacon Press, 1975).

48. See James T. Johnson, *A Society Ordained by God* (Nashville, Tenn.: Abingdon Press, 1970), especially pp. 37ff. See also J. Noonan, *Contraception* (Cambridge, Mass.: Harvard University Press, 1965). Please note the similarities of this view to that of the Hindu tradition. See Chapter Seven, Section B.

49. Edmund Leites, "The Duty to Desire: Love, Friendship, and Sexuality in Some Puritan Theories of Marriage," *Comparative Civilizations Review*, No. 3 (Fall 1979), pp. 40ff.

50. Ibid., p. 44.

51. See E. S. Morgan, ed., *The Puritan Family* (New York: Harper & Row, 1944), p. 29.

52. Quoted by Leites, "The Duty to Desire," p. 47.

53. See Johnson, *A Society Ordained by God,* especially Chapter IV.

54. Quoted by Leites, "The Duty to Desire," p. 52.

55. Ibid., p. 53.

56. The duties of passion, work, and governance are, I believe, the obverse of the monastic virtues of chastity, poverty, and obedience. The monastery is undercut as the center of the believing community and divided into two parts—the congregation and the family (the little church), both of which are anti-monastic. In these institutions everyone is to be a member—in the congregation by "election," in the family by necessity. No one was to be "merely an individual." By law everyone was to belong to some covenanted group. Indeed, individual family homesteads were not permitted in early Puritan New England. People had to belong to, and be settled in, a village and go out from there to work their farms. To be human was to live in a community of communities.

57. These observations are documented in a forthcoming book by Professor Leites; I had the opportunity to read several chapters of it in draft form. This chapter has to do with Locke and the Liberal view of marriage and child-rearing.

58. See G. Winter, *Love and Conflict* (Garden City, N.Y.: Doubleday, 1958); Elizabeth Achtemeier, *The Committed Marriage* (Philadelphia: Westminster Press, 1976); and John K. Yost, "The Traditional Western Concept of Marriage and the Family," *Andover Newton Quarterly,* 20 (March 1980), 169ff.

59. See R. E. Hall, ed., *Abortion in a Changing World* (New York: Columbia University Press, 1970), especially Volume II.

60. The best resource on this matter remains Daniel Callihan's *Abortion* (New York: Macmillan, 1970). See also the World Reformed Alliance and the Council of Catholic Bishops "Joint Statement on the Abortion Controversy," November 1979. See also E. L. Unterkoefler, A. Harsanyi, et al., *Ethics and the Search for Christian Unity* (Washington, D.C.: U. S. Catholic Conference Publications Office, 1980).

61. Massachusetts Historical Society, *Winthrop Papers,* II (1931), 294ff.

62. See Appendix II for a copy of the declaration.

63. The principle of choice in the formation of groups is pervasive. Article 13 speaks of the right of movement in a country, and the right to leave or return to any country; Article 15, of the right to change nationality; Article 16, of the voluntary family—a point that differs from the arranged marriage of India (see Chapters Seven and Eight); Article 17, of joint ownership of property; Article 18, of the right to religious conversion; and Article 20, of the rights of assembly and association.

64. The argument is not Hobbesian.

65. See Section B in Chapter Two and Section E in Chapter Three.

66. The term "government" includes both "political" and "legal" components. The decisive, social question is the differentiation of the sectors of society; the doctrinal one is whether the legal provisions include universalistic elements to which the particular regime must subject itself. The latter question depends both on whether there is a universal moral

law and on whether it can be known in a way that is sufficiently untainted by particular interests that it can govern them.

67. These provisions read as a modern translation of the "covenant renewal ceremonies" in the Bible. See Deuteronomy 6, Deuteronomy 26, Joshua 24, and Nehemiah 8.

68. See U. S. State Department, *Selected Documents*, No. 5, revised (Nov. 1978).

69. See my *The Ethics of Necropolis*.

70. See R. J. Barnet and R. E. Muller, *Global Reach: The Power of the Multi-National Corporations* (New York: Simon & Schuster, 1971).

71. Max Weber, *The Protestant Ethic and the Spirit of Capitalism*, trans. T. Parsons (New York: Harper & Row, 1958). For a survey of the intense debates surrounding this essay, see O. Stammer, ed., *Max Weber and Sociology Today* (New York: Harper & Row, 1971); B. Nelson, "Max Weber," in *Beyond the Classics*, ed. Glock, Hammond, et al. (New York: Harper & Row, 1973); S. N. Eisenstadt, ed., *The Protestant Ethic and Modernization* (New York: Basic Books, 1968); and Robert Green, ed., *The Protestant Ethic Thesis* (New York: Heath, 1960).

72. The argument is often called the "Weber-Tawney" hypothesis, but wherever that phrase appears, one knows that confusion reigns. See R. H. Tawney, *Religion and the Rise of Capitalism* (New York: Harcourt, Brace & Co., 1926). More recent views that support Tawney's general orientation can be found in Christopher Hill, *The Century of Revolution: 1603 – 1714* (Edinburgh: Nelson & Sons, 1961); and several of his other writings.

73. Marxist views of labor (see Chapter Six) are easily accounted for by Weber. Indeed, "socialism" can be seen, in Weber's terms, as capitalism without God, in which a whole society is a corporation.

74. The roots of the work ethic are probably deeper than those Weber identifies, and are quite possibly grounded in the twin purposes of the monastic discipline and renewal begun during the medieval period: *orare et laborare*. To say that the true marks of humanity, under the vows, are to pray and to work is not far from saying that labor *is* piety.

75. See A. Lovejoy, *The Great Chain of Being* (New York: Harper & Row, 1936).

76. E. Leites, "Conscience, Leisure and Learning: Locke and the Levellers," *Sociological Analysis*, 39 (Spring 1978), 36ff. Leites refutes the widely celebrated views of C. B. Macpherson, *The Political Theory of Possessive Individualism* (London: Oxford University Press, 1962).

77. See Richard Greaves, *The Puritan Revolution and Educational Thought* (New Brunswick, N.J.: Rutgers University Press, 1969).

78. See O. Von Gierke, *Natural Law* (Boston: Beacon Press, 1967).

79. Robert Heilbroner, *The Worldly Philosophers*, 5th ed. (New York: Touchstone Press, 1980), p. 35.

80. Ibid.

81. F. X. Sutton et al., *The American Business Creed* (New York: Schocken, 1962).

82. See my "Toward a Theology of Stewardship," *Andover Newton Quarterly*, 14 (March 1974) 245 – 66.

83. P. Wogaman, *The Great Economic Debate* (Philadelphia: Westminster Press, 1977).

84. Walter Rauschenbusch, *Christianizing the Social Order* (New York: Macmillan, 1912).

85. Ibid., p. 130.

86. Ibid., pp. 136ff.

87. Ibid., p. 145.

88. Ibid., p. 156 et passim (Chapter III).

89. Ibid., p. 160.

90. See Reinhold Niebuhr, *Moral Man and Immoral Society* (New York: Scribner's, 1932).

91. Reinhold Niebuhr, *The Nature and Destiny of Man*, 2 vols. (New York: Scribner's, 1939 and 1941).

92. Ibid., Volume I, p. 207.

93. Ibid., Volume II, Chapters 8, 9, and 10.

94. See D. Hollenbach, "Public Theology in America," *Theological Studies*, 37 (June 1976), 290 – 303.

95. Quoted by D. Hollenbach in "Public Theology in America," p. 60.

96. Jacques Maritain, *Man and the State* (Chicago: University of Chicago Press, 1951). See also P. Ramsey, *Nine Modern Moralists* (New York: Spectrum, 1962), Chapter 8.

97. A. Hennelly and J. Langan, eds., *Human Rights in the Americas* (Washington, D.C.: Georgetown University Press, 1982).

98. Ron Sider, ed., *The Chicago Declaration* (Carol Stream, Ill.: Creation House, 1974).

99. See Joseph L. Allen, "A Theological Approach to Moral Rights," *Journal of Religious Ethics*, 2 (1974), 119ff.; Lisa S. Cahill, "Toward a Christian Theory of Human Rights" (forthcoming); P. Shriver, "Theological and Other Rationales for Human Rights," National Council of Churches Background Paper, 1978; *Journal of Current Social Issues* (Summer 1978), entire issue; Mia Adjali, ed., *Of Life and Hope: Toward Effective Witness in Human Rights* (New York: Friendship Press, 1979); A. Müeller and N. Greimacher, *The Church and the Rights of Man: Concilium*, 124 (New York: Seabury Press, 1979); and E. Weingärtner, *Human Rights on the Ecumenical Agenda* (Geneva: World Council of Churches, 1983).

100. John Wilson, *Religion in American Society* (Englewood Cliffs, N. J.: Prentice-Hall, 1978), especially Chapter 17.

101. Ibid., Chapter 18. For a theological treatment of these themes by an actively ecumenical denomination, see Appendix III.

CHAPTER FIVE

Religion and Society
in a Marxist Land:
A Cross-Sectional Encounter

A. LIVING IN A DIVIDED WORLD

THE human needs which every society must meet are the same in Eastern Europe, of course, as they are in the West. Identification of the decisive institutions present in every successful society gives us a vivid indication of what these needs are. Provision must be made for education, health care, sexuality, and child-rearing, as these affect every person in society in one way or another. Common provision must also be made for the production and distribution of goods and services by technology and economics, for the accumulation and exercise of power by political and legal authority, and for the sharing of ideas and feelings through the media and the arts.

Exactly how these basic human needs are to be met, and how the social spaces to meet them are to be arranged, are questions that are not answered by pointing to the needs themselves. The questions are answered, in each society, according to two things: the metaphysical-moral doctrine that gives guidance to the whole of society, and the concrete organization of a community of commitment which makes the doctrine its creed, occupies the core of the society, and from that vantage point gives guidance to the relationships between the various sectors of society under the complex conditions of historical life. In fact, these two factors of governing creed and bonded community reflect the most basic, universal, and socially determinative human needs. The character of the creed will determine which other needs are to be given priority; which are viewed as the character of the core community will determine which structures and social spaces of society will be independent, which controlled, which powerful, which weak, and thus which human claims about rights and needs will be actually met. We have seen the ways in which America has been shaped by one cluster of influences.

It is appropriate that we begin our examination of the creed and the society

131

of the German Democratic Republic by initial reflections on Berlin. Berlin is a divided city. It is a symbol of a divided creed and a divided society, both as it struggles to overcome its own divisions and as it stands at the frontier of the Marxist-Leninist world as it faces the West. Berlin also is divided by the experience and the interpretation of history. We shall turn to a deeper, longitudinal analysis of this division in the next chapter, but we can identify something of the distinctive character of the G.D.R. by noting at this point the different ways in which the defeat of Naziism is treated in East Berlin and West Berlin. In the West the residues of the Third Reich itself and of the role of the British, French, and Americans in defeating Hitler have, for the most part, been removed. What monuments there are stand as testimonies against totalitarianism. The people on the streets are highly diverse in color, lifestyle, class, and interests. The rubble of war is gone; walking the Kurfurstendam is like walking the principal commercial streets of London, Paris, or Manhattan. The only visible remains from the War is the shell of a church tower with a tiny, rebuilt chapel at its base.

In East Berlin both public monuments which celebrate the defeat of National Socialism at the hands of heroic comrades and the physical marks of this defeat are visible on every street corner. The victory over Fascism, as well as the reminders of the suffering and sacrifice demanded, is constantly recalled as a turning point in the life of the nation—and, it is held, of world history. The People's Palace, the massive edifice of the Party—not the famous commercial street (Unter den Linden) which dead-ends near the mound of the bunker where Hitler died—is the center of East Berlin's life. The palace dwarfs the Evangelical Cathedral across the street. Still, the glass-and-steel construction of the palace reflects the image of that old, granite church and the repairs presently being made on it.

On the surrounding streets one can see the marks of bullets fired during the final, bloody taking of Berlin by Soviet troops. Piles of rubble from scattered craters stand as silent markers of a demolished chapter of German history. On the streets next to these grim monuments, red flags wave. On the fences blocking off these areas, placards proclaiming a new future exhort all to join the struggle for the new society, to achieve higher levels of production, to form greater solidarity of purpose and performance. They call for a constant reinvigoration of the revolutionary convulsion, the *historicus interruptus*, which divided the past from the future and began a new thrust into tomorrow.

Also highly visible is evidence that production, solidarity, and future orientation are making a difference. Everywhere, new construction is underway: a dramatic TV tower, new housing, industries, office buildings, public parks, and malls. It may be that the real economic miracle of post-World War II is not West Germany but East Germany. The Federal German Republic in the western two-thirds of the land not only contained the larger share of the heavy industry and technical leadership of Germany before and during the War, and hence had much more of an infrastructure from which to rebuild but it was aided by the massive infusions of the Marshall Plan. With a few exceptions in the southern industrial cluster of cities, the German Democratic Republic, which was formed in the eastern third of the land, was more agrarian. It was less developed before the war, more thoroughly destroyed by the war, and stripped of virtually all its remaining industrial resources by occupying forces after the war. It absorbed thousands of penniless, German-speaking refugees from other Eastern European countries. They began from nothing, and were aided only in the provision of defense and ideological guidance by the U.S.S.R.

It is not only in the construction and the growth of industry that one senses the changes in the G.D.R.; one can see it among the people on the streets. The clothing of people going to work in the morning or coming home in the evening is well-cut, if not very diverse; it is almost never elegant or striking. It is more like Chicago than Boston, more like Queens than Manhattan, more like Liverpool than London. The people wearing the clothes are healthy and well-fed. If there ever was a "proletarian mass" struggling to become middle-class in style and bearing, it is these people. They stand in contrast to those exceptions represented by the chauffeured cars of the leading Party members and the occasional appearance of a pensioner poking through the trash barrels.

The greatest symbol of division, however, remains the Berlin Wall. Visually it is imposing only in certain places. Here a major avenue comes to an abrupt halt; there an older road or smaller street has been rebuilt to detour around barriers, fences, and guard posts. The indirect routes by which one must travel around West Berlin to get to another part of East Germany remind one constantly of division. More subtly, dedicated workers, pastors, and professionals who have made a conscious choice to stay in the G.D.R. and to carry out their vocations in the context of the new society find the Wall an affront to their dedication. The Wall is, indeed, a sign of the felt insecurity of new government, an insecurity that is not entirely unwarranted. The number of those who preferred to move to the West before the Wall was built was unsettling: two-and-a-half million citizens left.[1] Now a number of blunt and closely enforced laws make attempting to leave a heavily punished crime, although West Germany caters to and encourages these desires for departure. It maintains very powerful radio and television broadcasting stations in West Berlin and along the border which needle the G.D.R. government and people in a variety of ways. The media of both East and West constantly compare the wonders of their own systems to the weaknesses of the other, and the Wall comes to signify a split perspective on the world as well as a physical structure dividing the countries.

All along the borders are garrison after garrison of Soviet troops. Thus the Wall also signifies a world division in spheres of political influence. Although G.D.R. citizens look first to their own government for political and social leadership, they are well aware that it is closely tied to Moscow. In fact, among the Eastern European countries, the G.D.R. and the U.S.S.R. are surely among the closest of friends, sharing more of the orthodox interpretation of Marxist-Leninist doctrine than most of the other countries who participate in the same cluster of cooperating nations. G.D.R. personnel carry out missions in Africa and Asia,

133

where direct Soviet presence would cause undesired reactions. They share the same friends, enemies, and policies.

Marxist-Leninist doctrine is the dominant guide in all social, human, and political questions. It was not entirely foreign to Germany—much of it was developed on German soil out of German philosophy—but by the time of the Wall, Marxism-Leninism became the only real option—except for a courageous minority church.

East Germany can be said to be dominated by a specific kind of socialism shaped in the aftermath of World War II by the Communist Party and modified internally by necessary concessions to the Christian churches—the only major organizations that exist outside Party and governmental control. We shall trace the deeper roots of this world view shortly, but even to understand the Wall itself, we must take a quick glance at the fateful dozen years which produced it. It was built in 1961. Twelve years earlier West Germany, under occupation, began to develop a parliamentary government centered in Bonn under the leadership of Konrad Adenauer. That same year, NATO was formed among the Western Allies. Talks between the Soviet Union and the Western Allies regarding Berlin had broken down, and the Berlin Blockade was put into effect. In East Germany the Communist Party absorbed smaller socialist parties to form the S.E.D. (Socialist Unity Party) and hold its first united party congress. The congress decided to follow a strict Marxist-Leninist line in alliance with the Soviet Union, and to mobilize all existing organizations into a people's "democratic, anti-fascist national front."[2] The S.E.D. moved systematically forward from that moment, gradually increasing its influence in and control over political, economic, legal, educational, medical, cultural, technological, and familial life. There were two exceptions to control: people could leave the country (but that ended when the Wall was built), and people could give primary loyalty to the church. That demanded swimming against the stream.

The churches in Germany derived predominantly from the Lutheran part of the Reformation, although there is also a history of the inclusion of Calvinists in the United Evangelical Church (Evangelische Kirche der Union), and there is a minority (eight percent) Catholic Church.[3] Historically these churches have been quite unlike the Conciliar Catholic, sectarian, or Liberal-Puritan traditions which influenced the United States. They were formed on territorial bases according to the dictates of the ruling princes. They did not share the theological-ethical or organizational presuppositions which shaped Switzerland and Holland, the English Reformation, and colonial America. The theological and organizational bases for "covenant" and human rights were not an overt part of this religious history.

The churches of the German Democratic Republic had, however, experienced the Nazis' attempts to take over the churches and to make them but another instrument of the Third Reich. They had also formed an independent "Confessing Church" to resist National Socialism and the attempted Nazification of the church through the so-called German Christians at Barmen in 1934 under the leadership of the great Evangelical Calvinist Karl Barth. They suffered with the best-known martyr of the movement, Dietrich Bonhoeffer, and reorganized themselves, after the war at Spandau, under the leadership of Otto Dibelius, so as to resist any future efforts to make the church a dependent instrument of the state or any political promise of salvation.[4] The churches thus resisted all efforts to make them a part of or an instrument of the S.E.D. or its National Front, even though much of the Party leadership and the church leadership had co-operated in resisting Hitler and had suffered together in concentration camps for that resistance, and even though much of the church leadership shared a deep distrust of "bourgeois democracy," "liberalism," "idealism," and especially "capitalism." The struggles during the fateful dozen years from 1949 to 1961 were intense. The church was reduced in size and visibility, but it maintained its integrity and proved by its actions that it was not an agent of the West, that it would not become merely the chaplain of the new regime, and that it would not fade away. When the Wall was built, the church became the only alternative body, with an alternative conception of reality, to the Party-dominated, Marxist-Leninist state.[5]

During these years the churches and the Party did not agree on what were and what were not fundamental human rights. Whether land could be confis-cated and redistributed without indemnity to previous owners was heatedly debated.[6] Whether parents would have a role in determining the shape and content of their children's education was a constant issue of contention.[7] Whether it could be a crime to advocate nonparticipation in state-sponsored "democratic" institutions was a major question.[8] Whether one could be a member of, or a functionary of, a political party—especially the S.E.D.—*and* a member of a church was intensely disputed.[9] The church was forced, by the circumstances and by the logic of its own confessional traditions, to clarify its view of human rights.

The Party was suspicious of any attempt to claim human rights on the basis of "idealistic" teaching and practice. It was not until 1975, with the signing of the Helsinki Accords, that the German Democratic Republic officially subscribed to a full statement about them. The Party connected concern for human rights with the Declaration of the Rights of Man from the French Revolution and partially appropriated in the Constitution of the Weimar Republic. Both the French and the German versions seemed to the Party to be ideological masks for the ascendancy of bourgeois interests. But by 1975, when the Party was firmly in control and wanted to be recognized as a legitimate regime in the world community, approving of human rights seemed advantageous. Helsinki recognized that the borders of the two Germanies were legitimate boundaries of sovereign nations, and it provided for diplomatic and economic exchange between countries related by NATO and by the Warsaw Pact. It also contained "Basket Three," explicit provisions for all subscribers to guarantee freedom of religion, press, information, travel, property, family life, dissenting opinion, and academic research. Church responses were muted. They wondered at the signing of a document which contained principles not previously acknowledged by Marxist-Leninist doctrine; they did not believe that the groundwork had been laid for that shift.[10] To thousands of other citizens the church's reservations were unknown—indeed, for many born or schooled after 1949, religion and the church are non-categories. They believed the Party. When the Accords were published by the government and heralded on West German television, some 100,000 people applied for exit visas within a week, and public demonstrations (associated with rock concerts) spontaneously broke out—before the matter was brought under control. The Wall had not been breached. If there is a universal moral law to which both "pluralist" and "communist" societies must subject themselves to find reconciliation, it was not to manifest itself internally in this form in this society at this time.

I first entered the G.D.R. to study and to discuss theological education with the churches just as the furor over these matters was beginning to die down, to settle again into the basic patterns which shape life in a divided society. I was able to return to the G.D.R. on ecumenical church business again in 1980 and 1983, most recently as a guest professor at *Das Sprachenkonvikt,* an independent seminary. I had in the meantime collected as many sources on that society as possible. What follows is a report, in the form of a cross-sectional analysis, of what I found.

B. EDUCATIONAL AND CULTURAL INSTITUTIONS

Figure 9.
The Educational and Expressive Sectors

Educational	Cultural/ Expressive	Legal
Familial	Voluntary	Political
Medical	Technical	Economic

In the G.D.R. both education and the several arts are viewed, officially, as instruments for the upbuilding of society. Both are guided by the Party and governed by the state. The educational system, in its basic form, was established by the Soviet Union during the early days of occupation (June 1946). It has been modified by the subsequent G.D.R. government, first in a Stalinist direction under the leadership of Hilde Benjamine (June 1955), and subsequently in a humanist direction by Margo Honecker, wife of the present secretary of the S.E.D. Education is compulsory for children eighteen and under.

The character of this education is overwhelmingly focused on basic skills, on Marxist-Leninist understanding of social history, and on the technical applied-sciences. These concerns also dominate the great universities and correspond with Marxist definitions of the human as "worker," having "control over the means of production." "In the G.D.R. work is brought into the educational process as a part of the contemporary technical, economic, and social complex. ... [The pupil] finds that school and work as an occupation are no longer separate categories or areas of life. ..."[11]

All majors, from biochemistry to theology (and those universities which had theological faculties before World War II have them still), are required to have also a major in Marxist-Leninist philosophy and political economics. In the schools, too, all history, government, and social science is taught in a strictly orthodox way. Marxist dialectics is the only available philosophy of history and social life for most students, and it is taught in a highly practical, not heavily theoretical or critical, fashion. Some students take this subject with great seriousness; others pass it as a requirement and without really holding it as their basic view of life. But since it is the only major philosophical system that is discussed in any detail, even those who do not fully adhere to it think and work in its terms.[12]

The disciplines are rather tightly defined, each one occupying its own place in an elaborate system of the sciences. Applicants are channeled into fields which are determined to have personnel needs in future decades, although preferences are followed where possible. Students are not admitted to a university but into a departmental program where they become a part of a student collective, working in a prescribed course of study. A small percentage of the population receives a university education. Class and political background factors, as well as aptitude and social need, are heavily accented in admissions policies. Interdisciplinary work, from all testimony, is difficult, and there is little interdisciplinary conversation.

All schools, universities, and educational institutions are funded and managed by the government. All education is free and standardized. Admission to places of higher education, or assignment to a trade school after elementary and secondary education, is determined according to ability and societal needs. No one is supposed to be trained for a field where jobs cannot be found; learning is for specific social roles. Few fail; many are "re-channeled." All must have some training to prepare for responsible participation in the upbuilding of the society. If age and health permit a person to work, it is unlawful for him or her not to have a job, and the preparation for the job is seen as a primal social responsibility of every citizen.

The only educational institutions which are outside this general pattern are the three independent seminaries and the several church-related training schools. Only the church as a corporate body may hold property besides that held in common by the state (and some smaller amounts held by individuals and families). Only these church-related institutions, beyond government institutions, can award degrees or certificates. These bodies are relatively small, although lively and structurally important in the society.

To my Western eyes these patterns of education seem to be rooted in the patterns derived not only from the Socialist Revolution but also from certain historic developments in East Germany which survive but have been modified or adapted to the present structure of the society. The German universities, for the most part, never developed the kinds of independency from Crown and Miter that were won by the Conciliar Catholics at the universities of Paris, Oxford, and Cambridge, and by the Puritans of Harvard and Yale. A university appointment was a government appointment. In Germany the principle of "freedom of the pulpit" was never translated into "freedom of the lectern." To be sure, the authority of the lectern developed in Germany, and especially in the great universities (such as the present Humbolt) restructured by the Enlightenment. At the hands of several generations of internationally important professors, the influence of scientific standards on German thought induced a kind of freedom based on competence and prestige. Some leading scholars became "literati" beyond criticism, people whose opinions were sought by political leaders. Nevertheless, institutional or structural freedom in the sense of an independent research and teaching center separate from governmental and ecclesiastical control never developed in German academia. This long and at times glorious tradition, at the highest levels of German society, meant that when Bismarck, Hitler, and the Communists came successively to power, the German universities were integrated into the social objectives of the regime with little difficulty.[13]

At lower levels of education, the *gymnasium* had dominated German secondary education for a long time. If students were promising, which usually meant they came from elite families, it was possible for them to attend this combination high-school and liberal-arts junior college. This unique German institution has now been virtually abolished,[14] and in its stead, based on the Russian model, are vocational schools for those who are preparing for vocations in the crafts and skills, and advanced secondary schools specializing in the sciences for those who are likely to enter the universities. Those who finish this training but do not enter the universities become technicians of various kinds through further work in specialized training schools.

At the elementary level the government also controls the design of curriculum and prepares students for full societal participation with special accents on technical and scientific knowledge along with Marxist theory. The activities of the school are closely linked with those of youth recreation, social life, socialist youth corps (Free German Youth, or F.D.J.), and Young Pioneers—the official,

138

Party-guided "scouting" program. The majority (ninety-five percent in 1980) of young people go through a "youth dedication" (Jugendweihe) near the end of their elementary-school life. Participation in these activities and in the dedication is often necessary for qualification for and recommendation to the more desirable advanced-education programs. The "dedication" has, in most locales, replaced religious confirmation, which was earlier linked with local school activities.[15]

I inquired several times whether there was anything like the Home and School or Parent-Teacher-Student Associations. In the United States these not only manifest historic "free-church" ecclesiological patterns (now secularized into voluntary associations) to influence local school policies; they also serve to prepare parents for informed voting on local school-committee elections. The responses indicate that although there is, of course, organized communication between parents and teachers, and there are meetings in which the parents are informed of the priorities and directions of educational policy, parentally organized activities to alter or review government educational policy would be considered strange indeed.[16]

In the G.D.R. education is essentially preparation for productive labor. It is closely tied to the essential understandings of the relationship of theory to practice. Theory and ideation are tools for social praxis. The life of learning and ideas and the quest for truth are not ends in themselves. That, in the predominant view, was the great fault and pretense of various idealisms ancient and modern: they were closely tied to individualistic theories which promoted the egocentrism of intellectual elites and obscured the truths of the real social world, in which the will of each social group was pitted against the will of others. Ideas and claims about truth are tools, and nothing more. They are validated only in practice, in aiding the human mastery of human destiny. Education, then, which always involves the personal formation of ideation and theory, is viewed in the G.D.R. as a means to the end of creative and productive participation in sociality, in serving the whole community in concrete, material ways. Education is, above all, to be practical, and such that one can find one's identity in serving the whole.

These ideas are not entirely new in Germany. They are very deeply rooted in parts of German history prior to Enlightenment liberalism, and can be seen as now given new expression in contemporary Marxist society. It is not difficult to see similar motifs in the organic medieval notions of society being held together by a "cosmos of vocations."[17] Such views were held for centuries by Conservative Catholics in Germany, and were also accepted by Luther. Each station in life has its own skills and knowledge by which the whole is served. Each person is known by his or her station: one is a farmer or a cobbler, a smith or a window maker, a musician or a soldier. With one's "calling" (Luther) or "status" (Catholic) comes the pattern of education that is available within the whole, pregiven, organic, coordinated plan and structure of society as established by God. It is true, of course, that the coordinated plan and structure of

139

society is not something, in the Marxist view, that is pregiven in the structure of creation, as had been classically held. The plan and structure of society is a new creation of human activity to overcome the fixed alienation which the old view reinforced. Hence, like the Puritans, Marxists hold that the basic structures for human activity can be fundamentally rearranged: "We can become what we are not." But unlike the Puritans, they do not see general societal patterns as subject to universal rights and particular vocations given by God and worked out in covenantal relationships. Instead, humans acting in solidarity and concert construct societal forms by their own will, wit, and action. Human agency alone is fully responsible for constructing and coordinating the norms, plans, and structures of society. These are not subject to any extrinsic limitations. Humanity, being organically interdependent, as the Conservative Catholic and Lutheran (and Hindu) views hold, and being free to alter things, as the Puritans (and Muslims) hold, is—as none of the others hold—the absolute center and cause of all that is really real and of fundamental worth and power.

Until the separation of church and state in the Weimar Republic's Constitution of 1918—indeed, until after World War II (for the full impact of the earlier, formal separation was not felt for the next twenty years)—the clergy of Germany had the prime responsibility for supervising the nature and quality of education in the villages; sometimes they also served as schoolmasters. These clergy also were to see that the officials properly provided education and that the students learned both their catechism and a useful trade. The energy and dedication that went into work and preparation for work through education were enormous, and promoted a particular form of "this-worldly asceticism," to use Max Weber's phrase. Germans believed in hard work. But the institutional structures of the common life wherein one worked out that vocation and manifested an intense drive toward creative labor were not transformed by Lutheranism, the Evangelical Calvinism that influenced parts of Germany, or the political traditions from the kaisers, Bismarck, and the Fascists. It was not until the Marxist Revolution that the institutional transformation took place. The Marxist-Leninist transformation occurred less by breaking the organic presuppositions of medieval social life than by depriving them of an ontological basis. The new solidarity and work structures, so decisive for education, were based on the metaphysical-moral vision of a reconstituted "scientific anthropology."

The exception to this new, organic work-ethic is found in the educational institutions of the now disestablished churches. The independent, church-related centers of education are deeply influenced by the legacy of German Pietism. Pietism was a movement of experiential, personal Christianity which originated among Dutch Calvinists and English Puritans of the seventeenth century in reaction to rigid dogmatic orthodoxy and doctrinal divisions of the Protestant, Lutheran, and Reformed churches. The more pronounced impetus to the movement in Germany was given by P.J. Spener,[18] who organized a series of Bible-study groups among laity and local pastors. His leading disciple, A. H. Francke, was a professor who also built a school for the poor, an orphanage, a publishing house, a medical clinic, and a remarkable research library in Halle which became a center of scholarly interaction between the various Calvinist, Lutheran, and sectarian theologians.[19] Later another great leader in the tradition, Zinzendorf, was to develop further the social-service outreach of this movement, creating and sustaining a variety of educational and medical-care institutions among segments of the population which were neglected by official bureaucracies. This was also the movement which gave rise to Lutheran and evangelical missionary work in many countries of the world, including India. Gradually the influence of this tradition not only began to dominate several higher educational centers but influenced John Wesley, the founder of Methodism, who is often viewed as the developer of eighteenth-century "late Puritanism" in England and America.[20] It was fascinating to see the architecture and organizational patterns of this movement, for they compared to those of New England Puritanism like nothing else in Germany. A Pietist church in Herrnhut or in some evangelized villages in India, for example, could have been transported to a New England town without comment from the zoning commission.

The dominant theology in these independent centers appears to the contemporary observer to be a continuation of Pietism modified by the legacies of the Lutheran Bonhoeffer, the United Churchman Dibelius, and the Evangelical Calvinist Barth, who gave expression to those forms of the gospel most capable of resisting Naziism in the Confessing Church. It is not clear that this tradition can, without further modification, help the church form its directions and maintain its structures in the face of a militantly secular, technological society.[21] What is clear is that these independent institutions are a modest but vital part of the church *and* of the society. More than any other educational centers in the country, they provide the opportunity for a relatively autonomous exploration of the relation between the deepest levels of religious, personal, and social meaning, and the structure, strengths, and weaknesses of the emerging new society. While individual voices and small informal groups of intellectuals can be silenced, these institutions have a relatively autonomous social space unparalleled elsewhere in the G.D.R.[22]

In regard to expressive institutions the situation is somewhat similar. Publication, radio, and television media are strictly controlled. Materials from outside the country are difficult to obtain, although reception of radio and the television programs from West Germany is good in most of the country, thus creating complications of several sorts. A number of books are printed in the G.D.R., works by East German authors and translations of both Eastern and Western writers, but these are carefully selected and printed in relatively small quantities. The most intriguing new works by G.D.R. authors disappear from the bookstores very quickly. I was informed that the limitation on Western imports and translations exists not only because of governmental policy—which is designed to prevent the literary celebration of that which is held to be "reactionary" and "dehumanizing," such as pornography, the glorification of war, the defamation of the world's proletariat, and falsifications of Marxist-Leninist teachings—but also because of quite concrete problems of the availability of paper and foreign exchange (which would be required to pay royalties to Western authors and publishers).[23] There are some intricate complications arising on this front, however. The G.D.R. had had long-standing trade and travel agreements with Poland, and Poland signed a trade agreement with West Germany in the early 1970s which involved the sale and distribution of literary materials. Since East Germans enjoyed vacationing in Poland (it being a relatively inexpensive and clearly interesting place to visit), they found it possible to purchase Western reading material there in German. Getting the material back across the East German border seemed to be a highly unpredictable venture: border guards were sometimes rather permissive and at other times quite restrictive. After Polish labor unrest began in 1980, control was tightened, and since 1982 the border has been closed entirely.

In spite of real restrictions, the Stalinist era of absolute control is past. Wider ranges of expression are allowed in all the arts than was the case a decade or so ago. Young artists connected with the Lingner Institute, for example, are exploring quite innovative forms of painting, as long as explicitly critical political and social content is excluded. Official publication, like official monumental art, is massive, heroic, and pedantic; but literature, sculpture, and music of a wide variety of styles, techniques, and intentions are being explored.

During one visit I attended a seminar on baptism and confirmation with theology students in Wittenberg. Later that evening several of the students invited me to join them for informal conversation to continue the discussion. After a while the students began to share their excitement about some of the new literature and paintings that were being allowed. They became animated and engaged in a most intense discussion of the relationship of symbolic action to organizational loyalties. They drew my attention particularly to a new book by one of East Germany's most celebrated authors. I wanted to know more about this author, and as a good-bye gift they gave me a copy of the volume, pointing out specific passages. I later read and reread these passages. The author was clearly an orthodox Marxist, but in exploring literary expression he had come to recognize the power of the intentional metaphor and the double entendre. Expressions that are most meaningful have multiple levels of meaning, and what at one level may be the most specific endorsement of Marxist-Leninist humanism may simultaneously be a most direct critique of the way things work in a socialist society. At the same time, such expressions gather into themselves echoes of intrapersonal dilemmas and place them in a perspective which both illumines the relationship of the self to the structure of society and the ways in which the self is, and can be, held in reserve. "Membership" in a community is both a liturgical-exterior act and one demanding authentic commitment that can transform formalism. Only after this reading did I find the inner connections between the students' passionate involvement in this literature and the questions raised by the deadly seminar on baptism. Baptism, for Christians, is a multileveled symbolic act of basic acceptance by God and by the community of faith. It is a decisive metaphor of membership. I realized that the students saw in this author's work clues for how to be faithful Christians and loyal citizens; membership questions require new symbolic interpretation in this social context. The students were thinking fresh thoughts about such issues, which could only be written between the lines in approved publications. How much mental reservation is permissible in any membership? Must membership involve a conscious decision, or is socialization and acculturation sufficient?

On May 15, 1978, an item appeared in *The New York Times* which indicated that the author to which these students turned had just been excluded from the G.D.R. National Writers Congress. This means that his works will no longer be published in that country or discussed by the approved literary critics. They will be discussed in the seminaries.

The double meaning—it seemed to be elsewhere. I became familiar with what is called the "Berlin wit," a kind of joke with several levels of meaning. Usually it both celebrated the present state of affairs and simultaneously harpooned the exploitation by an omnipresent leviathan.[24] I attended an introductory course in Hebrew in which the early lessons focused on correct understanding of Hebrew grammar and sentence structure. The text was the Book of Job. When I asked the instructor why she began with this text, she replied, "Think about it; then you tell me."

Some weeks later Professor Meeks and I went to the theater and saw a performance of J. Schwartz's *The Dragon,* one of the longest-running shows in East Berlin. By this time we had been alerted to look for the double meanings. Again and again the audience laughed outright at what seemed to be inappropriate spots. I made mental notes on lines that seemed to trigger such outbursts and found, on checking with those more immediately familiar with the present situation and the nuances of the German language, that again the lance was launched, sometimes from the inside. But the absolutely superb technical production, with some highly innovative set design and staging, and the power of these double meanings carried the play more than the quality of the writing and the overt message. Clearly, in technical mastery of material and metaphor, a kind of artistic freedom was being expressed.

In all, some one hundred permanent centers of drama are active, and almost double that number present performances seasonally. Theater is one of the liveliest forms of high culture in East Germany, although there are very few writing new plays today. I wondered to what one could attribute this relative license in the theater. A specialist on German language theater pointed out that there has been a long tradition of social drama in Germany. For nearly two centuries this lively art was often a chief source of satire on traditional thought, superficial piety, bourgeois lifestyles, and conventional bureaucratic stupidity.[25] The theater was not the center of establishment recreation, as it was in Puritan England, but a center of dissent.[26] Certainly the kind of theater which, in some ways, culminated in the works of the much-celebrated Bertolt Brecht was supportive of much of what the Socialist Revolution was about.[27] Thus it is ironic that this medium continues that longer tradition, and now does so with support from the government that is sometimes the target of its historic ally.

Philosophically, Marxism is rooted in a dramatic interpretation of history in which "man is the maker of all things." Fears about the lack of integrity in producing "effects" and about humans generating "artificial" structures and purposes are not present, as they were among the Puritans.

Music is another area of artistic expression in which interesting developments are occurring. Much of the music broadcast on radio and television is nineteenth-century *folk-lieder* in style, modestly modified by an imitation jazz or rock beat and electrified instrumentation. The law requires that music played at the dances in the various youth clubs be eighty percent East German; the remaining twenty percent may be from the West. The official reason for this, I was given to understand, has to do with copyright problems and foreign exchange policies. (In the minds of the youth, it has to do with stupid regulations by old fogies. Intentional violation of these regulations is a mild political protest too diffuse to control.) On several occasions a rock concert has been allowed. The one in Berlin in 1978 turned into a political rally, complete with chants about throwing the Russians out of the country. Since then, however, a gradual modification of government policy has taken place. G.D.R. rock groups are now sponsored for official performances, and on a Sunday in June 1983 I was able to hear "I'm a Honky-tonk Woman" played at an open concert in the People's Palace sponsored by the F.D.J. Friends told me that this is one manifestation of the official efforts to recapture the loyalties of young people, whose support had become less than enthusiastic.

More interesting to me was the way in which classical music is being performed. Much of the great music of Germany is related to the church. According to present official definitions, however, music is a "cultural" activity, not a "religious" activity, and hence may be controlled by governmental policy. Still, some of the great organs and choirs (as well as some orchestras) are in the churches, and several of these churches sponsor, with governmental approval, concerts on Saturday and Sunday afternoons for the performing of larger works. As I saw in May 1980, hundreds of young workers and intellectuals—the future leaders of East Germany—come to these concerts, bringing their scores along. These young people are not, in a formal sense, "religious." They seldom if ever attend religious services. Indeed, their motivations for attending seem to be related to a highly personal attempt to find the time and atmosphere for quiet reflection, linked with an attempt to reclaim a cultural tradition. They also demand artistic excellence, and they walk out if the performance is shoddy. Here again it is not difficult to see double meanings. All associations with the church—even these personal, aesthetic, and cultural ones—have in the G.D.R. overt and conscious social-political meanings. For the performers and for the audiences, the church provides a structured opportunity for freedom of expression and spontaneous meditations outside the ordinary strictures of "socialist realism."[28]

Today one cannot mention the arts in the G.D.R. without drawing attention to sports. Athletics is the most highly developed cultural activity in the country. The outstanding performance of the G.D.R. in the Olympics and other international contests is a product of an intensive and extensive cultivation of the physical arts among the people, with careful selection and development of promising youth. When I asked about the reasons for this, a party lawyer told me that sport is the contemporary "mass art," followed all over the world. Excellence in this field meant recognition of the achievements of the society by the workers of all countries. Sport also provided a creative channeling of human competitive instincts. Further, this form of the arts was fully participatory, not only spectator-oriented. At some level every human could engage in these arts, without special talent, and be better off for it.[29]

In looking back now upon my experiences with the arts in East Germany, there are three that stand out. One was my visit to the Pergamon Museum, that great reconstruction of an ancient Mediterranean civilization in a magnificent late-nineteenth-century building. One can hardly walk around and through that edifice without imagining the ways in which, at the height of the Prussian empire, grand ladies and gentlemen, scholars, and political leaders strolled through these halls and pored over these artifacts. The display surely provided a sense of civilizational achievement and excellence which these grand figures then saw recapitulated in Germanic terms in their own culture. It just as surely provided the occasion for much discussion of what it is that makes a civilization great, and why some fail. That experience left me with a question: What are the models upon which the present leadership draw as they, like responsible leaders in all cultures, try to find standards by which to measure and assess their own accomplishments? I posed the question several times. Nobody knew the answer, or whether there was an answer.

A conversation turned out to be my second outstanding experience concerning the arts. At a church-sponsored youth retreat at Mansfeld Castle, a number of theology students gathered for a weekend. After a busy day of lecturing, discussions, volleyball games, and planned entertainment (some delightful satirical skits about the Russians and the Americans being unable to find a bathroom as they got out of their spaceships on the moon—obviously done to show American guests how distant and foolish some of the Cold War competition is that forgets about simple human needs), a small group of students brought in the inevitable case of beer and sat down to talk. The conversation lasted nearly until dawn. At one point the discussion turned to the question of freedom of expression. A young woman and her husband, recent newlyweds, were both interested in literature and had read widely in English and Russian as well as German sources. "Is it better," she asked me, "to have full freedom of expression than to have controls? One can do all kinds of things when there is absolute freedom of the press and for the arts, but it costs nothing. Nothing is at stake, and storytelling becomes separated from serious decision-making. Exploration of all kinds is open, but it is without consequence. It *makes no difference* to anyone, not even the author. When there is a price to pay for what one says, the words get chosen very carefully, truth becomes precious, and the real meanings of words become personally and socially existential. Freedom, of course, is a good thing, but without a price it becomes degenerate and chaotic. Everybody wants liberation. To what end, this freedom?"

When I returned to the West, first to West Berlin and then to Munich, Tübingen, Frankfurt, and eventually New York and Boston, and visited the book shops and saw the movies and the television, I was unable to forget her question.

The third set of reflections on the arts derives from the fact that 1983 was both the centennial celebration of Karl Marx's death and the five-hundredth anniversary of Martin Luther's birth. Everywhere one could see displays, banners, and portraits of these two great figures. One also heard, everywhere, the standing joke: "Why does one see so many more festivities and pictures of Luther than of Marx?" "Because Marx has been dead for a hundred years, but Luther has been alive for five hundred." At another level this coincidence of dates has revealed several features of G.D.R. society that are worth noting. The primary form, the most primordial one, of cultural expression is language. And it was Luther's translation of the Bible which standardized and gave poetic integration to German. Germanic cultural identity is as much rooted in Luther's contribution as in any other single work of art, however one assesses the religious significance of this event. This language both bonds the German Democratic Republic with the Federal Republic next door, and differentiates the G.D.R. from its sociopolitical allies to the East. That cultural fact makes "the Wall" relatively ineffective at some profound levels of life.

Further, one can find indications among the people, and occasionally in Party documents, that the marvelous technological, economic, and comprehensive managerial strides made by the G.D.R. are not matched by the inner spiritual cohesiveness and spontaneous commitment which Party doctrine expects. In fact, one can sense a cultural torpor, a spiritual inertia. With some exceptions, cultural and artistic creativity seems derivative, like the rock music. Apparently this was one of several motivations which led to Party cooperation with the church to celebrate the Luther year. Perhaps Luther's spiritual vitality, seen now through the glasses of cultural genius and not so much in theological terms, could help the people recapture the creative energies that had once conjoined German Lutheran national identity and original creativity.

All this, however, seems to me to have led to a set of questions about cultural symbols which are not likely to be answered easily. These questions took shape in a small debate between an engineer in the audience and a professor at the lectern at the 1983 Kirchentag Lecture in Rostok on "Marxist Views of Luther." The engineer wanted to know whether religious change, represented by Luther, or social change, represented by Marx, best accounted for the basic transformations of culture and history. The professor could not offer a clear answer.

C. LAW AND THE FAMILY

Figure 10.
The Legal and Familial Sectors

Educational	Cultural/ Expressive	*Legal*
Familial	Voluntary	Political
Medical	Technical	Economic

Education and the arts are controlled by law. Much in the G.D.R. is controlled by law. Yet the legal institutions are, by Western standards, less developed in specific ways. For one thing, there are very few independent commercial companies (they make up less than six percent of the economy) holding property and doing business by contract.[30] Thus those kinds of legal action which preoccupy some sixty percent of all proceedings in the West are just not present. In other areas, divorce is a relatively simple procedure; inheritance and borrowing are strictly controlled and limited; and most medical costs are paid for by the government. Hence family and personal-finance law is, comparatively speaking, seldom evoked, although economic crimes such as taking too much interest, having unauthorized holdings, or stealing from the state are severely punished. There are, to be sure, cases of wife-beating, public drunkenness, and child abuse, as well as questions of legal guardianship and the like, which appear in the simplified family courts; but all evidence I could gather suggests that the judges and lawyers who work in these areas function more as "social workers" in cooperation with the work groups to which the people belong than as legal adjudicators.

Laws are carefully obeyed, and there is little overt or public criminality (criminals are harshly treated). Even traffic laws are obeyed scrupulously. In fact, the traffic law is something of a metaphor for the general structure of the law in East Germany. Traffic laws are conventions established by the common will to prevent harm to those active in the public domain (the streets). In socialist societies the public domain is much wider. All law is seen as a convention. Law has no fundamental autonomy from the general political, social, and economic will. What aids the common purpose is right; what inhibits or confuses it is wrong. To be sure, there is a constitution and there is a supreme court, but both are seen as instruments of the common will (as correctly interpreted by those who best know the true interests of the people). Thus political crimes are the most serious ones. Antisocialist assembly, propaganda, and agitation are considered treason, as are attempts to leave East Germany without authorization. Police presence and surveillance did not seem to me to be obtrusive. For older people who remember the Nazi days and some features of the Stalinist period, the suspicion of uniforms and police authority lingers on. They have a hard time being candid about religious, social, and political opinions, and stay away from "the law" as much as possible. Younger people are discreet, but not fearful, about what they say of a religious, political, or social nature in public places. The moderate anxiety, evidenced in the so-called "Berlin blick," a glance over the shoulder before a sharper critical comment is made, derives not so much from fear of arrest or punishment as from the fact that people are sometimes questioned about what they think they are doing. They may have to explain in great detail, even if they are allowed to go free, if a particularly diligent public official happens to be within earshot. The hassle is just not worth it. It is true, however, that I was advised to be discreet about what I wrote in letters, because there was a good chance that my mail would be opened and read. East Germans are quite careful at this point, for a wide range of things are viewed as subversive to socialist society.

Socialist law does not operate by absolute standards or abstract principles. It is governed by a sense of "proportionality." Actions are evaluated accordingly as they are proportional to the development of a genuinely socialist society or subversive to that development. All people, and especially the proper authorities, are responsible to examine or investigate every behavior according to its concrete social implications in a particular time and place and in terms of the particular political-economic stage of development of socialism, and the resistances to it, at that juncture.[31] Thus equality before the law does not mean that similar cases should be treated similarly over time, but that each case should be treated according to whether it entails greater promise or endangerment to society. Whether a particular action is judged to be constructive or antisocial depends on the actual social conditions in which the action takes place. Thus all involved are to be made conscious not only of what actions are proper and improper but of the real social conditions which determine propriety and impropriety.

The understandings of law are stated in the G.D.R. Code of Penal Law (Strafgesetzbuch der D.D.R.), which can easily be summarized:

1. Socialist law guarantees effective protection of socialist society, socialist state, socialist order, and socialist legality (Preamble).
2. Every act that is in contradiction to these is criminal (Article 1).
3. Every individual is guaranteed the opportunity to behave in a fashion appropriate to society (Article 2).

4. All state and social organizations are responsible for the prevention of criminal activity through scientific leadership and education (Article 3).

5. The dignity of humanity and the freedom to fulfill basic human rights by participation in the economic, political, and ideological life of society are protected by the penal law (Article 4).

6. If that dignity and freedom is violated, socialist justice requires differentiated application of penalties according to class (Article 5).

7. Changed political situations, especially as they reflect crises in the class struggle, alter the criteria for the evaluation of justice relevant to the classes (Sub-article 5, par. 1).

Law, its role and function, is obviously quite differently understood in the G.D.R. than it is in societies informed by the Catholic or Liberal-Puritan synthesis of the West (or, as we shall see, by Hindu thought). On the model of Marxist-Leninist law developed in the Soviet Union,[32] law is understood as a flexible tool or instrument which helps the working classes to inform a fully integrated society and gain control of the total socioeconomic process. What is legally right is what contributes to this greater good; what is wrong is what inhibits it. What is good is greater intentional and coordinated human command over all social, material, and economic processes. Thus human rights are essentially the duty to participate in the dynamics of this holistic process. Since Marxism-Leninism is the science of this process and its dynamics, known to those who concretely participate in the movement by praxis and those who scientifically clarify that praxis by strict adherence to Marxism-Leninism, what is lawful is what the movement determines to be lawful.

Even in a people's democracy, not everyone is a full participant in the movement. Hence the movement must structure the whole of the society so as to include as many as possible. One of the ways it does this is by forming a comprehensive state and giving that state, and all members of it, guidelines for cooperative actions. Law, in the form of "constitution," is such a statement of guidelines. The constitution, however, is to be interpreted by, applied by, and, if necessary, revised, altered, or revoked by the movement should the praxis of the movement, properly clarified by Marxist-Leninist science, deem that to be necessary.

Of course, the movement itself needs internal structure and focus—an executive committee, so to speak. The Party is legally assigned precisely that role. Its activities and discernments are prior to the law and the constitution; indeed, law and constitution are *expressions* of the practical actions and scientific determinations of the Party on behalf of the movement and for the sake of the whole. As scientifically clarified by Marx and made a historically organized force by Lenin, law is an important, temporary instrument of the Party for humanity, reflecting the universal logic of historical and social development.[33]

By law, therefore, an entire society such as that of the G.D.R. is conceived as a single corporation led by the "executive committee," the Party. Other organizations and individual preferences are in principle allowed if they do not

149

inhibit the structure or purpose, in practice or in theory, of this corporate whole. And, of course, the corporation may have numerous subdivisions and functional subunits to carry out specific responsibilities of the whole—such as factories, work brigades, unions, the army, schools, institutes, etc., each with a concretely operating "code."[34]

We have already mentioned the fact that in the G.D.R. the church is the only other corporate group of any size. But families represent another institutional arena which is particularly problematic. Nearly everyone belongs to and lives in a family. Families develop their own internal laws, rules, and patterns, and their own goals. Further, there are so many families that it is very difficult to structure a legal apparatus that can supervise all forms of familial behavior and assure that they are fully compatible with the corporate goals of the whole.

The Party in the G.D.R. has not maintained the efforts of some early Marxists to destroy the nuclear family because it was perceived as a strictly bourgeois institution. Instead, due to the practical resilience of the family in German life, and because of theoretical development which now recognizes the family as a basic social unit in society, the Party attempts to develop good and enduring familial relationships on a new model. Through socialism, it is believed, the basic social causes of alienated relationships have been removed. Now a new vision of socialist marriage is beginning to develop, one which contributes to and is supported by the legal structures of the society.[35] It is "the task of every individual and of the total society to contribute to the protection and development of every family."[36]

There are three ways in which official policy attempts to foster the family while at the same time integrating it into the corporate whole. First, the state participates in the education of the children by supporting parents with "appropriate measures, institutions and agencies, [so that] . . . they can exercise their rights and duties in the education of their children."[37] Concretely, this involves compulsory education in state schools for all six-to-eighteen-year-old children, nurseries for infants and preschool children through industry-based facilities while both parents work, after-school organizations and care centers, and subsidies for couples who bear several children. Second, health care for mothers and children is provided at reduced cost. And third, the state provides a cultural celebration of the "rites of passage"—name-giving at birth, a secular festive ceremony for marriage, and a socialist funeral at death.

It does not appear to the visitor that these strategies are working terribly well. Families tend to view home life as a respite and retreat from the public world, not an increasingly integral part of it. Not only do the churches resist the substitution of socialist rites for baptism, confirmation, and burial, but families who are not involved in the churches tend to seal off family life from "political invasion."

Family life in the G.D.R. is at once troubled, conflictual, intense, protected, and sacred. Family and sexual matters are not openly discussed, and it is something quite special when outsiders are brought into the family circle. Older-style male/female divisions of labor still obtain in most families, although the pressures for change are mounting. Nearly ninety-five percent of the women of employable age and health have jobs outside the home. Women are guaranteed equal opportunity in the job market, and financial security. One of the lowest birthrates in the world and a high divorce rate, cited variously as ending forty-seven to fifty-one percent of all marriages (and seventy-two percent of the marriages among those born since the G.D.R. was founded), also reflect major changes. The high divorce rate in part reflects the fact that women hold two full-time jobs yet have relative economic independence. If the man is more trouble than he is help, divorce is simple. Also involved is the lack of attention paid to family concerns until the last decade. The low birthrates reflect the availability of free birth-control measures and abortion without question for women sixteen and older.[38]

To counter the declining birthrate, the government has developed new inducements for larger families, and has made new housing for married couples with children one of its priorities. First steps were taken in 1972, and they were expanded in 1976 and 1978. The statistics for 1980 reflect a partial reversal of declining birthrates, for having children means quicker access to scarce housing. It has also reduced women's movement into leadership positions. Because employers are required to keep a pregnant woman's position open for a year, allowing time for childbearing and the early months of child care, they are reluctant to promote women into important positions. A cash bonus for second and third children is viewed as a partial recompense as well as an inducement to childbearing.

One of the features of family life fascinating to a Western visitor is the vocabulary used to describe familial, sexual, and child-developmental relationships. Unlike Westerners, the East Germans have not made the categories of such psychological theorists and clinicians as Freud and Jung a part of their language. When people talk about male-female relations, the stages of child development, or various dimensions of the emotional or erotic life, their terminology sounds like that of nineteenth-century novels. It is fashionable in some circles in the West to try to get beyond the influence of psychiatry and psychoanalysis, but it is something else not to have these basic terms in the working vocabulary of otherwise educated people. Psychological language in the G.D.R. is drawn from occupational therapy and sociological sciences, as befits the dominant Marxist view of the world. Only some church diaconic (social service) centers are more open to alternative psychological concepts and methods.

D. MEDICINE, TECHNOLOGY, AND ECONOMICS

The institutions dealing with health care in the G.D.R. are one of the most intriguing aspects of social life, with interesting relations to institutional religion. Health care is viewed as a right of all citizens, and the level of medicine is in some respects high on both the preventive and curative side.[39] General

Figure 11.

The Medical, Technological, and Economic Sectors

Educational	Cultural/ Expressive	Legal
Familial	Voluntary	Political
Medical	Technical	Economic

health care is readily available, inexpensive, and excellent, although medicines for the elderly and other "nonproductive" segments of the population are reportedly very difficult to obtain. Medical personnel have nothing like the excessively high prestige accorded doctors in America, and clinical work is dominated by professionally trained women instead of men. Life and accident insurance is available, but it is comparatively expensive considering its modest returns.

Large percentages of the population are elderly, due to the low birthrates, the exodus of many younger people before the Wall was built, and the increased life expectancy. Indeed, the G.D.R. has the highest proportion (sixteen percent) of people sixty-five and over of any country in the world. There are the usual percentages of those with severe mental and physical handicaps. It is clear that these people are given some care and support in the G.D.R., but it is not clear how Marxist-Leninists deal with irremediable personal senility, suffering, frailty, and death. Tragedy is, in orthodox Marxist-Leninist thought at least, primarily a product of false and exploitative social arrangements. Since these have been vanquished, at least in principle, by the socialist triumph, how is the society to deal with continuing frequencies of tragedy? If humanity is essentially defined in terms of how we concretely participate in production and in shaping the common will, what are we to do with those who can do neither?

Under the impact of the Pietist movement in German history, a long tradition of "diaconic" service to the sick and suffering, the aged, and the handicapped developed in church-related hospitals, institutions, and therapeutic communities. It is to these that the government has turned in recent years, paying the several church institutions approximately eight marks per day per patient for the care of these people. The churches own and manage 54 hospitals and convalescent homes, 36 homes for mothers, some 600 old-people's homes, and over 300 nursing stations.[40] Efforts to restore people to the larger community of production continue in these centers. All patients are to participate in occupational therapy to the limits of their abilities, and even those institutionalized for life make rather remarkable handicraft articles for sale and export. The waiting lists for these centers are long.

To be sure, one also finds public, non-church-related hospitals, nursing homes, and the like; but these seem to be reserved as "sick-care" centers for those needing temporary help before they can go back to work. There are also government medical personnel in the factories and industries. Workers who feel ill do not go to a medical station in these institutions unless they are referred by the trained personnel who visit them at the work site and confirm that treatment off the job is needed. I could get no reliable information on the political use of psychiatric medicine. Nevertheless, it is the Pietistic religious traditions from Francke, Zinzendorf, and their more recent disciples, Wichern and the Blumhardts, that formed Protestant diaconal centers of care. It is this church tradition which built the major medical centers for the handicapped, which staffs them and trains the personnel to deal with suffering in a deeply religious, humane, and loving atmosphere. Today many Party officials reportedly prefer Christian hospitals to government ones because of the compassionate care that accompanies equally good medical treatment. The contributions made by this tradition in education, family life, and health care remain as powerful and vital legacies, even if the sources of these concerns are now often forgotten.[41]

Technological and economic activities in East Germany, where they are not specifically designed to support one of the sectors of society already discussed, are in some ways the focal point of the nation. The televised evening news programs almost always begin with an item showing the workers and scientists making yet another breakthrough in efficiency, production, welding technique, plant organization, or automation. All economic activities of extraction, production, and distribution are managed by the state. Mines, farms, factories, systems of transportation, and stores are all divisions, as it were, of the governing corporation. The necessities of life, such as staple foods, clothing, and shelter, are subsidized. The unemployment rate is low, and America's toleration for higher rates is viewed as positively immoral. Underemployment, however, is frequent, and workers who perform poorly and are absent often are seldom fired. One is guided in job performance, if one does not work to capacity, by the unions of the farmer and worker organizations, whose role is to discuss, understand, and assist in the implementation of national planning policies as well as to deal with careless, undisciplined, and low-quality workmanship. At the same time, brigades of workers are privately critical of someone who is too zealous, sets too fast a pace, or becomes a true believer in exceeding production goals. Managers and engineers, too, see their role as one that involves the interpretation and application of technical and economic planning priorities to make official policies operational. But they are limited in their ability to fire or discipline workers. Replacements are hard to find, and a trained worker who performs poorly is better than no worker or an improperly trained one.

In Western societies the techniques of planning and the technology of design, toolmaking, and engineering are often in the possession of the economic corporations. These are structurally independent of the government, although they influence it and are influenced by it. In East German society economic institutions are under the control of the technological and planning leadership, and these are guided essentially by governmental policy through a vast and pervasive bureaucracy which has been dubbed "Red Prussianism." Students quizzed me several times about American policies in Latin America, especially Chile and Central America. And when I pointed out that we really have two foreign policies—one managed by the political sector of life and one by the giant corporations which sometimes carry the day—they expressed amazement at the distinction. The relative autonomy of market and corporate policy is intentionally destroyed in East Germany, along with the elaborate systems of finance, exchange, independent planning and production, and corporate jurisprudence that characterize Western economies. As the G.D.R. increasingly integrates itself into the world economy, however, new divisions of the government which specialize in these areas are developing rapidly.

The economic accomplishments of the G.D.R. are pronounced, and are celebrated at every opportunity. The G.D.R. has the highest standard of living of any socialist country in the world. Its technical capacity in electronics and heavy industry, in chemicals and trade, compares favorably, on a per-capita basis, to that of a number of West European nations. Yet there are difficulties on the horizon. The country's limited natural resources have demanded extensive use of high-polluting soft coals. Ecological damage by highly industrialized nations is not unusual, but in a society dominated by a Marxist-Leninist creed, a special problem arises. It is not a part of official ideology to believe that humanity is limited by forces and structures external to the social system. The notion of a universal, objective law of nature which limits humanity's control over its own destiny is not easily comprehended. The only ideologically viable way of dealing with this problem is to call for further, total mastery by more complete and efficient technological control, as directed by more intense political guidance.

In another area the fact that the Party, through the state, has taken responsibility for management of the whole society means that thousands of citizens do not feel personally responsible for much of anything in spite of the efforts to intensify committed participation. If anything goes wrong, it is seldom that any grassroots movement will or can be started to set it right. Initiative comes from the top, and increased cynicism about the top is clearly present among the people. Many workers "do their job" with diligence and precision, but otherwise "do their time" in shop-related political-education and solidarity groups, in worker brigades and union meetings. There is a pronounced psychic alienation from the political aspect of work.

Part of the reason for the alienation is the enormously cumbersome character of the decision-making process. In any particular effort on the medical, technological, or economic fronts, there are five institutions, each operating by "consultative centralism," that must be coordinated. At the most immediate level the brigade, production team, or workers' collective must understand, discuss, and endorse the objectives brought to it by the industrial-managerial hierarchy of the firm. The efforts of the firm, in turn, are coordinated by the state planning agency responsible for that area of governmental operation. The local workers' organizations are also integrated into one or another of the nationwide Front-related institutions—unions, guilds, peasants' organizations, and the like. All of these are coordinated and directed by the Party. Finally, an "invisible" but very powerful cluster of organizations makes up the security departments. These departments investigate and report on cooperative and reluctant attitudes and behaviors in all the other organizations. Party members often participate in all of these structures, wearing many hats; they form the policy-making, informational, and personnel links which hold these structures together. The investment of skills, resources, and numbers of people to maintain these bureaucracies as separate entities, yet to assure that they are united in policy, purpose, and program, is enormous. Upwardly mobile youth frequently choose one of these organizations as a ladder of success. But most people feel far removed from the machinations of these vast bureaucracies, and are only the passive recipients of their edicts.

I spent a long evening in Magdeburg discussing the comparative socioeconomic structure of German society with a scholar who had visited the West. He insisted that another problem is present in this area: a continuing class structure in the German Democratic Republic. The arrangement is somewhat different from that in America in three respects. First, there is not so great a difference in terms of income between those at the top and those at the bottom. Thus a bell curve of its income distribution would look shorter and fatter than one representing that of America. Second, wealth, as distinct from income, is largely abolished. However, it must be said that it has been replaced by less traceable and less measurable "privilege." Top government officials, high-performance athletes, selected orthodox intellectuals, and the like enjoy perquisites that the rest of the citizenry do not: access to summer-resort facilities, use of private or chauffeured cars, more desirable living-quarters, better chances for their children to gain admission to universities, wider availability of consumer goods produced outside the country, greater chances for travel, and less likelihood of being hassled by bureaucratic or police procedures. Privilege, not money, has become the coin of reward and the mark of "nonclass class." Political and social influence, not directly connected to personal or family wealth, become the medium of prestige and rank. The trading of "favors" is an intricate, well-hidden exchange. Third, some groups which are very high on the socioeconomic scale in the West are lower on the scale there, and vice-versa. Doctors and lawyers are rather clearly "middle range," whereas professors are very highly situated as a class. Independent businessmen are very marginal, although owners of small construction firms are doing very well, by all reports; some are called "red millionaires." Engineers, managers, bureaucrats, and highly skilled craftsmen stand between the higher and middle levels, although there are persistent rumors that through moonlighting (at exorbitant rates and sometimes only for Western currency) doing home repairs outside official channels, some craftsmen have earned considerable (and well-concealed) wealth. There are only a few areas where ethnic minorities (mostly Slavic, but increasingly Indo-Chinese) of unskilled or semiskilled labor endure poor and difficult living conditions—in contrast with, say, Harlem. People on pensions—nearly twenty percent of the population—have enough to subsist on, but meet many problems in daily life only with difficulty. If they have families in West Germany, they try to emigrate, because retirement benefits and old-age medical care are better there. The government has been rather permissive about emigration for this group.[42] The Jewish community, once Germany's largest minority group, was destroyed by Hitler. Fewer than two thousand Jews, many of them elderly, remain in all of the G.D.R.

The reason for these difficulties in the technological and economic sectors lies, I believe, in the character of the deep traditions of the nation as well as in the specific form of the regnant Marxist-Leninist creed (as we shall discuss more fully in the next chapter). In the West it is widely held that Marx believed in, and contemporary Communists hold to, an economic determinism. This is not the case. As we shall see, Marx held to the decisive importance of "the *means of production*" in determining the stage of historical development in a society. That, in ordinary Western vocabulary, would be a technological, not an economic, determinism. But this technological determinism is not absolute. A society is also dialectically shaped by the will of whoever it is that has control over the technology. On that basis a specific economy is formed. It is this matter of control which Lenin solidified in a specific direction by accenting the decisive role of centralized, coercive power and by giving specific political shape to the "dictatorship of the proletariat." As these doctrines have been incorporated into the public creed of the German Democratic Republic, they have legitimated a politically dictatorial domination of the technical abilities of a people, and reinforced a traditional passivity to authority.

E. POLITICAL INSTITUTIONS

All lines of authority guiding this mighty dynamo of technological-economic activity are traced through the political authorities and coordinated with the policies of the People's Army, and both are controlled by the Party in close association with Moscow. The political sector of society is the public integrative and coordinating center of all important activities and has an absolute control

Figure 12.

Political Institutional Sectors

Educational	Cultural/ Expressive	Legal
Familial	Voluntary	Political
Medical	Technical	Economic

over all powers of coercion. Externally this means that foreign policy is governed by the attempt to support revolutions which will extend Marxism-Leninism. In Africa, Asia, and Latin America, the G.D.R. is fully integrated into the Soviet Union's understanding of power. Internally every sector of life is inextricably interlocked indirectly through bureaucratic controls and directly through the Party's coordination of various organizations linked in a united Front. It is a contemporary return of an understanding of the term "political order" which makes politics the most comprehensive category for organized society and human community. Yet it differs from ancient, Renaissance, and French Revolutionary definitions of political realism in that the government is itself controlled by an organization which is not, in a formal, technical sense, governmental—in this case, the Party. The policy of the Party is understood to be decisive for the character of the society as a whole, for all members and for all constituent groups. We will trace the roots of this idea in the subsequent chapter.

The operational side of government is the technical-administrative bureaucracy. Bureaucratic authority is rationally and hierarchically organized and comprehensive in scope. If one were to speak of it in religious terms, one could only compare it to the ideal, organic, hierarchical structure of the ideal medieval Roman Catholic Church. Like that institution, it mediates the means of salvation to the people, guiding and informing all areas of thought and action. But the grace mediated is not of supernatural origin; it is the scientifically and technically derived rational-empirical interpretation of basic human purposes, needs, and means to fulfill those needs and ends. The relative efficiency and occasional officiousness of this bureaucracy penetrate and shape every dimension of life in

157

what one East German spokesman called a "conformed" or "integrated" society in contrast with a "pluralistic" society.

The power and efficiency of German bureaucracy are not entirely new with the socialist regime. The scope and influence of Prussian bureaucracy, especially under Bismarck's "state socialism," earlier expressed and confirmed a deep tendency in German history. The Nazis capitalized on these structures, turning them against the people as well as against neighboring countries with devastating results. Out of the ashes of that self-destructive, rationalistic, bureaucratic, politically centered collective life, the phoenix of the new bureaucracy, guided by a new civic religion of Marxism-Leninism, has filled the leadership vacuum. However, the concern to guide all aspects of society through comprehensive planning has pushed the efficiency of the bureaucracy to its limits. A Western political observer in East Berlin estimated the present efficiency at "about eighty percent of the U.S. Department of Health, Education and Welfare."

The official structures of the political order, however, are not fully self-guiding. The Party (the S.E.D.) is the nucleus which guides the rational, bureaucratic political order by "consultative authoritarianism."[43] It is made up of about eleven percent of the population. About sixty percent of the population belong to one or another branch of the National Front which it guides, making it proportionally more inclusive of population than most of the other Communist countries. However, estimates are that less than twenty percent of the population are actually active in Party or "Front" organizations. Within the Party, debate and discussion are, by all reports, intense and pervasive at lower levels until a consensus is reached about the actual character of human needs and the policies required to meet them. Any unresolved disagreements, or any which require clearance with Party policies, are referred "upstairs" for decision. At that point, in principle, debate ceases, and all join to implement the agreed-upon directives through the bureaucratic as well as the Party apparatus.

While I was in Germany, the Party Congress was in session, and many of its proceedings were broadcast on television. The reports of the various subcommittees were made by the chairmen of those subdivisions of the Party, speaking to and for the society as a whole. These reports were then unanimously and enthusiastically adopted in a celebrative liturgical set of actions.

Celebration may well be required. For on the one hand, all reports suggest that the overt signs of unity in fact mask very sharp disagreements within the vast and inclusive structure. There are echoes of internal political struggles of major proportions in the process of consensus formation. Indeed, several of my older conversation partners who have followed political developments in detail say that there is considerable insecurity precisely in the power structure because the coalition is not secure; there are cracks at the base, factions within factions, and divergent understandings of the ground on which the whole apparatus rests. As one wag put it, "The floors are slippery in the People's Palace." If these reports are correct, the celebrative and unifying experience of liturgical actions provides a sense of the kind of univocal unity sought.

F. THE DIVIDED RELIGIOUS SITUATION

In such a society it turns out that there are two religions. One derives from the Christian heritage and is present in the churches and in some educational and health-care institutions, as well as in the hearts and homes of innumerable believers. It appears less directly in the specific sense of "work ethic" and technical excellence as a matter of "vocation," as these derived from the impact of Lutheranism on the whole culture. The other is the political religion, of a humanistic and collective nature, which is organizationally centered in the Party, and elaborated ritually in "name-giving," "youth dedication," "state marriage," and "socialist funeral" ceremonies. This religion has located its understandings of what is really real, worthy and powerful, and genuinely holy in the creative social and material activities of humans as revealed in the "sacred" texts of Marx and Lenin. About sixty percent of the population remain on the church rolls (Steuerliste); ten percent of the population are visibly active in church activities; the present number of newborn infants being baptized is somewhat under twenty percent. Some thirty percent of the youth have some sort of church-related contact on a regular basis, although fewer than ten percent choose to be confirmed.[44] The relationship between these two religions is unsettled. Most of the clergy and many of the laity greatly appreciate the peace, stability, and relative plenty brought by the socialist society, and the relative equality of opportunity among the population as compared with the inequality of former times. Many express thankfulness that some religious freedoms remain basically in effect in the G.D.R. as compared with some of the sister socialist countries. But puzzlement and confusion exist as well. One elderly lay woman in Cottbus told me that she had said the Lord's Prayer every day for most of her life, and in that prayer she had asked the Lord to "give us this day our daily bread." For the first time in her long life, a socialist state which denies the Lord now provides her with her daily bread. "Is that God's doing?" she asked.

There is some evidence that the G.D.R. government and some theologians are ambiguous about the increased ecumenical concerns of the G.D.R. churches. On the one hand, they encourage closer contact with the Eastern Orthodox churches of the Soviet Union and other socialist countries. From a government standpoint it would be convenient if the East German churches developed a relationship to the state such as the Orthodox have. Some theologians also believe such a relationship would be good. Most church leaders, however, respond by developing closer ties with the World Council of Churches and other ecumenical groups more influenced by Western traditions, in which the church is involved in moral and spiritual discernment of political and social life. The government also encourages all church groups to speak out, when they are in ecumenical gatherings, on the necessity for peace. The church representatives do so, but many in a particular way. When the G.D.R. government or Party speaks of "peace," it means the disarmament of the West above all. Church delegates to ecumenical gatherings speak of the perils of nuclear armaments, but they also speak of the foundations for peace—human rights, freedom, and justice. The message is easy to read: if these are not present, Western disarmament alone may not bring peace. Outside the churches there is no social space in which to gather the information or to develop the ideological principles to think about such matters independent of the government. Indeed, in May of 1980, when a church official at a church synod spoke critically of the Soviet invasion of Afghanistan, a government official present as an observer became very angry. The issue was not only Afghanistan but the fact that the church continues to develop, among at least some portion of the population, an independent "public opinion" on sociopolitical issues backed by an independent, organized constituency. The deeper traditions of German Pietism, however, make such efforts ambiguous even inside the church.

Older church-leaders at the local level who no longer are the best-educated and most prestigious leaders in their communities feel displaced and useless. They are committed to their faith, and they appreciate the new possibilities for material, educational, and recreational life brought by the government to their people; but they also feel that the political-economic humanism of the prevailing secular religion is superficial and thin, and that the people are preoccupied by material gain. It does not in fact grasp the deeper reaches of human need, nor can it provide through its technological manipulation the means to meet these needs. Indeed, they are anxious about the apparent increased manipulation of the population. Still, most are resigned to the present directions; they sigh a lot and throw up their hands in simultaneous thanks and despair. There is nothing that can be done, they have decided, except to carry out one's role with a sense of duty, let the societal machine run, and prepare for retirement. Others hope quietly for the day when the Party will expand its appreciation for organized religion and reinstitutionalize a cooperative mutual support system between regime and piety. Every sign of concession is seen as potentially full of promise, yet they do not really believe the situation will ever fundamentally change.

The more vigorous church leaders, however, are presently engaged in a debate regarding how the church shall conceive of its own role in such a society. For some the answer is clear: religion deals with the inner heart; another realm entirely is the outward one, where Marxism-Leninism is a purely rational science. Few agree. More say that the answer is given in terms of the "diaspora," a term that recalls the dispersion of the Jews into the cities and local synagogues after they had lost political control of the pagan Roman Empire and the ancient temple was destroyed. According to this way of thinking, the essential task is survival and the building of a vigorous, disciplined religiosity which can preserve the tradition and keep alive the ancient promises of God and the hope for new days. An influential number in this group are pressing for more organizational integration in and among the church bureaucracies so that a solid, structurally cohesive "fortress church" will be able to withstand the power of intentional "secularization" (de-Christianization) of everything in the society. Critics see this as a prelude to voluntary "ghetto-ization of the church." For others, still a minority, an ecumenically oriented new tradition of the Free Church is aborning which can work creatively and constructively with many aspects of Marxist society, as the church in the past worked within—and not only against—Greek and Roman and old Germanic civilizations. This latter group agrees that it is necessary to build a vigorous, disciplined lay-religiosity, and is deeply engaged in work with families, women, young people, and the elderly. This group does not advocate withdrawal into "diaspora" conventicles, but tries to stimulate imaginative recovery of neglected traditions of the church, intensive contact with other church bodies, and, wherever possible, constructive participation in those aspects of socialist society which are most compatible with Christian thought and practice. Instead of "diaspora," this group accents "critical participation," implying that from within the church traditions one can find resources by which socialism in the Marxist-Leninist mold can be improved. A suppressed speech given by Heino Falcke is still quoted widely on these points.[45]

Both groups see the need for internal reorganization of church order, practice, and theological education, and are earnestly debating new ways of structuring these. Some of the most imaginative and least dogmatic are drawing from new directions in practical theology being developed by the Catholics (especially in Erfurt, where the only remaining center of Catholic theological education after the division of Germany is exploring very creative new models), and some of the efforts going on among the "sects" (the Methodists, the Baptists, etc.) who have never been rooted in the older official ecclesiastical structures on the Continent (although contact with these groups is sporadic, and the learned pastors constantly point out that the academic level is not as high as in the Lutheran and E.K.U. churches). Most agree, however, that the G.D.R. government is their government; they are loyal citizens. They believe that there are features of the present regime which commend it to Christians in comparison with anything they have known in the past. Yet in the theme of "critical participation" they imply that Christians have access to standards which surpass, and can thus evaluate, the ideology and structure of the society. Nevertheless, that society is the field in which they sow their seed and in which they may find unexpected treasures. They are also fully aware that the Party wants the souls of the people as well as their cooperation, and that the Party line offers a vision of human salvation which they believe finally to be false.

The ambivalent relationship between ecclesiastical and political authority is, I believe, deeply rooted in German history. Luther's classical distinction—drawn actually from one motif in Augustine about the "two kingdoms," the spiritual one and the worldly one—has been interpreted, reinterpreted, misinterpreted, abandoned, and recovered again and again.[46] In technical theological debates it is represented by the Meissen Theses of 1951 and by such theologians as Bosarak and Hanfried Müller today. This perspective holds that the spiritual kingdom has to do only with inward things, and that the secular Marxist government is legitimately the sovereign over all things external because it is truly scientific and rational and outside the concern of religion. On the other hand, a variety of scholars, such as the well-known older theologian Gunter Jacob and the churchman Heino Falcke, say that such an interpretation means that the inner cannot and should not decisively influence the outer; it relegates religion to the idiosyncrasies of personal hobby, "like growing flowers or keeping goldfish."[47] It is clear that the older relationships between church and state, which held from the 1555 Peace of Augsburg through the abdication of the German princes in 1918 to the attempt of the Nazis to control the churches, are broken. Most see that as an obvious benefit, although many critics of the Meissen position see temptations to an uncritical approval of present political authority, echoing the perils of previous ages in Germany.

On March 6, 1978, a new and carefully negotiated statement on the relations between church and state appeared in the Party- and government-sponsored newspapers. For several years there had been complaints from the religious communities about discrimination in educational and employment opportunities, and some growing hostility toward government policies that formally allowed freedom of religion but allowed very little opportunity to exercise that freedom outside the rituals of worship. The official agreement between the state and the churches speaks of government permission to build churches in the "new cities" and to rehabilitate or reconstruct old ones. Also, in a quite innovative move, the churches are allowed to offer TV programs—twenty minutes every other month. Also permitted is the possibility of prison chaplaincy, government-supported pension plans for church workers, and wider ecumenical relationships. There is a strong suggestion that some reimbursement will be made for the 40,000 hectares of property previously owned by the church which was collectivized some two decades ago.

By all reports that I have heard, the lower Party functionaries are distressed by this move. They have been led to believe that religion is the opponent and the opiate of the people and of scientific communism, and now there seems to be a new rapprochement between the Party and the church. One can, of course, understand some of the political reasons for this new relationship. The echoes of Helsinki and of a rather stinging report on freedom of religion issued in 1977 by Amnesty International still ring. One could also note that East Germany needs Western currency, and that much of the money for the rebuilding of churches is likely to come from the West. I think it is more important, however, to note that organized religion does not seem to be fading from the socialist society as anticipated, and that the continued loyalty and cooperation of the church people are sincerely desired. Some sources suggest that a recent, but not publicly available, Party report may have had a major impact: that Christians, although seldom in privileged positions, work harder than non-Christians; and that in job situations where there is a high concentration of Christians, there is less absenteeism, alcoholism, and stealing. Others point out that this agreement was reached just as a new program for universal military training was instituted in all G.D.R. schools—a move which only the church had reason and the capacity to protest. The churches objected at several points, but focused much more attention on the new agreements. What is not yet known is whether this new agreement will have a major long-range impact on the social system, or whether it will be a new version of the deep traditions of religion in that part of the world.

In nearly all the older church buildings the previous relationships are embodied in stone. Luther had to appeal to the princes to protect his fragile movement. Gradually the princes were acknowledged as the highest "bishops" of the region they governed. The churches of this time were built by nobility whose images and family coats-of-arms adorn the walls. High on the wall of the chancel, Christ and the saints or the disciples are painted. Only slightly lower, discreetly to one side, are the family balconies of the nobility. One step down, but usually in the center, is a high and exalted pulpit. Clergy preached mostly down to the people below, and only sideways and up to the political leadership. Between the elevated pulpit, from which the Word was preached, and the people below was the communion table, often rather small and partially recessed. The liturgical solidarity of the people in sharing drink and bread was made highly subordinate to the preaching from on high, just next to the magistracy. Whether the new agreements are the re-emergence of these old relationships is not yet known. But the depth trajectories of human civilizations are such that we must look at the historic roots of modern German society to see from whence it came and what motifs from the past are likely to shape its future. In 1979 a government committee of one hundred members, headed by the Party secretary, was formed to plan a "Luther Jubilium" for 1983, the five-hundredth anniversary of Martin Luther's birth. The federation of churches was invited to send members to plan this celebration. After considerable internal debate the church established its own committee, independent of the official one, and began to develop its own agenda. How to view Luther and his influence on sociopolitical as well as theological questions, and the relations between theological and sociopolitical loyalties, will be questions of paramount importance for both church and Party. The problems are intensified by the radical disruption of historical continuity in Germany caused by Hitler and the aftermath of World War II. No people can build a future without a sense of history, but the recent history of Germany has been disjunctive and destructive. To what in the deeper past can the people of the G.D.R. turn? How shall it be understood?

The theoretical as well as the practical questions that must now be faced by the two communities of faith are precisely how, and in what measure, to discern the claims of both the humanistic political authorities and the Party to have a grasp on that which is really real, worthy, and powerful. Is it a proper claim, to some degree, to be and bear that which is "holy"? Clearly Marxist-Leninist thought has brought about a transformation that bears within it many dimensions of a cosmopolitan ethic. How are its quasi-religious claims to be adjudicated, and in what measure are its structures, ideologies, and programs to be judged holy? To an analysis of the background of the most pertinent aspects of religious thought in the G.D.R.—Christian and Marxist-Leninist—we now turn.

1. R. Solberg, *God and Caesar in East Germany: The Conflicts of Church and State in East Germany Since 1945* (New York: Macmillan, 1961), p. 10.

2. Eberhard Schneider quotes a document from the first S.E.D. Party Conference:

Party discussion has ... made it clear that we are on the way to a new style of party. ... The Marxist-Leninist party is based on the principle of democratic centralism. This means strict adherence to the principle of election of administrations and functionaries and the accountability of those elected to the members. This intra-party democracy is the basis of the strict party discipline which stems from the socialist consciousness of the members. Party resolutions apply to all members without exception. ... The toleration of factions and groupings within the party is incompatible with its Marxist-Leninist character (*The G.D.R.: History, Economy and Society of East Germany* [New York: St. Martin's Press, 1978], p. 17).

3. The Lutherans and United Evangelicals constitute half the population. A small "free church" tradition, mostly Methodist and Baptist, also exists, representing only one percent of the population. See T. Beeson, "German Democratic Republic," in *Discretion and Valour: Religious Conditions in Russia and Eastern Europe* (Glasgow: Wm. Collins Sons, 1974), pp. 167ff.

4. See F. Littell, *The German Phoenix* (Garden City, N.Y.: Doubleday, 1960).

5. See Solberg, *God and Caesar in East Germany*, pp. 84ff.

6. Ibid., p. 34.

7. Ibid., pp. 46f. and pp. 188f.

8. Ibid., p. 107.

9. Ibid., pp. 84ff.

10. See the National Committee of the Lutheran World Federation in the G.D.R., "Concern for a Human World" (church document, 46 pp., n.d.), and the Committee on Church and Society and Secretariate of the V.E.L.K. in the G.D.R., "The Theological Relevance of Human Rights," trans. in J. Lissner and A. Sovik, *LWF* Report, 1 (Sept. 1978), 29 – 30. Many of the most significant resources in the G.D.R. churches are written as committee documents and reports and published in mimeographed form as church documents only. This reflects conditions in which (1) church documents circulated in this form are not subject to censorship, (b) collegial or socialized forms of research have become standard, and (c) relative anonymity of individual opinion is maintained.

11. Ministry of Education, "Education for Today and Tomorrow" (Berlin: Verlag Zeit im Bild, 1971).

12. In 1980 I had the chance to read the schoolbooks in history and government for the fifth, sixth, and seventh grades and compare them (upon return) with those of my own children. G.D.R. texts have very few references to persons (except as examples of classes or movements), almost no reference to dates (for specific events are seen as epiphenomena of the dominant structures of an epoch or period), and absolutely no reference to the socially or historically causative role of ideas. The focus is on the technology developed by the workers in a specific period; the social structure built on that base as some elites gained control, through manipulation of the social structure, of the fruits of the technology; and then the split as the elites developed fantasies to justify their pre-eminence and as the workers developed new technologies to regain control over their lives. The process began again in a subsequent period but was interrupted when Marx discovered this logic of history and therefore gave the workers the scientific tools to prevent the elitist takeover of the fruits of technology and society.

13. We shall examine the deeper historical roots of this pattern in Section D of Chapter Six.

14. One remains, but I was unable to get detailed information about it.

15. The battles over the discrimination against those who chose confirmation instead of dedication have at times been intense. (See Solberg, *God and Caesar in East Germany*, especially pp. 46 – 91 and Chapter 11.) Today the tension seems reduced in some areas of the country. It has been a custom since the nineteenth century for young people, after Jugendweihe or confirmation, to publish a small notice of thanks in local newspapers for the gifts and good wishes received at these moments. The notice serves also as a public

announcement of adulthood. For many years it was socially disadvantageous to announce confirmation in this way. In 1980, however, some public notices of confirmation appeared. I counted the number of Jugendweihe announcements as compared to those for confirmation in the papers of Naumburg; about five percent were for confirmation. Even more interesting, however, were two notices which thanked friends for gifts and good wishes for both. Such a thing was not possible from either the state or the church side in most of G.D.R. history. We shall return to the discussion of Jugendweihe in Section F of this chapter.

16. "Parents Councils" were in effect and quite influential as a part of the "de-Nazification program" until October 1955, when the Party ordered new elections for all the councils and set up provisions for nominations which assured Party-desired results. The elections were deemed necessary because of decisions by the Ministry of Education and by the Central Committee to remove courses in religion from all school instruction and to replace them with instruction on material prepared by the newly formed Society for the Promotion of Scientific Knowledge, an atheistic propaganda organization. Parents Councils resisted this move.

17. See note 18 in Chapter Three, Section C in Chapter Seven, and Section C in Chapter Eight.

18. F. E. Stoeffler, *The Rise of Evangelical Pietism* (Leiden: E. J. Brill, 1965).

19. J. T. McNeill, *Modern Christian Movements* (Philadelphia: Westminster Press, 1954).

20. J. R. Weinlick, *Count Zinzendorf* (Nashville, Tenn.: Abingdon, 1956).

21. See Arend Van Leeuwen, *Prophecy in a Technocratic Era* (New York: Scribner's, 1968), pp. 117f. Quite unconnected with Van Leeuwen's comparison of the Pietist concern for social service and Marx's concern for social change, the "Report to the Theological Commission" (May 1976) by Professor Douglas Meeks and me attempted to identify how theological education could be so developed in the churches' institutions to include a theologically based analysis of ethics and ecclesiastical history in relation to social developments.

22. See, for example, A. Stephan, "Johannes R. Becker and the Cultural Development of the G.D.R.," *New German Critique*, 1 (Spring 1974), 72ff.

23. Conversation with an S.E.D. Party-member and journalist, May 1976.

24. See Hanns Eisler, "Letter to a Musician—and Others," *New German Critique*, 1 (Spring 1974), 63ff.

25. Conversation at the International Symposium on the G.D.R., New Hampshire, June 1980: "The reason so few are today writing for the theater seems to be related to increasing uncertainty about what innovations will in fact be allowed in the production of untested dramas" (name withheld by request).

26. See point 3 in Section B of Chapter Four. Nor was the theater a place for sacred liturgies and lore of gnostic religion, as we shall see it is in India. See Section D in Chapter Seven.

27. D. Bathrich, "The Dialectics of Legitimation: Brecht in the G.D.R.," *New German Critique*, 1 (Spring 1974), 90ff. In 1983 I attended Brecht's famous *Threepenny Opera* in East Berlin. Tragically, Brecht has been so canonized that the play is "liturgically" produced in a mechanical imitation of the way he staged and directed it in the 1930s. Little of the lively innovation that he would have brought to every new historical moment is present any longer.

28. In 1985 Germany will celebrate the 300th birthday of J. S. Bach. Already state and church committees are planning how to deal with this great, classical church musician. It will be fascinating to see precisely how he is interpreted and represented by all concerned.

29. Jonathan Steele writes: "The Country's Gymnastic and Sports Federation has a membership of 2,660,000 [1977 figure], about one-seventh of the entire population." He goes on to speak of the selection and training programs for G.D.R. athletes (*Inside East Germany* [New York: Urizen Books, 1977], p. 195).

30. This represents about one percent of the population. Private corporations having no more than twenty-one employees are permitted—mostly in the construction industry.

31. J. Michas and G. Udke, eds., *Socialistisches Recht* (Berlin: Verlag die Wirtschaft, 1980), especially pp. 7 – 14.

32. See Harold J. Berman, "What the Soviets Mean by Human Rights," *Worldview*, 22 (Nov. 1979), 15ff.

33. See Imre Szabo, *The Socialist Concept of Rights* (Budapest: Akademiai Kiado, 1966).

34. See E. Poppe, *Menschenrechte—eine Klassefrage* (Berlin: Staatsverlag, 1971); and H. Klenner, *Studien über die Grundrechte* (Berlin: Staatsverlag, 1964).

35. See Herta Kuhrig, ed., *Familie in Geschichte und Gegenwart* (Berlin: Dietz Verlag, 1978). This volume contains a sustained critique of Western theories of the family as represented by such theorists as Freud, Cooley, Goode, and Parsons.

36. Preface, The Family Law of the G.D.R., Dec. 20, 1965.

37. Ibid., Section 3, par. 2.

38. See Steele, *Inside East Germany,* Chapter 9.

39. Ibid.

40. Beeson, "German Democratic Republic," p. 167.

41. Unlike any other East European country, the G.D.R. has a provision for conscientious objection to "universal (male) military service." Objectors must undertake "alternate service," and often do so in these "diaconic centers."

42. Name of conversational partner withheld by request.

43. P. C. Ludz, *The Changing Party Elite in East Germany* (Cambridge, Mass.: MIT Press, 1971).

44. I got these figures from a seminary professor in 1980. The rate of youth participation is very difficult to estimate because of a conscious decision by the church to have youth organizations which are strictly based in the local church and have no membership lists. Previously such lists were used by the Nazis to attempt to take over youth organizations. See Solberg, *God and Caesar in East Germany,* p. 45.

45. Most of the text was translated by Solberg in *God and Caesar in East Germany.*

46. See K. Hertz, *Two Kingdoms and One World* (Minneapolis: Augsburg, 1976).

47. Conversation with G. Jacob, May 1973.

CHAPTER SIX

The Socialist Creed:
A Longitudinal Interpretation

MARXISM-LENINISM is clearly the dominant ideological force in East Germany. In its present form it owes its most immediate debts to the influence of the Soviet Union, which took control of what is now the German Democratic Republic at the end of World War II. In every official proclamation of the Party, overt and sometimes obsequious reference to the solidarity of the two governments is made, and fidelity to the Marxist-Leninist line of Moscow is overtly expressed. Of all the Communist countries of the world, perhaps no regime is more "orthodox."

The basic social orientation of Marxism is not at all foreign to Germany. In spite of a small, persecuted group of Communists who worked in Germany from the 1840s until the founding of the G.D.R., Marxism in its main outlines was exported from Germany in the nineteenth century and only reimported as a ruling philosophy at the end of World War II. It had a certain affinity with patterns of life and thought that existed in Germany for centuries. In the period of its exile, Marxism was revised in a specific political direction at the hands of Lenin. In his Bolshevik efforts he adapted it to a country ravaged by World War I, to a situation in which pluralistic democratic traditions, which Marx thought promising for Communism, were fragile at best, and to an economy which was more based on agriculture and peasantry than the already industrialized societies out of whose womb Marx expected socialism to develop. Lenin gave Marxism a centralized, disciplined political power-base by which Marx's expectations could be fulfilled. When this Leninized Marxism was reintroduced to Eastern Germany after World War II, it seemed highly pertinent to the devastated, semi-feudal economy with no coordinated political center after the defeat of Hitler.

At the other decisive level, that of doctrine, Marxism is a world view held with religious intensity. It finds its focus in a specific, human-centered creed that emerged out of a deep trajectory of continental intellectual and social developments. This creed represents the second great revolutionary tradition of modernity, born out of continuous confrontation with Catholicism, the Liberal-Puritan synthesis, modern Christian ecumenism, and non-Western cultures since the failure of the Council of Constance. The understandings of religion and of society are different in this tradition, and thus the definition of the nature and basis of human rights is quite distinctive. We shall focus on a longitudinal analysis of these deeper trajectories in this chapter.

A. REFORMATION AND RENAISSANCE IN GERMANY

At one stage it appeared that Germany might well go in the direction of the English Reformation, with its struggles for liberty through the clarification of a public theology and the creation of an independent, reformed church. Between the time of the Council of Constance (which had burned Huss and deposed the first Pope John XXIII) and the Reformation of Luther a century later, a vast array of small populist uprisings in the cities and among the peasants took place. Here it was a protest against the imposition of new duties by feudal lords; there it was the preservation of old "common law" privileges against the incursions of new "Roman" legal arrangements; elsewhere it was resistance to restrictions imposed by the traders of the free cities upon workmen. In almost every case religious reform was the central issue, although many of these movements were strongly tinged with ethnocentric nationalism as well as economic and political protest. In all of these sporadic uprisings there was a concerted movement against feudal authority on the land, ecclesiastical hierarchy in the church, and the privilege of "bourgeois confraternities" in the towns. The moves made by the workers and the peasants were of several kinds. First, like Huss, they insisted on full participation of laity in the Mass by the full sharing of bread and wine. This implied an antihierarchical mutuality, by equitable participation in sharing in the "staff of life," that had both theological and sociopolitical meanings. Second, many defined themselves as "covenanters," invoking an Old Testament motif of bonded membership and freedom from imperial political authority. Third, they appealed to a universal, divine law, taught by Moses and the prophets and by Jesus Christ in Holy Scripture, as the guide to both ecclesiastical practice and civil procedures. In affirming this they resisted the authority of tradition and reason represented by technical theology, and insisted on lay access to the Bible. Fourth, they accented the power of the Holy Spirit, which they saw appearing in the movements of "direct inspiration" among the people, as a primary locus of God's presence and a harbinger of social transformation. And fifth, on the basis of the above they protested economic exploitation in the forms of rents to absentee landlords, usury, and high taxes.[1] In most of these movements radical clergy such as the famous Thomas Müntzer were at the center, providing both the organizational skills and the ideological leadership, and "proving" by the "spiritual analysis" of Scripture that if ecclesiastical and political leaders did not obey "God's righteousness" and meet the needs of the people, they should be put to the sword by violent revolution.[2]

By 1525 this movement was crushed, systematically and brutally, in Germany. It was crushed in part by the Conservative Catholics, who became more intensely committed to traditional hierarchical society. More significantly for our purposes, it was crushed also by the Lutheran and Renaissance-oriented princes. For while the Lutheran and Renaissance thinkers brought with them decisive revolutions, they were not to be in the direction of human rights or a grassroots organization among the people. Meanwhile, what was left of the Peasants' Revolt went "underground" into the small, withdrawing conventicles of Anabaptist sectarianism—attempting to avoid contact with both the established churches and political power, and producing, within their communities, a work ethic and ecclesiastical discipline that approximated some aspects of the Liberal-Puritan synthesis in form and style.[3]

We can perhaps best see what the forces were which conspired to crush the peasants if we look briefly at the three great contending forces of Europe, which represent different resolutions of the religious, social, and political strife that was occurring on the Continent at this time. They are Luther, Machiavelli, and the Catholic Response (to be discussed in Section C). In the first two figures we can see how, for Germany, the failures of Constance bore fruit: internal faith became increasingly separated from outward reasoning in society; the "universal church" was more clearly broken into regional bodies; theology became more and more "confessional" and "fideist" (increasingly distinct from philosophy); and ecclesiological concerns became more and more separated from constructive legal and political theory.

Luther's turmoil was born out of a deep, inward personal experience, and focused the attention for much of modern religious thought on inward experience. He rebelled against the monastic life wherein he had hoped to work out that inner struggle. For a thousand years before the rise of scholasticism and the crises which led to Constance, many held that monastic life was the model par excellence of true piety and learning. It was the center of the church and the sacred arena for encounter with God—beyond the worldly cares of family, politics, and economics. In the Augustinian monastery to which he went, much of that older tradition was maintained.[4] Luther was deeply influenced by that tradition, yet even there he found that the striving for a higher, more complete fulfillment of the monastic ideal was impossible. It forced him not toward the joy and peace of God but into despair.

Luther came to believe that the presuppositions of monasticism were false. Monasticism presumed that humanity had at its core a basic goodness which by discipline and nurture could know and attain spirituality. The world of spirit, like the empirical feudal world, was constituted by a great chain of being. One could, through discipline and spiritual consciousness, climb the ladder toward God. Luther saw in monasticism a Pelagian element that did not take account of the radical evil at the depths of the will, perverting mind and heart.[5] At the core of our being is an evil so rooted that no one, even by the most intensive and rationalized discipline and effort, could dig it out or lift us out of it. Only the power of God's utterly irrational mercy and grace can "justify" us. In Jesus Christ that power is at hand as a free gift of grace from God, known by faith.

If this is true, reason cannot comprehend what is at stake. The authority of reason in theology has to be challenged. Humans are, to be sure, rational creatures in some respects, and we need to develop whatever rational possibilities we have; but finally the head is always in the employ of the inner disposition of the heart.[6] Only when that is purified can reason assume its proper role. Reason is the necessary handmaiden of human life, but it cannot lead. Thus law—all law which attempts to guide moral life by rational articulation of principles: the Torah, phariseeism ancient and modern, Roman law, monastic rule—is but empty legalisms. The law is "rationalistic"; it cannot guide or grasp the holy. It leads to exterior "works-righteousness," not to the transformation of the heart. It may serve as the exterior dike against the more grotesque public evils, but it does not touch the heart. Indeed, it drives one to the gospel. And those who insist on the law while denying the gospel are Christ-killers in their hearts. Luther saw in Judaism,[7] in the spirituality of the monastic idea, and in the Roman Church, as well as among the radical sectarians, an exterior concern for law and reason which betrayed all he had discovered—a new freedom of the will in direct obedience to God's grace, beyond legalism and "Aristotelian faith."[8]

There was another key set of issues in Luther's repudiation of monasticism. In it he saw a denial by organized religion of indigenous culture, of the family, and of the nation.[9] The rise of monasticism had brought about a spiritual subordination of "worldly language," family, and nation—salvation is not to be found in the worlds of vernacular, erotic affections, or political loyalty. Luther saw a negation in this subordination, a deprivation of the real meanings which people find in ordinary, earthy communication, family, and nationality. Further, since the real meaning of the gospel had to do with the inner heart and not with outer and worldly forms at all, participation in local culture and family and national identity had nothing to do with salvation. Indeed, marriage and patriotism might serve as proper barriers to worse evils so that the depths of the soul might be freed for the gospel, which is best understood in the native tongue.

These moves by Luther meant, in principle, a certain democratization of the gospel. First, no longer were the "higher" parts of faith to be worked out by those having a special monastic vocation. All people could grasp the points of grace and faith and work them out in the world—in German, in the family, and in the midst of the political economy. Second, it pointed to a powerful religious use of culture—especially art, music, and language. These became the vehicles of propagating the message to the masses. They were to be clearly and imaginatively employed in the vernacular so as to reach each soul. Third, it meant that the true church really is an *invisible* church. Only God knows what is in the heart.[10]

If the true church is not visible in the monastic orders, or anywhere else,

170

what happens? The family and the nation as visible centers of experienced authority become the realms for dealing with exterior, social matters. In one sense the logic of this position implies a return to certain features of Greco-Roman civilization, where life was dominated by family and *polis*. It is between these that the early church had long ago driven a wedge and founded a social space from which it proceeded to relativize the power of kinship and kingship. Luther developed his arguments on Germanic-feudal notions of human relations, not on Greco-Roman ones, but the power and authority of family and nation were reasserted. The visible church, in such cases, became a "territorial church"—a church primarily organized by and for families in a geographic-political region controlled by a prince. The primary purpose was speaking the gospel of grace and faith to the inner soul, while the paternalistic state and the authoritarian family dealt with external matters. The gospel, the family, and the state, of course, were understood to be mutually supportive.

We must recognize, of course, that not all this was planned by Luther in his initial break with the church. Much of it—especially the political side—was reinforced by the sheer force of necessity. When the Roman-controlled imperial troops marched in his direction, they threatened not only his person and doctrine but also the standing and privileges of the German princes. They defended him with the sword; he defended them with the Word. In the long run this orientation in "word" undercut the democratizing tendency of his gospel message. Many of the German peasants and artisans who had become increasingly restless as the newer legal and social systems further and further encroached upon their traditional modes of life—forcing them off the "commons" and binding them more tightly and more impersonally to authority—had taken up Luther's message with enthusiasm. Again and again they appealed to the learned doctor as a champion of the people. But when they attempted to act out that message—as many of the radicals did at that time—Luther revealed his true colors: he insisted that the radical doctrine he preached was only for the inner heart.[11] In this, Lutheranism much more nearly approximated the Eastern Orthodox and mystical strands of Christianity (and of evangelicalism everywhere) than those of Conciliar Catholicism, Calvinism, or Free-Church sectarianism in the West. In exterior matters this meant that the traditional structures of society and the traditional authority of rulers were to be obeyed. Insofar as Luther had a developed social theory, he held to the medieval notion of a hierarchical integration of groups in various vocations, all communally related in an organic social cosmos of order. These were the orders of creation which should rule everywhere. There were public matters, of course, that had to be decided; but they were to be handled by concrete analysis of the situation, by the technical rationality of philosophy and political prudence, and by the traditionally constituted authorities. They had nothing to do with the salvation of the soul.

It is the last point that makes Machiavelli so important for this discussion. Machiavelli was writing as Luther was undergoing his turmoil (and, as shall be important later, as Vasco da Gama was opening trade routes in India and Columbus was informing the world of America). Machiavelli set forth a view which had great influence on subsequent German intellectual development, and especially on political theories which led to the present "civic religion" of East Germany. For as Luther separated theology from the encumbrances, in his view, of philosophy and political-legal theory, Machiavelli freed philosophy and political-legal theory from theology. Metaphorically speaking, Machiavelli is tails to Luther's heads: both left their impression on the common coin of continental social spirituality.

Like Luther, Machiavelli had a sense of the evil in the human heart. He saw people driven by their interests as creatures willing to exploit the neighbor for gain.[12] He too saw religion as an inward matter and doubted that external observation was adequate for discerning the true state of inward meaning. Indeed, various claims about inward matters only led to contention, fanaticism, and division. The true church, if there was one, was indeed invisible. In contrast to Luther, however, Machiavelli held that it was the outward, not the inward, that makes the basic difference in life. As an advisor to princes, he saw that what counted in social life was the outward *appearance* of things. *That* had social and political consequences. Thus the wise, rational, and prudent prince would *appear* pious and ethical. He would do this in order to coordinate and integrate the loyalties of the population, to consolidate power for the political community, to build a genuine civic religion which, in contrast to the merely inner piety and esoteric ritual of Christianity, would cultivate proper respect for authority and the heroism of military valor on behalf of the *polis*.[13] The salvation of humanity in the concrete, objective world was to be found in political life, in civic virtue.[14]

Like Luther, Machiavelli distrusted the capacity of grand theory about universals to guide us. What could guide our behavior was not reason in the speculative and contemplative senses which some monks presumed would lead us to God, but practical, scientific reason known by observation. What works in experience is what counts. And what works in experience is the application of rational means to desired ends. The first thing that must be known in social-political life is what produces what and how to control the means-ends relationship.

Closely related to the focus on objective political salvation and mastery of technological reason is a distrust of law, which Machiavelli also shared with Luther. Law, he points out in *The Prince*, is legalistic. It binds us up; it prevents the dynamic movement of the concrete will in the context of political life; it inhibits expediency and is cumbersome. Law, to be sure, has a certain exterior usefulness. People respect it, and thus it is an instrument, a tool for political order. As Luther set aside the law for reasons of the heart, Machiavelli set aside the law for reasons of state. For Luther this guaranteed the freedom of the Christian unto salvation. For Machiavelli it secured the freedom of the sovereign to exercise the kind of prudent will which could save the body politic.

Machiavelli also shared with Luther the appreciation of the family and the state with a due respect for the hereditary elite, although in his context the state was the city-state, not the nation. (The fuller development of the idea of national sovereignty had to await the work of Bodin, a half-century after Machiavelli's death and thirty years after Luther's.) Indeed, he wrote to give advice to a "ruler family." It is this that becomes the center of loyalty and the agency of social salvation. It is this "ruler family" that was to seize and manipulate government to insure survival and success. Many commentators, of course, see Machiavelli as having utterly secularized life. In fact, he has relocated the sense of the holy, giving a new definition and center to holiness, to what is ultimately reliable (and in this anticipates Marxism-Leninism). What is truly sacred is political-economic community. Its medium is a technically and politically competent patriotism. It is focused on the sovereign will, not of God, but of those who have the best *interests* of the community in mind and on this basis marshall, control, and realistically exercise political power.

The Lutheran and Machiavellian responses to the intellectual and social crises of the late-medieval period articulate a major theme of continental thought which was to become decisive for subsequent European life. It represents a fundamental break between the inner and outer meanings of life, a break which the Conciliar Catholics and the Liberal-Puritan synthesis, and more recently some Neo-evangelicals and most Christian ecumenists, have tried to overcome. The second great Western trajectory of life and thought is essentially a struggle with the consequences of these twin orientations, symbolized by Lutheran evangelical orthodoxy and Machiavellian political "realism." In all "orthodox" evangelicalism since the Reformation, there has been a tendency on one side to so accent the inner, the spiritual, and the individual dispositions that the exterior, the material, and the sociopolitical dimensions of life are neglected. On the self-consciously religious side, the gospel is not preached to the whole person but to an abstracted self. In consequence, theology becomes separated from political reflection as a constitutive voice. God is seen as belonging to an utterly alien reality, which is "wholly other" to sociopolitical and legal life. Sociopolitical questions become a matter of national sovereignty, governed by technical calculations and worldly interests of state. On this side of the coin an empirically based "humanistic" philosophy and a strategy-centered analysis of history devoid of normative religious theory come to resist moralism and "perfectionism" in public matters. This entails a benign attitude toward purely inward accents in faith *so long as they remain absolutely private.* The consequence of this is that whenever Machiavellian, technocratic power holds sway over a given political region, it is often privatistic, evangelical faith that is tolerated; and often it is only the purely inner-evangelical faith that can find its way among the people. Evangelical "orthodoxy" is the complement of the absolute, rational state—not only by historical accident but by the fundamental logic of both positions.

The complementarity of evangelical orthodoxy and political absolut. n, however, remained unstable. It had a tendency toward dualism which, ultimately, both positions resisted. From the theological side the vision of one true God meant that at some level the dualism of inner and outer life had to be overcome. The Christian doctrine of incarnation resisted an absolute division between spirit and body. There could not be two truths, one for the inner self and one for the outer society, one for the spiritual realm and one for the material realm.[15] From the standpoint of political realism, the particular crises of community life, as in the repelling of outside invaders or the quelling of rebellion, demanded a fuller commitment than exterior, mechanical obedience. And the ideas which were preached and taught, no matter how focused on the inner self, had consequences for material well-being. In these situations loyalty and dedication to the salvation of, and to the salvific efficacy of, the body politic stood paramount. Political leaders needed the inner commitment, not only the outer functions, and wanted the souls, not only the bodies, of the population. If the collective body politic was the instrument of salvation, nothing short of absolute commitment would suffice, and specific movements for the common welfare were almost messianic in claim.

The immediate influence of Machiavelli's writings on the structures of German life is not clear. What is clear is that during the century after the Peace of Augsburg (1555), each prince was given the authority to decide which religion all the subjects were to adopt under the principle *cuius regio, eius religio*. The will of the ruling class was the determinant of piety. Not everyone was pleased. In 1618 war broke out again. Germany consisted of a great number of local princely or church-governed states and autonomous cities, often at war with one another over land and political-religious issues, an easy target for foreign powers. The Peace of Westphalia in 1648 fixed again the boundaries of these territories, and focused all social-political thought on the salvation of these particular communities by Machiavellian means.

Two aspects of this period are especially important for our topic. First, the cities further developed a system of rights for their members. Reinhard Bendix states the matter this way:

> To be the citizen of a hometown was a communal status granted by one's neighbors. It involved all aspects of life, not just one's civic status. And as it tied the individual to his neighbors through life, honor, and property, so it deepened separation from all outsiders. . . . "To be without citizenship meant to have no right to pursue a citizen's trade, usually no marriage and no right to an established home . . .!" [This created a *Burgerschaft* which] . . . used its powers of exclusion to maintain the status quo . . . [and produced a] cleavage between the patriciate and the artisan class. . . .[16]

Rights in Germany were privileges conferred by community action in the context of political identity. They did not pretend to be universal in derivation or significance. They were functional prerogatives intimately related to economic interests.

The second major aspect of this period was the power of personal, local rule. Many princes were attracted to Luther's doctrines, for whatever their intention they induced a strong inward sense of duty to arbitrary "Higher Power."[17] Frederick Wilhelm in East Prussia was able to use the piety of Lutheranism and the new techniques of military organization developed in the Thirty Years' War to develop the most integrated and disciplined of the German states. His Machiavellian efforts from above, supported by Lutheran piety from below, established the model for a number of significant and enduring patterns in German life. At stake is a highly individualized religion and a highly rationalized, collective political identity.

The history of many European movements in thought and social life that influenced Marx, Engels, and Lenin could be written in these terms. In each period of German history between the crushing of the Radical Reformation and the present, these are the terms in which life is understood. Attempts to overcome these dualisms mark the greatest moments of European religion and continental philosophy and politics.

B. PIETISM AND THE FRENCH REVOLUTION

Under the influence of the efforts by some English Puritans and a number of Dutch Evangelical Calvinists to develop a dynamic lay religiosity that could be effective in the community, Philipp Spener and, later, August Francke developed German Pietism on Lutheran grounds, adapting it to the intellectual and social situation of Lutheran orthodoxy and absolutist politics. The purpose was to cultivate a personal, ethical Christianity by Bible study, nurture of spiritual growth, and a direct, immediate love for the neighbor. As pointed out in the previous chapter, these movements broke the bonds of "pure" inwardness and began ministries in the interstices of the social-political system. Schools, orphanages, and dispensaries for the poor were founded, and a gathered group of committed laity were brought into fuller positions of authority and leadership in the established churches. An elaborate system of diaconal service was developed as lay Christians formed Lutheran "orders" for service, living among and caring for those caught in the cracks of the social system. Over time this movement was to give impetus to the "Innere Mission" and was to provide many of the models for the "welfare" policies of Bismarck. As Pietism was becoming a force among the people, Hobbes' reaction against the Puritan revolution was having a wide impact on all continental political theorists. This heir of Machiavelli[18] radically accented the notion of state sovereignty as the locus for the material preservation and bodily salvation through communal solidarity, and severely stated the critique of all intermediary groups. In Prussia the notions of sovereignty were quickly taken up by Frederick I, who, significantly, crowned himself king in 1701.[19]

Frederick I assumed absolute control over all areas of social life and founded the "benevolent despotism" that was to last until the French Revolution. He founded the University of Halle in concert with Lutheran Pietist scholars, and established the Academy of Science, at government expense, to improve the technological development of the country. He reaffirmed traditional governmental control of the arts and the sciences while simultaneously subsidizing their rapid development. His successor, Frederick Wilhelm I, shared little love for the trappings of royalty but marshaled his considerable administrative skills to rebuild the treasury and to reform the army, the courts, and the structure of civil service in such a way that all the lines of an increasingly efficient bureaucracy ran up to him. Frederick the Great followed him, and he too followed in the steps of Machiavelli and Hobbes in his practice, which was modified by his fundamental dependence on the agriculturally based aristocracy called the Junkers, a residue of feudal arrangements. Frederick the Great, himself a Renaissance humanist of considerable accomplishment who believed that each soul had to go to heaven in its own way, increased religious toleration. Further, he solidified his alliance with the local feudal aristocracy by draining swamps, rebuilding villages, and granting monopolies, while obtaining from the Junkers both taxes and the leadership for local militia of trained peasants to secure borders while he was involved in expanding the empire, thereby consolidating bureaucratic and traditional authority. The efficient and formidable, if rigid, social system prevented any efforts among the people to develop structures for self-government, but allowed Prussia to become one of the leading European powers. In this the orthodox and pietistic evangelicalisms of the church were welcome allies, cultivating the virtues of hard work in one's pregiven vocation, personal love in interpersonal relations, and obedience to established authority. Indeed, Frederick the Great viewed even the different ecclesiastical traditions as troublesome. He demanded that Lutheran and Calvinist churches in Prussia be united, and at one point tried to appoint himself as papal vicar over Silesia. However, because of his learning and piety, as well as his military and political genius, Frederick the Great was very aware of the dangers of his own moves and of the perils of a purely Machiavellian approach to social order. In 1745 he wrote a fascinating and revealing study, *N. Machiavelo Regieriengskunst eines Fursten*. The ideas in this book were fleshed out even more thoroughly in his more pious *Political Testament* of 1752. In both he defends his view that his military and political expansionism was not a Machiavellian move but an attempt to re-establish an integration of civil order so as to allow a society in which the freedom of purely personal inner spiritual life and the "right order" of rational, hierarchical outer life could be realized. The sovereign does and must rule over the other classes, but the sovereign is also accountable to universal natural law for the welfare of all other classes. From this basic conviction Frederick the Great set about the task of expanding industry, rationalizing agriculture and commerce, cultivating the arts, extending education, reforming the law, and establishing the administrative bureaucracies in all these areas, dominated by the new "middle classes" and with lines of authority all leading to the sovereign party. Here a pattern was established, one characteristic of an aspect of German social life from that time, through Bismarck's "welfare state" of the nineteenth century, until the present. It is the paradigm of public "enlightened absolutism" with tolerance for any purely "irrational," personal interest—such as religion.

Meanwhile, in France and England new movements of thought were developing which challenged the very foundations of an intuitive, purely inward religion linked with the "reason" of objective political arrangement.

In England this possible direction of the Reformation had been mitigated by the Liberal-Puritan public theology and covenantal social thought, giving rise to fresh definitions of human rights, parliamentary democracy under law, and the limited state, as well as to new theories of the corporation influential for the Industrial Revolution.

In France, however, the response to the breakdown of the Council of Constance and to the Renaissance and the Reformation led in quite different directions. France became increasingly tied to Spain (in the Peace of 1559), where the Conservative Catholics were the strongest. There the Inquisition was in full force against intellectuals and Protestants, and a pronounced devotion to the sacraments was a decisive mark of true Christianity among the simple people. France also was deeply influenced by the Council of Trent, which was held in the middle of this century and which attempted, without success, to re-establish the unity and reform of the church attempted long ago at Constance. This time the perceived threat came from Luther and Calvin, who were seen as heirs of Huss. Some Conciliar Catholics were optimistic at the start of this council, and pressed for an open rapprochement with the Protestants. Indeed, in 1551 Protestant delegates came to the council, but their demand that the council be declared superior in authority to the pope was dismissed by the majority. In this council a specifically Roman-centered, patriarchal Catholicism, what I have called Conservative Catholicism, was victorious. The primary characteristic of this form of Christianity was the claim of absolute, centralized authority in all religious matters and the willingness to use political authority to enforce conformity. In France the nobility was deeply concerned about the efforts to evangelize the peasants to Lutheranism and the growth of Calvinism among the urban leaders and intellectuals. Both threatened the fragile harmony of the regime. In long and complex struggles, Conservative Catholicism and royal authority managed jointly to put down the threat. By 1600 and throughout the next century, the sovereign was absolute. And by the early 1700s Louis XIV was able to grant or revoke "rights" at will; all rights were civil rights and existed at the behest of the sovereign. But at several points the Church in Rome allied itself with the enemies of France, making the old coalition unstable.

Meanwhile, other ideas were being imported into France. Ideas about the "individual" and about "social contract" from Machiavelli, Hobbes, Pufendorf, Grotius, and Locke were circulating among the intellectuals, as they tried to figure out the true origin and nature of social life.[20] Clearly an absolute, arbitrary rule by a single figure, such as Louis XIV in the state or a foreign power, such as the pope in the church, had not been able to assure justice or peace.

No single figure better grasped the precariousness of the situation or gave a stronger answer to it than Jean Jacques Rousseau. Scholars debate the degree of influence he had on the French Revolution. Some consider it to be quite minimal, but few dispute the idea that Rousseau expressed concerns which were central to the Revolution. The central problem, as he saw it, was how to reconcile the primal freedom of the individual—the inner essence of humanity—and social-political authority, so necessary for unified national life, while overcoming the arrogant presumptions of authority and privilege assumed by royal families and high-ranking clergy. Rousseau specifically reacted against Calvinism (he had spent some of his earlier years in Geneva), and he borrowed from Hobbes and from the liberal, deistic theorists of England who had developed an economic contract theory. Rousseau, however, gave the contract theory a specific thrust that led him into the Machiavellian "realistic" directions of a totally "secular" political community. The contractual relations which he accented in his famous *Du contrat social* were not in the first place economic agreement between private persons to form mutually advantageous exchanges. That "English model," in Rousseau's view, led to all sorts of alienating relations between "master" and "slave" whereby the freedom of the poor and weak was exchanged for the bread and protection of the other. It led to unequal dominance by the few.[21] Instead, contractual agreements were to be by individuals *with the whole of society*. Thereby was constituted the political or *civil community*, which would be the *inner* fabric of the state. Thus the state became nothing other than the *formal* structure representing the whole collection of citizens, and not some party or group given the task of governing by traditional authority. Humanity, viewed as a series of individuals, was in effect contracting with itself to create a unity, a total community. This new creation had no real existence separate from the individuals who constituted it. Thus it was not the "will of the prince" which was sovereign; the "will of the people" became the princely power. "The whole community" was the moral equal of "individuals" understood as a total unity, acting by a single motive power. In this a nation could find its integration and salvation.

In forming this contract, humanity does two things. First, it regains its essential liberty, its autonomous right to determine itself against all the artifacts which historic civilizations and superstitious religions have engendered as heteronomous powers over individuals and nations. Second, it integrates the primal and inward human nature with public political and economic structures by constructing a civil state into an almost mystical union. Further, by giving over freedom and property to the civil state, we gain genuine equality, for each is in the same relationship to the whole. Thus it is in the interest of each to overcome all private preserves of privilege and interest. Each self becomes an indivisible part of the whole, and each will thus find that general altruism is the best guardian of the self.

The guide to this altruism is the "general will"—the direction of the affections and the interests to the whole. It gains expression in the sovereignty of the whole by issuing laws through the mechanism of government. Laws, indeed, are the public articulation of the general will arrived at through collective procedure. Law is made by government and directed toward the shaping of a community that can overcome private wills and private interests. Law is not discerned or discovered; it is not rooted in universal first principles. Law and all principles of right and rights are constructed as human artifacts. One knows, indeed, the legitimacy of a particular law when one knows whether or not it reflects the general will and gathers into itself the affections and interests of the majority who best speak for the whole community. Thus law has a moral character, but one invested by the autonomous will of people acting in concert. Morality is not something that can stand over or against the general will. Classical understandings of "natural law" or "divine law" are thus turned on their heads. Indeed, minorities who oppose a law rooted in the general will cannot lay claim to the law. They must obey the government which represents, in a formal way, the will of the majority. Minorities are, as it were, "forced to be free"[22] by being forced to conform to the law which expresses the general will and therefore the true interests of all parts of the whole. *That* is what is "natural" and, indeed, "divine." It is not so much that the majority, merely by the fact of its power, can arbitrarily decide anything that it wants. That would simply mean "might makes right," a position Rousseau vigorously opposed. It is rather that in commitment to the "general will" the ground is laid for relevant discussion and clarification of our true interests. That is what "scientific" means. The public—or most of it—will come to discern what it is in fact that they really want, what is actually in their general interest, and what in fact best serves the interest of each member, if they have this solidarity. In this way the general will is rationally clarified and the will of the majority becomes rationally stated in positive law. On this basis citizens can establish definitions of "civil rights" beyond which there may be no appeal.

The chief enemy of this view is organized religion. In this the revolutionary power of Rousseau's ideas became most overt. On the one hand, religion holds that there is another order of reality beyond the human empirical one which can be used to judge the empirical human order. On the other hand, in organized religion, whether represented in the predominant Catholic traditions which asserted absolutism from the top, comprehending all other associations, or in the Liberal-Reformed traditions which focused on the importance of concrete mediating institutions between the individual and the whole—especially the church but also the family, the university, and the collegium of professionals[23] —groups were held as particular realities *beyond* the domain of the state. In these several views society was an association of associations, each possessing a kind of sovereignty that could not be suppressed by individual wills or by the will of the political community as a whole. That is the problem for Rousseau. Such pluralism fails to bring wholeness. Worse still, Christianity looked beyond nations to universal humanity. However nationalized any specific religious tradition, Jewish and Christian traditions maintain something of a transnational—

indeed, an otherworldly—element that is always a threat to the civil state. For Rousseau it was precisely these features that had enslaved humanity on the one hand and given license to foreign intervention on the other. Thus he argues in *Du contrat social* that no "partial society," especially one which is in league with foreign powers, should be allowed to exist. Such factors corrupt and undercut the general will and draw humanity into bondage, alienation, and privilege. They dissipate dedication to national unity. Precisely what is required is a permanent revolution by which the people of a nation reclaim the primal nature of their liberty, equality, and fraternity by dissolving everything that stands between or beyond the integration of the individual and the general will.[24]

The inner commitment to this permanent "humanist" revolution, says Rousseau, is to be cultivated by a "civic religion," a term which Saint Augustine had attributed to Varro, the Roman poet who eulogized Caesar's exploits. Rousseau develops the idea more extensively than any other figure prior to its usage by twentieth-century American liberals who, like Rousseau, broke with the quest for a public theology in favor of an individualism linked with a progressive, activist political program based on common social experience and developed a new interest in "civil religion." The reason a civic religion is needed is functional. It shapes opinion, it penetrates to the souls of persons, and it bends the individual will away from egoism and toward an attitude conducive to the general will. In Rousseau's view a specifically civic religion is to be cultivated by the issuance of general dogmas, subscribed to by all, inculcated by public education, and controlled by the "censor." The school promotes genuinely social attitudes; the censor controls antisocial ones. The function of both is to shape opinion in forming the general will.

It is precisely these ideas that were lifted up in the French Revolution. Here a new synthesis of the inner-personal life and the outward political life, overcoming the stale artifacts of tradition and undercutting the basis of the ancient regime, came to a highly practical expression. Heads rolled with the swish of the guillotine, and social institutions long sanctioned by conciliar theory of the relationships of groups and estates, as well as the holy water of Conservative Catholicism, were transformed. Here was the basis for a new, purifying "antireligious" doctrine that could be practiced with "religious" zeal. New idols to reason were set in Notre Dame. All of Europe was shaken by the echoes of this movement.

Not all went as planned. It did not seem to be the general will that emerged but the will of specific groups who were organized. The Declaration of the Rights of Man was issued, but it supported the political power of the emerging bourgeoisie more than the interests of the whole people. Unlike the Liberal-Puritan alliance in England, which gave guidance to the middle classes, demanding that they see themselves under a universal moral law and the watchful eye of a just and wrathful God, the civic religion of the French Revolution gave license to whoever could capture the instruments of government. When Napoleon was able to do that better than others, he became ruler, lawgiver, emblem of the general will, the consolidator of private interest and body politic. The hopes of Machiavelli and Hobbes seemed to have been fulfilled; the impact was enormous.

C. A BRIEF EXCURSUS: CATHOLIC RESPONSES

The impact of these ideas is important for understanding the reactions of the Catholic Church against "democracy" and "human rights" for several centuries. It is also important to understand why Europeans seldom turn to organized religion when human rights questions come up. From the rise of Luther until the papacy of Leo XIII (1878–1903), the history of Catholicism was resistance to "modernity," especially in the areas of social thought. The church was challenged from two sides. On one side the challenge was spiritually and ecclesiastically made by the Lutheran accent on personal inwardness rather than "objective" sacrament and doctrine, and the exterior reliance on national or regional political authority rather than on the organized, "universal" church. From the side of social and political theory, the Renaissance ideas of Machiavelli seemed to be actualized by the French Revolution, with its vicious attack on the church, the clergy, and Christian doctrine. On both sides the church saw tendencies toward a libertinism in which all basic values and social forms were seen as nothing more than a creation of the human will. Life was to be governed simply by voluntary choice. To give coherence to life, both movements authorized absolute political authority—one embodied in the prince, the other embodied in a diffuse "general will" which was to be sovereign in all things, including a fabricated religion. Indeed, the power of the political sovereign extended to things spiritual as well. The settlement of the Peace of Augsburg (1555) had established the principle that the religion of a territory should be determined by the prince of the region in Germany. And when the secular, rationalistic religion of the French Revolution came along, it appeared once more that religion was to be a disposable item according to the will of a regime.[25]

Throughout this period the Catholic Church had little contact with Calvinistic notions. Switzerland was isolated, Holland was small, New England was remote, and the English church had already broken with Rome over other matters. Hence the fundamental understanding of Protestantism was "Lutheranism," or the radical sects; the basic perception of democracy was the terror of the French Revolution, which the Lutherans, with a traditional loyalty to traditional worldly authority in political matters, also resisted.

When economic theories began to develop with vigor in the eighteenth and nineteenth centuries, they appeared either as utilitarian liberalism or Marxism—both equally atheistic to Catholic eyes, both radically voluntaristic, and both critical of any attempts to speak of universal moral laws. Neither "modern" economic theory had a definition of humanity as rooted in the image of God or related to basic intermediary institutions such as church and family. Instead, the utilitarian liberals celebrated individual autonomy while the Marxists critiqued individual autonomy as a form of alienation and called for a new communality of autonomous humanity as a "species being." The former appeared to subject humanity, in the wonders of freedom, to the dehumanizing greed of the competitive market; the latter appeared to make humanity the instrument of a violent, revolutionary collectivity. In these movements Rome saw but the rehearsal of Lutheran subjectivity and French Revolutionary "totalitarian democracy," even if Lutheran social thought was quite traditional and the theorists of the French Revolution had a place for individual will.

As David Hollenbach has shown in his superb book, *Claims in Conflict,* it was not until the social encyclical *Rerum Novarum* of 1891 that the Catholic Church was able to re-enter the mainstream of Christian commentary on human rights and re-engage the central motifs of modernity, and then only with ambivalence and reservation.

We must return, however, to the other European responses to the French Revolution. Lutheranism and Catholicism, the dominant religious forces, were unable to respond constructively—Lutheranism because such matters were "exterior" and not related to the gospel, Catholicism because it was forced into a defensive position. Philosophy, not theology, had to take up the hard questions; the ideology of political power and party, not the covenants of churches and other "sacred" associations, became the forum for creed and the context of "salvation." The result was "civic religion" in philosophical and political, ideological form.

D. IDEALISM AND HUMAN AUTONOMY

In Germany the response was very complex. Frederick the Great, who was in constant contact with the French Enlightenment philosophers and host to several at his summer castle, Sans Souci, knew that fundamental changes were on the horizon. He began legal reform as the first major step, calling for the drafting of a new code of law which would embody the ideas articulated by Rousseau but adapted to Prussian conditions. The code, the Allgemeine Preussische Landrecht, was not completed by the time of his death, but it was concluded and promulgated by his successor, Frederick Wilhelm II, in 1794. It contains many of the provisions for "individual rights" which had been stated in the French Declaration of the Rights of Man in 1791, but it also contains a corporate, collective view of the whole society in which the state is coterminous with the general will and welfare of all members. Alexis de Tocqueville wrote of this code:

> [In spite of its reliance on views of individual liberties at several points], ... more than half [of this work] was borrowed from the Middle Ages, [with] ... provisions whose spirit borders on socialism. Thus it is declared that it devolves on the state to provide food, work and wages for all who

cannot support themselves. . . . The state is bound to provide establishments for relieving the poor. It is authorized to abolish establishments which tend to encourage idleness, and to distribute personally to the poor the money by which these establishments were supported.[26]

This code also abolished the relative autonomy of various estates. No particular group—peasant, burgher, or even nobility—had its own continuing organization.[27] Only the Jews were given special status—a disadvantaged one—until late in the nineteenth century, for this society was viewed as a "Christian State." Indeed, clergy were paid entirely by state taxes. In little more than a decade, even the status of the family as an organization independent of the nation was challenged.

In 1808 Johann Gottlieb Fichte delivered his famous "Addresses to the German Nation." It was a central thesis of these lectures that Prussian weakness in the face of the French Revolution and the rise of Napoleon were due to the selfishness of the German people. To overcome this, nothing was more important than the development of a new national identity by reconstruction of the school system. Children were to be removed from the control of their families and placed in a system of unified educational institutions. Fichte developed a vision of "state socialism" in all of education, one endorsed at the university level by the prestigious Wilhelm von Humboldt. Education in both school and university was to develop secular, technologically competent, and committed citizens able to cultivate their own abilities to the fullest and yet dedicated to the values of the state—which would have a monopoly on culture and education. As H. W. Koch points out, these are also the patterns which were eventually adopted in the Soviet Union and other Eastern European countries influenced by the vision of the redemptive, enlightened French Revolution.[28] One critical difference remained, however. Christian clergy—often the most educated persons in a village—were given the responsibility to supervise the local educational system. This system supplemented their income, accented the learning of the clergy, and bound them more closely to the state bureaucracy.

The tensions between the notions of "individual freedom" and "social solidarity" were never fully integrated in either the Prussian judicial code or the educational system. The tensions represented the persistent dilemma in continental thought and German life specifically since Machiavelli and Luther. The problems were so pervasive and complex that they became the central focus of German philosophy.

In this regard two philosophical developments are of direct importance to the formation of contemporary Marxist society and ideology. The two philosophers who triggered these developments are Kant and Hegel. Kant, who wrote while Frederick the Great ruled and the French Revolution was in full swing, represents the response, in philosophical terms, of the Evangelical-Pietistic side of Lutheran Germany struggling with the new humanism that both empiricist philosophy and the French Revolution seemed to imply. Hegel represents the political-philosophical side of this same crisis. Each thinker, of course, is enormously subtle, and we will lift from their thought only certain key motifs that became decisive for Marx.

By the French Revolution and the fall of Germany to Napoleon, as much as by David Hume (who had given Rousseau a place to live when he was in exile), European thought was plunged into chaos. Immanuel Kant, the greatest figure of the continental enlightenment, responded to Rousseau and Hume. Both—one on political grounds, the other on epistemological grounds—had raised the radical question as to whether there was any objective, knowable order of things to give guidance in thought and life. Without that, both science and political ethics seemed impossible. Everything seemed destined to dissolve into arbitrary will, arbitrary power, and chaos.

Kant did for the Continent what Locke had done for the Anglo-American traditions. Out of a profound skepticism he set forth a powerful argument for a principled liberalism. But he differed from Locke in that he saw the principles as entirely dependent on the internal structure of the human mind. In a "purely rational" fashion he took up the challenge from nominalism, mediated through both the religious traditions of Lutheran Pietism and the political theory of the medieval nominalists, that universals in the objective sense could not be known. There is a split between subjective knowledge, which seems so particular and immediate, and the world outside the mind. It is an enormous gap, a distance as great as that between the stargazer and the heavens above. Yet, Kant argued, internal to the observer are certain logical and necessary structures of mind which, if we but turn the light of critical thinking on them, allow us to grasp the relations between things and to construct scientific judgments about them. By spelling these out, we can arrive at "enlightenment," and thus at a reliable science from within, even if we are still removed from any objective order.

If this is possible in science, surely it is also possible in practical matters— in ethics. Here, however, it is less a question of knowing what *is* than of knowing what is *good*. This is especially a problem if everything seems to center in the will. But Kant saw in the problem the clue to the answer. He writes: "Nothing in the world—indeed nothing even beyond the world—can possibly be conceived which could be called good without qualification, except a good will."[29] In solid, nominalist, Lutheran and Pietist fashion, and in concert with the individualism of the contractualists, Kant focused attention on radical inwardness. The good is intrinsically good, whatever other experience a person has and whether or not it accomplishes its intentions. External matters do not count. But Kant proceeds further. He argues that everybody knows this. It does not need to be taught to people but only to be brought into the light—by enlightenment. People have been looking in the wrong places for morality—in society, in the cosmos, or in the empirical calculation of consequences. What is needed instead is to focus the spotlight of reflection on the human self, understood as will.

When we focus on the will, we find two things: structure and freedom. The good will does what it ought, and it can do this because it has an internal principle. We call it "duty," and we know it by reason. The good will is one that bends itself to duty, known by the internal principle of reason. This internal principle is as universal as the will itself, and hence "universalizability" becomes the test of its genuine reasonableness. We ought to do those things which everybody knows in the heart would be reasonable for everyone, always, to do.

Whether people in real life actually do the good is irrelevant. The question is whether there is, in principle, something to guide the will. Kant was concerned about how we know that principle. Whether we do what is good or not is another question. In another essay he suggests that we may in fact be a race of devils.[30] But that is not the point. We know how far we are from morality precisely because we have, in the very structure of the subjective will, universal principles of the good, knowable by reason.

We not only find structure in the will; we find freedom. The will is that which chooses. There is the universal, rational principle by which we ought to choose, but there is still the choice itself. If choices are imposed from without, the will becomes bent to what is not its own, and the self is governed by "heteronomy," something that is not intrinsic to our nature. However, if the will chooses that which is internal to itself, it both gains the freedom of "autonomy"—of self-rule—and a pattern of moral order. We act in concert with our own nature. Freedom means the acting out of one's internal resources, the core of which is the rational will.[31]

The implications of this are several. First, Kant supplied the philosophical basis for a genuinely "human" moral guidance-system which was lacking in the earlier Protestant and Renaissance strands from Luther and Machiavelli through the Pietists and Rousseau. Second, he provided a way of linking liberty and authority by placing both squarely in the heart and mind of the individual. Political arrangements by implication are but an expression of rational human will; properly structured, they have as their chief function the preservation of human autonomy. And third, he provided the basis for a new interpretation of religion. Religion, at least traditional Christianity in its claims about God's being, eternal truths, and revelations, is not so much false as misstated. Religion is, in fact, veiled human morality. When it is authentic, it is compatible with the structure and freedom of the good will; when it is false, it claims more about "objective" reality than can possibly be sustained and becomes "heteronomous," imposing something alien on human inwardness. We begin to treat each other, and ourselves, as means, not ends—as the source and norm of value. This latter set of motifs gave impetus to the Ludwig Feuerbach's views, from which Marx drew many of his interpretations of religion. Religion is projected anthropology. Autonomous human will, rationally understood, is the center of value, the locus of the holy.

Hegel, the most important philosopher in the university of which Fichte was chancellor, was dissatisfied with Kant's solution. It seemed to focus on the individual separated from, abstracted from, history and society. And the logic, the reason to which Kant appealed seemed divorced from empirical reality. The polarities of the personal-social and the ideal-real seemed still unbridged.

Hegel recognized that both philosophy and religion in Germany had tended to produce tension, contradiction, and separation. Spirit was separated from nature, and the moral self from the world's historical process. He wanted to overcome these and find the basis of genuine integration, of actual unity. This he attempted in his famous "dialectic," in which he saw opposites entering into one another and reshaping each other in a new synthesis. The logic one could find in the mind was not the logic of a constant order, as Kant had claimed, but a dynamic logic of action and reaction, penetration and transformation, thesis, antithesis, and synthesis. The mind not only reflects on nature, discovering in its own character the structures necessary to interpret it; the mind is actively reflected in nature. Not only does the self finds its inner logic within itself, but it transcends subjectivity and finds its fuller career in interaction with others. Thus the logic of the mind and of the self must be understood in the realm of the objective order, a world of cosmos as well as mythos, a world of social-institutional order as well as personality wherein the ideals can become incarnate.[32]

In working out his vast and complex philosophy, Hegel restored to priority many of the issues of social life that had been swept aside by Machiavelli, Hobbes, and the British contract theorists, and that were, for the most part, neglected by Luther, the Pietists, and Kant, although the vision he sets forth sounds remarkably like the Pietist-Prussian society.[33] The inner moral spirit, he argues, in an amplified echo of Rousseau, has to find embodiment, and it does so in property, family, civic community, and state. The human spirit which creates these makes them absolute. Property makes objective the personal, individual will. In marriage the self finds fuller self-realization in the ethical union of mutuality, each completely identified with the other, and each shares property with the other. The family naturally grows into a clan and a people, expanding the self to a personal other, eventually to create a civic community. The civic community organizes life between the family and the state by establishing an economic system, by developing a structure for the administration of justice, and by supporting corporation and guild. These create rights. But the spirit behind all of these comes to greatest fruition in the state—"the actually existing, realized moral life. . . . All the worth which the human being possesses—all spiritual reality, he possesses only through the state. . . . The state is the Divine Idea as it exists on earth."[34] Civic religion is supreme.

So here we have it. The Luther-Machiavelli division of inner and outer, shaped by the rise of the Pietist-Prussian state, the absolutisms that led to Rousseau and the French Revolution, and the philosophical celebration of individualism and then statism in Germany constitute the line that stretches from the failure of the Council of Constance to the immediate precursors of Marx. Rights are what human will decides on rational grounds. This is the line of giants on whose backs Marx works to form the second great revolutionary tradition of the West—now heard around the world. The Hegelian synthesis itself had not been fully stable, of course. Almost immediately it was cracked open as Kierkegaard applied, with great brilliance, the logic of Hegel—not to the world-historical process as did Marx but to the inner life of the self in a characteristic Lutheran and Pietist way. Yet apologists for political absolutism, both Prussian and, subsequently, Nazi, tried to use Hegel to sanctify state power.

E. MARX'S "CIVIC RELIGION" AND THE CRITIQUE OF HUMAN RIGHTS

Marx, drawing explicitly on many of the figures here treated, gave Hegel a new turn. Marx believed that these figures were all influential in breaking the ideological masks of feudal power and establishing a new mode of social existence. Each contributed to the shattering of old chains in thought and political life. According to Marx, however, none of these fully realized how they were simultaneously forging new chains, the oppressions of bourgeois society. They failed for three essential reasons. First, and on one side, they all accented the "abstract self." They all in various measures presumed the primal reality of the inner heart, personal affections, private will, inner moral law, or the individual personality of ruler or citizen. Marx argued, in contrast, that humanity is not individuality first; humanity is a "species being." Individual, inner existence is a product of social interactions without which the self has no existence. Viewing humanity as "individuals" was a result of an alienated state of society.[35] Second, previous theorists failed because they focused questions of public authority on the state. However, the state is not some pre-existent entity but a specific creation of the constellations of power in a particular environment. Besides, the state is always rooted in a specific territory. But humanity, as a species being, is not confined by such political geography. There is a universalism in humanity which no state can contain. To attempt to establish such a state is imperialism. Every particular state and its laws tell us who won in the most recent struggles, not what human life really is in its fundamental structures. A specific state may, indeed, be the enemy of human society.[36] And third, all these thinkers presumed that ideas—theological and philosophical ideas, political theory, declarations about the rights of man, the innate principles of the mind, the logic of spirit becoming incarnate in history—can and do make the fundamental difference in life. In fact, they do not, according to Marx. History, life, and thought work from the bottom up, not from the top down. It is fundamental human need that gives rise to the will and focuses energy. More than anything else, concrete, material, human action to meet needs shapes our identity, our communities, and our ideas. "Production" (and its forms) determines relationships; relationships determine ideas. Precisely because this is misunderstood, argues Marx, every one of these great transformations of thought, although they shattered the more mystifying ideas of religion, ethics, and feudalism, became a mask for very earthy interests.[37] Did not the radical accent on "the personal" actually support the interests of private property in France and Prussia? And did not the apologies

187

for political community become the legitimizing canopy to hide the dominance of the new bourgeoisie over the workers and peasants? And do not this personalism and this patriotic statism contain within themselves lies about their own character which prevent both persons and nations from recognizing the true character of their life? Do they not dehumanize?

Marx believed these things. The continued flourishing of both more explorations of inwardness and thrusts toward imperial nationalism seemed to confirm his views.

More and more workers became alienated from the communal tissues of life by a capitalism sustained ideologically by individualism, "idealism," and statism. But true to the dialectical cunning of history, which Hegel had correctly recognized, Marx held that these very movements were producing a new class which had no "personalism" to defend, no private property to protect, and no state which represented their interests. Further, they found the intricate philosophies and spiritualities designed to protect and enhance the state, "privacy," and inwardness irrelevant to their very material needs. These movements were producing a class that had no use for patriotism, for they were the cannon fodder of aggrandizing adventures. This new class had no need for the illusions of religion or idealistic philosophy. They could, because they had to, see things directly, clearly, realistically. This new class was free to be "more scientific" than the "scientisms" of humane and kindly social thoughts with objective detachment.[38] The realities of the situation thus purified their wills and their minds; and for the first time in human history, the social basis was formed for a truly empirical, scientific, unencumbered human will that could seize control of its own destiny. True autonomy was on the horizon. It was a species-wide autonomy, found in solidarity with this new class. The workers of the world could unite, throw off their chains, and fulfill the universal, dialectical, world-historical process of constructing a genuine humanity.[39] For these reasons, according to Marx, all previous history and philosophy is but prologue. Discontinuity, not continuity, is the reality of the present. Nothing which has been done or thought in the past counts, except as forecast. Here is the foundation of a messianic revolutionary humanism that could overcome the historic misalliance of Jewish, Christian, or idealistic speculation and nationalism. A "substitute church," a new redemptive community, the proletariat, could find a point of integration in the rational will of a new, socialist "civic religion."[40] What was holy above all else was the purified, absolutely autonomous company of the committed, united by their real interests, dealing concretely and scientifically with the actual processes of meeting concrete human need, beyond any constraint of universal moral law derived from "nature" or God.

The implications of these views for human rights are quite specific. Marx himself deals with human rights extensively only in one context, and that is in the context of a discussion of religion. Although there are a few other scattered and passing references,[41] it is in the early essay "On the Jewish Question" that we find the most sustained perspective to which he returns time and time again in later work.

Bruno Bauer, a fellow radical Hegelian, had published the article "The Jewish Question" just as Marx had completed a summer of study on France and America. The Jews were petitioning for greater emancipation in view of the inferior status they had in German society as codified since the Allgemeine Preussische Landrecht. Marx used his response to Bauer as an occasion to speak to the German situation more generally, to lay out his developing theories of the relation of religion and society against the "idealism" of Hegelian thought, and to refute both American and French understandings of human and civil rights. Bauer had argued that because Jews—and Christians, for that matter—held to specific and concrete claims about revelation and faith, above and beyond all reason, no state should grant specific privileges or rights to them. How could a rational, enlightened state deal with such special claims? The state could deal only with universal, rational human rights. Jews as Jews and Christians as Christians could make no general claim. In fact, Christianity itself should not be state-supported. Religious groupings themselves had to be overcome first; only then could a liberal, secular, philosophically guided state grant rights to all on an equal basis.[42]

Marx responded by endorsing Bauer's critique of the Christian state, but he sharply criticized the political order and allowing freedom of religion in civil society. Indeed, a state may break free from the constraints of religion, but members of the state might still be in private bondage to it, still living an alienated existence. Religion in this case is no longer the basis for the deficiencies of the political order, but it still remains as the symptom of a deeper defect. Such was the case, Marx argued, in America, where the political sphere was emancipated from religion but religion flourished. Religion is not the spirit of the *state* but reflects the fragmentation and privatization of *society*, as can also be seen in the arena of private property. Ownership of property is no longer involved in qualifying a person for voting, but this freedom of the *political sphere* from economic privilege in an official sense does not mean that the power of property is undercut. Indeed, in the *society* at large it flourishes even more. In both religion and property arrangements, differentiation, division, and conflict are intensified. They become expressions of the fact that persons are separated from the community. Thus vigorous, pluralistic religion in society, even with a "secular state," represents the decomposition of humanity.[43]

Insofar as Christianity accents the sovereignty of the individual soul, political democracy can, says Marx, be called Christian. In passages that recapitulate the dualism of Luther and Machiavelli, however, Marx argues that it is an individuality lost to itself precisely because it is an individuality cut off from society.[44] Hence a purely secular state appears as an alien, objective, atheistic "other." In contrast, the "Christian State"—such as that of the Pietist-Prussian alliance celebrated by Hegel—is not really a Christian state at all, for it only uses Christianity as one of its means.[45] The *real* state, the democratic state, does not need religion. It can relegate religion to the arena of privacy. It can grant or withdraw religion's civil rights much as it grants or withdraws the rights of private property. In a rather obvious reference to Rousseau and the French Revolution, Marx argues that in times when

> the political state as such comes violently to birth in civil society, and when men strive to liberate themselves through political emancipation, the state can, and must, proceed to abolish and destroy religion; but only in the same way as it proceeds to abolish private property . . . , or in the same way that it proceeds to abolish life, by the guillotine. . . . But it can only achieve this by setting itself in violent contradiction . . . , by declaring a permanent revolution. [This] . . . ends necessarily with the restoration of religion, of private property, of all the elements of civil society. . . .[46]

The Christian "political democracy" and the secular, "liberal, social contract," by which he means the French view as anticipated by Rousseau and culminating in the Declaration of the Rights of Man, establishes only "civil" rights.[47] Bauer had argued that only by sacrificing the civilly bestowed "privilege of faith" which allowed each person and group to preserve its particularity could we ascend to the higher cultural level of universal human consciousness. Bauer thought that was more nearly approximated in America and in the French state. But Marx argues against this, quoting from the early constitutions of several colonies, which he reads through the spectacles of the French Declaration of the Rights of Man. In his view these are simply the rights of the dominant members of a bourgeois civil society—that is, "of egotistic man, of man separated from other men and from the community. . . . It is a question of the liberty of man regarded as an isolated monad, withdrawn into himself."[48] Marx then summarizes his *Critique of Hegel's "Philosophy of Right"* to show that these understandings, rooted in changing commercial relationships, brought about the downfall of feudal society but had not brought about human emancipation. They had only established abstract bourgeois rights as reflections of a phase of historical development. The question of Jewish rights and of Christian rights had become, for Marx, the question of what specific social elements and forces in society had to be overcome to establish a genuinely human order—which also meant the abolition of Judaism and Christianity.[49]

In Marx's view, if we look realistically at why Jews and Christians are so eager to preserve human rights, we find that both are masks or covers for the love of money, property, and bourgeois dominance.[50] Jews particularly are the object of Marx's wrath here, for they represented to him a monied aristocracy most obviously separated from material labor and from political power. But Christians, in his view, are increasingly "Judaizing" themselves in the same directions.[51] Both the Christian and the Jew avoid the grasping of the real human problem. Each "only know[s] how to objectify his essence by making it into an alien, fantastic being; so, under the sway of egotistic need, he can only affirm himself and produce objects in practice by subordinating his products and his own activity to the domination of an alien entity, and by lending them the significance of this alien entity: money."[52] It is this latter motif that plunged Marx into his more scientific analysis of bourgeois society, culminating in his famous *Das Kapital.*

It can be seen in these and other writings that human rights for the Marxist tradition are expressions of particular historic consciousness born out of specific social conditions. However, human rights concerns, like religion itself, point to the genuine attempt by humanity to regrasp itself. All this issues, in short, in the establishment of a "divinized" humanity, free to determine all things, under no heteronomous rule. This is practically to be achieved by the creation of a genuinely socialized civil society of interdependence and solidarity not subject to any alien power—God, property, state, money, or individual interest—but only to the guidance of those who represent the whole of real humanity. In *The Communist Manifesto* he called for the adoption of human rights "for the working class." The redemptive community will begin the new liberation; the proletariat represent this universal humanity. Guided by enlightened realism, they must thus seize control of all abstract individualistic and political forces. They must, therefore, negate both the transcendental privacy of Christian piety and the rational, technical power of Machiavellian princes and their bureaucracies. And they must surpass the artificial, bourgeois social contract of Rousseau, actualize in practice the rational autonomy of Kant, and reverse the dialectic of Hegel. In doing so, they must acknowledge that there are alienated, privatistic individuals, represented by religious sentiment, who have to be dealt with. They must also acknowledge that the real facts of political regime have to be reckoned with, until the full transformation has taken place. On these foundations the core vision of the movement deriving from Marx is an organized reconstitution of social relations on the basis of a material, empirical, socialized community that has no other basis than the integration and absolutization of human needs and solidarity of will. It is a materialistic, "humanistic" civic creed, echoing in Enlightenment language many of the themes that were suppressed by established religious authority and the princes in the Radical Reformation and the Peasants' Revolt, now seen as human issues expressed theologically and not at all as theological issues expressed humanly.

In 1980, in the special exhibition of the Museum of German History, the first display was a quotation from Lenin. V. I. Lenin had come to Berlin in 1895 by order of the illegal Russian group, the "Marxist Circle." There, in the Königlichen Bibliothek, he studied the works of Marx and wrote, "The Doctrine of Marx is almighty because it is true." More of the formation of the present ruling creed of the G.D.R. is owed to Lenin than the confirmation of a true believer. Lenin, more than Marx, gave the creed a social-institutional support system by shaping the Party in much of Europe and especially in the Soviet Union after World War I. In close contact with the leading German Communists, such as Rosa Luxemburg, Lenin forged the "executive committee" of the revolutionary masses into the "dictatorship of the proletariat" and resisted all efforts to "revise" Marxism toward liberalism on the one hand or to move toward a social democracy on the other.[53] Lenin's Party seized control of the very core of society and controlled everything from that position, not as an outgrowth of altered means of production but as a political act which would bond humanity into a new solidarity which would intentionally restructure the means of production. The now-modified traditions from Machiavelli through Rousseau displaced all previous partial syntheses of European history as the most powerful, civilization-forming force of the modern world. What is right is what serves the revolution![54]

When the Marxist-Leninist civic creed was established in the Soviet Union, the rights of all persons and groups were overtly subordinated to those of the working class. As the Party representing this class gained fuller control of the government, it was not "negative" rights, delimiting the power of the state, that were accented; it was "positive" guarantees of rights to produce, rights to technical education which aids human mastery over human destiny, and rights to participate in the building of a new society that were set forth as goals and guides for the state and for the state bureaucratic authorities. It is precisely these motifs which also became the pattern in the German Democratic Republic. The individual has rights only as a *member* of the socialist *society*, controlled in principle by the triumphant working class, which, in turn, guides the actions of the state and which requires of the state the active protection of all social rights. The individual has proper claims against bureaucratic structures when the structures prevent full participation in the socialist civil society. Indeed, elaborate, Party-guided organizations focused on the factory, office, or profession wherein one works are designed both to guide the worker toward fuller participation and to correct any structures that prevent fuller participation.

Most significant for our comparative understanding is the fact that independent intermediary organizations—except the church and the nuclear family—between the self and the whole society and between the society and the state are obliterated. More precisely, multiple groups are coordinated so as to find their governing and central expression in the one, united Party, which, representing the whole society concretely and the whole of humanity in principle, guides both individuals and the state and leads them to fulfillment. The Party is, as it were, the one true church. Personal opinions and the formation of private groups in particular social solidarities may not be publicly expressed in an independent fashion and are seen as criminal, for they undercut the very prospect of genuine humanization according to the official civic religion.

F. THE MARXIST-LENINIST CRITIQUE OF RELIGION— CHURCH RESPONSES

According to the leading official East German sociologist of religion, Olaf Klohr, Marxism understands religion not according to the question of the truth or untruth of its creed but as a social, economic, and historical phenomenon. In *Marxism und Atheism heute* he argues that religion must be understood first in its sociological dimensions rather than in terms of a theory of cognition or voluntary "bonding." Ethics, religion, metaphysics, and other forms of ideology and consciousness can no longer take on the appearance of independence. They have no being, no history, no meaning, and no development separable from the material ground and circumstances of their origins. Consciousness does not determine existence; existence determines consciousness.

Having stated this fundamental viewpoint, Klohr states five theses that represent the basis of a "Marxist-Leninist sociology of religion":

1. Religion is a specific form of social consciousness which, in the final analysis, is conditioned by material, social conditions, and determined as to its contents.

2. Religion in its contemporary expression is primarily a social phenomenon which derives from a class society.

3. Religion is therefore only a social factor insofar as it is institutionalized in a church with all its accoutrements and forms of life.

4. Religion and the church are, nevertheless, in no way only passive products of social relations, but in turn influence politics, morals, law, and philosophy and thereby play an active role in social life.

5. Insofar as religion and the church are finally determined by social relations, attention must be given to the relatively independent developments so that they do not develop determinative social power.[55]

On the basis of these five theses, Klohr looks at Christianity, paying particular attention to modern theologies in which concern for "one's fellow man" is a central theme. He concludes that the decisive difference between humanitarian theologies and Marxist atheism is that the former obscure fundamental human relations by placing them on a mysterious undergirding, whereas the latter forms such relations on a primarily rational and empirical basis.

He goes on to point out that religion is not a natural or spontaneous thing but a convention growing out of specific conditions. Atheism is not a spontaneous matter, either. The theoretical and practical affirmation of the world is something that must be attained and is not gained by mere negation of religiousness or faith. One must actually free humanity from the conditions of slavery and suppression and make it actually possible for humans to become lords of their world. Then the old dream of humanism, of which one finds many traces in Christianity, can become a reality. Only then will scientific atheism as the theoretical expression of practical relations be fully possible. In an oblique way Klohr then moves briefly to an argument for tolerance. It is foolish to suppress religion, he suggests, quoting Engels, for the need for it still remains.[56]

Further, since an approximation to a fully socialized order has, thus far in the humanizing progress of world history, been realized only in certain nations, no transnational power or other sovereign state can serve as the judge of various definitions of socialist rights, or develop any procedure to enforce human rights. Such universal concepts are surely abstract and have no real meaning—especially if they are thought to be rooted in God or a universal moral law. Indeed, critical assessment of socialist definitions of rights by appeal to such things as the United Nations' Declaration of Human Rights is seen as the effort of capitalist societies to encroach upon the freedom of socialist ones, an imperialist effort to recolonialize the workers at the hands of the feudal or bourgeois powers.[57]

The capacity of the worker's movement, centered in the Party and its official civic creed, to overcome the confessionally rooted religion on one side and the power of the rationalized bureaucracy on the other appears stalemated to the outside observer. On the one hand, organized religion has not remained in its purely inner personalism. Lutheran piety has been forced by revolutionary events more nearly to approximate Catholic, Calvinist, and radical sectarian notions of public responsibility. The Lutheran-influenced churches are facing funda- mental philosophical and social questions which they much earlier put aside. They must show that they have something to say about God, membership, and justice in an altered environment where thousands are unfamiliar with biblical or theological modes of thought. To baptize one's child, to be confirmed in the church, to seek a church wedding or burial are political acts. The private cannot be so neatly separated from the exterior, societal questions. The confessional divisions which loomed larger in the past under the impress of Lutheran or- thodoxy seem less divisive now as Lutherans, Catholics, and sectarians have to ask daily how to remain faithful in a new situation and how to preserve the social space to be faithful even to the differences. Structurally, vigorous moves are being made to form "councils" of churches which work with the people from the ground up and not only from the top down. Aspects of the Pietist heritage, which sometimes overlooked confessional differences, seem to be in resurgence, promoting a kind of sensitive interpersonal life and disciplined, local ecclesiastical life while functioning within the limited interstices of socialist structures. It may be that such developments will provide East Germany with greater prospects for "socialism with a human face" than other Eastern Euro- pean efforts seem to have achieved. What is emerging is a "church in socialism," one that is neither a "church for socialism" nor a "church against socialism." To this outsider, what is significant is the growing interest in human rights within the G.D.R. churches, precisely insofar as they have claimed and thus far maintained the absolute right to exist. The heritage is itself redefining its own understanding of the genuinely human by accenting the claim of God on us to serve the neighbor and to demand the social space to do so. Marxist-Leninist socialism of the established civil creed does not yet know how to adjust itself to *this* claim; much of its critique of religion has a different kind of religion in mind.

Yet it is clear that Marxism-Leninism in the G.D.R. is more than a scientific body of knowledge for guiding society through political economy. It is increas- ingly a religious movement seeking the souls of all. Nowhere is this more clear than in the liturgical forms which have been worked out to provide a substitute set of "sacraments" for the people. Liberal thinkers in the tradition of Kant and Fichte as well as Goethe broke with the Jewish traditions and Christian churches in the nineteenth century and formed a "philosophical church" called the "Free Thinkers," dedicated to scientific humanism and national development. At the turn of this century and through the Weimar Republic, that group split into two factions, the smaller supporting the republic and the larger supporting the radicals influenced by Marx. Ernst Thälmann, one of the latter, was a founder, along with Rosa Luxemburg, of the present Communist Party in the G.D.R. In an autobiographical essay he writes that the most important moment of his life was his "dedication" as a youth to that movement. It gave him a purpose in life. Today the "youth dedication" (Jugendweihe) is the cultic "confirmation" ritual of most of the East German young people. Similarly, socialist "name-giving," wedding, and burial services have been created to displace baptism, church weddings, and religious funerals.[58] The problem of inwardly linking the individual with the whole remains a critical, still unresolved issue in this highly conformed society. Nevertheless, it is easy to adapt De Tocqueville's observations on the French Revolution to the present G.D.R. situation: Marxism-Leninism functions

> in relation to this world in precisely the same manner that religious revolutions function in respect to the other: it considered the citizen in an abstract fashion, apart from particular societies, in the same way that religions consider man in general, independently of time and place. It sought not merely the particular rights of . . . citizens, but the general political rights and duties of all men. [Accordingly] since it appeared to be more concerned with the regeneration of the human race than with the reformation of [the nation] . . . , it generated a passion which, until then, the most violent political revolutions had never exhibited. It inspired proselytism and gave birth to propaganda. It could therefore assume that appearance of a religious revolution which so astonished contemporaries; or rather it became itself a kind of new religion, an imperfect religion it is true, a religion without God . . . , but one which nevertheless inundated the earth with soldiers, apostles and martyrs.[59]

At the same time, the notion that the worker's movement, through the Party, should grasp control of the state and its bureaucracy to shape a genuinely human society has raised expectations high. Again, to the outside observer peril seems to lurk in this assumption of duty. If responsibility for everything is claimed, and power is so concentrated that no other authority can restrain it, disenchantment with leadership is compounded when anything goes wrong. Yet no alternative structure of action or influence except the church is at hand, and no transcending principles except theological ones are available to evaluate the standards of those who lead and define on behalf of the whole society. And church and theology are marginalized wherever possible. These aspects of the contemporary situation are made more complicated by the fact that many habits of mind and procedure remain as legacies from the ruins of Prussian and Nazi days. To the ordinary citizen the bureaucracies of Party and government seem still to be alien powers, each a heteronomous authority, not yet under control, hardly an expression of true autonomy, hardly of theonomy. The secular, "humanistic," civic creed of East Germany and the communities of faith must wrestle still with the legacies of Luther, Machiavelli, and Rousseau. The quest for the true religious basis of human rights in a Marxist-Leninist, conformed society remains.

1. I am indebted in this section to several sources. See N. Cohn, *The Pursuit of the Millennium: Revolutionary Messianism in Medieval and Reformation Europe and its Bearing on Modern Totalitarian Movements* (New York: Harper & Row, 1961). The most complete treatment of the religious groups in this period is G. H. Williams, *The Radical Reformation* (Philadelphia: Westminster Press, 1962). For the connections between the medieval Catholic efforts at reform and these movements, see especially M. Reeves, *Joachim of Fiore and the Prophetic Future* (New York: Harper & Row, 1976).

2. See T. Müntzer, "Sermon Before the Princes" (1924) in G. H. Williams, ed., *Spiritual and Anabaptist Writers* (Philadelphia: Westminster Press, n.d.), pp. 47ff. The heroic role of Müntzer in the G.D.R. was assured by the fact that Engels wrote "The Peasant War in Germany," celebrating Müntzer, in 1850. Engels saw in Müntzer the anticipation of the Marxist Revolution, a way of viewing the movement still widely held in schoolbooks and public museums in the G.D.R. Interest in Müntzer was renewed by the East German philosopher Ernst Bloch, but the best research now being done in the G.D.R. is represented by Wolfgang Ullman. See his "Das Geschichtsverständnis Thomas Müntzer," in *Thomas Müntzer* (Berlin: Evangelische Verlagsanstalt, 1977).

3. I refer, of course, to such movements as those of the Swiss Brethren, the Mennonites, the Hutterites, and others. See G. Lewy, *Religion and Revolution* (New York: Oxford University Press, 1974), especially pp. 116ff.

4. I had a chance to visit that cloister in 1980. Most fascinating to me were the gravestone on the floor and a stained-glass window in the chapel where he conducted his first Mass. The gravestone was that of Johannes Zackarias, lawyer of the Council of Constance, who led the case against John Huss. The window depicted the life of Saint Augustine. Novices had to kneel before the gravestone and meditate at the window. This is especially interesting in view of the fact that after Luther had gone through his own spiritual struggles, he clearly chose Augustine's *Confessions* over Canon Law. Luther was later accused, by the jurist von Eck, of repeating Huss's errors. See A. G. Dickens, *Martin Luther and the Reformation* (New York: Harper and Row, 1967), pp. 43 – 59.

5. Luther, *On the Freedom of a Christian*. (Because there are numerous printings of Luther's works, I shall refer only to the titles unless I offer a direct quotation. This pattern will also be followed in regard to Machiavelli, Rousseau, Kant, etc.)

6. This accent was not new in German theology. When the Germanic tribes were converted many centuries before, the variety of Christianity which they adopted was Arianism, a view which entailed a distinction between the object of reason and the object of faith. The German mystics—such as Meister Eckhart—also made this distinction, celebrating the intuitive above and beyond all rationality.

7. Luther's profound anti-Semitism is rooted in this theological principle. He was instrumental in designing one of the pillar capitals on the Predigenkirche in Wittenberg. It portrays Jews holding their law books and suckling on a great sow.

8. Luther reports reading with enthusiasm Augustine's writings against the Pelagians. See H. Boehmer, *Martin Luther* (New York: Meridian, 1946), pp. 138f.

9. See Luther's *Judgment on Monastic Vows*, *Treatise on the Marriage Estate* and *An Open Letter to the Christian Nobility of the German Nation*.

10. See S. A. Lakoff, *Equality in Political Philosophy* (Boston: Beacon Press, 1964), pp. 25 – 36.

11. Luther, *Against the Robbing and Murdering Hordes of Peasants*.

12. See his "Aphorisms on the Nature of Man."

13. See *The Prince*.

14. See *The Discourses*.

15. This is the source of the constant struggles about the "two-kingdom theory" in Luther. See K. H. Hertz, *Two Kingdoms and One World* (Minneapolis: Augsburg, 1976).

16. Reinhard Bendix, *Kings or People* (Berkeley: University of California Press, 1978), pp. 381 – 82. The quotation which he includes is from M. Walker, *German Home Towns* (Ithaca, N.Y.: Cornell University Press, 1971), p. 33.

17. Bendix, *Kings or People*, p. 155 and p. 160.

18. Leo Strauss is correct, I believe, in making this connection explicit. See his *History of Political Philosophy*, 2nd ed. (Chicago: Rand McNally, 1972), pp. 271 – 92.

19. In this portion of the chapter I am especially indebted to H. W. Koch, *A History of*

Prussia (London: Longman, 1978); Bendix, *Kings or People*, especially Chapters 5, 10, and 11; and C. Hinrichs, *Preussentum und Pietismus* (Göttingen: Vandenhoeck und Ruprecht, 1971).

20. J. W. Gough, *The Social Contract*, 2nd ed. (New York: Oxford University Press, 1957), pp. 147ff.

21. See his *Discourse on the Origin of Inequality Among Men*, ii.

22. See Gough, *The Social Contract*, p. 171.

23. Rousseau is specifically working out an alternative to both Bodin, who tried to move toward a more conciliar position, and Grotius and Althusius. See Sheldon Wolin, *Politics and Vision* (Boston: Little, Brown, 1960).

24. See C. Dawson, *The Gods of Revolution* (New York: Minerva Press, 1975).

25. Wolin, *Politics and Vision*, especially chapter 10.

26. De Tocqueville, *L'ancien regime et la revolution*, quoted by Koch, *A History of Prussia*, p. 143.

27. See Koch, *A History of Prussia*, pp. 142 – 46.

28. Ibid., p. 174.

29. Kant, *Critique of Practical Reason*, trans. Lewis Beck (1949; Westport, Conn.: Garland, 1977), first sentence of the first section.

30. See his *Perpetual Peace: A Philosophic Essay*.

31. See A. Levine, *The Politics of Autonomy: A Kantian Reading of Rousseau's "Social Contract"* (Amhurst, Mass.: University of Massachusetts Press, 1976).

32. See his *The Phenomenology of Mind*, especially the preface; see also *The Encyclopaedia of the Philosophical Sciences*.

33. See his *Philosophy of Law*.

34. Hegel, *Philosophy of History*, trans. J. Sibree (New York: Dover, 1956), pp. 40f.

35. See "The German Ideology," especially Part I, in R. C. Tucker, ed., *The Marx-Engels Reader* (New York: Norton, 1972), pp. 110ff. This is the best, most easily accessible collection of Marx in my judgment. Subsequent references to Marx's works will be drawn from this volume unless otherwise indicated.

36. *Contribution to the Critique of Hegel's Philosophy of History*, in *The Marx-Engels Reader*, pp. 11ff.

37. *The Eighteenth Brumaire of Louis Bonaparte*, in *The Marx-Engels Reader*, pp. 436ff., and *Critique of the Gotha Program*, ibid., pp. 383ff.

38. See "The German Ideology." See also T. Ogletree, "Ideology and Ethical Reflection," in *Selected Papers of the American Society of Christian Ethics*, 1972.

39. See *The Communist Manifesto*, in *The Marx-Engels Reader*, pp. 331ff. See also N. Bancroft, "Does Marx Have an Ethical Theory?" *Soundings*, 62 (Summer 1980), 214ff. Bancroft specifically is arguing against E. Kamenka, *Marxism & Ethics* (London: Macmillan, 1969). D. G. Trickett has correctly challenged Bancroft's critique in my view. See his "Karl Marx and Ethical Theory" (A.S.C.E., Jan. 1979).

40. E. Kamenka is correct, I believe, in connecting these motifs to Rousseau. See "Marxian Humanism," in E. Fromm, ed., *Socialist Humanism* (Garden City, N.Y.: Doubleday, 1965), pp. 106ff. This entire symposium is a very valuable resource.

41. Almost all these references are found in the works cited in notes 35 – 40.

42. See D. McLellan, *Karl Marx: His Life and Thought* (New York: Harper & Row, 1973), pp. 80ff.

43. Marx, "On the Jewish Question," in *The Marx-Engels Reader*, pp. 24ff. See especially pp. 28 – 29 and p. 33.

44. Ibid., p. 30 and p. 37.

45. Ibid., p. 34.

46. Ibid., p. 34.

47. Ibid., pp. 39f. and p. 44. This view was refuted in 1901 by the revisionist Georg Jellinek. See *The Declaration of the Rights of Man and of Citizens*, repr. ed. (Westport, Conn.: Hyperion Press, 1979).

48. Ibid., p. 40.

49. Ibid., pp. 45 – 51.

50. Ibid., p. 48.

51. Ibid., p. 50.

52. Ibid., p. 50.

53. Lenin, *The State and Revolution in the Essential Left* (New York: Barnes & Noble, 1961), pp. 147ff. For the best sympathetic treatment of Lenin's development, see Bastiaan Wielenga, *Lenins Weg zur Revolution* (München: Kaiser Verlag, 1971).

54. See U. Huar, *Mensch und Politik in Geschichte und Gegenwart* (Berlin: UEB Deutscher Verlag, 1978).

55. See my "Christianity and the New Exodus in Eastern Europe" (1968) in *The Religious Situation*, ed. D. Cutler (Boston: Beacon Press, 1978), pp. 887ff.

56. See also E. Hinz, "Toward a New Interpretation of Religion and Atheism," unpublished paper, 1980.

57. See Mollnau, Schoneburg, et al., *Macht und Recht: Einheit oder Gegensatz* (Berlin: Staatsverlag, 1976), pp. 39f.

58. In these efforts one can discern a partial, vulgarized recovery of motifs from the German enlightenment. These liturgical forms are deeply influenced by E. F. Heckel, *Die Weltrutzel der Welt* (1899), as appropriated by E. Thälmann. See *Handbuch zur Jugendweihe* (Berlin: Volkseigener Verlag, 1974), p. 39.

59. De Tocqueville, *L'ancien regime et la revolution* (Magnolia, Mass.: Peter Smith, 1900), Book 1, Chapter iii.

CHAPTER SEVEN

Religion and Society in India: A Cross-Sectional Encounter

A. INTRODUCTION TO A TRADITIONAL SOCIETY

THE encounter with India draws into our horizons concerns that are not prominent in either the U.S.A. or the G.D.R. From the distant perspective of many Indians, Liberal- and Puritan-influenced pluralist societies seem very much like Marxist-Leninist conformed societies. Temperate climate, compulsive work habits, taste in everything from clothing to music, attitudes toward health, education, and family life blur the distinctions which seem so important to East-West differences in the northern hemisphere. Indeed, from an Indian point of view, even one informed by the inclusion in the Constitution of both parliamentary-democratic procedures in government and socialist principles in economy, many sociopolitical differences also seem more a part of Cold War pushing and hauling than directly a part of the real possibilities for India. They seem Western, foreign, and "unnatural."

It is also the case that from South Asia, the philosophical and religious presuppositions of socialist and Christian thought appear to be quite similar. It is true that socialism is in principle atheistic and materialistic, a fact that deeply troubles those loyal to the predominant traditions of Hinduism. Yet several philosophical traditions within Hinduism are also atheistic. Further, the activist, scientifically engaged social theology of the Catholic and Reformed missionaries seems, from the standpoint of traditional Indian belief, also to be materialistic and possibly irreligious. Both presume, to use Calvin's words, that humans "can become what we are not," or, to use Marx's words, that we are most human when we "support every revolutionary movement against the existing social and political order of things." To the Hindu both are unnatural, out of phase with the true, eternal, natural laws of the cosmos, the frenzied product of those who do not know who or what they are, the artificiality of those who have lost spiritual depth.

These things I knew from some formal study of Indian thought and history before going to India. It is a deep and long tradition, rich in philosophical nuance, religious subtlety, and social pertinence. One can see in it analogues to ancient Greek and Roman natural philosophies and to religions which have been displaced by Christian and Enlightenment thought in the West. But nothing quite prepares a Westerner for direct exposure to India.

The mass of people, especially in and around the cities where travelers inevitably start their visits, is overwhelming. People in all shapes and conditions move in gentle waves through the streets and markets. There is nothing threatening or hostile in these tides of humanity, but it is disorienting. Odors, sounds, colors, and gestures are unfamiliar. The ordinary cues to guide the routines of daily life are not clear; and only slowly does one begin to be able to discern what is friendliness to strangers and what is show for commercial advantage, what is humor and what is deception, what is respected and kept therefore at a distance, and what is considered disgusting and therefore kept distant.

Even more slowly one becomes aware of the richness of complexity and contrast. This is no simple, or primitive, or undifferentiated society, even though in Western economic terms it is "undeveloped." Every spectrum by which observers classify societies in India must be broad, with many, many gradations in between the extremes. There is great and graphic poverty, but there is also great wealth. There is much that is ancient and traditional, but there is much that is brand-new. There is magnificent beauty and subtle aesthetic sensitivity; there is also gross ugliness and crudity. There is a radical individualistic element and a profound corporative sense. There is elaborate eroticism and the most intense ascetic repression imaginable. There is open generosity and blatant cruelty. There is the fiercest competitive and acquisitive commercialism I have ever seen, and there are solidaristic communal forms of mutual support and sacrificial sharing. There is high learning and incredible ignorance. India is a living museum of human joy and triumph, of misery and defeat. The contrasts of Manhattan, let alone East Berlin, pale by comparison.

I had gone to India after completing a study of the relation of Christian theology and ethics to complex society in the West, to see whether similar structures of belief and society correlated cross-culturally. I had thought to draw comparisons and contrasts in a project that would take, perhaps, two or three years. My wife, a musician, was interested in Indian music and yoga. Thus we arranged a sabbatical in South India in 1973. We tried to prepare ourselves for this encounter, but the vastness and richness of Indian civilization and the variety of journalistic and scholarly opinion on every aspect of Indian life prevented rapid progress. Further, living in India is complex for outsiders. Immense problems of coping beset the visitor. My wife and I discovered that mailing a letter sometimes took half an hour; cashing a check sometimes consumed an hour; preventive and curative medical attention was regular and demanding, although there is little that one can get in India that cannot be treated. In these and dozens of other little ways, coping is a constant preoccupation. The division of labor is fantastically refined, yet similar or related functions are seldom clustered for Western efficiency. Hence daily operations are extremely time-consuming. For millions without Western incomes and professional connections, coping is the basic feature of daily life.

I went to India again in 1976, after being in East Germany. The questions of human rights were particularly intense at that time due to the Emergency proclaimed by Prime Minister Indira Gandhi. I returned to teach on the subject and to engage in rather regular conversations with C. Duraisingh and Somen Das, two young, brilliant Indian scholars who had come to this country for advanced study. I am still very much aware of how much there is to digest, to read, to check with specialists, and to pursue; but I am now at a point where I must attempt, even with hesitations and apologies to those who have spent a lifetime living in or studying India, an interpretive overview of religion and society in India as it bears on human rights in comparison with American and East German cultures.

I must add one further qualification: I conducted most of my study and had most of my experiences in South India. We were centered in Bangalore, guests of the most gracious United Theological College, under the leadership of R. Chandran, and given greatest scholarly stimulation by M. M. Thomas, perhaps India's leading living theologian, and M. N. Srinivas, clearly one of India's best sociologists. Our most intensive travel and research was done in Karnataka, Tamil Nadu, Kerala, and Andra Pradesh. We traveled as tourists in the great northern cities, but most of my impressions and observations are distinctly southern.[1] Only subsequent study would reveal whether they pertain also to the northern states.

I have already suggested the complexity of life in India. One can hardly speak of it except metaphorically. It is a beehive in slow motion. It is a vast honeycomb, with many pockets of activity and sweetness, many spots of emptiness. Except after seasonal rains and along the coasts, India is honey-colored— soft browns, sepia, and yellow. In the villages, where more than eighty percent of the people live, life gives the appearance of being divided between the drones and the workers, with all engaged in preprogrammed, ritualized functions and showing little concern for whether it is the tenth, the fifteenth, or the twentieth century. One scholar, who spent much more time in intense study of village life than I was able to, spoke about the honeycombed personality structure produced by traditional village life—multiple, many-sided compartments for multilateral relationships, each connected to, but simultaneously separated from, other little compartments of living.[2]

The cities are more complex. In part they are overgrown, overpopulated, and intermingled villages which have had their preprogrammed, compartmentalized, and ordered lives cracked open. The sweetness becomes a sticky mess, although the workers and the drones keep the compartmental plan in their memories and their instincts. In difficult times people flood to the cities. The city is liberation from the fixed and constricting patterns they have known.

It is also terrifying and insecure because the guidelines for living are not clear. In part the cities are only homogenized villages; in part they are enclaves of modernity. Structures of nontraditional industry, commerce, education, communications, and law—clear imports from the West—govern "ritually neutral" features of life.[3] The momentum of the novelty introduced by these enclaves, which appears so slow, so organically evolutionary, and so cautious to Western eyes as it ripples through society, is experienced as dramatic and rapid by Indian friends.

The people are friendly and inquisitive. At the least signal of openness, conversation begins. Schoolchildren and university students, rickshaw drivers, and shopkeepers are shyly eager to try their English. Every bus ride or tea break is an occasion for immediate sharing of life histories, in much greater detail than one sometimes wants, as well as for cross-examination about how much money one earns, how much the watch costs, and the state of one's digestive tract (the functioning of one's alimentary system is of constant and pervasive interest). If these opening inquiries are dealt with candidly, conversation again and again turns to family life and religion. On one bus ride I happened to sit next to the head of the Department of Agricultural Sciences at a major university as we were traveling through a fascinating farming region of Andra Pradesh. New techniques of irrigation were being introduced and production was changing from consumer to cash crops—especially sugar cane—bringing all sorts of shifts in the socioeconomic structure. After the usual preliminaries I attempted to get this knowledgeable expert to explain to me all that we were seeing. I pumped him with questions from material I had read about economic development, government planning, irrigation, the impact of the introduction of a money-economy, and the receptiveness or resistance of these farmers to new techniques. He was not at all interested. He wanted to speak of important things—family and religion. He had a new grandson, and he had a new *guru*. I learned a great deal about these in the next three hours.

Religion and the family. These are the foundations of traditional Hindu life and, to a substantive degree, contemporary Indian life generally. While to understand Western and socialist societies one must begin with *doctrine,* one begins with family and religious *practice* in India. I spent a good deal of my time with Indian Christians and Westernized Hindu intellectuals, many of whom are Marxists to one degree or another, and less time with traditional Hindus, Muslims, and the sprinkling of Buddhists and Jains who can be found. Conversations with villagers and urban poor people had to be conducted through translators, and the sense of modesty or embarrassment, as well as deference to a white Westerner (a colonial legacy), made these conversations more difficult. But when a basic level of trust was established, the topics of interest were the same. The major exception to this occurred in conversations with that segment of the population which was more urbanized—those who had lived in the modern, industrial cities for at least a generation or who had chosen Western religious and intellectual patterns. Among these people, of whatever socioeconomic level or faith, a third ingredient was added: nationalism. Family is of primary concern, for the family is, for most, still the absolute center of social life and loyalty. By "family," Indians mean the extended kinship system, not only the "nuclear family." The latter is but a single link in an elaborate and finely forged fence of inclusion and exclusion. Family in this extended sense is the social center of meaning, membership, and identity. The blissful, peaceful calm and order of the traditional "joint-family" patterns (as celebrated in traditional lore), which connected the individual also to one's vocation and subcaste (*jati*) and thereby to caste, are under pressure in the cities. It is doubtful whether the joint family was ever quite so prevalent, peaceful, and ordered as people now, somewhat romantically, present it to be; but it is surely the case that both family structures and family duty, as a matter of religion, are under pressure and are often now a source of conflict and burdensome obligation. Still, they are the core of social life.

Closely related is religion, specifically in the sense of "rite." Religion in India is less "institutional" than in the American sense and less "private" than in East Germany. It is more diffuse, more pervasive in daily life, more directly connected with the ritual activities of relationship and work in and between the extended family, the *jati*, and thus the caste. Especially important is the increased spread and development of the several, century-old devotional, or *bhakti*, versions of Hinduism. *Bhakti* is increasingly important among the urbane and intellectual leadership, among whom the direct connections of daily family life, occupation, and religion are less obvious. As we shall see in the next chapter, Hindu *bhakti* apparently derives from internal Hindu reform movements in response to Buddhist success among the people. It is, in some ways, the "Protestantism" of Hinduism. The *bhakti* traditions are also supported by a fresh synthetic tradition of Hindu philosophy developed in the last hundred years called the Hindu Renaissance. Ram Mohan Roy, Tagore, Keshub Chunder Sen, Ramakrishna, Vivekananda, Tilak, and Aurobindo represent several generations of leaders who had gotten Western educations but consciously chose Hinduism. They offered reinterpretations of the meanings of Hinduism that have not only influenced the West but provided the basis for an urbane, "evangelical Hinduism" that is presently converging with both older *bhakti* devotional practices and newer lifestyles to produce the basic religious vocabulary by which contemporary educated Indians, including a number of Christians, express the basic meanings of their life and faith. Gandhi was, in many ways, a product of this emerging synthesis, and although his movement is, for all practical purposes, dying, it is in Gandhi that the connection with nationalism comes to its fulfillment.

Only slowly did it begin to become clear to me what discussion of these matters, which appeared in conversation after conversation, was all about. It was, I now think, an attempt to discover *what* I was. My being and the beings of my conversation partners were determined by family, by the state of religious enlightenment seen in the quality of enlightened mind and personal religious devotion, and by nationality. These are the key indicators of what one *is*. One can only recognize what one is, and live it out. Our "being" is an ontological given. The central task of life is to know who we are and fulfill what we are. The understanding of the world around one consists in finding out other people's "being." Justice to another person depends on finding the right compartment in which to place him or her. To use another metaphor, life is organized like a giant filing cabinet, and each group of persons has a slot. In the honeycombed world of the village, the slots are clear and recognized by all. In the world of the cities where the slots are less clear, one must find the right clues to organize things and put them in their correct slots. By grasping patterns of family and piety, one can read the clues. Thereby things can be treated according to their proper place in the whole scheme, as they ought to be.

During my first visit I heard about a local movement in Karnataka to organize a strike among road workers, in sympathy with other road workers who had been clearly exploited and nearly starved and worked to death in a government-sponsored but locally managed project. The movement was to begin with a fast (a necessary act of purification) near a road-building project where the laborers had their huts. It was sponsored by a coalition of Christians and socialists who intentionally played down their own family and religious connections in order to focus on solidarity with the workers. I joined the fast and had the conversations between the sponsors and the workers translated. The workers laughed at and ridiculed the leaders of the movement. "Look at those silly people!" my translator reported the workers saying. "They think things can be different. Is it not our *dharma* to do this? They don't even know who *they* are!"

There is social change going on in India.[4] One sees it in the presence of more bicycles in the rural areas—a fact that signifies a new range of human transportation, technology, and communication. One reads about the political shifts before, during, and after the Emergency and the formation of new political coalitions in opposition to this or that regime at national or regional levels. Technical studies confirm that India is increasingly self-sufficient in food production, and that starvation is much reduced, even if malnutrition remains a problem in localized parts of India. The population growth itself is a force for change, although no one is sure in which direction, and in spite of the fact that the rate of growth has been decreasing for a decade. The enclaves of "modernity" previously centered in the ports are daily expanding their influence in education, medical care, and mass media (especially radio and movies). Careful longitudinal studies have shown that whole subcastes in particular regions have moved up the social scale relative to their neighbors by adopting new styles of life, by altering patterns of diet (toward vegetarianism) and of intermarriage, by forsaking polluting work (leather-working), and by obtaining new priests.[5] As to whether there is a fundamental reorganization of the categories and predetermined compartments of life—that question is more difficult to answer.

During my 1976 visit I read with detailed care Gunnar Myrdal's *Asian Drama*,[6] the most massive single compilation of social data gathered about social change and development in South Asia yet published. I also read Louis Dumont's *Homo Hierarchicus,*[7] perhaps the most sympathetic assessment of the caste system that has ever been written by a Western scholar. V. S. Naipaul's literary portrait, *India: A Wounded Civilization,*[8] also appeared while I was there and was the occasion for many debates. During my semester there in 1982, the discussion about Naipaul had been displaced by a more intense debate about Salman Rushdie's prize-winning novel *Midnight's Children,* perhaps the most revealing and delightful treatment of India yet written. I gathered and digested all the critiques of these materials I could find by Indian authors, and discussed at length dubious points with Indian scholars and long-term Western observers. The results lead me to the following conclusion. These authors in large measure are correct; there is change *in,* but not yet fundamental change *of,* the system. Dumont, of course, sees advantage in this; Myrdal sees this as a problem; Naipaul sees it as tragic; Rushdie see it as "fate." Dumont, like most of the Indian critics of Myrdal and Naipaul, finds considerable resilience and wisdom in the complexities of Indian patterns of religion and family as they join in caste. Professor C. T. Kurien of Madras, in one of the most articulate recent studies of social development,[9] also sees ways in which the caste traditions of India, by selectively appropriating elements from the West, are able to provide resources for a cosmopolitan ethic. What is clear is that the most pronounced change *in* the system has been taking place in the twentieth-century Indian cities, and that ancient patterns of society and religion are emerging in new ways to form an alternative "neo-traditional" ethic to that of either the Liberal-Puritan West or Marxism-Leninism. It is this which I shall try to portray by using the cross-sectional, analytical map.

B. Family, Caste, and Soul

We begin, in India, with discussion of the family. In a sense all discussion of sociality begins here. While to the Western observer voluntary associational or technological-political and economic structures seem to be the most obvious ways of interpreting problems of continuity and change, to the traditional Indian the key to understanding stability and change in the society is the family. Western observers, schooled in the long and deep debates under the impress of either Christian ecclesiastical reflections or Marxist political-economic ones, have developed certain self-conscious and critical ways of thinking about social arrangements, covenantal relationships, and political-economic order. In part because most Indians do not experience these as the decisive arenas of meaning in their lives, they maintain a certain cool distance from these categories, even if they have gotten a Western education and are quite articulate and knowledgeable about them. (As we shall see, Indian Christians and Indian Marxists are exceptions to this rule.) Whenever one begins to talk with Indians about changes that are difficult, decisions that are central to their lives, obligations that are most sacred, problems that burden their souls, the topic is the family.

Figure 13.

Family and Religion, the Bases of Caste in India

Educational	Cultural/ Expressive	Legal
Familial	Voluntary	Political
Medical	Technical	Economic

In most of India the traditional ideal of the family is the "joint family," a three-generational, hereditary, usually male-dominated kinship pattern to which each nuclear family relationship is subordinate.[10] This kinship structure is the decisive center of all social "membership" and personal identity, with prescribed relationships to father, mother, brothers, sisters, male children, female children, and in-laws. Procreative pairs are formed by arranged marriages which are themselves as much familial alliances as the joining of individuals. The joint family is also the nucleus of the subcaste or *jati,* and it is through this that the individual is linked to the general pattern of caste, which in turn shapes the decisive status and the determinative sociopolitical and economic structure of the society. The castes are sometimes as large as smaller European nations, although the *jati* is the more immediately functional group. The noncaste peoples also have status groups and a sense of group identity that function as subcaste in spite of (a) the nonrecognition of these as proper by Hinduism and (b) the attempts of the government since Independence to reduce emphasis on and discrimination based on caste. To have a family place in a *jati* by family connection is to have a place in the general scheme of things, to belong in a network of rights and duties, claims and obligations of the society. To have no such place is to have no social being and hence no rights.

The most important single event in the life of an Indian is, thus, the wedding. Long negotiations go into the selection of the mate, negotiations in which not only the qualities of the potential husband or wife are discussed at length but family histories of the parties are thoroughly investigated. As children approach puberty, they—especially the girls—are kept under closer and closer supervision, until marriage arrangements are ready to be consummated. "Love marriages," those in which individuals choose their own mates, are often still seen as somewhat corrupt by definition, although they occur increasingly among the educated classes. Some of the most highly educated and liberal parents told us with pride of just how liberal they had been in allowing their daughters up to four "values" of parentally proposed candidates. Dowry, too, is an important consideration, and poorer families will go into lifelong debt to see that a sufficient dowry is available for a proper match and to provide for a proper wedding. The wedding, with its fiscal and familial-alliance character, fixes the status of the next generation, and one can trace the upward, downward, or non-movement of a family-*jati* in the social hierarchy by the pattern of arranged marriage. The family-*jati* and caste are the outward and visible signs of the inward and spiritual status of the group, as acknowledged by the surrounding groups, in Indian society. This is true in spite of the fact that most Hindus believe that each individual has an immortal soul which may achieve spiritual status far beyond that of his or her group. Professor M. N. Srinivas has rightly stated that these patterns represent the core of Hindu society, and that all the hundreds of Indian intellectuals who denounce caste with such vigor and speak to Westerners of its decline seldom, if ever, defy these patterns in practice.[11]

The family, in its extended forms of "joint family," *jati,* and caste, not only decides social status but is also religious. Hindu priests and astrologers play a great role in weddings. The astrologers are important, for they are called upon to discern whether the conjunctions of these persons and families are metaphysically sound, whether this proposed social arrangement fits into the entire cosmic structure. They not only investigate the astrological backgrounds of the parties involved but seek an auspicious date for the wedding. The priests certify that both the cosmic structure and the gods as invoked by sacred rituals are properly confirmed as the couple—*and their families*—are joined. I use the passive voice, "are joined," in a somewhat special sense. Westerners are familiar with weddings in which vows are taken by the parties as they, in the eyes of God and a congregation, form a covenant—or at least, in the eyes of the state, a contract. But no vows are taken in a Hindu wedding; no choice or statement of intent is a part of the ceremony. The husband and wife are recipients of a complex social, cosmic, and mythic process which is religious in its essence. They are understood to be not agents in the upbuilding of a covenantal or civic society but participants in an eternal cosmic order.

What is religious in India is itself familial in orientation. The great religious epic poetry of India, notably the *Mahabharata* and the *Ramayana,* is replete with images of family life. Philosophy, ascetic instruction, adventure, and conflict, which also pervade these great stories, are all done and experienced in service of securing, maintaining, and celebrating the desired family relations, all of which have symbolic and transcendental meanings. The older Brahmanic traditions which focus on the ancient sacred hymns and ritual sacrifices have increasingly become adapted over the centuries to proper devotional activity in the "home" or in the "home of the gods," the temple.[12]

The temples are tremendously interesting to the Westerner. In many of the temples where worship is going on, non-Hindus are not welcome, at least in the inner sanctum, without special arrangements and permission. But access is easily gained to most other parts of the larger temples and to nearly all of the smaller ones. I spent my most interesting time at three worship centers in Tirupati, the great temple complex for Venkataswara; in Madurai, the marvelous temple city of Manikshi (and Shiva); and, in western Karnataka, the three temples of Somnathpur, Halabid, and Belur, built at about the same time that Chartres was being built in the West. Somnathpur had been defaced by the Muslims in struggles long ago and thus was no longer an active worship center. Because it has now become a government-protected museum, we could study the various parts of it in detail and at our leisure without feeling that we were intruding on people's worship. From this older and least active center to the most recent and active center at Tirupati, one can see a long and deep tradition of familial imagery as the focal point of Hindu worship.

The bases of these several temples are laid out according to astrological symbols. Religion is understood to be rooted in the order of the cosmos. Surrounding the bases are various representations of royalty, such as elephants, fortress-like walls, and carvings of royal guards and warrior kings. The political order is seen as the exterior guardian of inner religious functions based on cosmic order. The centers of worship are the images of the gods who live in a joint-family set of inner rooms, decorated by or centering on the *lingam* (male) or *lotus yoni* (female) symbols in the case of the Shiva temples, or an image of one of the *avatars* (incarnations) of Vishnu and his consorts in those dedicated to this other great "sect."[13] Each aspect of the ritualistic daily routine of the god-family is an occasion for religious ritual activity—from rising in the morning, bathing, and dressing, to preparations for the evening's private intimacies with the inevitable spilling of "precious fluids." Further, the ritual calendar is arranged primarily according to the celebrations of the anniversary of the courtship of marriage of the god and the goddess; the births of the children, who are also worshiped and who can intercede with the parental gods; the various jealousies and reconciliations; and specific relationships to other relatives. Indeed, the dominant pattern of piety and the content of the prayers deal with the cycle of love, fertility, birth, initiation, and life, and familial relationships. Each of these motifs also represents a metaphysical-moral "truth" about what is real and what is not real, about separation and union, about engaged duty and detachment. Every temple has, at some prominent points, quite overt and sometimes rather athletic erotic carvings celebrating sexual intercourse as dramatically as Christian religious art portrays Christ's suffering on the cross or Marxist art celebrates the Revolution. In Tirupati, where I was admitted to one of the "prayer chapels" to the side of the main inner sanctum, the priest looked very surprised to see a Westerner in the midst of the gathering before the idol, but he quickly recovered and performed a purification rite over me and graciously asked, through a friend who could translate, the names of my family so that he could pray for them, their fertility and tranquility.

There has been a long and complex debate among scholars of Indian religions as to whether there is in any sense a "congregation" in Hinduism.[14] It is clear that various temples have constituencies which tend to be drawn from particular clusters of families and subcastes. In some temples, such as those at Belur and Halabid, one can see rows of stone benches near the inner sanctum on several sides of a raised platform. In older times the sacred lore was told on these platforms in the form of liturgical, classical dance—in the presence of a gathered body. A Hindu worshiper told me that the practice of temple dancers tended to degenerate into temple prostitution and was discontinued. But for the most part my own observations tended to support those scholarly works which suggest that the primary sense of the "holy community" remains in the extended family, concretely centered in the *jati,* with links to caste, and it is *this* membership which confers ritual privilege and social status—not, as developed in the West, an organized ecclesiastical group which certifies that a covenant is valid to both family and state, or, as in socialist society, the government, which certifies marriage through socialist ceremony. A newborn is initiated into a caste family, not a congregation or a party. There are orders of priests which serve families or subcaste groupings, and this pattern is extended to those "families of gods" who find residence in the temples; but outside of monks or given groups of disciples around a *guru,* there is no sense that I could discover of membership in a community of faith except through the family. The individual finds religious meaning by participating in family ritual in the home or in the home of the gods.

More educated Indians say they feel less need for these rituals, but one of the most fascinating studies of the meaning of this religious accent on the family is a book too much neglected by Western scholars in my judgment. P. Spratt, a Protestant minister's son, became a British Marxist and labor organizer who went to India in 1926 to help "bring the revolution." Over the years of struggle, especially in southern India, including several periods spent in prison for sedition and conspiracy, he began to wonder why the revolution did not, and apparently could not, take place in India. He began to study aspects of the popular Indian, especially Hindu, ways of looking at the world, and finally wrote *Hindu Culture and Personality.*[15] Certain motifs in his work seem to me to have grasped certain dynamics of the dominant Hindu conception of what it means to be human, and thus are directly pertinent to our comparative study of religious ethics and human rights.

Spratt points out that part of the Hindu understandings of family, and thus of both anthropology and society, rests in metaphysics, especially the metaphysics of the "soul" and its relation to the body. The soul is an eternal substance, a "life force" which resides, temporarily, in a specific human form. The most celebrated philosophers of India disagree as to whether the individual soul is, is the same as, is like, or is different from the eternal "cosmic soul"; but they tend to agree that the body is an exterior vessel for the soul, although the body must also be seen as ultimately related to the cosmic soul, much as a bottle partly filled with water floats in the ocean.[16] This exterior body must be appropriate for the soul in that it is the means by which the soul can express its own particularity by taking its proper place in the eternal and universal cosmic order. However, the body can contaminate or hinder the expression of the soul when it is not kept pure, restrained, and disciplined, or when it is allowed to be blemished. The precise connection between body and soul is debated in various schools of Hindu thought and represented variously in a vast array of local practices; but a widespread governing image is one in which the bodily fluids, which are a chief material manifestation of the primal, creative energies of the soul, are "drawn from all parts of the body and hence represent the whole essential person, the soul."[17] Here we find the predominant point of connection. It is through the "life force," conceptualized as semen, that the "soul" becomes embodied. The gods are those who have this in abundance; the goddesses are those who receive abundantly.[18] For humans, who live at lesser degrees of intensity, the concentration and preservation of these fluids become critical concerns. The creative powers of the universe are at stake. Indeed, Gandhi speaks in quite similar terms in explaining his own dedication to *bramacharya,* celibacy and self-control.[19] In a sense, the body-soul energy is a microcosm of the universal macrocosm, and hence each person is complete within himself or herself, because of the relation of this energy to the universal soul. Obviously, if this energy, which "materializes" most immediately as "precious bodily fluids," is totally self-contained, it becomes impossible for other bodies to be created to receive other eternal souls. Only a rare few are sufficiently enlightened to see the macrocosm's full meaning in the microcosm of the self; only a few can gain such full self-consciousness that they are released from the world of rebirth. Hence endogamous groups as secondary, social microcosms are seen as the repositories of the "gene pools" of "soul energy," each with its own ritual, social, and economic life in the hierarchy of cosmic order. Most narrowly drawn in the family-*jati,* the boundaries of this gene pool of soul energy are more widely drawn in the caste.

There are many qualitative gradations of the soul energy, and hence it is necessary to have many gradations of caste vessels to contain them. Of course, the spiritual power of the inner soul may become sufficiently enlightened to recognize its affinity with the cosmic soul. Such great souls are beyond the need for procreative vessels; they transcend all the empirical gradations of vessels that are necessary for social order. Short of full spiritual realization, however, one's being as a concrete social person is decisively influenced by the quality of the social exterior vessel. Over time, of course, with the transmigration of souls, the qualitative awareness of one's inward spiritual condition and the disciplined attention to the appropriate qualitative vessel mean that the soul may progress to fuller realization of its place in the whole ocean of meaning. Or through neglect of this inner dimension, or failure to attend to the proper care of the vessel, the soul may revert to a lower status. Hindus disagree as to how far into the human, animal, or vegetable world this hierarchical structure of vessels extends, but there is the pervasive sense that there must be eternal, multiple levels of vessels to accommodate the multiple levels of qualitative soul.

The formation of a family in such a world view is not, then, the mere joining of a man and a woman together in love. Love in the romantic sense is an art, to be cultivated by the sciences of the emotions and the techniques of the body between parts of the vessel who have regard also for the other's soul. The formation of a family is a metaphysical-social action by which the proper and appropriate vessels are formed or preserved to provide a temporal home for the individuated souls. Those who negotiate and arrange weddings, as well as those who get married, are engaged in solidifying and confirming the secure structure of the vessels and providing an appropriate context for that which is most worthy, most powerful, and most holy.

In Spratt's view all of this entails a particular variety of human narcissism, a concentration on the inner energies and powers of the self and the cultivation of the psychospiritual powers. However, it is a narcissism which extends beyond the self in two ways. First, the inner energies are interpreted in connection with an elaborate and sophisticated religious metaphysics which sees the whole universe in terms of the emanation of a natural energy which in its highest reaches is pure spirituality. When this is recognized, the self realizes that it is divine, and the self is reabsorbed into the cosmic force. Second, while still a part of this world, the narcissism is focused less on the self than on the social vessel which holds the self. Preservation of the purity of the vessel, for the sake of both the soul and the metaphysical structure of society, becomes a compelling duty.

Whether or not Spratt is correct in all his arguments, it is very clear that kinship patterns, presently still the link between nuclear family, joint family, and *jati*, are a metaphysically powerful force in Indian life. Divorce is rare; much time is spent keeping family relationships alive and on an even keel. Unlike their Western counterparts, cousins and uncles—often several times removed—are sources of immediate aid in times of trouble, intergenerational relationships are deep and long-lasting, and young people are much less independent of wider familial responsibility and control well into adulthood. Indeed, most Indian intellectuals who have experienced socialist or Western societies are more sharply critical of the "breakdown" of family in these societies than anything else. They see this as both a symptom of and a cause of spiritual and moral degeneration in those societies which have lost rootage in the cosmic, natural order. If the discrimination and oppression of caste are to be overcome, so they argue, at least the extended family must remain as the central vessel of moral and spiritual nurture, as the vertebrate support of decent social order.[20]

Some Indians are offended by overt use of psycho-sexual interpretations, such as Spratt's, in looking at such matters. To them, these things are not sexual or physical in any sense but are metaphysical realities of consciousness, desacralized by such "demythologizing" treatments. They see these things stated only in the more degenerate forms of Tantric Hinduism, with its overtly erotic speculations. Other Hindus see in such analysis a reductionist tendency to treat the biophysical dimensions of sexuality as more important than they are. To correlate sexuality with religious belief and social practice avoids the spiritual point about the fundamental problem: the relation of the inward soul to the eternal or cosmic soul. The body with its fluids—and for some, indeed, the caste—is only an inevitable fact, never the vehicle of purity. The physical vessels are to be trained and restrained so that the real self is freed for higher consciousness beyond such material preoccupations.

No Indian whom I met, however, was able to make a clear break with the three cardinal marks of familial *jati* or caste purity: *connubium,* commensalism, and vocation. In one way or another, deep loyalties to restricted patterns of intermarriage, close attention to what and with whom one eats, and pervasive assumptions about the kinds of work that are appropriate to distinct groups determined both attitudes and behavior in society.

The development of spiritual self-awareness can, in the Hindu view, transcend the questions of vessels and sexuality and move immediately to the recognition of the spiritual fact that the water in the bottle is of the same essence as the universal ocean. Many of the great feats of the *rashi* and the *yogin* (holy men) are beyond the question of vessels and gene pools. They are, however, also beyond family and caste and beyond society generally. Further, there are many stories of the gods eating from the leavings of the low caste or the outcaste, who are recognized by the gods as in fact more enlightened spiritually than the highest-ranking Brahmin. It is, to use a technological metaphor, as if there were an independent spiritual escalator outside the hierarchical ladder of *jati,* genepool, soul-energy groups. One can transcend these things by developing consciousness of the inward essence of the soul and surpassing all that is of exterior, bodily, and familial concern. One can bring the body, or the family, under programmatic discipline and ritual control. Or, in *bhakti,* one can neglect the body and family entirely, engaging in caste-negating, but spiritually insightful, inversions of prescribed, ordinary behavior. The intensity with which such views are argued by Hindus, however, seems on the face of it to suggest that these issues are very near the core of all they consider holy.

After hearing a scholarly paper by one of the leading Indian experts on psychic research, a man trained in medicine and psychiatry in England and the United States and head of a prestigious research project on the spiritual powers of the Yogis, several Indian Christians and I had a chance to spend an evening with him. We talked long into the night, and it became very clear that although he considered himself a nonreligious, nonpracticing Hindu, his driving motivation for intense research and publication was an attempt to prove two things: first, that there is a psychic-spiritual power which can transcend all physical laws, and second, that where the physical laws are present, they are cosmically given as a hierarchical chain of reality. The higher levels of this physical chain of reality are manifest in humanity, where "breeding" is decisive. He argued, in brief, that the Hindu caste system, although "of course" overlaid with all kinds of superstition, nevertheless had at its core the fundamental scientific insight of eugenics, a scientific insight confirmed by the longest scientific experiment ever conducted by humans on humans. The castes had practiced eugenics for centuries, and the evidence was very clear. Those who came from the highest, more pure, and most disciplined castes were by nature emerging into leadership positions in the new India now that casteism was illegal. Indeed, when Indians (from the upper castes) went abroad—to Africa, to the Mideast, to Southeast Asia, and increasingly to the West—they immediately proved themselves mentally and psychically superior to those groups which had practiced indiscriminate interbreeding. The tone and mood of this man was in no way condescending or arrogant; the entire discussion was conducted with scientific restraint and cautiously worded argument, supported by a large number of references to statistical studies collected by his institution in Hyderabad and by others. There are groups which treat these matters much less dispassionately. In Delhi and Calcutta I visited a number of bookstores where I was surprised to find Hitler's *Mein Kampf* available in large numbers. I asked one shopkeeper about this, and he was quite candid in telling me that some high-caste peoples among his customers are deeply impressed by Hitler's theories of the "natural" racial superiority of Aryan peoples.

But quite contrary to the immediate hostility to implicit arrogance felt by Christian and socialist outsiders to such reading of the data, the Hindu ethos produces a kind of tolerance not fully present in Western or Marxist societies. Most noticeable is the enormous variety of religious and philosophical opinion and belief. It is very difficult to say what is orthodox in a Hindu thought system, and there is no institutionally prescribed public theology or civil creed. The first impression is that radical polytheism reigns, that it is a world swimming in multiple centers of divergent meanings.[21] But the pervasive images suggest an alternative logic. Every diamond has many facets, and each facet is a part of the single whole viewed from a different perspective. Each soul, indeed, is at its own level of awareness, of its own essence, and each sees the world differently as it discovers its own microcosmic reflection of the macrocosm. Some are higher, some are lower, but each is equally valid. There is thus a gradation of proper behaviors, a hierarchy of ortho*praxis* with regard to the maintenance and care of the appropriate familial-*jati*-caste vessel which guides the ethics of each cluster of souls. On this score all is governed by a fixed, rigid, and ritualized discipline. At the same time it is clearly recognized that there are, and must be, many vessels and many ideologies to accommodate the enormous variety of soul energies and levels of awareness. Thus India has developed a kind of tolerance for a wide variety of idiosyncratic doctrines, beliefs, and gods. Indeed, Hinduism has found it relatively easy to absorb tribal groups and colonies of "outsiders," from the ancient Jews in Cochin to the Parsees around Bombay to the Orientals around Calcutta to, most recently, the Tibetans. Fur-

213

thermore, when groups become Buddhists or Jains or Sikhs or Lingyat, they too are seen as another vessel for a particular "state" of one "kind" of soul energy.

The Muslims and the Christians and the Marxists, however, have had greater difficulties, for they all hold that some things are true *and others false*. Theirs are all traditions of ortho*doxy*. For these groups it is not essentially a matter of where one is on one's spiritual pilgrimage that determines the essentially or relevantly true. Truth is objective, not subjective.[22] The vision of eternally fixed, hierarchical social order, while sometimes held by these groups, is understood as subject to change—change on the basis of an objective logic or force, by God's will or human will. The last may be first; organizational and social change may be brought about by the social instrument of change, the church or the party (or the "brotherhood," as in Islam).[23] These movements expect and look for change in social history. The highborn may marry the lowborn. Gene pools are not central to social identity or group formation in principle. As I have pointed out, change occurs in Hinduism also, but it is essentially the change of subjective spiritual self-discovery and growth of awareness. It is the inward change and growth that is of immediate and most pressing concern. "Outward" change also occurs, in a sense. M. N. Srinivas from one perspective and D. G. Mandelbaum from another have shown that over time the subcastes adopt new modes of internal discipline and engage in increased or decreased practices of intermarriage with those caste groupings immediately adjacent in religiosocial status, gradually over the generations manifesting upward or downward mobility as a group, expanding or contracting the endogamous unit. This, however, is basically change of group subjectivity and the subjective acknowledgment by others.[24] The expectation of dramatic social change, or the finding of meaning in the reform or revolution of the social order on the basis of an "objective" truth, is outside the Hindu metaphysical-moral vision. The fundamental structure of the metaphysical-moral vision is a universal, cosmic order which all truly enlightened souls would recognize. This creates a crisis for any convert from Hinduism. Many of the converts to Islam, Christianity, and Marxism were converted as groups, and as such they experience a constant struggle between identity as members of the family, *jati*, or subcaste and as members of the new "movement" against "natural law."[25] From the standpoint of this study, what is central in all of this is the metaphysical-moral foundation for human rights. Hinduism does not hold that all are created equal. Nor does it hold that individual needs, voluntary associational membership, and socioeconomic class are central to what it means to be human. These are not, and could not be, the basis for rights. All rights are essentially the privileges of duty to be what one is, socially marked by proper maintenance of the ritual obligations which concentrate, preserve, purify, and perpetuate soul energy in accord with the hierarchy of the spiritual-material cosmos. While all humans have, in some measure, this soul energy, they have it in different degrees. Hence a structured inequality is fundamental to Hindu anthropology and society. To deny this, in the Hindu view, is both an empirical and a spiritual failure.[26]

C. HEALTH, TECHNOLOGY, AND PURITY

Figure 14.
Health Care and Technology as "Caste-Specific Purity"

Educational	Cultural/ Expressive	Legal
Familial	Voluntary	Political
Medical	Technical	Economic

I have already mentioned in passing the health-care problems in India. They are pervasive in most tropical areas of the world, and are compounded in places like India by the raw facts of poverty and malnutrition. Things are improving; since Independence, life expectancy has risen from about twenty-nine years to nearly fifty years. Interesting for our purposes are the ways in which the profound sense of family-*jati*-caste, socially and religiously understood, influences the patterns found in health care and therapeutic institutions in urban and urbanizing areas. The classical ways of dealing with health care are preventive and involve prescribed ritual ways of taking care of the body. In classical religious literature and in contemporary edifying discourses by religious leaders, detailed instructions on what may not be eaten and drunk are prominently featured. One may take into the body only certain foods, and these may be prepared only by certain groups. There are several theories of how far soul energy extends into the animal and vegetable worlds in the process of transmigration. An Indian's diet depends on which theory he or she embraces: only some will eat beef, more will eat chicken or mutton, even more, eggs. Still others are vegetarians; a few are only fruitarians. To ingest certain foods would, in all these views, contaminate both the soul-energy purity and its physical vessel, destroying personal health and introducing impurities into the gene-pool group. Ordinarily one may not eat or drink with, or accept food and water from, people of lower castes, although some lower-caste servant groups are considered ritually and physically acceptable by virtue of their caste functions as cooks or food-servers. Functional preventive health-care is directly linked with theories of caste purity and the dangers of pollution. Similarly, there are prescribed ways of carrying out one's toilet and of adorning the body. These are a constitutive part of the ancient wisdom of India, but even those who no longer know or study the sacred texts are under their influence.

I happened to be staying for a few days in a student center in Andra where some thirty-five or forty advanced and rather Westernized students were also coming to take M.A. exams in education, literature, and liberal arts. Drawn from several parts of southern India, these bright and well-schooled young people engaged in animated and excited conversation about ideas, exams, job prospects, and the like, using English as their common language. When I asked about caste concerns as discreetly as I could, I was assured that they had left such concerns behind. By the end of the second day, however, deep hostilities had surfaced. Each group was accusing the others of being "dirty" and "ruining our health." Each group had its own procedures of bathing, eating, cleaning the teeth, and otherwise dealing with the daily bodily functions. They accused the director of the hostel of hiring food preparers who were not clean. From all I could see, facilities and preparation standards were quite high for a student hostel, but the sense of ritual purity with regard to daily health-care revealed the persistent sensibilities of classic connections between caste sensibilities and health care that still pervaded perceptions. One low-caste Shakespeare scholar, who had studied caste practices in order to cope with the world she was entering, interpreted the caste patterns for me as she pointed out the self-chosen seating, eating, bathing, and hand-washing practices of the several groups which quickly formed. The purity and health of the vessels were of obvious and present passionate concern.

On another occasion my son came down with a high fever. Everyone we knew heard about it in a matter of hours and came to offer elaborate advice as to what caused it and how to cure it. The level of knowledge of basic physiological functions, and of what affects what, differs quite markedly from the science of Western countries. Various broths and ways of preparing yogurt, "well known for its cooling effects," were suggested in detail. Finally we took my son to a Christian missionary hospital for tests and treatment. That caused further anxiety among some of our friends, for in India hospitals are used in only the most extreme cases. As my son gradually improved, we had a chance to note the tensions between the forms of medical care there and the beliefs and practices of the patients. For example, there is no food service in the hospital. There could not be. Nothing that was prepared by a single kitchen would be acceptable to the patients with caste backgrounds different from those of the preparers. Each patient had some relative in attendance to help with the bathing and, if necessary, hair-cutting and the like, as well as food preparation, for all of these are seen as "therapeutically" important. There is considerable anxiety also about getting injections, and these are a chief topic of conversation among attendants and patients. Injections involve the introduction of foreign fluids into the bodily system, and, leaving aside problems of sterilization, it is just not clear whether or not this is ritually neutral.

Hospitals, clinics, nursing homes, mental-health centers, as distinct institutions with a set of values and perspectives on the world different from those of family-*jati*-caste, are for the most part a Western import. They represent something of a problem in the thinking of urban and urbanizing peoples. Providing traditional preventive and maintenance medicine was a function of the priesthood and of other specific groupings within the caste structure: barbers, midwives, and the makers of various herbal potions. For large sections of the population, this pattern of differentiated social function remains. But, as we shall see in other sectors of life, the introduction of another kind of differentiated institution—in this case a medical institution specifically organized around curative functions—creates a conflict. One noted ophthalmologist told me that recent governmental policies in regard to Indian medicine have been highly dysfunctional. In the last century most of the better hospitals were founded by missionaries. The government, under one of its socialist five-year plans, also founded a number of hospitals and related institutions in the years since Independence. Decisions were evidently made to develop new training institutions for medical personnel and to insist that the highest international standards be applied. The result has been the training of a great number of highly qualified medical professionals in India. Unless the newly trained doctors and nurses join the staffs of missionary or governmental hospitals, however, they frequently find it difficult to establish a practice in India. There is little place for them in traditional Indian social life. Not only are people too poor to pay for their fancy services, but Indians who recognize other kinds of pollution and purity as they bear on physical and bodily health have a highly ambiguous place in the community life of all but the elite in modern urban enclaves. As a result one of the key exports of modern India is medical personnel. They emigrate to the commonwealth countries; render service, in return for good oil money, to large segments of the Arab world; and, I understand, dominate medical services in parts of East Africa. A number of Indian medical personnel whom I have met in the West clearly reveal in the course of conversation that they often send large portions of their earnings to their families and relatives (*jati* relations) in India, and frequently return there to find appropriate mates for their children when they reach marriageable age.

Preventive social medical facilities in the form of drainage, sewage, pure-water supplies, and the like are welcomed in the villages. These innovations often engender disputes among the *jatis* as to who should have the rights of control over and access to the wells. Questions of the purity of fluids taken into the body are as important as economic development and advantage.[27] Except in large cities these projects are primarily the work of Christian missionaries (or semisecularized missionary programs such as the Peace Corps). In the cities they are the projects of government when socialists gain influence. Those who bring these improvements seldom stay or become a part of the ongoing pattern of social life at the local level, and frequently these facilities fall into disrepair and disuse when the donors depart.

While I was in Bangalore in 1976, a large medical conference was held at the college where I was staying. I inquired of the delegates (both Indian and Western) whether there were characteristic illnesses which were predominant in India and how these compared with those of the West. On the one hand many of the illnesses are geographically specific and are often contracted because of general malnutrition, as one would expect. On the other hand it was most interesting that the greatest numbers of reported psychosomatic illnesses cluster around various forms of depression for infertility and impotence. The most difficult medical and surgical problems, however, are caused by venereal diseases and by primitively induced abortions among the poorest of the population. Heavy drinking and wife beating are fairly common among this segment of the population also. An enormous sense of guilt is often an additional burden for the people being treated for these problems. Suicide is not infrequent among those afflicted with these several "family medical" problems, according to my informants. Government policies regarding birth control, whether of the informational variety or of the "forced sterilization" type reputedly a part of the Emergency policies, are relatively unsuccessful, ignored, or resisted. The state of Kerala, of all the densely populated nations and provinces of the developing nations of the world, is the only region to show dramatic success in birth control. Kerala has the highest percentage of Christians and Marxists, and hence the highest percentage of female literacy in India. Otherwise birth control does not make sense in the metaphysics of family-*jati*-caste life, or in the economies of a society where survival in old age depends on having relatives and children to take care of one. What other downward trends there are in the birthrate, according to more recent data, began before the intentional programs to control fertility were introduced, and seem to correlate with urbanization.

The concern for the purity of the vessel as determined by *jati* groupings is played out also in the technological arena. Classically each group or subgroup has its own technical set of skills. This set of skills is twofold in nature. One part of it has to do with the performance of specialized functions in the social ecology of the community, from street cleaning and clothes washing to farming and tax collecting. Particular skills and mastery of techniques are required at each point. Each of these tasks has a relative "purity status" assigned to it, and each village is organized according to the relative status of the various groups, with those who dispose of dead animals at the bottom and those who are custodians of spiritual lore at the top. Each group also has a distinctive ritual function in the life of the community, one which reinforces the network of specific claims and duties. In the complex conduct of a wedding or a temple festival, for example, only those from such-and-such a caste can perform integral parts of the ritual. The variety and complexity of these technological/ritual functions, involving fascinating inversions at certain points, is clearly documented in the vast number of intensive studies of village life.[28] Community life is intricately interlocked by an eternal mutuality of a highly differentiated, technological/ritual complex of roles. Change is feared in some regards, for a break-

218

down of a part means a threat to the whole. The *jati* groupings are key indicators of technological complexity and interdependence, with each group possessing a very narrow range of skills and competences over which it has singular command. If one were not a carpenter from a particular caste, one would never think of repairing a broken cartwheel oneself. One would not have the tools, would not be interested in the mechanics, and would possibly violate one's purity status. Furthermore, one would deprive the proper members of the proper caste-grouping from performing their particular technological role and thereby deprive them of claims to the service which one was properly to render to or for them.

Karl Marx argued a century ago that the industrialization of India was bringing the only revolution that India had ever known, one that would destroy the structure of the means of production upon which Indian social life rested.[29] Max Weber at the turn of the century speculated that the introduction of the railroad by the British for commercial reasons would bring about new ways of organizing social life, for it would introduce a "ritually neutral arena" in which new, voluntary organizations such as the Brahmo Samaj could find the social space to modify the culture from within.[30] Industrialization and modern communication systems, where they have occurred, have brought less a revolution than a new refinement of social life. Older handicraft technology has survived, but it is increasingly "industrialized." Handcrafted artifacts are produced in traditional ways by traditional groupings. They are increasingly sold at home and abroad as consumer goods through mass-marketing methods. Commercial castes, government-sponsored cooperatives, and urbanized peasants have in scattered instances begun to develop new techniques of nontraditional trade. These techniques are not fully woven into an established commercial network of approved obligations. More industrial places of work are increasingly thought of as ritually neutral. Those who perform special technical functions and develop particular technological skills in factories, for example, no longer connect their specific technological work with specific ritual functions in the community. The tasks performed there are neither pure nor impure. They are like plowing in the agricultural economy, which was, in some measure, done by nearly everybody.

Within the work situation, technological operations are again divided into very precise and limited operations. These are hierarchically graded, sometimes according to technical skill involved—more frequently, in firms not started by Westerners, by kinds of materials worked with. Leather, for instance, is lower than cotton, and cotton lower than metals. (Metal does not have life soul; cotton, derived from plants, may; leather, from animals, most surely does or did.) The correlations between previous ritual/skill/caste hierarchies and new technological rank are overwhelming. Low-caste peoples perform low-level, although ritually neutral, technological functions; middle-caste peoples perform middle-level technological functions; and high-caste peoples are the engineers and managers. The exceptions to this are of great interest in conversations and scholarly literature. In a real sense, technology has changed many things, but more remains the same. Very few would think of performing tasks outside the bounds of their narrow, precise skill.[31]

At the same time, ritual functions continue to be observed outside the technological arenas. People who may be machinists in a factory or mine are treated, outside the job situation, according to their relative diligence in maintaining or upgrading the patterns of their family-*jati* of origin. If an individual's job situation brings relative wealth and the possibilites of higher socioeconomic status, he or she will often make increasing efforts to enforce higher dietary, religious, and intermarriage constraints, thereby seeking higher ritual status for his or her family and subcaste.[32]

In general I think it is fair to say that the Indians of the twentieth century have selectively adopted Western technology and incorporated it into the emerging society. Such feats as the detonation of an atomic bomb are surely testimony to that. But they have adopted it on their own social terms and on the basis of complex, interdependent, and hierarchical social groupings, and the technological innovations are used to reinforce the "natural law" of family-*jati* ranking. They seldom have adopted a Western scientific world-view, and are sharply critical of its presuppositions about humanity and nature and their relationship. Technological means of extraction, production, and distribution are tools, nothing more and nothing less. They are not primary causes in society or consciousness in themselves but are instruments which "natural," spiritual, and social groups use for their own purposes; they can be adapted to Indian life without fundamentally altering the dominant meaning systems and social patterns.

One night at the home where I was staying in Bangalore, a faucet washer gave way when there was a surge of water pressure. Water gushed into the bathroom and woke the whole family. I had brought no household tools with me to India and could not fix it by hand. I sought out the night watchman, but he had no tools either, and no idea of where to find any. He would be willing, he said, to wake up someone and send him for a plumber. I said I thought I could fix it easily if only I had a wrench. We then awakened several Indian friends in an attempt to borrow a wrench. None of them had one, and they clearly indicated that they would not know what to do with one if they did. The mysteries of the technology of faucet repair was the social responsibility of other groups, and only crazy Westerners would think of doing it themselves. We later learned that changing electrical fuses and planing down a sticky door brought us into interdependence with still other groups who had, as did no one else, the skills and tools for these technical operations. Technological mastery of specific kinds of tools and skills is proper only for the designated groups. This differs from practices in both the United States and, to some extent, the G.D.R., where general mechanical and technical skills are more diffused throughout the social system (although the German tradition of the "cosmos of vocations" is still a force in this socialized country). No household, at least in America, is complete without a rather complex supply of hand and power tools, and growing up means gaining some personal acquaintance with their use. In India, only among some sectarian Christians and some Marxists whom I met did I find people taking pride in the fact that they had several skills to offer when they applied for work, and were even willing to work with anybody and try anything. In that country, it seems to me, the specialized access to these tools and skills is not only a function of the general economic level but a function of how one understands human nature and social organization through the metaphysical-moral spectacles of the Hindu world-view. Each group has a right and a duty to a specific set of functions in an intricate network of holistic interdependence. To modify this technological specificity is to disrupt the holistic natural and spiritual order of the social cosmos. Technology is thus being adapted to Hindu presuppositions more than it is changing Hindu social life.

The most widely diffused technical facility in Indian society is technique of a quite different sort. The techniques of controlling the body and for nurturing the soul, so as to bring the soul into harmony with cosmic forces, are widespread. The feats of the *yogin* are part of the folklore of India and a strange, fascinating occasion for curious skepticism on the part of outsiders. Neither the public theology of the West nor the civic religion of Marxist-Leninist society has a meaning structure by which such techniques are regarded as important. Even if Westernized Indians show before Westerners their disdain for such practices, institutes for teaching of yoga continue to grow. Indeed, in the West, too, they have gained a constituency among those who have little contact with either Christian churches or radical political parties, and who search for a realignment of body and soul with the natural and spiritual patterns of the universe.

D. EDUCATION, THE ARTS, AND CONSCIOUSNESS

Figure 15.
The Expressive Sectors

Educational	Cultural/ Expressive	Legal
Familial	Voluntar	Political
Medical	Technical	Economic

Educational life in India is in some ways comparable to health care and technology. As there must be careful attention to the bodily vessel and the performance of particular skill through the purity of *jati* practice, so there must be careful nurture of the mind and the discovering of one's groups, particularly by spiritual praxis. Learning is highly regarded throughout India, whether it be the traditional Brahmanic learning, study under a *guru,* or modern forms of learning introduced by the British for the training of clerks. The wise soul, the cultivated pundit, the master of sacred texts, the university graduate—are alike honored. In the prescribed life-cycle of the faithful Hindu, one entire period of life is given over to the stage of being a student, and another to contemplation. The kind and amount of education an individual has had are decisive criteria for making arranged marriages. About thirty-nine percent of the population is literate, and a number of efforts are being made to increase that figure in spite of resistance to formal education in some areas. Some pious Hindus are fearful that the Western forms of schooling will break classical traditions. Some higher-caste people do not want the same curriculum taught to peoples of different castes; in their views such efforts fail to recognize the different levels of soul readiness of different groups, and besides, it makes the servant castes "uppity." Vedic learning is, for the most part, confined to the higher castes. Some lower-caste peoples doubt the efficacy of government-sponsored book-learning. It takes the children away from traditional jobs for youth (such as goat-herding), whereby the mutual interdependence of landlords and workers is maintained and patterns of inter-*jati* obligations are sustained. But for the most part the regard for education is high and intense.

It is not clear that the motivation for education is the same as in the other societies we have surveyed. Education is not focused on the clarification of the objective truths of God or God's creation, as in the Judeo-Christian (or Islamic) traditions, or on the preparation of workers for technical mastery and achievement, as among the Marxists (and Western "vocational training" programs). Rather, education is appreciated for its capacity to bring the individual to greater inner awareness and fulfillment—an improvement of and realization of the spiritual-mental powers that already reside within. As I will note more fully in the next chapter, the key form of evil in Hindu society is considered to be ignorance—especially ignorance of one's inner essence. It is not "sin" or social "alienation." As the microcosm of the whole, the soul's consciousness is the key to full understanding. Education, both in its classical forms and in the ways in which its more recent patterns are adapted to Indian society, is almost preconsciously experienced as the discovery of, or the bringing to the surface of, what is already present.[33] Hindu teachers and students frequently point out how ancient spiritual texts in fact anticipated most recent discoveries, from aviation to thermodynamics to mathematics. Contemporary teachers of everything from electrical engineering to ethno-musicology more often than not assume the attitudes and authority of the *guru* as much as those of the Western "professional" or the socialist "expert." The rather vocal unrest in the urban universities of the past few decades in part parallels student protest around the world, but a number of acute observers suggested that they were convinced that the incompatibility of the impersonal educational concerns and methods of these universities was in constant tension with the felt needs of the students. The overt conflicts were also inner conflicts between life worlds and the kinds of meanings that education was presumed to be able to provide. Many of the other wise most progressive educators fully approved of the rather draconian measures taken by the government during the Emergency to force the students into the singular educational role of fulfilling the needs of their souls and minds by intellectual development.

Western patterns of education, introduced by the colonial government, were designed to prepare administrators and workers for the vast worlds of colonial bureaucracy and corporate management. It was not the British education of Oxford and Cambridge, with its accent on critical thought and creative research; it was the London system of examination focused on "correctness." Much of what went on under this educational policy could accrue to the fiscal and social prestige of the family and *jati* which sent its bright young people through such training. Today the vast bureaucracies continue, and much of the attitude toward education is of precisely the same order. If education could not fully satisfy the inner quest for inward and enlightening self-knowledge, at least it could provide the correct behaviors for finding a secure position for oneself, and hence for one's family, in the bureaucracy (which was "ritually neutral"). One could then conduct one's life in *two* arenas of orthopraxis, one religiously neutral and external, and the other religiously and spiritually important, although now less wide-ranging in its total influence. Formal technical education prepared one for the externals; studying under a *guru,* for what was ultimately more important. In both arenas there seemed to me to be a passivity among the students. On the one hand they dutifully recorded ideas, then faithfully memorized and regurgitated them on exams. This occurs in every culture I have heard about. Yet there is another ingredient here, I think. Namely, ideas are not seen as either true or false, to be tested and criticized. Ideas are either exterior tools to be used in obtaining a degree and a position, or the expressions of the spiritual status of the teacher, of his or her subjective truth. As either, they are accepted. If a student becomes really interested in an idea, it does not seem to indicate that a common truth has been discovered, but either that an advantageous tool is grasped or that the awakening of the student's inner spiritual consciousness is similar to that of the teacher. In this latter case the sharing of ideas becomes subordinate to the sharing of a "presence." Students will attach themselves to teachers without any particular interchange being necessary. Those without this experience in formal educational settings gain spiritual wisdom by sharing in the "presence" of a "great-souled" person such as Satya Sai Baba, the very popular "god-man" of South India who presents his "visage" to his followers in frequent appearances. He and hundreds like him are the "educators" of the masses.[34]

It is interesting that it is through such "god-men" that Hindu motifs are increasingly being exported to the West. The great and learned scholars of the Hindu Renaissance who evoked such movements as the theosophy movement and who intrigued Western authors from Schopenhauer to Schweitzer to North-rup are now succeeded by figures such as the Maharishi and such movements as Hare Krishna and Transcendental Meditation. These forms of "evangelical Hinduism" still play an enormous role in the popular culture of India. However, their days may be numbered as new forms of urban-based popular culture emerge.

The chief vehicle of the new popular culture is the film. India makes more movies per year than any other country in the world, and, through the use of gas-powered generators, the movies are flooding from the cities of Bombay, Madras, and Calcutta to those villages that are still without electricity. These films, in roaring color, are mostly family-centered love stories, filled with action and adventure. They inevitably involve religious and moral conflict, the larger-than-life soap-operas of Indian culture, with the heroic triumph of wisdom and piety over wickedness. They are as replete with popular, edifying moralisms as they are with technical information about how, for instance, a blender works to grind the spices for food. One cannot see one of these films without seeing "Classic Comics" renditions of the great epics of Indian literature in modern garb, for the stock stories are thinly veiled fantasies based on classical themes.

The chief forms of cultural expression and the arts have always been religiously oriented in India. The *ragas* of both Hindustani and Karnatik music are directly tied to religious symbolism and sung as variations on religious hymns.[35] The dance is designed with a vocabulary of several hundred gestures by which the stories of the gods may be acted out for the edification of the people, although Muslim music and dance, with less overtly religious overtones, and sometimes nonreligious erotic motifs, have also influenced the traditions in ways seldom acknowledged by Hindu teachers. These forms of art and religious cultural expression have been passed down from *guru* to student for centuries, and parts of them are still dealt with only by oral tradition. With the introduction of the printing press by missionaries, and with the first dictionaries and polyglot editions of the various sacred traditions being made available by them and by Western Orientalists (so that they could study the languages and religious traditions and know what they were wrestling with), there began a process of "universalization" of the Hindu traditions. The particular schools of oral tradition could be compared and corrected; the different strands of the tradition could be traced. All of this led to the Hindu Renaissance, which I have already mentioned, whereby the literary analysis of the deeper and broader meanings of Hindu poetry, lore, and stories was made more widely available to fresh interpretative comment. With the development of the movies, this process has gone one step further, for now the arts and the riches of the ancient lore not only are available locally or to scholars but are accessible in simplified forms to all. The consequences are enormous, for although there are clearly Hindi,

Bengali, and Maharashtran traditions as well as southern ones, a consciousness of a common Indian style and a common Indian culture is emerging that is much deeper and broader than could previously be recognized. Musical scores of movies are what people hum in the streets; the meaning of stylized dream-sequences of dance in the movies fill the imaginative gaps which signify the passage of time, sexual intimacy, or inner struggle. The hero and heroine who adjust to change while holding fast to the universal, fixed principles of the common tradition become the models for living. Movie stars play leadership roles in some political parties that operate on the national scale. They are popular symbols of the blending of the new into the tried and true.

E. LAW, ECONOMICS, AND POLITICS

Figure 16.
The "Collective" Sectors

Educational	Cultural/ Expressive	Legal
Familial	Voluntary	Political
Medical	Technical	Economic

Law is another area of the social system which is undergoing change in India. Since many of the governmental patterns of law were dominated by foreigners for nearly four hundred years, first by the Moguls and then by the British, there was something of a hodge-podge legal structure at the time of Independence. Further, with some notable exceptions such as the banning of *sati*, neither the Muslims nor the British basically interfered with religious law which regulated large segments of community life—especially matters of family, *jati*, and caste. Every religious group had its own tribunals to deal with family and caste matters, and this was basically separate from civil law and commerical law, which were handled by the rulers. When India gained its independence and the time came for the formation of a constitution, British parliamentary and Marxist socioeconomic motifs were included. A severe test of India's commitment to its constitutional tradition occurred in the last decade. In 1973 the critical question had to do with the relative independence of the judiciary. The government, to carry out some of its social reforms, wanted to have the judiciary under the closer control of political powers. Only then, it argued, could it properly control both the controverted practices of religious laws with their ties to caste, and the independent commercial corruption at the hands of both multinational corporations from the West and an internal "domestic colonialism" of the Indian, bureaucratic ruling classes. Some progress was made toward the political control of the judiciary until accusations were made that the chief political officer, Indira Gandhi, had used illegal means to maintain political power, and that she was basically supported by precisely the "domestic colonialists" whom she said she wanted to control. A vast struggle ensued, and an enormously widespread debate followed, comparable in scope and implication at least to the American debates about Viet Nam and Watergate. Steadily things moved toward the proclamation of the Emergency and the suspension of ordinary judicial procedures and rights. Some twenty-seven constitutional amendments were pushed through parliament or were in the process of becoming law when, in a stunning turn of events, the ruling party was unseated in elections which all observers had thought would be a *pro-forma* ratification of the Emergency policies.

In 1976, during my stay in South India, the Emergency was in effect; arrests without warrant were possible, and *habeas corpus* was voided. The press was censored, and political demonstrations, student rallies, and labor activity were illegal. Friends discussed the situation in hushed tones, and asked me to be careful what I wrote in letters or took through customs. Enormous numbers of the Westernized intelligentsia, especially in the cities, were rather sympathetic to the Emergency, for unrest among labor groups and students was abruptly ended and anticaste protests from below were no longer visible. New food-distribution policies under the Emergency controlled the price of grain for the urban poor, pacifying this potentially explosive mass which had broken the customary social constraints of traditional village life and not yet found new coherent structures to guide daily living. There were a number of protests from specific Hindu intellectuals, especially in the Gandhi tradition, but only three groups which I could discover were taking the risk of speaking out against the voiding of the independence of the law from political manipulation: some Muslim lawyers, centered in Hyderabad; Marxist labor-leaders centered in the port cities (and not connected with the Communist Party of India, which backed Indira); and some Christian leaders, especially in the Christian Institute for the Study of Religion and Society.[36] These were woefully small minorities. If there were other voices, I could not detect them.

These groups evidently voiced concerns which were much more widely held. More resistance to Indira, however, seemed to be generated by stories about experiments in forced sterilization and about poor relationships between Indira and her son. Bad family-related matters raised anger. As the political shell around the prime minister and her cabinet began to crack, of course, other leaders began to speak out more vigorously. They pressed for the recovery of judiciary independence and democratic procedures. They joined old Hindu caste groupings on the right who had wanted above all to keep the traditions of religious law entirely outside of government control but use the government to enforce it. As is well known, this odd coalition of the "Janata Party" won. It was as if the right and the left joined to void the middle.

This strange coalition could not actually rule successfully for very long. It does seem that those who fought for an independent judiciary and democratic law governing political process have won a resounding victory which will surely be a legacy of modern India to the future. But the failures of the Janata Party to unite in anything except opposition to the Emergency brought its downfall. More and more the party turned to caste politics, and Indira's Congress Party returned to office by stressing nationalism and a "secular" state—that is, one in which no caste dominates but all castes are represented.

One of the most interesting features of contemporary Indian political life is the way that the caste is becoming the basis for political organization. In a sense that has always been the case, and the politics of the local communities were managed rather rigorously along caste lines, with elected "councils" to negotiate disputes and to keep all in order. Increasingly, as national political operations extend into economic planning to shape local life, and as means of communication improve to make people aware of wider common problems and prospects, the wider and more diffuse caste connections are becoming the basis of wider political solidarities. Coalitions between castes who might not eat together, and who certainly would not intermarry, form the basis for voting patterns as much as any other political force. When I mentioned earlier in this chapter the nationalism that is part of the essential loyalties of urban peoples in addition to family and caste, it is this phenomenon that I had in mind. The traditional *jati* structure is breaking down among that fifteen percent of the population in the cities. Although some see this as the inner decay of the caste system, it is more likely that caste will increasingly have a bipolar arrangement—one part centered more distinctly in the nuclear family, and the other part centered in the political and economic solidarity in the public realm.[37]

At this time it is not clear where this will lead and how much of the intercaste "council" idea will be brought into parliamentary arrangements. What is clear is that the increased solidarity of the lower-caste groups, already begun at least symbolically by Mahatma Gandhi's renaming the outcastes Harijans ("people of God"), and the constitutional provisions of "one man, one vote" will mean that these groups will have to play an increasing part in determining their own destinies. Many of the most overt forms of ritual and social discrimination are already outlawed, although they are still widely practiced. By law, also, certain numbers of positions in bureaucracies and nationalized industries and in the universities are set aside for Harijans. Nevertheless, there is no radical movement for change among these groups visible in any numbers. They want freedom of access to places of worship, and enough to eat and drink. They also want relief from unscrupulous moneylenders who prey upon the poor, from whom they must borrow large sums to provide dowries and weddings for their daughters. They want a reduction of the arbitrary violence and beatings wreaked upon them when they deviate from prescribed technical or ritual activities. If possible, they would like a little plot of ground which they could farm themselves. Through political solidarity it is possible that some of these wishes could become realities. Nevertheless, it is clear that no radical change can, at the moment, be expected from these groups. They participate too fully in the traditional Hindu social metaphysics, and they do not have the social, political, or economic power to mobilize over a long term.

For several hundred years, when India was under the control of the Muslim Moguls and the Christian British, these groups had everything to gain and little to lose by conversion to alternative world-views with their attendant pressures for social rearrangements. For the most part they did not convert. Even today, where the Marxists are active in Kerala and Bengal, some of these groups vote Communist en bloc if the party seems to be moving ahead on the changes mentioned above. But there is relatively little inclination to forsake the basic social philosophy of Hinduism with its family-caste, solidarity-group grounding.

F. POVERTY AND ECONOMIC DEVELOPMENT

These patterns in the various sectors as I have tried to represent them throughout this chapter all affect economic life. Vast numbers of Westerners, whether of a liberal or a Marxist orientation, have focused on economic life in the past several decades. The liberal economists who have written about "development" and the socialists who have argued from a presupposition of economic determinism have alike attempted to discuss economic factors without reference to these other forces. One of the chief merits of Gunnar Myrdal's vast work on the economics of the area is the recognition that economic development in India is nonsense descriptively and programmatically if careful attention is not given to other aspects of the social system.[38] His sometimes-polemical critique of both orthodox liberal and Marxist economic myopia strikes home again and again, whatever other deficiencies his work may have. It is surely also the case that Westerners and Eastern Europeans who go to India are so overwhelmed by the relative poverty and painful struggle for economic subsistence among large portions of the population that they are temporarily blinded to the ways in which the economic functions of the society are in large measure controlled by noneconomic functions of the society. Change in the economic structures may affect relatively little until these other areas of living are taken into account. So far as I can see, a combination of myopic economic theory and "Lady Bountiful compassion" have conspired to blind development economists to what is going on and what can happen in India.

I have elsewhere attempted to show, following the lines of thought of Weber and Myrdal, that most of the economic factors which are held by economists to produce modern economic structures have been present in India for a long time without the same results produced in Puritan and Marxist societies.[39] From ancient times India has had a number of these factors:

—extensive trade
—credit-interest rates for complex finance operations
—a commercial stratum of the population
—philosophies of rational enlightenment
—large political units of relative peace
—state contracting and public works
—technically skilled craftsmen
—independent merchants
—occupational specialization
—acquisitiveness and rational calculation of gain
—group solidarity among laboring classes, etc.[40]

Yet neither market-oriented corporations nor government-planned economic development has occurred to parallel the developments of Puritan and Marxist societies until recent conscious efforts have been made to introduce Western and Marxist models. What did develop is a radically free commercial market for small-scale producers and consumers as the exchange mechanism between families. This works in the interstices of the traditional, mutual interdependence of the family-*jati* in the village, now given a wider range of freedom in the cities. Larger patterns of production and distribution are labor-intensive operations owned and managed by family or caste groupings and financed by intricate marginal loan-arrangements (or by government loans if one can make the right connections, through family or caste, with the right government officials). A bribe, which there is often viewed as a broker's fee for service, usually has to be paid to get even the most direct and legal things done in these financial arrangements if one operates outside caste ties. National economic planning and control of the economy are not very effective, although the central government has been trying to make them more effective in a constant struggle since Independence. A Swiss economist who was in India studying the situation while I was there told me that about thirty percent of all economic activity is conducted using "black money," black-market deals, bribes, private arrangements, and untraceable funds. A Danish colleague who had worked on economic development there for five years put the figure closer to forty percent. What is also fascinating is that although there is a pronounced struggle for subsistence among the poorer groups and a considerable drive for wealth among the already privileged, what gains are made are put immediately into consumption—food for the poor, ostentatious houses and gadgets for the rich, and wedding feasts and temple gifts as large as people can afford.

The point is that economic activity is simply not a basic locus of meaning. In the social spirituality of India, humanity is not *homo economicus*. If anything, humans in this life are to be understood as *homo ludens*. We "play" our socioeconomic roles, and all economic and social rights are subordinated to a larger metaphysical-moral vision. There is no poor peasant who does not want to be rich, and there are very few wealthy families who do not see that they get richer. They fret about economic matters intensely when it comes to questions of how to divide the family belongings among heirs and in the face of numerous needs and claims from relatives near and far, but economic activities of extraction, production, and distribution as such are not laden with basic meaning.[41] These are neither "vocations" wherein one manifests faithfulness to God's providence, as in Puritanism, nor the clue to the social meaning of history wherein humanity overcomes alienation, as in Marxism. They are necessary facts of life. It is better to have more than less, but people do not find their core identities in relation to economic activity even if they identify others by their outward marks. When people work, in the fields or in business, when they barter at the market or negotiate loans, they work hard at it, but with a certain detachment. Given the level of health and the general level of nourishment, no one can watch a group of Indian construction workers, for example, and doubt that they work hard. Yet it does not, finally, entail fundamental meaning. Duty must be done, the body must be fed, the network of extended family obligation met, the nation built up, and the rules of these games must be followed; but the meaning of life is elsewhere.

It is fascinating in this connection to see what happens in secularized business or professional families in America and Europe when one of the sons or daughters becomes a convert to Hare Krishna, Transcendental Meditation, or the like.[42] The parents go to great extremes to enlist religious, political, and economic institutions to reclaim their lost children and to get them into some significant economic position where they can find meaning for their lives and be "of use" to themselves and society.[43] The children, of course, directly challenge the social metaphysics and morals of the society by turning to the East.

Among some segments of the Indian economic community, the growing awareness of the interdependence of the whole nation economically and the wider significance of extended caste-alliances have brought about a new dedication to economic activity as the obligation of the parts to the whole. Each group must do its part, or the whole falls apart. Hopes are set forth for a new, nationwide interdependency, harmoniously interacting with natural ecological laws, each group having its own "appropriate" lifestyle and technology. Westerners are perhaps most familiar with these views through the writings of E. F. Schumacher.[44] Certainly there will be areas in which ritual and social conceptions of purity will dominate in ways quite different from those of societies shaped by the Liberal-Puritan synthesis and Marxism-Leninism. Even more, it will be a very difficult struggle to find out whether such a society can manage economic survival internally and find creative ways to interact externally. Gunnar Myrdal at one point, after noting that this fifth of the world's population accounts for only about three percent of all international economic life, suggested that the entire subcontinent could slide into the Indian Ocean with scarcely a ripple in the world economy.[45] Still, for all the problems and the precariousness of Indian society at this time, one can find, emerging out of a long and deep history, a revitalized vision of a "natural law ethic," rooted in the cosmic order and discerned by spiritual enlightenment, that is a major alternative conception of the basis for human rights in religion and society.[46] To that history and vision we now turn.

---

1. I am deeply appreciative of the work on South India done by John Carman; see his "Report from South India," in *The Religious Situation*, ed. D. Cutler (Boston: Beacon Press, 1969), pp. 395ff.

2. Joseph Elder, "Industrialism in Hindu Society," Diss. Harvard 1959.

3. See M. Singer, *When a Great Tradition Modernizes* (Delhi: Vikas, 1972), especially pp. 325 – 31.

4. See M. S. A. Rao, *Urbanization and Social Change* (New Delhi: Orient Longmans, 1970); A. B. Shah and C. R. M. Rao, eds., *Tradition and Modernity in India* (Bombay: Manaktalas, 1965); R. S. Khare, *The Changing Brahmans* (Chicago: University of Chicago Press, 1970); S. Dasgupta, *The Hindu Ethos and the Challenge of Change* (Calcutta: Minerva Associates, 1972); and B. Kuppuswamy, *Social Change in India* (Delhi: Vikas, 1972).

5. M. N. Srinivas, *Social Change in Modern India* (Bombay: Orient Longmans, 1972), Indian edition.

6. Gunnar Myrdal, *Asian Drama*, 3 vols. (New York: Random House, 1968), especially Volume I.

7. Louis Dumont, *Homo Hierarchicus* (Chicago: University of Chicago Press, 1970). The power and scope of this work derives in part from the fact that Dumont shares certain fundamental assumptions about humanity and society that are themselves close to Indian views: cultural forms derive from "spiritual insights" and, in large measure, determine all other aspects of social existence; the "Old Regime" of France, before the Revolution, is superior to and more truly human than either Marxist or "bourgeois individualist" societies; to utilize categories from the West in discussing Hindu conceptions is to fail to see an alien system of classification and thus to miss the meaning of hierarchical, organic society. See R. Darnton, "What's New About the Old Regime," *New York Review of Books*, Apr. 3, 1980, especially p. 29.

8. V. S. Naipaul, *India: A Wounded Civilization* (New York: Knopf, 1977).

9. C. T. Kurien, *Poverty and Development*, CISRS Social Concerns Series, No. 17 (Madras: CISRS, 1974), Chapter 5.

10. See I. P. Desai, ed., "Symposium on Caste and the Joint Family," *Sociological Bulletin*, 4 (Sept. 1955); Singer, *When a Great Tradition Modernizes*, pp. 288ff.; P. D. Devanandan and M. M. Thomas, eds., *The Changing Pattern of Family in India*, rev. ed. (Bangalore: CISRS, 1966); and Indian Social Institute, *The Indian Family* (New Delhi: Sterling Publishers, 1972).

11. M. N. Srinivas, *Caste in Modern India* (Bombay: Asia Publishing House, 1962).

12. S. Stevenson, *The Rites of the Twice-Born* (London: Oxford University Press, 1920).

13. The use of the word "sect" differs greatly from Western usage. See J. Carman, "Report from South India."

14. This debate was sparked largely by Max Weber's seminal work, *The Religion of India*, trans. and ed. by Hans Gerth and Don Martindale (Glencoe, Ill.: Free Press, 1958), which argues that there is not. See also Bradley Hertel, "The 'Congregation' in Indian Religious Life," paper delivered at the annual meeting of the American Academy of Religion, 1975.

15. P. Spratt, *Hindu Culture and Personality* (Bombay: Manaktalas, 1966).

16. These views are also set forth by P. M. Rao, *Contemporary Indian Philosophy* (Bombay: Bharatiya Vidya Bhavan, 1970); and G. M. Carstairs, *The Twice-Born* (London: Hogarth, 1957).

17. Spratt, *Hindu Culture and Personality*, pp. 163ff. et passim.

18. See also G. Parrinder, "Hinduism," in *Sex in the World's Religions* (London: Sheldon Press, 1980).

19. See E. Erikson, *Gandhi's Truth* (New York: Norton, 1969), pp. 192ff. and p. 374.

20. See my "Social Ethics East and West," in S. Amirtham, ed., *Man in Indian Society* (Madras: CLS Press, 1978).

21. See A. Daniélou, *Hindu Polytheism* (New York: Pantheon Books, 1964).

22. Truth *is* objective, although in both Lutheran-Evangelical Christianity and in Marxism-Leninism a subjective element plays a critical role, as we saw in Chapter Six.

23. It is precisely because he challenges such assumptions that Dumont (*Homo Hierarchicus*) is able to offer such an appreciative view of caste and the Hindu view of reality. In this study Dumont represents a tradition of Western scholarship which sees the loss of the organic, hierarchical world of the *ancient regime* in Europe at the hands of the Reformation and the French Revolution and its successors as a loss of human reality. See A. Gould, T. M. Madan, et al., *Contributions to Indian Sociology*, New Series, No. 5 (Dec. 1971), for a special symposium on Dumont.

24. Srinivas, *Caste in Modern India*; and D. G. Mandelbaum, *Change and Continuity*, Vol. II of *Society in India* (Berkeley: University of California Press, 1970), especially Chapter 27.

25. I use the term "natural law" here in the classic, Western sense to draw attention to the analogies between certain Hindu assumptions and those of the classical "conservative" traditions in the West.

26. T. W. Organ, *The Hindu Quest for the Perfection of Man* (Athens, Ohio: Ohio University Press, 1970), especially Chapter VIII; I believe it is essentially correct on these points.

27. I learned this in conversations with numerous Baptist missionaries and Peace Corps personnel in Karnataka in 1973. I am especially indebted to John B. Slattery, director of the regional Peace Corps projects.

28. See, for examples, S. C. Dube, *Indian Village* (Bombay: Allied Publishers, 1967); A. C. Mayer, *Caste and Kinship in Central India* (Berkeley: University of California Press, 1960), especially Chapters IV and V; and William and Charlotte Wiser, *Behind Mud Walls*, rev. ed. (Berkeley: University of California Press, 1970).

29. Karl Marx, *The First Indian War of Independence* (Moscow: Progress Publishers, 1959); this book is based on a series of articles prepared for the *Daily Tribune* in the 1850s. See also Trevor Ling, *Karl Marx and Religion in Europe and India* (New York: Harper & Row, 1980), especially Chapter 6.

30. Weber, *The Religion of India*; cf. Ling, *Karl Marx and Religion in Europe and India*, especially Chapter 7.

31. These motifs are of great interest to Singer, *When a Great Tradition Modernizes*, and Myrdal, *Asian Drama*.

32. See Srinivas, *Caste in Modern India*.

33. The analogies to those theories of consciousness developed in the West by C. G. Jung are striking. See "The Psychology of Eastern Mysticism," in Vol. 2 of *The Collected Works of C. G. Jung*, ed. G. Adler et al., trans. R. F. Hull (Princeton, N.J.: Princeton University Press, 1972).

34. See K. Singh, "Godmen of India," Special Holi Issue of *The Illustrated Weekly*, Mar. 18, 1973, passim.

35. I am indebted to my wife, Jean Stackhouse, for most of the materials in this section. See her forthcoming volume on Karnatik music.

36. See *Religion and Society*, the double issue on the Emergency, 24 (June and Sept. 1977).

37. Compare C. von Fürea-Haimendorf, "Caste and Politics in South Asia," in C. H. Phillips, ed., *Politics and Society in India* (London: Allen & Unwin, 1963). See also Donald E. Smith, *South Asian Politics and Religion* (Princeton, N.J.: Princeton University Press, 1966), Part II.

38. See Myrdal, *Asian Drama*.

39. See my "The Hindu Ethic and the Ethos of Development," *Religion and Society*, 20 (Dec. 1973), 5 – 33.

40. Hence none of these factors can be seen as the primary causes of "modernization" or the development of human rights.

41. See D. C. McClelland, *The Achieving Society* (Princeton, N.J.: Van Nostrand, 1961). See also M. Weiner, ed., *Modernization* (New York: Basic Books, 1966); and especially J. Huizinga, *Homo Ludens* (London: Granada, 1949). Huizinga began as an Indo-European philologist, and his references to Hindu motifs appear constantly in this study.

42. H. Pope, Jr., *The Road East* (Boston: Beacon Press, 1974).

43. H. Richardson, *Deprogramming* (Toronto: Toronto School of Theology, 1977).

44. See especially E. F. Schumacher's *Small Is Beautiful* (New York: Harper & Row, 1973). It is, I think, no accident that the portrait of Gandhi dominates the cover, although Schumacher calls his moral vision "Buddhist" (Chapter 4) in an apparent, but unsuccessful, attempt to divorce it from the classical metaphysical-moral vision and social hierarchy of Hinduism. M. E. Spiro, however, has documented that even the most isolated Buddhist efforts have not succeeded in this divorce. See his *Buddhism and Society* (New York: Harper & Row, 1970).

45. Gunnar Myrdal, *The Challenge of World Poverty* (New York: Pantheon Books, 1970).

46. See, for example, the appeal to these motifs in several papers delivered at the World Council of Churches Conference on Faith, Science and the Future held at the Massachusetts Institute of Technology in 1979. See Roger Shinn, ed., *Faith and Science in an Unjust World*, Vol. I (Geneva: World Council of Churches, 1980), especially the presentations by Charles Birch, pp. 62ff.; M. Palihawadana and N. Matsugi, pp. 138ff.; and C. T. Kurien, pp. 220ff.

CHAPTER EIGHT

India's Social Ethic: A Longitudinal Interpretation

A. ANCIENT ROOTS

THE traditions that have informed and are still shaping modern India are long, deep, and complex. No single chapter, and perhaps no single author, could do them justice. The multiple streams of influence from the past and from abroad are so diverse and are viewed so many ways by so many scholars that it is only with hesitation that I dare speak at all. Yet the particular social spirituality of Hinduism is highly influential even today in India's understanding of human rights. It is rooted in ancient and basically continuous traditions, although it has been cross-pollinated by many non-Hindu winds of thought and society that have swept across the subcontinent, blowing the dust of ancient soil and exposing, but not dislodging, the indigenous flowers. As we shall see, in the last century a hybrid has come into existence which is still bearing fruit. Indeed, the metaphysical-moral vision of this tradition represents a major option for belief and sociality—one which has analogies to numerous elements of Western history and countercultural movements.

When the troops of Alexander the Great invaded northwest India several centuries before Christ, they found a rich and high civilization already in existence. Among the things which impressed the invaders were subtle religious and philosophical modes of thought which rivaled those of Homer, Plato, and Aristotle. Not only were there many local and tribalistic patterns of worship and social organization, but a sophisticated body of grand literature and high learning was widely established.[1] In the Vedas were ancient hymns, chants, ritual texts, and treatises celebrating the powers of the cosmic order. The Vedas prescribe those prayers and rites which are to guide humanity in understanding, and cultically re-enacting, that order so as to assure the right order in society and consciousness. These texts also reflect the dominance of ancient Indo-Aryan tribes over indigenous ones, and speak of social rank in terms of color (*varna*), the term still used for caste. Of more recent origin, a body of literature called Upanishads represents a revised interpretation of the older Vedic sources. In the

234

Upanishads, written by ascetic monks, a more speculative set of minds is at work. The connection between the human soul and the cosmic order is not primarily a ritual one; it is one of spiritual understanding (of what the Western intellectual traditions have called *gnosis*). Through symbolic reinterpretation, concern is less focused on prescribed religious behavior and more focused on intuitive knowledge of the internal and external forces which determine life and life's meanings. This later classical tradition of the Upanishads, called Vedanta, or "coming at the end of the Vedas," quests for a principle of unity by which all things may be understood. It issues in an identification of the deepest character of each soul (Ātman) and the ultimate being of the universe (Brahman). The essence of the self and the character of the universe are identical and eternal. Thus by introspective self-discovery one could come to know the secret of life. This is what is really real, and transcendental awareness of this identity is the truly saving knowledge. By such realization we are saved from the distractions of the world and are enabled to renounce the apparent contradictions of experience. Different souls, however, are at different stages of awareness of this saving knowledge. This has two implications: first, it means that there have to be different gradations of humanity; second, it means that a particular soul may have to undergo a number of rebirths or reincarnations (*samsāra*) in the illusory world until it reaches full enlightenment.

These doctrines of cosmic order and ritual on the one hand, and gnosis, hierarchy, and transmigration on the other, combined to form Brahmanism. This set the pattern for most subsequent Indian thought. Both the Vedic ritual texts and the Upanishadic speculative ones were frankly elitist, establishing the social dominance of holy men over all other groups and functions in society, even where other groups had control of political and economic power.

There had been resistance against these traditions, to be sure. The Jains and Buddhists had repudiated the ritual and social hierarchy of the Vedas and cast doubt over the utility of the philosophical speculations of the sages who composed the Upanishads. Already by the time that Alexander invaded India, they had begun to develop modes of simple devotion, belief, and popular piety which captured the imagination of the people beyond the priests and holy men. Both these movements originated among the Kshatriyas—the warrior-king classes which had been subordinated by the possessors of ritual and spiritual wisdom. They appealed to other constituencies as well. For a while these heterodox movements threatened to displace the Brahmanism of the Vedas and the Upanishads, for while they shared the presuppositions of the need for disciplined action and enlightenment, they promised a way to enlightenment which required neither the elaborate ritual enactments of the Vedas nor the intense, speculative asceticism of the Upanishads. A series of local dynasties were formed on heterodox principles. Under their protection Buddhism in particular spread rapidly and became the dominant religion in many parts of the subcontinent. Thus it was a rich and complex social and intellectual world which was in existence by 327 B.C. when Greeks accompanying Alexander brought some of these ideas back to the Mediterranean world.[2]

The religious and social concerns of the Vedas and the Upanishads were not to be displaced by either internal heterodox movements or exterior influence. Indeed, what we now call Hinduism was formed out of the Vedic and Upanishadic traditions as they underwent revision in response to internal and external challenge. In an extensive movement lasting some five hundred years, the influence of Buddhism was gradually displaced among the people, and the antihierarchical sentiments were undercut as the caste system was firmly consolidated. New epic poetry was penned which both captured the religious imagination and gave a prominent place to popular devotion, incorporating many of the local and previously tribal gods and goddesses in overarching narratives. Perhaps most important, however, was the systematic ordering of Sacred Law. The incapacity of the Buddhists to provide either a normative theory of social order or a committed constituency able to carry their philosophy into the formation of lay organizations meant that in house after house, temple after temple, and princely court after princely court, the Hindus were able to regain dominance.[3] In these moves Hinduism was formed. It consisted of a vast array of particular beliefs and practices that attempted to encompass, or at least provide a place for, all parts of society. The key organizing principle of Hinduism is the idea of *dharma,* a spiritual, moral concept of the eternal law of being. It was based in the Scriptures, interpreted by the Brahman caste (which stands at the peak of the social pyramid), and applied to all questions of the inner soul, social interaction, and the cosmic order. It found its most systematic articulation in the Sacred Law.[4]

Dharma, variously translated as "right order," "virtue," and "religious duty," is given in the very structure of things. The "ought" is found in the depths of the "is." It is the inner law which is to be discovered and lived out. It may be found by the path of knowledge, that is, by discovery of what one essentially is; it may be discovered in dutiful action, that is, according to the selfless carrying-out of one's social role; or it may be found in devotional love of God, that is, by direct, intuitive, spiritual communion of the inner self with cosmic reality. Each path brings the person to true self-discovery and thereby to the discovery that, at the deepest reaches of the inner self, the Ātman is the same as the universal soul, the Brahman. Each path, of course, has many degrees and stages, and each stage has particular and appropriate orientations and disciplines proper to it. But the final stage is one of release (*moksha*) from all gradations, distractions, and illusions that are a part of the material world, and the transcendental attainment of the bliss of union with the universal spirit, beyond right and wrong, beyond good and evil. All of this structure and each moment along the several paths are governed by the universal moral order within them—by *dharma.*

On the path toward final release, two sciences are especially necessary while we are still bound to this world. One is the science of polity, by which we master the world of politics, civil and criminal law, and economics and wealth. This has to do with material gain (*artha*), a proper human activity, one which is necessary to human society. All who are spiritually ready for this activity should carry it forth with intelligent dispatch, using all the skills and stratagems proper to gaining the maintaining command over land, people, and riches. The other is the science of love, the art by which we cultivate the attractions of pleasure and sexuality (*kama*). All who are spiritually ready for this activity also should know its many parts, study its several forms, and master its possibilities. Both material gain and pleasure, both regime and sexuality, however, are to be carried out under the guidance of *dharma*, the eternal Sacred Law which guides virtuous conduct. *Dharma*, *artha*, and *kama* require each other to be whole. Indeed, material wealth and true pleasure flow from *dharma*. If we pursue pleasure only for sensuous enjoyment, or political and economic power only out of fear or avarice, we forsake *dharma*. We may gain fleeting moments of illusory glory, but we gain neither integration with the spiritual law of the cosmos nor closer approximations to release (*moksha*) from these worldly matters.

These themes are accented again and again in hundreds of different but interlocking ways in the great literature of this creative period of Hinduism. It pervades the Laws of Manu, the great codification of the *dharma* that governed marriage, inheritance, and caste rules. The *Artha Shastra* and the *Kama Sutra* deal with polity and sexuality in great detail. These themes are peppered throughout the *Ramayana* and the *Mahabharata,* the great epic poems of devotional life; indeed, they culminate, in some ways, in the *Bhagavad Gita,* the Song of the Lord, the "new testament" for many Hindus. It is clearly these themes which are taken up as the point of departure by the later great philosophers of India, who elaborate the metaphysical and epistemological bases for them.

In South India these themes are perhaps most articulately stated in the *Kural,* the work of Tiruvalluvar, a Tamil priest of the third century A.D. His work has been claimed by Hindus, but also by some Buddhists and Christians. More recently it was selected by UNESCO as one of the works which is appropriate to the study of human rights.[5] The *Kural* has three main parts: *Dharma, Kama,* and *Artha.* After offering praise to God and the natural order as they present to us the vision of true virtue as recognized by seers of old, Tiruvalluvar turns to the study of those virtues proper to home and family. Subsequently he takes up the arts of wealth and rule, wherein the arts of government are seen as requiring both a shrewd deviousness and a dutiful detachment.[6]

In all these sources it is instructive to see, for our purposes, these three motifs intertwined in dominant views of "humanity" and "rights."

The entire society was understood as a human representation of a sacred cosmic order, populated by a multiplicity of hierarchical familial groups, within which are individual souls, each soul being a microcosm of the whole. In a cycle of rebirths (or, as some sources report, in the more immediate intensity of devotion through *bhakti*), each soul eventually experiences all possibilities. In the meantime each finds a temporary place and knows that in the general scheme of things it is only temporary. It can thus be endured with detachment.

If one held such a view, a complete interpretation of the world and society would be theoretically possible. Everything could, in principle, be related to everything else; nothing would be contrary to anything else. To be sure, things would be perceived differently because different perceivers are at different places in the cosmic whole. If one believed this, it would not be necessary for everyone to know the whole, so long as a few could interpret the whole for the many. One would only have to know and carry out the duties of one's own being at a particular stage and station of the universal spiritual-moral economy.

B. ANALOGIES TO AND DISRUPTIONS FROM THE WEST

In many respects the portrait of society in India as conveyed through this classic literature is not far removed from the spiritual order of the Middle Ages in the West, prior to the Council of Constance, the Renaissance, the Reformation, and the development of both the Liberal-Puritian synthesis and the eventual humanistic "civil religion" of Marxism. It has certain social affinities with Conservative Catholicism and Imperial Calvinism, and a number of similarities to the Transcendentalists of America and the Romantics of Germany.

Further, like the West, India underwent a variety of changes as this tradition entered into the cultural and social patterns of the various regions of the subcontinent. In region after region, as various dynasties and linguistic groups became predominant, Hinduism was adopted by various groups in specific ways, adapted to the particular needs of quite different social arrangements and cultural achievements, and is therefore remembered and practiced in a variety of ways. Thus each region has its own "golden age," with the moments of highest religious consciousness often memorialized in distinctive and divergent forms of temple construction, liturgies of worship, and specifications of Sacred Law. These can be seen most especially in the Puranas, the poetic *bhakti* songs composed around Vedantic themes; these contain references to multiple deities and express in the nonclassical languages the local traditions of regional Hinduism. Those who live by the Puranas of medieval Hinduism are thus sometimes skeptical of attempts to overcome popular religion by returning to some "purer" earlier form, much as Catholics devoted to the "saints" resist the development of modern Conciliar Catholicism. Until today the linguistic divisions which symbolize these differences most dramatically to thousands have remained as powerful guardians against any simple reduction of Hinduism to any singular classical interpretation. The "great traditions" of the classical age are mediated by, fused to, and often in tension with the "little traditions" of local and regional practice.[7] There is some parallel to the tensions felt in the Medieval West between, for instance, Frankish, Spanish, and Latin Christians (and tensions among all against the Reformation). There were, however, basic differences in what was viewed as "the natural order of things." First, the Christian view of natural law is one which could not lead humanity into fulfillment or perfection. What is "natural" is in fact "creation," a product of a divine reality other than nature itself. Creation is not the extension of divine being into existence but an act of loving, personal reality. Creation is thus taken with great seriousness, but the order of the cosmos is not the final guide for social behavior.

Second, the West had the church, organized in principle on different, "nonnatural" bases than those of other centers of loyalty and meaning in society. In India the priesthood became hereditary according to "natural" family groupings. They served the natural constituencies of kinship and regime, adapting to local practices, and were able to bring the whole of society under their influence. They made, in effect, the whole "natural" society into a sacred, highly differentiated, organic entity, with no distinct or centralized religious creed or community. The Brahmins had special spiritual and liturgical functions, but so did others. They were really only on a higher level in an integrated social pyramid. Family and regime were integrated into the regionally diverse, hierarchical caste system, whereas in the West family and regime were subordinated in principle to a centralized, doctrinally focused church. Further, each individual, whatever the family or political connection, was in principle under the equal ministry of that church. The person, as person, came to the new community formed at the communion rail, whatever his or her natural abilities and background. Family power and political power were viewed as having within them (precisely when they were at their noblest, and not only at their weakest) constant temptations to sin and evil, to domination and idolatry, precisely because they were a good of God's creation but not continuous with the goodness of God; hence they were subject to pride and arrogance.

Third, when Islam began its expansion into India, there were sharp repercussions like those that had occurred in the West.[8] Like Western belief systems, Islam had a real notion of sin and a hatred of idolatry, even if it did not have the church. The Islamic invaders in India were victorious. Although there had been Islamic colonies in India since the eighth century, large-scale invasions began only in the eleventh century. It was not until the thirteenth century, however, that Islamic power was consolidated and widespread on the subcontinent. The coming of the Muslims began a long chapter in Indian history. From the Sultanate of Delhi (1211 A.D.) until modern India's independence from the British, large parts of India were under non-Hindu political domination. First by the Turks and then by the Moguls, who consolidated an efficient and extensive reign, the integrated and holistic system of thought and society established by Hinduism was cracked open before the Westerners arrived.

Islam brought with it a prophetic religious orientation with a fundamentalist view of the one God's Holy Law—a view which differed sharply from that of the diversified, pluralistic piety of Hindus and the many levels of Hindu Sacred Law. Law for Muslims was not rooted in the organic and hierarchic structure of being, something that could be discovered, developed, and fulfilled by cultivation of that spark of the divine innately present in all forms of human life. Law was posited by the one God in one form, itself a product of his almighty and sovereign will that stood over and against pluralism, the world, and all merely human knowledge of it. The governance of humanity was to be guided by one purpose only, by the enforcement of those policies which brought the people to confession of the one true God and obedience to the one law. Humanity and the human community were created for submission to God, *not* for self-realization. Politics and religion were essentially the same thing: an opportunity to serve God in history.[9]

In some ways the introduction of Islam into India had few effects. For the most part, in the villages, it merely substituted a new set of tax collectors for the old ones. Most often the local agents remained the same; they merely handed over the revenue to Muslim instead of Hindu rulers.[10] Islamic political rulers were, in many respects, "a caste" outside "the castes," an elite, from the Hindu perspective, with their own *dharma* and piety that functioned in the social hierarchy but had somehow escaped traditional categories. Over the centuries, as some outcaste groups were converted to Islam, they became subcastes scattered among the various *jati* of the social pyramid. As some worshiped the eternal soul in the form of Shiva and others in the form of Krishna, still others worshiped Allah. In these ways Islam represented a change in, but not a change of, the system.[11]

In two related ways, however, Islam brought a revolution—some might even suggest that it brought the first major transformation in India in at least two millennia. It had two sides: one was religious, the other legal. In religion, Islam, growing out of many of the same Semitic roots which had shaped Christianity, held that belief, lifestyle, religious community, and ultimately salvation are given by God. Other false views were wrong and to be rooted out. Humanity cannot—neither by ritual, by knowledge, nor even by spiritual devotion—discover its own essence and cultivate it to perfection, to self-realization or fulfillment. The microcosm of the soul is *not* like, a part of, or the same as the Soul of God. There is no way that what is already within us can be enlightened, trained, or refined so that it becomes fully divine. God is other than humanity. The multiple temples and shrines are not refractions of a single light that is seen through many prisms but the anthropomorphic projections of false human inventions on an idolatrous cosmic screen. Indeed, the religious problem is precisely the opposite of what the Hindus hold. The soul, which is quite different from God, must subject itself utterly to the all-ruling God, who is utterly beyond.

It is true, of course, that a mystical strand of Islam, Sufi, had developed very early.[12] Sufi accented the paths for cultivation of the soul. In India it flourished in many ways and was eventually accepted in modified forms by some orthodox Islamic leaders, by many simple believers, and by some Hindu thinkers as an authentic form of religious experience. It formed the basis for the later syncretistic religion of the Sikhs. Certainly it had direct affinities to the *bhakti*, the devotional patterns of popular Hinduism. But for the most part this strand

240

of Islam was subordinated to the more pronounced motif of subjection to the heteronomous rule of the one, invisible, transexperiential God. The will of God, and not the experience of the soul, known through the revelations to Mohammed, and not through gnosis, introspection, or human speculation, was the clue to the whole duty of humanity. Accountability to the sovereign God, and not mastery of the sciences of the soul, of politics or pleasure, was the guide to righteousness. The historical enactment of God's will in thought and deed, not the achievement of a harmonious social pattern in accord with some eternal cosmic order, was the ideal. The goal of life was not release from the cycle of rebirths or the full integration, in consciousness, of the Ātman-Brahman, but a kingdom of God to come in the future in which all of God's will would be historically fulfilled and concrete human identity maintained.

The implications of this prophetic, theological view for human behavior are most apparent in Islam in Law. The Koran itself is understood as the law book for life; indeed, the Word of God is the very incarnation of God's will and power.[13] The greatest thinkers of Islam were more often pious lawyers than theologians, philosophers, saints, or sages. Within a few centuries after the death of Mohammed, an elaborate body of religiopolitical jurisprudence had been developed. The provisions developed by the legal scholars in numerous commentaries were proclaimed and enforced by godly rulers wherever Islam went. When a wide consensus was obtained by practical acceptance within Islam, the legal mandates were understood as orthodox and any departure was viewed as heretical. Highly typical of this genre of work as it was worked out in India is the late-twelfth-century *Guidance in the Holy Law*, which specifies the proper behavior of Muslims in the areas of duty of worship (prayer, almsgiving, fasting, and pilgrimage), in social life (the legal treatment of wives, children, and slaves), in the proper rendering of judgment or punishment in regard to drunkenness, holy war, and infidelity (to Allah), and in the conduct of economic matters (thefts, loans, gifts, wills). Where these forms of behavior were followed, there was true Islam. The Shi'ite and Sunni branches of Islam might dispute the relative merits of family heredity or political authority as the true basis of succession to Mohammed's charisma, but it mattered little to the Muslims whether one knew one's own "essence." The decisive question was what one did in subjecting oneself to the one God and in obediently carrying forth that God's revealed Holy Law. Thus the enforcer of the Law is an agent of God's will. If there is prophecy with no enforcement, the commands of God will not prevail. If there is familial or political authority without prophecy, there may be the pretense of orderly society, but there will be no reordering of life toward the one God.[14] Thus authority informed by prophetic religion is a sacred trust, and to this all are to be obedient. It is not surprising that political rulers assumed increasing public dominance over the traditional custodians of Indian religious life—most obviously over the priestly authority of the highest Hindu castes, but often over the pious lawyers of Islam as well.

The significance of this double transformation brought to India by Islamic religion and law is that those elements in Hinduism which accented regime and political governance of the sciences of material gain had to be muted. Many of the Islamic rulers were tolerant people. The Mogul Muslims especially followed a policy which allowed freedom of religion in private life at least. Hinduism, in effect, retreated from the public domain and focused, in social life, even more intensely on family-caste structures in regional societies as well as upon personal devotion. Certainly there were Hindu rulers in some princely states, but they too became more like the Islamic warrior-rulers, beyond the control of traditional Brahmins, than a part of the whole, organic tissue of corporate life set forth in classical Hindu visions of social order. *Dharma* was maintained, but it was more focused on, and expressed by, *kama* and *varna* than *artha*. Perhaps it would be more accurate to say that the political-economic prescriptions of *artha* became split—one part of it had centered on the science of political regime to assure and secure the peace and stability of the whole body, and the other part had centered on the prudent steps to assure both the common wealth and the mastery of material gain for one's self and family. When Islam took over and set the pattern for regime, family and caste became more self-regarding and more concerned about material gain and power in the face of their relative decline in public, political, and legal influence. The patterns of economic control of the land, except for taxes to the rulers, fell more and more into the hands of the dominant castes, less and less constrained by the organic interdependence which it had been the *dharma* of the Kshatriyas to sustain under Brahmanic guidance. Caste domination became more clearly class domination. The structural symptom of this was the sharper division of the law into two areas: one, to be adjudicated by the political ruler, had to do with "public" behavior—murder, theft, treason, and the like; and the other, to be handled by the Brahmins, had to do with "private" behavior—marriage, inheritance, caste relations, temple privilege, etc. The latter became the vehicle of the Hindu understanding of life, since questions of polity and public justice were in the hands of others.[15] In both classic Hindu Sacred Law and Islamic Holy Law, these two areas were interwined. With Islamic rulers and Islamic law governing a Hindu society, they were more sharply segregated. The Islamic rulers, themselves socially conservative in many respects, supported the Hindu practices which inclined the people to the least turmoil. Caste, except perhaps in the academic and courtly centers, became even more rigid and powerful in the social life, kinship patterns, and political aspirations of Hindu India than its early metaphysicians had envisioned.

C. CHRISTIANS AND COLONIALISM

Christianity also was introduced to India on a significant scale during the Islamic rule. There had been small colonies of Christians in India for many centuries—some tracing their origins to the evangelization of parts of South India by one of the original disciples of Christ who (according to legend) followed trade routes set by King Solomon, who had sent out a colony of Jews to southwest India. Others found their roots in Syrian Christianity several centuries later. But these communities had remained small and localized, functioning much as odd *jati* in the predominantly Hindu world even where they were faithful believers. Modern Christian movements began later.

As the Moguls were threatening the dominance of the Turks in the Islamic world, as Machiavelli and Luther were writing and studying in Europe, and in the same decade in which Columbus discovered America, Vasco da Gama cast anchor off the shore of India. This event opened trade routes long closed by the Turks, and began the formation of trade cities around the natural ports of India's coast. For nearly a century thereafter, Portuguese, Spanish, and French Catholic missionaries, following the traders and committed to winning the world to the Roman faith as against the heresies of the Protestants at home, moved among both the Hindu and the Muslim people, converting some Hindus, fewer Muslims, and establishing churches and colleges here and there. More often they engaged in debates, conversations, and the reporting of what they found. This reporting made the East and the West more familiar with one another. Francis Xavier, the great Catholic missionary, spent some four years in India, saturating the lives and minds of converts with the Conservative Catholicism of the Council of Trent.[16] When he left, others followed. Some, such as the Jesuit Robert de Nobili, began the serious study of Hindu languages and practices, a study that was to be taken up by successors and was to have enormous conse- quences.[17] One successor, Joseph Beselie, wrote a poetic interpretation of the gospel in Tamil, using the South-Indian literary style so effectively that the work has become accepted by Indians as a classic. More frequently it was the spiri- tuality of Thomas à Kempis which was taken up by Hindus as a form of religion which proved the universality of Hindu-like perspectives.

Just as consequential for the formation of modern India was the English Charter, in 1600, of the East India Trading Company, followed soon after by Dutch and Danish companies. (This was, of course, the same company which brought tea from India into Boston Harbor in 1773 and inspired the Boston Tea Party.) For over the next two-and-a-half centuries, corporations such as the Company did for economic life in India what Islam had done for law: namely, they introduced into economic centers, as Islam had into political centers, an alternative leadership and an alternative set of assumptions about human life and interaction, driving the classic ideals of *dharma* further from the public domain and increasingly concentrating them in the "private," "religious" realms of family and caste. Faithful Hindus especially began to adopt the "external" habits of Western commerce and technology as pragmatic paths to wealth, but they had little sympathy for the religious or "liberal" social motivations which drove their Western business associates. Further, these traders brought with them Protestant chaplains and, eventually, missionaries whose orientations and preaching were in greater contrast to classical Hindu life than were those of the earlier Catholics, informed as they were by the ideals of Trent and still struggling against the Conciliar Catholics and the Protestants. Indeed, most of the early chaplains sent out with both Dutch and British trading companies seem to have spent more of their time—when they interacted with Indians—arguing against the Catholics who had been converted than seeking new converts.[18] A few, however, such as the Dutchman Rogerius, found it necessary to engage the analysis of Indian life and thought for their own benefit and for those back home, much as the Catholics also had done. Through such early writings a new mode of descriptive, interpretive analysis of Indian tradition was made available both to Western and, eventually, to Indian scholars. What seemed a structural, eternal part of Indian life and practice was lifted into consciousness, where it could be compared and contrasted with other possibilities.

The Danes were the first to decide to enter the Protestant missionary field. However, they could find no Danish clergy eager to go. They turned to their brother Lutherans at the great Pietist university of Halle and secured the services of Bartholomew Ziegenbalg. He not only extended the tendency to attempt an analysis of Indian culture, anticipating the foundations of modern ethnology and anthropology, but he translated the New Testament into Indian languages for the first time. Further, he made a fateful decision consistent with his Lutheran Pietism. The meaning of the gospel was inward and personal; exterior matters of polity and regime were not decisive for salvation, although they were of scientific and practical human interest. Hence what was necessary was a distinctively Indian form of piety and church order, unencumbered by Western ecclesiological theories or practice. This orientation, carried on by any number of subsequent evangelical missionaries, especially in the nineteenth century, blended rather well with the growing division of "public" and "private" realms brought about by the impact of Islam in law and the corporations in economics. Missionaries of this persuasion wanted the soul of the individual believer. Everything else they would leave to the structures of this world.

The economic success of the corporations, however, was beginning to undercut the political regime of the Mogul rulers, which was already weakened by internal decay. The structure of Islamic rule depended so much on geniuses at the top that when weak leadership came to power, things did not hold together. Less by design or intention than by the combined indirect effects of the acids of modernity and the reassertion of traditional power by local princes, the Muslim empire began to break up. The East India Trading Company became, by the time of the American and French Revolutions, the allies of the local princes or the outright managers of territory. Sometimes, the Company used highly dubious machinations to gain an advantageous position. Elsewhere local princes became exploitive "warlords" living off booty and brigandage. In these areas, such as in Mysore, the troops employed by the Company, some of whom had also fought against the Americans in 1776, appeared more as deliverers than as conquerors or conspirators for gain. Of course, it was first of all a trading company and not, in the narrow sense, a political entity that came to power, and it was not until 1858 that the British government itself stepped in after it became clear that the Company, as a corporation, could not rule. Earlier, in the face of the French Revolution, the English Parliament had authorized the company to assume some political functions—especially to prevent France from becoming as dominant in Asia as it was becoming under Napoleon in Europe. This move was also "justified" by those influential utilitarian liberals, James Mill and his more famous son, John Stuart Mill, both employees of the Company. India became the first "third-world" country dominated by a transnational corporation, which brought with it a rather unfettered form of utilitarian capitalism and commercialism protected by imperial power.

The increased range of influence and administrative responsibilities of the Company demanded two other changes which were to be of long-range consequence. One was in education; the other was in the area of public law, now vacated by the Muslims. To maintain its extensive economic activities and to carry out the administrative duties which had fallen to it, the Company needed bureaucrats and clerks. The Christian missionaries had already established several schools and colleges, and the products of these schools proved to be those best able to meet the growing need. But they were far too few, and their concerns were too broad. The Company itself established its first school in 1784, and a number of colleges soon followed, but for a generation or more a rather sharp three-sided debate raged. Should the curricula of these schools focus on India or Western materials? Should courses be conducted in the indigenous languages or in English? And should they follow the patterns of Cambridge and Oxford, or the "applied" patterns of the "utilitarian" experiment of the University of London, much influenced by the theories of Rousseau, Fichte, and Bentham? On each question the second option won. A liberal form of British education was introduced, with the primary focus on languages, law, and "practical" training. The missionaries, however, were not to be outdone, and their interests were other than the training of commercial clerks or supporting the Company. Indeed, they frequently were critical of Company policy, and the Company often prevented missionary activity. At the hands of Calvinist missionaries, whether Free-Church Calvinists (like the sympathetic Baptist William Carey) from 1800 on, or more Evangelical Calvinists (like the rigid Scotch-Presbyterian Alexander Duff) from 1830 on, the focus was on a comparative and critical examination of the religious and philosophical tenets of Christianity and Hinduism. The key question centered on the true foundation for knowledge, belief, and public reform. Both the Company and the missionary forms of education deeply affected India. One provided a basis for technical, bureaucratic, and commercial work, a new, pragmatic *artha* outside the traditional behaviors governed by *dharma*. It gave to India a modernized, indigenous elite and the foundations of a capitalist, industrial segment of the economy. The other proved eventually to be a leaven in the renewal of Hindu philosophy and ethics, one that set the pace for spiritual and moral reform from that time until the present.

We should not fail to note at this juncture the dominant tendencies in British life and culture which had repercussions in India. Queen Victoria came to the throne in mid-century and represents a recovery of Anglo-Catholic conservatism in religion. A wide breach opened between science and religion, with religious sentiments focused on the Neo-Platonist views of Coleridge and Shelley. The lush, post-Romantic and medievalistic writings of Tennyson, the Brownings, Rossetti, Swinburne, Matthew Arnold, and especially Rudyard Kipling dominated cultural life. The Oxford Movement, with Cardinal Newman's attempt to restore the Anglican Church to previous medieval spirituality, dominated religious debate. His chief enemy was Liberalism. Indeed, Liberalism in its utilitarian form was pervasive in both religion and sociopolitical thinking. Religion was strictly a matter of "private opinion," and public life was governed by a technical calculus of costs and benefits amid the booming trade, the industrial expansion, and the opening of new markets in the colonial regions. During this period the class structure of England, which had been relatively open since the Cromwellian Revolution, became firmly fixed. England became the model of "capitalism" upon which Marx focused his study. This is the Victorian England which assumed responsibility for the governance of India.[19]

Decisions made by the Company (and eventually by the British government during the Victorian period) with regard to law were of major consequence. When tribunals had to be established due to the displacement of older Hindu Sacred Law by the Muslims and then the displacement of Islamic rulers, the British brought with them procedures of justice and principles of right that had been developed out of the common-law tradition as revised by the Liberal-Puritan synthesis but now were dominated by the neo-conservatism of Victorian England. The public law, in the Liberal-Puritan view, is an approximation of universal moral law which may be known by "common grace" in the form of self-evident truths. Before and under this law, each person has a standing and a right to an impartial hearing. Further, with the notion of limited government, the burden is on the civil authorities to prove guilt in criminal cases. Otherwise, innocence is presumed. Each person is seen as equal before the law, whatever one's estate or social condition. Justice is thus best served when all ties of blood, class, birth, group membership, previous behavior, and religious opinion are left out of consideration, for then the court has a greater chance of being fair, impartial, and unprejudiced. The moral law being known in some measure, the purpose of the procedures is to determine the particular, relevant facts of the case, scrupulously leaving out anything that could bias our understanding of them, and then to apply the principles as codified or as given in precedent.

The Hindu understanding of law, both as classically stated in Hindu texts and as often practiced locally throughout Muslim rule, was quite different.[20] In the Hindu view it was precisely the social ties of persons—ties of family, caste, and religion—that were the clue to the identity, the being of persons, and hence to the *particular* cluster of rights and duties by which they were to be judged. Life was sufficiently circumscribed by traditional patterns of behavior that everyone knew when an infraction had been committed. The problem was not to establish guilt or innocence but to find a way to restore harmony between the groups and to bring wayward individuals back into the *dharma* of their proper family, *jati*, or caste, thereby restoring cosmic harmony in some measure.

In the face of concrete cases where the two systems came into direct conflict, the British found that their system was constantly subverted, both because litigants did not understand it and because it was not relevant to the real decisions which they felt people had to make in their own contexts. The British made a number of responses. In some areas, such as *sati*, the traditional religious-legal requirement that a Hindu widow cast herself on the funeral pyre of her husband, the British held to Western sensibilities, which they held to be universal: they outlawed the practice. With the help of some Hindu scholars, they were also able to show that the practice had no precise authorization in the Sacred Law. Nevertheless, other Hindus saw this as the imposition of a Western, culturally relative, moral view which showed no appreciation for the absolute, eternal, and sacred bonds of Hindu marriage, which existed even after death.

Much more frequently, the British, under the neo-conservative influence of Victorian understanding, attempted to leave matters of family, caste, and religion entirely alone—in the hands of local judicatories and village elders. When cases had to be tried in formal proceedings, they turned to *maulvies* and *pandits,* Muslim and Hindu authorities on classical texts. These became advisory officers to the courts, there to instruct the Western judges on what the traditional law was. To make certain that there were enough of these to serve the courts who also knew something of English procedures, the British founded law schools which offered instruction in both legal traditions. These moves had several consequences. On the one hand they reinforced in many areas the authority of classical Hindu law and of the Brahmins who were its custodians, re-establishing in positions of public visibility a way of thinking about social order that had been displaced since the arrival of the Muslims. In cases involving Muslims, *maulvies* were used, undercutting in fact the claim that the Holy Law was universal and making Islam into something of a specialized caste within the whole pluralism of caste groupings. On the other hand the establishment of the law schools, which admitted students from a number of castes, not only from the Brahmins, and which demanded the printing of copies of the Sacred Law for study, meant that detailed and expert knowledge of Hindu lore became accessible to non-Brahmin groups. Simultaneously it meant that new utilitarian-liberal theories of Western law, based on the principles of Bentham and the elder and the younger Mills, were introduced to Indian leaders. When the Western theories of national sovereignty "of the people" and the equality of all reached India through these channels, at the time highly compatible with the commercial, economic, and Imperial theories by which the Company operated, the Hindus gained an understanding of Western thought patterns no longer so directly connected with the alien religion Christianity. If the missionary colleges brought about crosscurrents that issued in a renewal of Hindu religious and philosophical thought, and if the Company schools brought about a wider familiarity with commercial and technical life, the focus on law brought about a new interest in political and legal thought. Western law was Indianized; Hindu lawyers selectively adopted motifs from Western justice. Most especially, when independence came, a constitutional government was formed, with specified civil rights and liberties justified on utilitarian grounds.

D. THE HINDU RENAISSANCE

It was out of this mix that the second transformation in India was born, a transformation still in progress and uncertain as to final outcome. It is the Hindu Renaissance. If the first transformation of India, as I argued earlier, was the Islamic/British severing of Hinduism from its public forms in law, economy, and politics and their driving its notions of *artha* increasingly out of their proper "public" arena into closer ties with family and caste (*kama* and *varna*), the second transformation is the critical renewal of Hinduism at the hands of those Indian philosophers, poets, educators, and lawyers who had been influenced by the clash of Hindu, Islamic, Christian, and Western liberal ideas. The leaders of this movement attempted to transcend the clash by returning to their roots, to form out of the genius of their own rediscovered identity a cosmopolitan spiritual and moral vision which could include the best of all, but to leave behind disruptive, degenerative, or divisive elements from their own as well as from other traditions. Out of that renewal they have attempted to re-establish Indian control over economic, legal, and political life on that recovered basis. The Hindu Renaissance is, in brief, the mother of Indian nationalism that has attempted to extend, once more, *dharma*-related *artha* beyond family, *jati*, caste, and private religious opportunism into a renewed, holistic, social and civilizational order.

In its origins the Hindu Renaissance was not primarily a political, economic, or legal movement. It was neither a "revolution of the saints" in the Puritan sense nor a "revolution of the masses" in the Marxist sense. It was first of all a revolution of cultural consciousness. Engendered by linguists and philologists, litterateurs and translators, journalists and publicists, poets and lay philosophers educated by Christians, for the most part, it drew heavily on the help of Hindu Brahmins and *pandits*. As it turned out, the necessities of the colonial economy, law, and administration demanded a support group of scribblers who eventually brought as many changes to India as the economic, legal, and administrative structures from abroad had brought. All this came to focus nowhere more sharply than in Calcutta, where the College of Fort William was established in 1800 to train Company functionaries.

As David Kopf has brilliantly documented,[21] an odd cluster of intelligentsia was formed around this college. Consisting of Westerners who had become proficient in Indian languages for all sorts of motives, their Indian assistants, and networks of relations set up by interaction with Hindu beneficiaries of the Company, the crosscurrents of cultural exchange began to flow. A few Westerners "went native"; an occasional Indian became foppishly British. Some Hindus resisted every foreign import, and some Westerners replicated enclaves of pre-Victorian England. Other Hindus professed admiration for the teachings of Jesus, although baptism of a convert was rare, and several Christians became apologists for Indian scriptures, although seldom did they leave the church. Within these boundaries fertile minds began a series of programs in research and publication which were to transform India's self-understanding, to bring about the possibilities for a reassessment of Hinduism around the world and, in little more than a century, a movement for liberation and self-rule that would produce one of the twentieth century's first "new" nations. At the time, what these minds agreed on was that the state of Indian social and intellectual life was poor. It needed invigoration desperately. They differed on how that was to be achieved. There were few known models within Indian memory to show how that might happen. The Europeans, of course, brought with them models from the West, and as these became known to Indians they were variously adopted or adapted by them also.

Several of those gathered by Governor-General Hastings in the late eighteenth century were, like him, classicist by inclination. That is, they believed that the material, political, and moral "success" of the West was due to the reappropriation of classic Greek and Roman wisdom in the European Renaissance after the Dark Ages. In a comparable fashion they became convinced that India would be renewed both by exposure to these same classics *and* by recovery of India's own neglected classics. Indeed, India's classics could also become tutors of a world more cosmopolitan than even the Western Renaissance men of letters imagined. Others in this cluster were more intrigued by the "principled liberalism" of Locke, Kant, and others. They were questing for a new "natural philosophy" whereby the universal, natural structures and dynamics of life could be exhumed from the encrustations of superstition past and present, and seen in all the diversities of particular cultures.[22] Some of the scholars around Calcutta held that these structures could be found in the universal, structural similarities of grammar and of laws which are necessary everywhere for governance. Still others saw in the Protestant Reformation the model of renewal—whether they took as their ideal Luther's translation of the gospel into the vernacular or Calvin's demand for clear and learned preaching as a guard against idolatry, empty ritualism, and immorality in the common life. Only a very few saw the French Revolution as a model, and British Company men were very quick to scent "Jacobin" drifts and to stamp these out. In all cases the language and literature of India were to be mastered as the keys to bringing India out of its intellectual and social stagnation.[23] For about half a century a prodigious amount of materials—dictionaries, grammars, translations of the Vedas, Upanishads, and Puranas, critical editions of Hindu Sacred Law, commentaries, journal articles and histories in scholarly and popular forms—poured forth from the presses of Calcutta, each a product of Western and Indian scholars working together. In the West it was the publication of translations by William Jones, H. T. Colebrook, Charles Wilkins, William Carey, Edwin Arnold, and others which shaped the thought of Schopenhauer, inspired the American Transcendentalists,[24] gave succor to the Romantics, who celebrated intuitive thought against scientific rationalism, and became the basis for Max Müller's monumental scientific work in comparative linguistics. In India a new pride emerged, a new awareness of great legacy from the past and, with it, a new historical consciousness and new challenges. As the presses mediated Indian thought and history to the West, they also propagated Western ideas in the East.

Increasingly battles began to develop between various factions among the Calcutta intelligentsia, between those who would purify the past and thus find a model for the future, and those who would synthesize East and West in the present to create a new future; between those who were drawn to Indian modes of consciousness which could be gently infused with Western knowledge, and those who were committed to Western models of living and learning, expressed through Indian idiom; between those who would recover the ancient classics for all humanity, and those who would selectively use them for contemporary utilitarian purpose; between those who saw Christ as the fulfillment of the religion of India (as Christians held him to be of the religion of Israel), and those who saw Jesus as a sage equaled by the Hindu ancients.[25] On the British side these battles became questions of Company, scholarly, and Missionary Society support. Various individuals, projects, and policies debated these issues, not only in Calcutta but in the chambers of London counting houses, learned gatherings, and Parliament. India was the jewel of the British Empire, and what happened there had consequences at home. At the hands of a Liberal-Puritan coalition led by the great antislavery advocate William Wilberforce and supported by Macaulay's classicist "Minute on Indian Education," the door was opened to more aggressive policies of Westernization.

The same battles were more important for the Indians. To the Indians it became a matter of identity and destiny, a matter of personal and cultural existence. The reaction was typified by Ram Mohan Roy and his friends, Debendernath Tagore and Sri Ramakrishna. Ram Mohan Roy sought to immunize Hinduism against the growing epidemic of evangelical missionary activity by developing a revived Hinduism which could be adapted to the needs of the day in a "useful," "practical" way. In brief, he accepted the ethics of Jesus as seen in the Sermon on the Mount, and the utilitarian decision of the Mills. But he took his stand with the ancient Vedantic literature, in which he was the most sublime and universal expression of precisely those motifs of which Jesus spoke. In these traditions that India had bequeathed to the world, one could find the most profound statement that in each person was a spark of the divine, which, when properly cultivated, could fulfill its potential, recognize its rootage in the Absolute, and transcend the divisive dogmas and superstitions of corrupt popular religion. Mill's utilitarianism provided a critical principle by which anything judged "not useful" could be left behind.[26] In more devotional terms Tagore and Ramakrishna accented similar motifs. They focused on religious experience and spiritual insight as the way to the universal Truth shown in

Hindu scripture. The process of "spiritual realization" discloses that all religions strive for the same Absolute. Spiritual realization is possible because humanity is at base metaphysically grounded in it. The quest is the same, the goal is the same; only the degree of self-realization, which is also God-realization, differs. All creeds, rites, and dogmas — indeed, all systems of ethics and of science—are but the one Truth showing up in its many forms according to the spiritual awareness of particular persons and groups. One becomes free from all this apparent division when one realizes the essential unity of things. Then one could recognize the universal worldwide brotherhood, and then practical programs for social and cultural progress would be "natural." These authors became the framers of the new Hindu vision that increasingly dominated India in the nineteenth century. Their ideas were taken up and given fresh statement by Keshub Chunder Sen, who was closer to Evangelical Christians, by Swami Vivekananda, who was closer to the Western Transcendentalists, by Surendranath Banerjea, who was steeped in the thought of the British utilitarians, by Dayanande Saraswati, who was closer to the teachings of the orthodox Brahmins, and by Rabindranath Tagore, who was closer to the *bhakti* poets of old. Whatever their differences, they all shared the fundamental world-view, the organic hierarchical transcendentalism, of classical Hinduism with its celebration of the spiritual divinity of humanity and its recognition of the varieties of earthen vessels.

These revitalizers of the Hindu traditions found in the spiritual philosophy of their past what Louis Dumont has more recently argued in anthropological terms.[27] The "higher" and "more pure" spirituality entails a distinction between "that which is encompassed" and "that which encompasses." As the spiritual soul, the closer it approximates the cosmic whole, is more able to encompass all the apparent contradictions of life, so a renewed spirituality, on Hindu terms, among the people at large was soon to give rise to a sociopolitical attempt to encompass all of the diversities of India into a new whole which would be the basis for a new cosmopolitan vision. A spiritual nationalism was born, with a mission in the world.

The response of the Muslims was quite different. They felt that this Hindu revival was a reassertion of paganism, possibly a sellout to Christians, clearly a repudiation of the great achievements of Islamic rule, surely a relegation of Islam to but one of the many caste sects of India, and in any case a denial that Islam, after nearly seven centuries in India, had a place there. Certainly it made the one true prophecy of Mohammed but another apparently divisive creed which should be overcome by spiritual recognition of the unity of things. The Muslims resisted the incursions of Western education, and adjusted only slowly to the new synthesis of India's second transformation. They were decisive in fomenting the "Mutiny" of 1857, which forced the British to abandon working through the Company and assume direct political rule; but it was, I think, inevitable that Islam could not live comfortably in this emerging new situation in spite of the enormous creativity of some Muslim leaders—especially in cultivating a sense of history which classical Hinduism did not have and in preserving a sense of normative legal theory that was more universalistic than that of ancient India. Islam was self-consciously a political religion, much more so than Hinduism at that time. Eventually, of course, what are now Pakistan and Bangladesh, where Islam was strongest, were to break with India, leaving Hindu orientations even more social and cultural space in which to develop within India proper.

Develop they did. Borrowing openly from Christian evangelistic techniques to reach the heart of individuals and just as openly from utilitarian theories of social progress by public reform, a series of Hindus began to celebrate the great past of India and to call it once more to its *dharma*. As the vast bureaucracies of British rule began to integrate and coordinate the now-united administration of India, demanding more and more educated Indians to staff the machinery of government, the ideas from Calcutta spread, and minds moving on parallel paths in other parts of the country began to converge. The desire to clarify, rediscover, and live out the distinctive *dharma* of Hindu organic, hierarchical, spiritual transcendentalism became the overarching drive of Indian leadership throughout the subcontinent. No longer could Hinduism be confined, as it had been since the Islamic and British arrivals, to personal, family-*jati*, and caste practice. It must pervade the whole. The National Congress was founded and increasingly became the vehicle of this sentiment.

The leaders in education and the arts made the connections first. In B. C. Chatterji's widely read novel *Abbey of Bliss,* Hindu heroes resist foreign rulers in the name of the Mother goddess. But "Who is the Mother"? "It is the country. . . . We own no other mother." "Thou art wisdom, thou art law, thou our heart, our soul, our breath. . . ."[28] More overtly political leaders were soon to follow. Tilak, celebrating the resistance of his native Maharashtrian people against foreign domination six hundred years before, assumed leadership of the Congress and wrote: "The common factor in Indian Society is the feeling of *Hindutva* [devotion to Hinduism]. I do not speak of Muslims and Christians at present because everywhere the majority of our society consists of Hindus. We say that Hindus of the Punjab, Bengal, Maharashtra, Telangrana, and Dravid are one, and the reason for this is only Hindu *Dharma.*"[29] And when Tilak was imprisoned for his inciting activities, he wrote a commentary on the *Bhagavad Gita* wherein Krishna reveals to Arjuna that he must fight out of duty to *dharma,* to fulfill his inborn destiny of caste *and nation.* At Tilak's request another figure led a delegation to Congress. Aurobindo had been given a thoroughly Western education, at no less a place than Cambridge. Upon his return he rediscovered India through the leaders of the Hindu Renaissance. Becoming a convert to the neo-Vedantic views they held, he was inspired to say, in a lengthy speech that had immediate impact, "Nationalism is not a mere political program; nationalism is a religion that has come from God." He was imprisoned for his radical work. But in prison he again was inspired: "Something has been shown to you . . . and it is the truth of the Hindu religion. . . . That which we call the Hindu religion is really the eternal religion; because it is the universal religion which embraces all others." "It is for the dharma and by the dharma that India exists."[30]

This new accent on overtly militant Hinduism is understandable in view of the deep traditions of Hindu life, and the "extremists," as they were often called, were simply trying to reintegrate the private and public aspects of the classic Hindu teachings. To put it another way, they were attempting to reunite *dharma* with *artha,* the science of polity and material gain, in the face of a historic situation wherein *artha* had failed, or had at least been displaced. In the nineteenth and early twentieth century, these figures led the way, constantly looking over their shoulders for Western writers who supported their directions. The writings of these leaders are peppered with quotations from the utilitarians, Bentham and the Mills, and later in the century from Ruskin, Tolstoy, and Mazzini, the Western romantic nationalists. It was not clear which way this new *artha* would go. It could be more spiritual in the neo-Hindu sense, or it could be quite practically material and scientific in the utilitarian Western sense. Both tendencies were in the ancient *Artha Shastra;* both had been powerful in the formation of the Hindu Renaissance. One was focused in a new way in the National Congress; the other was present in the technical, bureaucratic system from which many of the members of Congress earned their daily bread.

Indeed, some of the Indian nationalists trained in economics, administration, and law were beginning to recognize the emergence of new *artha* theories in the West at the hands of the socialists. They were not long in beginning to apply these new concepts on the Indian scene as but extensions of what they had also learned from the French Revolution and the utilitarians. By 1897 Dadabhai Maoroji was advocating the socialism that was arising in the British Labor Party. Romesh Dutt analyzed the poverty of India and attributed it to the exploitation by imperial foreign rulers shortly thereafter. Within a decade Lajpat Rai saw Marx's diagnosis of capitalism as so scientifically valid that "there is now practical unanimity among Western thinkers about the indescribable evils of the capitalist system."[31]

E. A NATIONAL DHARMA?

But perhaps no two figures represent this tension more than the next generation of Indian national leaders, Gandhi and Nehru. These internationally familiar figures are but the late personifications of the "social spirituality" and its tensions that I have described in this chapter. In one we see the culmination, the embodiment, of Hindu organic transcendentalism. Trained as a lawyer, committed to the neo-Vedantic thought of the nineteenth century, Gandhi gave leadership to a movement, as he said, "based entirely upon truth. It is an extension of the domestic law into the political field." "It is a path of national God-realization, attained through simple duty, self purification and self rule."[32] Nehru, no less a nationalist, turned increasingly away from overt religious concepts (except in a great appreciation of "the spirit of the Indian peoples"). He had met many socialists and Communists at a conference in Brussels in 1927, and he had visited Russia the same year, coming away with a great appreciation of the economic and educational strides made in the decade after the Revolution. Further, he saw in socialism a model for modernizing holistic, "organic" societies in contrast to the pluralistic, voluntary societies of the West. He eventually became a lifelong advocate of governmental economic planning and development, although his socialism was less that of Marx than of R. H. Tawney, George Bernard Shaw, and Harold Laski. It used a pragmatic, reformist socialism that could restore the material well-being of his people while preserving the "natural" ties of social solidarity.[33]

If Gandhi played the role of the religious sage, instructing the people by word and example in the public implications of *dharma,* reminding them of their sacred past as recovered by the "new Brahmins" of the Hindu Renaissance, Nehru played the role of the dynastic king—respectful of religious authority but fulfilling his *dharma* by practical attention to the peace, progress, and prosperity of the community through a modernized *artha.* He worked with others to get socialist as well as Western democratic statements of human rights included in the constitution. The turning point for India came in the 1931 convention of the Congress. Some five thousand delegates from all parts of India gathered in Karachi to spell out the kind of government they would have once the British were to leave. Under Gandhi's guidance a series of "fundamental rights," taken directly from the traditions of Gandhi's British law training, were articulated—freedom of association, of speech, of press, of conscience and religion; religious neutrality of the state; adult suffrage; equal rights for both sexes; and equal access to all public facilities and callings by all castes.[34] Nehru's concerns also were included, for provisions were passed which demanded a living wage for industrial workers, protection against unemployment, maternity leave for women workers, and the abolition of serfdom.

Whether we speak of the intellectual developments of the nineteenth century, of Gandhi's charismatic leadership, or of Nehru's utilitarian socialism, caste raised its head at every turn. The nineteenth-century intellectuals criticized caste where it denied the spiritual dignity of each soul and where it led to violent repression of low-caste or outcaste peoples; but they seldom if ever challenged the fundamental presuppositions of an organic, hierarchical society rooted in interdependent *jatis* as the necessary series of vessels for spiritual development. It is true that the great lawyer Ambedkar saw the persistent dangers of caste in even Gandhi's and Nehru's efforts. He tried to organize a Neo-Buddhist movement.[35] Ultimately this effort failed, although it did leave a series of laws that further mitigated the most degrading outcaste laws. As already pointed out, Gandhi had renamed the outcastes Harijans, the "people of God." This new name symbolically offered a new dignity to these masses, but even this effort seems to have brought about the cooperation of the Harijans with Hindu nationalism more than anything else. Gandhi almost never attacked caste directly—certainly not its metaphysical presuppositions. Nehru worked for the economic betterment of low-caste peoples, but like the ancient rulers, the Muslims, and the British, he left its structure basically intact. And his daughter, Indira, when she succeeded him in an old-fashioned dynastic way, took several actions to equalize public law for all citizens and to provide compensatory benefits for the depressed peoples. Nevertheless, she continued to work with and support the dominant castes in most ways. When she did begin to challenge caste by strengthening the nation-state and the bureaucracies—in a more totalitarian direction—the caste leaders left her without support in several regions and joined the coalition to defeat her. Her recent recovery of leadership, by all reports, is due to the widespread perception that she, more than any other figure in present political leadership, represents a "secular" re-enactment of the ancient arts of power and wealth, *artha,* projected on a national scene. All others still have *artha* dominated by *varna.* Yet even then doubt remains. It appeared for nearly a decade that she was grooming her son Sanjay to take the reins of power when she stepped down. Since his death, another son, Rajiv, has emerged as the heir apparent, and the perpetuation of family-based dynastic leadership appears to be likely.

In this long history caste had become the most effective organizing principle besides the central government. It is understandable that the Congress wanted the support of the people, that most of the people were in villages where caste was intact, and thus that Congress should use caste channels in a utilitarian fashion to gain and sustain support, but without overtly accepting the familial-*jati* and caste definitions of *dharma* as guides to national policy. Instead, national policy is governed by an imported utilitarian socialism, using caste networks as bases for political self-interest brokering.

The results of this deep trajectory of human rights have produced a cosmopolitan "social spirituality" which differs from both the "public theology" of America and the "civic religion" of Marxist-Leninist societies. Its view of humanity and of rights is distinctive. Metaphysically it is the most individualist of the three traditions. Each soul is absolute and divine. Thus an enormously wide tolerance is permitted—in belief and in the individual quest for meaning—a motif that is often much appreciated by and that is quite similar to Unitarianism in the West. At the same time, a metaphysical naturalism has issued in a social orthopraxis, with highly ritualized forms of behavior, which governs hierarchical relations between groups and the daily cycles of life within groups. As Ralph Buultjens writes, "There are many levels of truth and all are valid, there are many levels of rights and all are valid . . . , [but] different rights are attached to each step. . . . [All levels of] rights bring obligations, and the failure to perform obligations can reduce or deprive an individual of his or her rights. . . ."[36] At the same time, imported views of "unalienable and inherent rights" and of a social duty to equalize the economic status of all people are officially enshrined in India's constitution and defended by Christians, socialists, some Muslims, the few remaining Gandhians, and urbanized intellectuals.

The most decisive question for India, and for Hinduism as a metaphysical-moral vision which claims universality, is twofold: Will the new utilitarian *artha* of Indian nationalism be fully integrated with *dharma*, and will *dharma* be understood in universalistic categories entailing human rights, or return to the logic of the Brahmanic hierarchy of gene-pool communalism centered in the particularities of family, *jati*, and caste?

If the latter is the case, India is likely to return to a form of "Oriental despotism." This option clearly represents a spiritual, organic communalism deeply attractive to many disenchanted with pluralist democratic or Eastern European "commissar" republics.

I suspect, however, that the key to new directions for the new India will be found among those groups presently marginal to most of the society—the Christians, the Marxists, the Gandhians, the urban enclaves of intellectuals, urbanized peasants, and Muslim modernists.[37] These are the tiny groups cognizant of the rich legacies of Indian life, most articulate about the critique of casteism, and most dedicated to the creation of new kinds of social solidarities *not* based on pregiven identity.

---

1. The most important one-volume treatments of Indian social history and thought are the following: Max Weber, *The Religion of India*, trans. and ed. by Hans Gerth and Don Martindale (Glencoe, Ill.: Free Press, 1958); A. L. Basham, *The Wonder That Was India* (New York: Grove Press, 1954); W. C. Smith, *The Modernization of a Traditional Society* (Bombay: Asia Publishing House, 1965); and William T. de Bary et al., eds., *Sources of Indian Tradition* (New York: Columbia University Press, 1958). I am indebted to these sources throughout this chapter. See also R. Hindery, *Comparative Ethics in Hindu and Buddhist Traditions* (Delhi: Motilal Banarsidass, 1978).

2. Direct influences are not easy to trace, but most histories of both Gnosticism and early Stoicism in the West offer some nod to the fact of contact and possible influence.

3. I think Max Weber's arguments regarding the incapacity of these heterodox movements to displace Brahmanism are essentially correct (*The Religion of India*, Chapter 9).

4. See S. Das, "Contemporary Indian Understanding of Dharma," Diss. Boston University 1979.

5. See T. W. Organ, *The Hindu Quest for the Perfection of Man* (Athens, Ohio: Ohio University Press, 1970), p. 218.

6. See Tiruvalluvar, *Tiruvacagam*, trans. G. U. Pope (Oxford: Clarendon Press, 1960).

7. The distinction between "great" and "little" traditions and the pertinence of the cultural-historical materials for the concrete analysis of society and comparative ethics are presumed throughout this volume. Much of the scientific argumentation regarding the pertinence of this method has been worked out by people with special interests in Asia. See M. Singer, *When a Great Tradition Modernizes* (Delhi: Vikas, 1972); M. N. Srinivas, *Religion and Society Among the Coorgs of South India* (London: Oxford University Press, 1952); and C. Geertz, *The Interpretation of Cultures* (New York: Basic Books, 1973). See also the works of Weber, Dumont, Mandelbaum, and Spiro to which I have referred.

8. On Islam in India, see W. C. Smith, *Modern Islam in India* (Lahore: Minerva Books, 1947); H. A. R. Gibb, *Mohammedanism* (New York: New American Library, 1955); and V. B. Raju, ed., *Religion and Politics in Medieval South India* (Hyderabad: Institute of Asian Studies, 1972), especially the papers by M. G. Pause, R. A. Alvi, A. Ahmed, and M. Hasan.

9. W. C. Smith, *Islam in Modern History* (Princeton, N.J.: Princeton University Press, 1957).

10. A. Maddison, *Class Structure and Economic Growth: India and Pakistan Since the Moghuls* (London: Allen & Unwin, 1971).

11. K. M. Panikkar, however, argues that the Islamic belief in a theistic God stimulated a number of Hindu thinkers to reinforce some aspects of *bhakti* toward a more exclusive monotheism. Islam also brought with it a new language among the rulers, displacing Sanskrit. This meant that the regional dialects would become more important vehicles of Hinduism and social identity. See *A Survey of Indian History,* 4th ed. (Bombay: Asia Publishing House, 1971), pp. 144ff.

12. See A. Guillaume, *Islam* (Baltimore: Penguin, 1954), Chapter 8.

13. My colleague, William Holladay, spent several years teaching the Christian Scriptures in a university in the Mideast where contact with Muslim scholars was a daily event. He points out that this constitutes one of the most important distinctions between Islam and Christianity. Both speak of "the Word of God," but in Christianity this "Word" is most fully present in Jesus Christ, that is, in a historical, living human. In Islam the "Word" is in the "words" of revealed scripture, the Koran. Only biblicistic fundamentalists hold such a view of Scripture in the Judeo-Christian traditions.

14. See K. W. Morgan, *Islam—The Straight Path* (New York: Ronald Press, 1968), especially Chapter 8.

15. See, for example, the topics considered in S. Venkataraman, *A Treatise on Hindu Law* (Madras: Orient Longmans, 1972).

16. See Stephen Neill, *The Story of the Christian Church in India and Pakistan* (Madras: C. L. S., 1972), especially p. 35. See also K. S. Latourette, *History of the Expansion of Christianity,* 7 vols. (New York: Harper, 1937 – 1945), especially the sections on India: Vol. 1, pp. 231 – 33; Vol. 2, pp. 280 – 84; Vol. 3, pp. 247 – 84; Vol. 6, pp. 65 – 214; and Vol. 7, pp. 274 – 315.

17. One of the founding documents of all Western study of comparative religions was by Abbé A. J. Du Bois (1765 – 1884), *Hindu Manners, Customs and Ceremonies.* See E. J. Sharpe, *Comparative Religion: A History* (New York: Scribner's, 1975), pp. 145ff.

18. See Neill, *The Story of the Christian Church in India and Pakistan,* Chapter 3.

19. See C. Wilson, "Economic Conditions," in the *New Cambridge Modern History,* Vol. XI: *Material Progress and World-Wide Problems,* ed. F. H. Hinsley (New York: Cambridge University Press, 1962), pp. 49ff.

20. In preparing this section on law, I am indebted to the superb summary of issues, with excellent bibliographic references, of L. I. Rudolph and S. H. Rudolph, *The Modernity of Tradition* (Chicago: Chicago University Press, 1967), Part III.

21. David Kopf, *British Orientalism and the Bengal Renaissance: The Dynamics of Indian Modernization* (Berkeley: University of California Press, 1969). I am indebted throughout this section to his work.

22. This concern is represented still by such writings as Dale Riepe, *The Naturalistic Tradition in Indian Thought* (Seattle: University of Washington Press, 1961); and, in a clearly Marxist-Leninist mold, by B. Wielenga, *Marxist Views on India* (Madras: C. L. S., 1976).

23. Kopf, *British Orientalism and the Bengal Renaissance,* Chapters 2 and 3.

24. In 1976, on the occasion of the U. S. Bicentennial, the Indian government commissioned and published a major volume on the relations between India and the U.S.A. It has extensive references to the influences of Indian ideas on the American Unitarians, on Emerson, Thoreau, Alcott, Whittier, Channing, etc. See M. V. Kamath, *The United States and India, 1776 – 1976* (Washington, D.C.: The Embassy of India, 1976), especially Chapters 2 and 5.

25. See Kopf, *British Orientalism and the Bengal Renaissance;* and de Bary et al., eds., *Sources of Indian Tradition,* especially Chapters XXI and XXII.

26. See de Bary, ed., *Sources of Indian Tradition,* pp. 573ff.; and Kamath, *The United States and India, 1776 – 1976,* pp. 35ff.

27. Louis Dumont, *Homo Hierarchicus* (Chicago: University of Chicago Press, 1970); see also F. A. Marglin, "Background Notes on L. Dumont's *Homo Hierarchicus,*" Harvard University Center for World Religions, May 1980.

28. See the translation in de Bary et al., eds., *Sources of Indian Tradition,* pp. 709ff.

29. Tilak, in *Sources of Indian Tradition,* pp. 717f.

30. Aurobindo, in *Sources of Indian Tradition,* pp. 728ff.

31. See S. Ghose, *Socialism, Democracy and Nationalism in India* (Bombay: Allied Publishers, 1973), especially Chapters 1, 8, and 9. See also B. Wielenga, *Marxist Views on India.*

257

32. See his *Hind Swaraj: Collected Works of Mahatma Gandhi*, Vol. III (Delhi: Government of India, 1963), p. 43.

33. J. Nehru, *An Autobiography* (London: John Lane, 1937).

34. See William Shirer, *Gandhi: A Memoir* (New York: Simon & Schuster, 1979), Chapter 9.

35. T. W. Wilkinson and M. M. Thomas, *Ambedkar and the Neo-Buddhist Movement* (Madras: C. L. S., 1972).

36. Ralph Buultjens, "Human Rights in Indian Political Culture," in K. W. Thompson, ed., *The Moral Imperatives of Human Rights: A World Survey* (Washington, D.C.: University Press of America, 1980), pp. 112f.

37. These are the groups most cultivated by the Christian Institute for the Study of Religion and Society.

CHAPTER NINE

Toward Comparative Evaluations

A. A BRIEF COMPARATIVE SUMMARY

IN the preceding chapters I have attempted to show that the contemporary debates about human rights bear within them fundamental questions about what it means to be human and how society ought to be organized. Further, we have seen that these fundamental questions have been answered in divergent ways by three distinctive metaphysical-moral visions. Each of these three visions entails an understanding of the "holy" and renders an ethic. Each ethic is highly religious in a double sense: each involves the embracing of a general doctrine about humanity in relationship to the ultimate powers of the universe, and each involves the bonding of persons in community to a specific social-institutional matrix which deeply affects the shape of these complex societies. In the bonding, critical understandings of "membership" appear which determine who may and who may not make claims to which kind of rights. By tracing the longitudinal development of each of the three "creeds" and by showing how the institutional locus of primary memberships affects other sectors of society in a cross-sectional analysis, we have been able to give an account of the divergent functioning of human rights concepts in the different societies, each of which claims universality of significance and all of which have fundamentally influenced the development of whole civilizations. Each civilization has been more or less able to meet most of the basic human needs which are present throughout the world, as identified by the universal presence of the decisive sectors of society. At a number of points we have also been able to see correlations, analogies, and interpenetrating influences between these three major possibilities. On these bases we have been able to identify the basic understanding of human rights that is creedally centered in a "public theology" and socially centered in the churches and voluntary associations of the West, in comparison and contrast with the definitions of human rights creedally centered in the "civic religion" of Marxism-Leninism as socially centered in the class structure and Party. Both of these have been compared with and contrasted to those conceptions of rights in traditional societies as exemplified by the "social spirituality" of India and

259

as centered institutionally in the hierarchies of kinship and caste and in utilitarian nationalism.

These three metaphysical-moral visions, supported and sustained by distinctive ways of organizing society, are not in agreement. Some areas overlap; analogy and interaction are present. Conversation between the three is not utter nonsense. It is possible for a person from one culture to enter into the world of the global neighbor in sufficient measure to recognize common humanity. Yet the metaphysical accounts and social ethics of what makes us all human are sufficiently different that at critical points the positions are mutually exclusive. One cannot logically hold all three positions at the same time; a society cannot organize itself along all three lines simultaneously. One may be an Indian Christian, an American Marxist, or a German mystic, but one cannot with consistency be a Christian and a Marxist-Leninist, a Hindu and a Christian, or a Marxist-Leninist and a believer in a hierarchical cosmic order.

As we have seen, no one of the three possibilities is fully integrated or complete within itself. The public theology of the West has involved an uncomfortable alliance of Puritan and Liberal motifs which appear today in the ambiguities of both ecumenical Christianity and the vast array of pluralistic organizations in capitalist democracy, where disabilities according to race, sex, and class remain. The civic creed of Marxist-Leninist countries has not resolved tensions between inner personal loyalties and outer collectivism, either in the relationship of official orthodoxy to explicit non-Communist religious groupings or in the areas of family life, the arts, education, and science. More disturbing internally is the fact that large segments of the proletariat remain alienated; walls have to remain to keep them from leaving; the quest for autonomy is heteronomously directed. The social spirituality of India is based upon a disjunctive reclamation, on the one hand, of traditional Hinduism with its transcendentalist yet "naturalistic" attempt to adjust all behavior and social order to the cosmic order and, on the other hand, of imported, utilitarian economic practices and technology—an importation which breeds social change and the erosion of traditional society. *Artha* is not yet integrated with *dharma; kama,* as worked out in family-*jati,* tends to reign in psyche, utilitarian opportunism in national political life.

Nevertheless, each of these three possibilities claims to be based on a universalistic, metaphysical-moral set of principles which could overcome not only its own remaining limitations but those of the other positions as well. Each recognizes that its own vision is not yet complete. Every Christian knows that the Law of God, the fulfillment of the Kingdom, and the Love of God are still besieged by sin; and every principled liberal knows that "self-evident truths" do not seem evident at all. Every Marxist-Leninist knows that Communism in its full glory has not yet arrived, that capitalism, with its celebrations of egocentric and ruling-class interests, is still powerful, that Marxism-Leninism has not captured the loyalties of the people, and that organized religion is not fading away. So also every German Evangelical knows that the designation of a "two-kingdom theory" does not solve the problem of the relations between the two kingdoms. In India every Hindu knows that much of the world is still caught up in spiritual ignorance and a lack of social discipline, and that every Western import from movies to computers weakens traditional religion yet strengthens some castes. Hence the promise of human rights is unfulfilled everywhere. Yet each also holds that a deeper grasp of the full meanings of the basic presuppositions of its own creed and a more intense commitment to making its own vision of social order effective throughout the world would bring about more humane societies and lead to the fuller actualization of human rights. Thus each creed with its distinctive way of organizing society claims to be universally true in principle. We are confronted with three relatively complete views which we can now summarize, in the following charts and figures, at the levels of both creed and social order.

A SUMMARY OF THREE CREEDS

	UNITED STATES	GERMAN DEMOCRATIC REPUBLIC	INDIA
Sources:	Conciliar Catholic, Reformed and Sectarian Christianity in alliance with Greco-Roman and Liberal philosophy.	Lutheran Pietism and Machiavellian political realism as transformed by Enlightenment Philosophy, French Revolutionary politics, and materialist economic theory.	Ancient Hindu tradition as modified by Islamic, Christian, Western-liberal, and social influences.
Modern Version:	The "great transition" to urban, differentiated "democracy."	Marxist-Leninist orthodoxy with an appreciation of Luther as a cultural hero.	Hindu Renaissance, Nationalism, and the drive toward modernization.
Chief Form:	Pervasive "public theology," often veiled in "democratic," pluralist ideals, and an intense "work ethic."	Official "civic religion" of scientific socialism as developed by Marx, Engels, and Lenin, with "humanistic" concessions to church religions.	Pervasive "social spirituality" with appeals to both traditional wisdom and utilitarian social-economic techniques.
Modern Exemplary Figures:	Eleanor Roosevelt, Martin L. King, Jr., Pope John XXIII.	Lenin, Rosa Luxemburg, and E. Honecker.	Gandhi, Nehru, Indira Gandhi.
Human Nature:	Humans are relational, willing creatures, sinfully out of relationship with God and neighbors.	Humans are an ensemble of social relationships developing in new ways as the means of production and society change.	Each self is an eternal part of the universal "oversoul" residing in a temporary social and material vessel.
The Ideal Pattern for Life:	Pluralist ecumenical community of communities, each part a voluntary association of persons living in love under universal moral law.	The integrated, classless society where conflict is overcome and all needs and interests are met by the autonomous human mastery of the world.	Hierarchic, universal, and social order, each level in a network of mutual ritual obligations, functional duties, and rights according to purity.
Ideal Rooted In:	God's Law and Purpose	The Will of the People	The Eternal *Dharma*
How Known:	"Revelation," discerned by reasoning together in voluntary association.	"Scientific" analysis of history and society, as promulgated by the revolutionary vanguard.	Development of "consciousness" through disciplined, communal living-out of being.
How Made Actual:	Covenantal bonding for worship and mutual edification to guide conscience and common action.	Revolutionary praxis and ideological reflection to guide praxis.	Ascetic discipline, intense devotional life, and orthopraxis in primary community.

	UNITED STATES	GERMAN DEMOCRATIC REPUBLIC	INDIA
Sources of Evil:	Sin/Pride	Alienation/Capitalism	Ignorance/Materialism
Strategies for Overcoming Evils:	Submission of prideful will to Will of God and reconciliation in community as tested by "common grace."	Progressive social action in concert with the inevitable forces of social history.	Enlightenment by education, development of consciousness and disinterested performance of duty.
Central Social Organ and Mode of "Membership":	Church, by baptism or confirmation, and/or voluntary association by agreement and qualification.	Party by participation in proletarian struggle, youth consecration (Jugendweihe), and Party selection.	Caste, by family and subcaste (*jati*) connections, and initiation ritual; nation by birth.
Target of Action by Central Social Organs:	Representative conciliar and parliamentary bodies—local, national, and international.	Communist lands and eventually the world through proletariat triumph, guided by Party.	"Natural communities" of family, caste, and nation; world through example and exhortation.
Perceived Internal Threats:	Moral failure of the churches on racism, sexism, and classism; "secularization," "confessionalization," and "liberalization" of theology.	Use of Party position for familial or "clique" advantage; organized religion which prompts loyalty to "mythic" nonsense.	Casteism which oppresses outcastes; communalism which divides the nation religiously.
Perceived External Threats:	Political centralization, amoral economics, and the "new" spiritualistic cults.	Imperialistic bourgeois capitalism and reactionary, spiritually sanctioned feudalism.	Imported Western lifestyles and militant, violent atheism, or alien religions.
Human Rights:	Determined for all humanity, for all times, by the *imago dei* and God's redemptive grace, as reported by Scripture, Tradition, and Reason, demanding justice for all and the reformation of all "natural" societies.	Determined for humanity in praxis according to the stage of socioeconomic development; principles are promulgated as landmarks of prevailing pattern, or as goals for social achievement.	Determined for each person according to membership in a particular network of graded claims and duties, spiritual rank, and role in the "natural" groupings of hierarchical social ecology.
The Most Important Right:	Freedom of Religion and, by extension, of all speech and association; in these, persons and society can be transformed toward a universal ethic.	Participate in *the* movement: remake humanity by reconstructing society; thereby fulfill human potentiality by making human will sovereign over all.	Be what you are—find your spiritual or sociometaphysical niche and live it out.

Figure 17
The Dominant Social Structure
of the United States

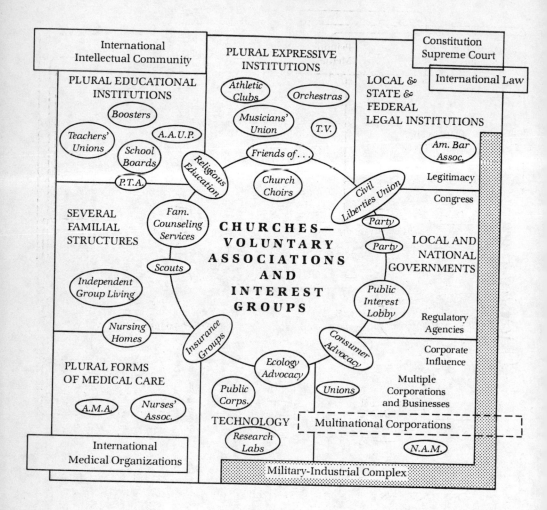

Note: Every sector influences every other sector directly and through the voluntary sector. No effort is made here to include either all important groups or all lines of influence and control. Such lines would overlap each sector and representative groups.

Figure 18
The Dominant Social Structure of the
German Democratic Republic

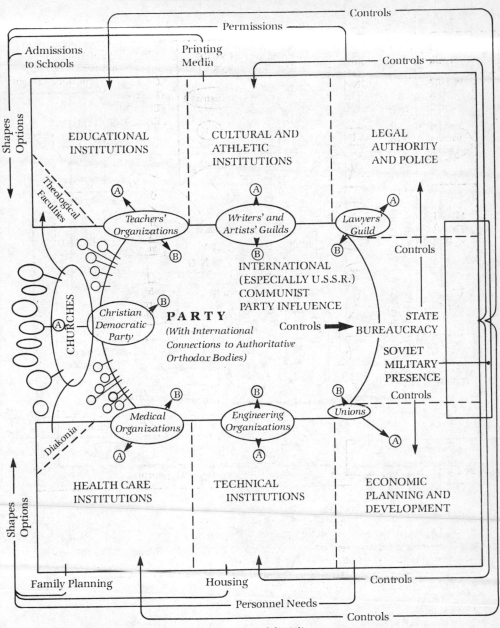

A = Guidance, information, encouragement, and discipline
B = Advocacy, feedback, suggestions, consensus formation
○○ = Family units

Figure 19
Dominant Social Structures in India

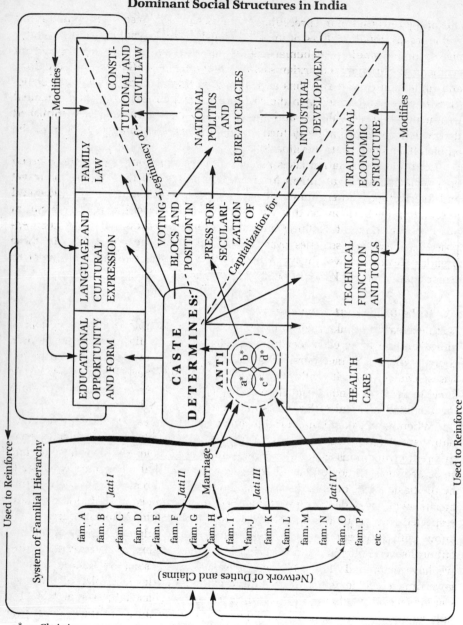

a* = Christians
b* = Westernized Hindus and some Neo-Buddhists, Parsees, etc.
c* = Marxists
d* = Urbanized peasants

Note: There is much overlap in these four groups. All these attack casteism, but frequently follow *jati* patterns in marriage and politics.

B. TOWARD EVALUATION

One of the purposes of the preceding chapters has been to set forth longitudinal and cross-sectional analyses of three religiously rooted social ethics that render diverse understandings of human rights, and to do so in such a way that an ecumenical Christian, a Marxian socialist, and a modern Hindu could recognize and understand the derivations and the social implications of the basic structures of creed and bonding in the respective social ethics. If both the extended treatments of these cultures and the summary just given have accomplished that, it is now appropriate to turn explicitly to another major purpose of the whole effort: comparative evaluation.

Continuous evaluation takes place implicitly when one encounters a creed or a social pattern that differs from one's own. One of the reasons for travel and for reading is to encounter alternative perspectives and social modes and to broaden our horizons so that we do not become parochial and provincial in our lives and thought. Nothing human is foreign to anyone who has been exposed to ideas and societies over wider ranges of time and space. In these broader encounters we always evaluate. We judge this or that to be better or worse than what we know in our own habitats.

1. Is Judgment Necessary?

Is it necessary to make such judgments? Is it not possible to accept the fact of pluralism and to let each society, each religion, each culture attend to its own course while we pursue ours? In some areas of life that would seem to be the wisest choice. Does it really make a difference whether people stand, sit, or kneel to pray? Is it not a matter of indifference whether people worship, make love, or hold political rallies in Tamil, German, or English?

When we speak of human rights, however, it is not easy to retreat to cultural pluralism. Human rights as a term implies universality. Yet, as we have seen, different civilizations define the truly human in sufficiently different ways and structure society into sufficiently divergent patterns that what some consider to be the basic rights of humans are violated by others. To argue that each culture has its own way of dealing with human rights and that each ought to be equally respected is to argue that there are no universal standards which humans can know with sufficient surety to make intercultural judgments. Such a view of cultural sovereignty fails to take seriously the truth claims of the several cultures we have examined. The members of each of these societies believe that the governing creed to which they adhere contains basic principles of universal significance. If we do not evaluate these claims as potentially true or false, but only as idiosyncratic opinion developed out of the triumph of some forces over others in cultural conflicts, we neither engage these cultures at their deepest levels nor allow our own culturally determined presuppositions to be challenged. Furthermore, in cases of cultural contact or confrontation we would leave the door open to the displacement or destruction of one culture by another.

Questions of truth would not be involved, only questions of cultural triumph. Human rights as a basic ethical concept would be entirely voided by such an approach, for in the final analysis might would make right. One could raise no objection to the exclusion of whole groups of people from any claim to human rights so long as that exclusion was consistent with reigning cultural understandings.

Perhaps it would be possible to avoid judgment by temporarily suspending our evaluations and allowing the divergent possibilities to continue to develop over time with the hope for eventual convergence. The power and influence of the three creeds and societal patterns we have examined suggest that, in some regards, we will have to do that whether we want to or not. No one of the three is ready to collapse or fundamentally alter its present orientations. But recognition of the fact that each of these options is likely to endure for some time does not relieve us of the necessity of evaluation. Each of these three societies, driven in part by the basic metaphysical-moral visions which give a sense of ultimate legitimacy, is also backed by international economic and political power. Indeed, all three are defended by nuclear weaponry. Public decisions as to how any one of these societies is to interact with the other two involve quite determinant decisions about which social models ought to become more influential or less influential in the future. Further, internal decisions have to be made in each society as to whether the social policies of that nation will operate exclusively in terms of its own basic creed, or whether they will adapt insights, motifs, and social-organizational models from other traditions. After all, the possibilities of reliance on a public theology organized in voluntary communities, reliance on a socialistic civic religion organized by party, or reliance on a social spirituality organized through natural kinship-based communities are present in each of the societies.

It is possible, for example, to assess racism as a sin before God and humanity which needs correction by the transformation of the heart, reconciliation through the church, and voluntary associational action to bring equalization of political, economic, and educational opportunity. Or it is possible to see racism as a product of class conflict based on the present stage of socioeconomic development in bourgeois society, to be overcome by the revolutionary triumph of the proletariat. Or it is possible to see racism as a distorted form of the inevitable, natural hierarchy of ethnic groupings, to be corrected by the closer adherence of each group to its own inner being. Each interpretation implies a fundamentally different social ethic and a distinctive strategy for understanding and enacting human rights. None of the societies can avoid making judgments on such questions, judgments which shape both creed and social organization.

At the immediate level, personal and small-group decisions also have to be made in each of the societies as to how we will spend our time, invest our energies, and shape our loyalties. Thus it is not possible in either public policy, group effort, or personal decision to avoid judgments by suspending efforts at evaluation. To hope that suspension of judgment will lead to convergence presumes a world in which neither public nor private decisions make any difference. This teleological suspension of the ethical is a chimera. None of the three options we have examined holds that to be a real possibility. Sooner or later we have to decide whether one or another of these is more or less true than the others. At such a point, confrontation occurs.

Perhaps it would be possible to avoid direct and confrontational judgment by appealing to some entirely different standard than those held by these three great world-historical options. Perhaps we could in some scientific or philosophical manner identify the real, basic needs of humanity and then evaluate all possibilities equally insofar as they meet these basic needs. The problem in this approach is the definition of what is "real" and "basic." Which metaphysical-moral vision shall we adopt in order to identify what is real and basic? We have seen repeatedly that definitions of what is real and basic depend on the fundamental definition of what is holy. If that is so, we cannot avoid encounter with the basic religious world-views. In terms of intellectual sophistication and capacity to develop various sciences, these three religious perspectives are surely among the most comprehensive and compelling that have ever been developed. They have been able to shape vast and dynamic civilizations. Yet at certain fundamental points they are both mutually exclusive and exclusive of any other possibility that might be developed.

Perhaps it would be possible to select those points on which the several traditions agree and find those principles which are universal in the sense that they are held by all major options. If we hold to a universal natural law in morality, then surely we could find the *consensus gentium* by abstracting the shared principles from all the cultures. Is it not the case that all societies condemn murder, stealing, and lying, and that all approve of kindness, fidelity, and honesty? It is certainly true that one can find certain kinds of behavior censured or sanctioned cross-culturally. But in the area of human rights, the logics of the three metaphysical-moral visions we have examined move the common elements in different directions. Murder is differently defined according to divergent definitions of membership in humanity and society. Is abortion murder? Is assassination in the service of the revolution murder? Is it tantamount to murder when systemic hunger and high death-rates for certain groups of outcastes are viewed as results of the inevitable and moral laws of the cosmos? Is capitalist profit, the expropriation of private property during collectivization, or uncontrolled usury among peasants in India stealing? And so on one could go. The apparent agreements among all peoples regarding certain "universal" ethical norms suggest that there are such things as universal principles, but the disagreements as to their contents force us to carefully examine and judge between the basic background beliefs by which they are understood and between the functioning of these norms in social practice. All natural-law ethics point toward the possibility of universal moral principles, but each natural-law ethic is in fact influenced by a particular faith tradition which gives it content. What, after all, is "natural"? Creation as God made it, or as fallen? The dialectic of history? The eternal, spiritual order of the cosmos? It appears that we have no choice but to make a choice. If human rights presents us with a situation in which we are confronted with a personal, group, civilizational, and world conflict in which we have to make decisions, perhaps we must simply exercise our will and make a leap of faith, embracing the religious or social perspective which seems most comfortable to us. Perhaps we have no choice but to be purely "confessional." If we believed this to be the case, however, we would undercut all truth claims about human rights, for all views of human rights would be simply a matter of subjective decision. We could decide to act on our chosen definition of human rights, but if anyone else decided differently—to deprive us of the right to hold that view, for example—we could make no persuasive claim about our own right to hold our view. In fact, our retreat to confessionalism would authorize the other's confessional decision to constrain our belief or action as well. All definitions would be arbitrary; universalistic judgments about human rights would be impossible. Will would be in contest against will; and, again, might would make right.

Clearly evaluation and judgment are necessary. We have no choice but to make a choice, yet the choice must be grounded in something more than cultural subjectivity or personal choice.

2. Is Judgment Possible?

Focusing on the religious and social aspects of human rights forces us to recognize that every view of or action on behalf of human rights is freighted with meanings out of a particular tradition, and that we are forced by concern for human rights to make decisions about these traditions. The critical question that immediately arises is whether it is possible to transcend the particular matrix of one or another of these traditions to make securely grounded judgments. In fact, this critical question has two aspects. In the first place the question is whether something of universal significance can arise out of a specific religious and social matrix, and in the second place the question is whether persons and groups can sufficiently transcend their own cultural and historical situations to give a fair assessment of both another tradition and their own. Both questions hinge on the relationship of particularity and universality. Is judgment possible?

It does appear, from the study of these three metaphysical-moral visions in their sociohistorical contexts, that some aspects of creed and social organization transcend their particular cultural confinements. Some specific notions, however contextually developed, seem to point to, to grasp, to unveil, indeed, to reveal motifs of import far beyond the particular matrices themselves.

I have no doubt that the ways in which each of these particular traditions speaks and acts about its own universalistic sensibilities are highly conditioned. Cultural myopia, rooted in egocentric sins, Machiavellian interests, and cosmic ignorance, besets us all. But does it so confine us that all basic interpretations of universal principles and all attempts to evaluate human values cross-culturally are utterly trapped in what many call the "hermeneutical circle"? That is, are our capacities to interpret the human condition so bound up in the credos and social fabrics, the conditionings and historical patterns of our own perspectives that we can speak meaningfully about human rights only to those who already share our presuppositions and social environment? If that is so, it is impossible to interpret and evaluate any other culture's fundamental religiosocial synthesis except by the imperial imposition of inappropriate categories.

Surely modesty about our capacities to surpass our own loyalties and bias must be the first response to the question of judgment. Certainly caution must be our guide in trespassing any boundary of open tolerance. Undoubtedly restraint and willingness to listen must attend every effort to find some basis for judgment and evaluation. Yet, as we have just seen, judgments do have to be made, and the question is whether we have a secure foundation upon which to make them. Human rights suffer as much by timidity as by dogmatic and arrogant ethnocentrism in making normative judgments. On what basis can we face the task of judgment with careful courage? Only, I think, by asking what is true.

To approach the question of truth in this area, I think we have to raise certain simple but fateful issues. Is the human condition such that all heaven and earth depends on our human decisions and human actions? If so, humans are and ought to be masters of life. Does what we do, as humans, determine everything? This is the view predominantly held in the G.D.R., and held by minorities in all lands. It is the position held in one way by "evangelicalism" wherever the primary focus is on "justification by faith alone," and whenever faith is held to be a "blind leap." (This is not the case when the focus is on "justification by grace.") When justification by faith is central, the human decision to believe, utterly beyond reason or precisely against reason, becomes the determining factor of salvation and meaning within the human heart. An arbitrary fundamentalism tends to result. In a quite different form this is the view also held by Marx and Lenin with regard to society. Social forms are constructed out of willed human actions; history is determined by the social relations humans build on the basis of the technological, economic, and political mastery of nature and destiny. Such constructions are also "beyond" or "against" reason in the sense that reason does not provide any universal moral categories to guide life. Such categories are themselves a construct of human actions and interests.

In both cases humans are called upon to decide the fate of soul and society. The message is to rise up, to throw off the chains, to seize human destiny in a predestined act of will. Humanity is to become what it is not by an existential decision and action that is predetermined by the logic of human history. All are to become masters of all and servants of none by becoming masters of none and servants of all. Humans assume the godly power of making the absolute decisions according to the autonomous law of human action. The chief human right is to participate in the whole and not to be ruled by any partial or heteronomous power. Otherwise there are no universal rights.

Or is the human condition such that we always shall be what we are, and cannot be other than what we are? Is it true that the law of the universe is such that each must accept and live out the various eternally recurring stages of life in accord with the natural, hierarchical structures of being? Is the primary task to develop our consciousness of who we truly are so that we can more appropriately fit into the divine ecology? This is the predominant view of Hinduism, although it has adherents in many cultures, especially those influenced by some modern psychological recoveries of *gnostic* wisdom, and those who hold that the natural law of classical cultures and the "ancient regime" was the true order for humane living. In this perspective humans are called upon to accept their being, to get in touch with the natural harmonies within the soul and in society, and to cultivate the natural virtues. Within us we humans have a piece of the universal spiritual reality which needs but to be cultivated. The primary human right is to be what we are; this differs for each person and each group of persons.

Or is it the case that we are sinners—that is, that humanity stands under a power, a purpose, and a moral law that we cannot make or unmake, that we cannot be or actualize in our own existence. If this is the basic human condition, we are called upon to "own"—that is, to accept as guiding for our lives— principles which we do not construct and which we cannot cultivate out of our own resources. We stand in a relationship to an "other" by which we are empowered and called to obedience. We are called to bond ourselves to that which we are not and cannot be, recognizing all other persons as having a dignity because *the* Other is in relation to them. On the basis of these relationships, clarified by mutual, rational discourse, we find a constitutional basis for respect for all "others," we find a courage to transform "natural," hierarchical relationships of sex and kinship toward a new, voluntary mutuality, and we find the will to subordinate the pretentious wills of class, party, and regime to principles of righteousness. Persuasion and the force of just law struggle to control all principalities and powers, yet sexuality and political regime are affirmed as signs of grace. They, like education, medicine, technology, economy, and art, must be granted a social space for freedom under moral law.

As a convert to the Liberal-Puritan synthesis and through that to ecumenical Christianity, I have become convicted that the last of these three views (treated first in this book) is the truest description of the human condition. This view preserves freedom and is rational; it is potentially universal and practically creates in particular settings the social space whereby the concrete social structures are opened up so that most basic human needs are likely to be met over time with a minimum of destructive violence. No society is yet pervasively shaped by this perspective, although the structural prospects for influence are most open in the pluralistic democracies of the West, precisely because of the previous influence of this tradition. Yet these societies neither know their own foundations, apply their deepest internal principles consistently, nor cultivate the public theology which can renew them from within. In large measure the fault lies in the shape and preoccupations of institutional religion, particularly at the grassroots level (I shall return to this problem shortly).

Nevertheless, I embrace this third view for several reasons. As pointed out, this view preserves freedom and is rational. The human condition is one which involves both freedom and ordered pattern. Form and vitality are both realities. The Liberal-Puritan and ecumenical Christian postures preserve both— freedom in the most basic sense, for it is based in a transcendent point of reference by which people may be abstracted from the determinative patterns of psyche and culture. When the first Hebrew bowed his head to an ethical God, beyond his own or any other culture, freedom was born. Freedom is a real possibility because there is God; because there is God, there is a basis for real freedom. Freedom—in this fundamental sense of relationship to something beyond determinate human capacities and human construction—finally has no metaphysical foundation in either Marxism-Leninism or Hinduism. To be sure, there is the prospect of the freedom of absolute human autonomy in Marxism-Leninism and of the final release (*moksha*) in Hinduism; but absolute human autonomy does not free us from human limitation, and in practice it always leads to the heteronomy of the strong over the weak. The final release of Hinduism is but the final stage in a totally determined process, and in practice it requires a strictly regulated ritualization of every aspect of life.

The basis for freedom is also a basis for rationality. The God of prophetic Judaism, Conciliar Catholicism, Liberal-Puritanism, and ecumenical Christianity is morally reliable. Perhaps we cannot prove God rationally, but God and God's righteousness cannot be refuted rationally either. Certainly this third option cannot be refuted on the basis of its own presuppositions, and it may meet the basic tests of rationality.[1] One can, however, rationally challenge Marxism-Leninism and Hinduism on the basis of their own presuppositions. Marxism-Leninism does not have a fundamental place for the causative role of ideas or persons in human history, yet the entire movement is inconceivable without the influence of traceable philosophical and religious ideas on Marx, the ideas of Marx on Lenin, and the role of each, as personality, in reshaping history. If ideas are not really causative, why are the press, education, the arts, and preaching so tightly controlled? Hinduism does not have a serious place for the role of history, modernization, and social change, yet Hinduism is the product of a series of traceable historical influences, modernizations, and social changes which preoccupy its authors and advocates. Marxism can be shown to be inadequate also by pointing to India: the introduction of new modes of production have not involved the fundamental altering of basic Hindu creed or social bonding. And Hinduism can be shown to be inadequate by pointing to Marxism-Leninism: the domination of some over others in the caste hierarchy can be shown, at least in part, to be rooted in class interests and not only in spiritual purity or natural social and cosmic order.

Critiques from these two other perspectives could be made against the Christian traditions I have traced. Much of what has been set forth as Christian

273

teaching is rooted either in the interests of the ruling few against the ruled many or in denials that there is anything like a hierarchy of natural spiritual excellence. But the Christian traditions of Conciliar Catholicism, Liberal-Puritanism, and ecumenical Christianity already know that. Such challenges do not refute the presuppositions or challenge the foundational doctrines. Because Christians believe themselves to be sinners, they know that the faith and the church are constantly distorted, and thus must be constantly reforming themselves, against self-interests, in accord with the fundamental principles of universal righteousness. Christians also recognize that some are wiser, stronger, and more advantaged than others, but this implies greater duty to the ignorant, weak, and disadvantaged, not privilege or status.

To argue that this view is rational does not mean that all who think logically or scientifically will automatically become believers. Nor does it mean that only those who are believers have any insights about universal human rights. On the contrary, persons may remain skeptics or agnostics on matters of belief for all sorts of reasons and still hold that there is a universal moral law. Principled liberals hold just such a position. Indeed, they may enter into the clarification of universal principles by critical reflection and mutual edification. They may work diligently for the implementation of human rights around the world. In the final analysis, however, they have no metaphysical ground for their moral vision, and no basis for claiming the absolute right to organize voluntary associations for such purposes.

I also suggested, in giving my reasons for embracing this third view, that this view is potentially universal and highly practical in that it creates the social space which allows society to meet the most basic human needs. This view is potentially universal precisely because it presumes the equality of every human person in regard to the most basic facts about humanity: all are children of God, all are equally loved by God, and all are sinners. Whatever discernments and discriminations are necessary and proper in making judgments about who is more capable, more virtuous, stronger, or wiser in this or that area of society— politics, economics, education, law, the arts, technology, etc.—at one point, the most fundamental one, all are equal. Thus all humans are called upon to reach out to all neighbors and to see that their human rights are not violated, whatever their role or station in life. The Communist and the capitalist, the Brahmin and the outcaste are everywhere to be equally regarded. This cannot be said of either the Marxist-Leninist position or Hinduism in either theory or practice. Further, in creating the concrete social institution, the church (and comparable voluntary associations), a social space is provided which relativizes the absolutistic authority "naturally" residing in familial-ethnic identity and in the custodians of coercive power, the political regime. Only a God who is not and may not be identified with a particular gene-pool or pattern of intimate relationship, only a God who is not and may not be identified with any particular principality or civic power can provide both the ultimate legitimacy for and the motivation to construct an open society. An organization dedicated to this reality can concretely hear the cries of human needs and demand that they be attended to by those sectors of society which are caught up in sustaining and extending their own profit, prestige, or power. Such an organization also provides the protection of group solidarity for individual persons. The rights of persons are less likely to be violated concretely in social practice when an organized but disinterested constituency becomes the advocate for persons whose rights are threatened. Individuals without such protection can be easily silenced. Marxism-Leninism and Hinduism contain within them no basic provisions for these features of creed and social organization except as they have been influenced by Hebrew prophecy and Christian insights.

We can summarize the arguments about the basis for judgment in comparative evaluations in two brief statements:

1. A creed which holds that there is a metaphysical reality other than humanity, but which humans can know in some measure, provides a basis for both freedom and rationality; only a metaphysical reality which transcends the accidents, determinations, and subjectivism of a particular culture, history, social arrangement, or group and belief can be the basis for reliable cross-cultural judgments, for genuine universality, and for practical implementation of human rights in diverse social contexts. Marxism-Leninism and Hinduism (and their Western correlates), in making humans divine, tend in principle to dehumanize by denying either freedom or reason.

2. The kind of social group most likely to bring about a concern for human rights in all societies is that kind of group which does not have direct power but which actually and practically bonds people into communities of discourse and solidarity which have no other purpose than the reconciliation of humans to one another throughout the world under a transcendent norm and power. Freedom of religion, in the concrete social sense of the right to organize groups on a voluntary basis around ultimate concerns for the sake of all, is the primary social factor in the historical actualization of human rights. The political party, which lives by seizing power, and caste, by definition and in practice, do not operate on a voluntary basis, see themselves under a moral law beyond themselves, or work for all.

C. WHAT THEN SHALL WE DO?

The first and critical test of whether such a social organization with such a creed is living according to its own deepest insights is whether or not it applies its internal principles against its own beliefs and social organization and the various institutions in its own social context. The process of reformation is constant. This is what was implied in the Bible and the organization of the early church, anticipated among Conciliar Catholics, made historically powerful by the Liberal-Puritan synthesis, and presently adopted, in principle, by both ecumenical Christianity and the United Nations. At its core it is based in nothing less than the drive for religious liberty. This drive was not and is not based in an individualist concern to believe anything one wanted, however irrational, but a drive to form "supra-natural," unmanipulated communities of faith under the love and law of God, for worship, mutual edification, and care, according to actual needs. From this basis communities of faith can and do offer a critique of spiritual pretense and arbitrary power—and they have an absolute right to do so. Where communities of faith are free to form, to speak freely about God's law, purpose, and love, to rationally articulate universal principles of justice, and to act for the redemption of the people in response to concrete needs on these bases, the theological understanding of human nature is renewed. Human rights can then be extended in political, economic, intellectual, and material directions. Where freedom of such religion is denied or the legacy of these traditions forgotten, the rights of people to speak of their needs for jobs, bread, homes, families, spiritual enlightenment, and power to decide their own destinies are soon also subverted. In one sense voluntary bonding for the open proclamation of truth and the communion-sharing of bread and drink form a paradigm of what is required of all societies for human rights.

Patricia W. Fagen, after surveying contemporary international human rights developments, confirms this view when she concludes that human rights advocacy "can only occur where there exists some institutional umbrella that can protect human rights advocates and offer both political and material support for human rights activities. . . . Almost everywhere, the churches play the most critical role. Religious groups, when internally strong, are the least vulnerable institutions."[2] The fact that many churches have not used their hard-won freedom in genuinely covenantal ways to speak the truth about oppression and denials of human rights only indicates the constant need for re-reformation today no less than in the prophetic periods of biblical history.

All human rights, to be sure, depend on enforcement for their long-term effectiveness and realization. Enforcement requires power. Churches do not have the psychosocial power of caste in India or the coercive authority of the Party in socialist lands. That is not necessarily a disadvantage. No person or human community is sufficiently beyond the power of sin that human rights can be actualized without the presence of coercion. Hence every struggle for human rights is likely to involve force at some point or other. But power cannot create or sustain itself; it cannot even direct itself. The exercise of power is always in the service of a purpose beyond the power itself. The critical issue is the ethical legitimacy of the purpose. Every power that comes into being tries to claim that its existence is legitimate. The point, however, is that power is never self-legitimizing. A creed with a committed constituency is required. Human rights derived from a godly covenant and concretely exemplified in pervasive networks among all the people of the earth offers the criteria by which such claims may be adjudicated. When power is exercised against human dignity in violation of community, it must be judged as illegitimate and resisted. A transcendentally based religious creed provides the conceptual framework to do that; a religiously bonded community provides the social and psychic support-systems which all but the most saintly and courageous need to fight for the actualization of creed. The criteria by which we know the difference between legitimate and illegitimate power involve not only political discernment and social action but, more importantly, theological discernment and the formation of active, involved, participatory faith communities. At the practical, social level the eschewing of the overt powers of familial or political authority means that communities must exercise all influence through the convictions and the consciences of the people. If the people do not believe something makes sense, and if they do not choose freely to bond themselves to it, it will not be powerful.

In brief, the most spiritually profound and socially revolutionary principle with regard to the realization of human rights was not enunciated by any ancient seer who spoke of the achievements of human excellence on the basis of spiritual consciousness and good breeding, or by any radical who focuses on the material needs and historical conditions which beset humanity, but by Saint Peter when he said, "We must obey God rather than man." When the heirs of Peter forget that point and fail to organize outside the "natural" contours of familial and political authority, human rights are in peril. At the same time, operating from that base, familial and political life can be reformed and transformed in directions which make sense to the people and which they can freely choose.

It should be clear by now. The evidence from the deep trajectories of history, from cross-sectional analyses of the functioning and structures of society, and from comparative evaluations is that judgment may not be avoided and action is required. In order to hold and maintain a human rights position that is in principle universal, it is necessary to affirm something like those doctrines, and to construct something like those social patterns developed historically by prophetic Judaism, Conciliar Catholicism, Free-Church Calvinism, and aspects of the principled-liberal tradition. When we are dealing with religion, we are dealing, of course, with explosive matters that have deep and long-range consequences. When these are distorted, the consequences are destructive and persistent. Thus the first responsibility is to develop those creeds and social organs that see themselves under a divine moral mandate and which renounce the direct use of coercive power while still attempting to influence every sector of human society.

From a Marxist perspective it could be argued that this is merely a bourgeois, middle-class suggestion. In one sense the Marxists are correct. These are the traditions which have given rise to, or have been adopted by, the middle classes in ancient Mediterranean cities, in medieval cities, and in modern cities, and which reflect their interests. Indeed, one can state the matter in a stronger fashion at this point: the decisive class for the future of humanity is the middle class. All should join it. When people are too poor or too rich; when they are powerless or so powerful that they can be corrected by no one; when it is not possible or necessary for them to enter into covenants and councils for mutual edification and correction; when they see themselves under no law that protects them from exploitation or no law that condemns the exploitation; when purpose is reduced to survival or has no end larger than self-realization—when this happens, something is fundamentally wrong with the world. We know it is wrong because we are in fact *under* a constant, reliable higher reality which demands equity and mutual care. The critics of the middle classes wrongly see this truth as mere convention.

From a Hindu perspective such a view does not seem truly spiritual. On the one hand, it seems too bound up with earthly matters to be truly transcendental. On the other hand, it does not seem to support the spiritual particularities of family loyalty and national culture; it seems to erode the absolute structures of the hierarchical cosmos which are the visible vessels of the multiple levels of spiritual excellences. In one sense the Hindus are correct. The position argued for here is one in which human spirituality is not separable from the material vessels, and the vessels are not fixed in order of rank. The "incarnational," "covenantal" perspective that stands behind these comparative evaluations does imply that contemporary Hindu perspectives bear within them valuable insights about the need of spiritual excellence, the importance of extended, stable families, and the legitimacy of resistance to imperial power from abroad. But the presuppositions of Hinduism as they have been developed internally and, under external pressures, have become institutionalized do not go far enough. Hinduism leaves too little space for the formation of innovative groups not rooted in the inherited status of family, caste, or nation, groups that can confess a creed that is not only a celebration of what one "is" by inheritance but one that provides beyond that a basis for prophetic critique of what one is. *Artha* cannot be opportunistically conceived and fundamentally governed by *dharma*. If the spirituality of cosmic order leads us to an inevitable and irrevocable hierarchy of authority that leaves no place for universal principles of equality to work their way into new constellations of civilizational organization, something is wrong at both the creedal and societal levels.

All this is not to say that a committed Communist or a pious Hindu is not as deeply religious or as profoundly human as anyone influenced by Jewish or Christian traditions. Nor does it mean that each must become a Christian in order to endorse human rights. At present many Communists and Hindus (and, for that matter, Liberals) cannot develop an appreciation of Christianity. The forms in which they have been exposed to it have been supportive of precisely that which stands opposed to universal ethics and human rights. Conservative Catholicism, with its affinities to Caesaro-Papal "Orthodoxy," and Imperial Calvinism have both betrayed too much of what the tradition contains, making Christianity a tool of repressive class warfare and polluting all decent senses of spiritual excellence. The pietist and evangelical traditions have made theology irrelevant to scientific and social life, and made it too often a matter of obscurantist, irrational confessionalism. Surely a God who is just and merciful will not condemn the devoted Hindu, the dedicated Marxist, or the concerned liberal-humanist who has seen only these forms of Christianity and so rejects it.

Nevertheless, it is not special pleading or arrogant myopia which claims that in a specific minority tradition, deriving from ancient Judaism, early Christianity, Conciliar Catholicism, Liberal-Puritanism, and ecumenical Christianity, a set of basic insights and social patterns have been developed which are in principle of universal importance precisely because they grasped aspects of human nature which point, in the way that other traditions and modes of thought do not, to valid truths about belief and social order. If that is the case, as I have come to think, the guidelines for action can be drawn.

What we are to do in the first instance is to quest for the truth about what is universally valid, a task we can undertake only if we believe that there is a reference point for all truth, and that things are not merely a matter of perspective. We recover the past and study other cultures to understand the present and to focus our designs for the future. In recovery of the past we begin to see how decisions made in one specific context have long-range consequences for subsequent generations and civilizations, often far beyond the intentions of the moment. We begin to see that particular decisions about bonding into this or that group, in attempts to discern or actualize a truth that transcends us, about making creedal commitments *under* that truth and forming support systems to keep our testimony to that truth alive in history, are of world-historical importance.

In doing this, we also begin to see how decisions in one area have consequences in other sectors of society. The relationship to family or nation, the loyalties to economic group or party, the structures of education, the arts, law, medicine, and the rest are all potentially affected by the kinds of bondings we make and the kinds of social spaces we construct for these various institutions of human life. Each decision we make in this regard is freighted with implications for subsequent understandings of what is human and for what rights are to be protected or abridged.

In becoming aware of the "deep trajectories" that have shaped modernity, and in becoming alert to the systemic cross-sectional implications of specific social bonding, we find that we are driven to ultimate questions of a metaphysical-moral order which give us a critical base from which to make judgments. The test of whether we are at that level shows up in a very simple way: Do we apply these tests reflexively? That is, do we apply them to our own groups of primary loyalty? This test would mean that the castes, for example, would become immediately self-critical about their own spiritual excellence. It would mean that the Party would become immediately self-critical about the actual, practical overcoming of alienation by allowing more choices, views, and organizations among the people. And it would mean that the church would become immediately self-critical about its covenantal fidelity, its spiritual excellence, and its class exclusiveness.

In the final analysis Christians will have to leave decisions on many of these matters to the Hindus and the Marxists. We cannot, must not, make their decisions. For ourselves, however, choosing to be ecumenical Christians for the sake of truth and humanity involves a conviction that in the final analysis

Christianity provides a better, a more universal basis for this self-critical function than the alternatives. It means that we bond ourselves to the church as "catholic," truly universal, and "always reforming, always in need of reform." In *this* way we can be also truly evangelical; in this way we have a basis for the liberal appreciation of other traditions. We are able to make these choices by God's grace.

Coming to that conviction, however, puts a heavy burden on the ecumenical church. At the practice level it suggests that the church must become the instrument not only for self-reform and universalizing concern but also for critical reconstruction of every sector of society. It is one of the scandals of the church that it historically fought for freedom of the pulpit, and extended this principle to academic freedom and freedom of expression for the press and the arts, but that it only occasionally uses the freedom it has won to expose the pathologies of the social system and the silliness of much that passes for information or learning. The churches have, in principle, the metaphysical-moral vision and the social space to inform the professions, to extend the concern for human rights in medical ethics and legal areas such as abortion and penal reform; but only occasionally does that happen. The area of political economics in the West remains so much under the dominion of utilitarian liberalism and consumerism, and so far removed from converted efforts by the churches, that disciplined thought or action on a covenantal basis in this area is rare. At this point, surely only a recovery of Puritan frugality coupled with an ecumenical concern for the poor and hungry of the world can allow credibility to attach to the churches' concern for human rights.

In brief, the hard-won visions of the tradition must be reinvigorated and reconstituted so that *re-conciliation* and *re-formation* in a genuinely universal context become live options.[3] The Puritan tradition must be integrated with that and must itself become genuinely covenantal, specifically in regard to the covenants of economic life which that tradition has never fully articulated. Covenantally it must *purify* once more the economic structures of the modern world. And liberalism must be transmuted into a genuinely *liberating* movement, linking together in consensus around international law those "self-evident" principles which in fact derive from profound religious insights.

To accomplish these visions, hundreds, thousands, millions of specific decisions, connections, and relations must be made. Persons must join, participate actively in, and sacrificially give to nongovernmental, nonfamilial, ecclesial associations, building linkages to and sharing resources with comparable groups in Western, socialist, and traditional cultures, and demanding in the name of God the right to do so.

*　　　*　　　*

The world is in the midst of a great Kulturkampf, a great struggle as to what principles and which groups will dominate humanity in the future. The question

280

of human rights is a centerpoint of the controversy. Like all battles, this one will be won or lost in the trenches. It is for this reason that after working on this book for several years, I dedicated it to seminarians in America, Eastern Europe, and one of the most sophisticated parts of the Third World. On the basis of this work, I invite, I plead with religious leadership to recognize the significance of what they are about. The cumulative decisions evoked by hundreds and thousands like them demonstrably have brought about dramatic improvements in human rights when their efforts are viewed in a comparative perspective over time and space. Great thinkers have made striking contributions for which we are all indebted, but these ideas have become historically powerful and effective only when filtered through the preaching, teaching, personal and social-organizational transformations at the grassroots level as shaped by grassroots leadership, to involve the people in the great questions of creed and ecclesiology, doctrine and society. At a time when basic human needs are not met for millions, at a time when the theological capital of ecumenical Christianity is at a low ebb, and at a time when the viability of voluntary associations of all kinds is being threatened in many societies, it is tragic that clergy forfeit efforts to speak of universal truth by becoming more "confessional" and leaving "reason" to "the world," by getting caught up in such short-term immediacies that they remain historically ignorant, or by focusing on such local problems that they fail to see the universal meaning of their efforts. The prospect of a public theology is undercut. This same clergy preoccupies itself with petty efforts to discover self-identity by second-rate psychology laced with Eastern mysticism and flirts with the latest radical slogans in pretentious attempts to be relevant. Communities organized around such tendencies deserve to become increasingly marginal in intellectual and social history, and they will get what they deserve. The price, however, will be the loss of firm doctrinal and social-organizational bases for human salvation. All three societies could become increasingly dominated by familial elites or centralized, single parties.

Against these possibilities there is also the possibility that we will enter a new era of theological renewal and ecumenical interaction. Paul Tillich was only slightly premature when he announced, a generation ago, the end of the Protestant era—an end which had to involve simultaneously the fuller actualization of the "Protestant principle" of prophetic thinking and acting.[4] It is possible that this will give rise to a new missionary outreach to all humans and for human rights in all societies. Such a prospect invites "the improvement of socialism," as Heino Falcke has argued so effectively in the German Democratic Republic, the "indigenization of Christianity," as M. M. Thomas has argued so well in South India, and "the democratization of the economic order," as Walter Rauschenbusch and others have argued in the United States.[5] If these directions are taken on the basis of a renewed, ecumenical public theology,[6] re-conciliation and re-formation are more likely, and human rights will be more fully actualized.

1. This is one of the most important contributions of Ronald Green's seminal work in comparative religious ethics, *Religious Reason* (New York: Oxford University Press, 1978). I disagree with his interpretation of Hinduism, however, after preparing this study.

2. P. W. Fagen, "Bibliography on Human Rights ..." (Washington, D.C.: Library of Congress, 1980).

3. See G. Baum, "Catholic Foundation of Human Rights," *The Ecumenist*, 18 (Nov.-Dec. 1979), 6ff.

4. Paul Tillich, *The End of the Protestant Era* (Chicago: University of Chicago Press, 1948).

5. See the treatment of these figures in Chapters Four, Five, and Seven. See also John Cort, "Can Socialism be Distinguished from Marxism?" *Cross Currents* (Winter 1979 — 80), pp. 423ff.

6. In my judgment a model for such an effort was developed by the United Church of Christ in 1979. See Appendix IV.

Appendices

Appendix I

January 17, 1977

President-elect Jimmy Carter
P. O. Box 2600
Washington, D.C. 20013

Dear President-elect Carter:

We write to convey our urgent concern about the State Department's superficial treatment of human rights violations. We have been very heartened by your statements on human rights throughout your long campaign and believe that you will share our frustration with the present State Department's way of dealing with human rights.

On January 1, 1977, the House International Relations Committee released partially declassified human rights reports by the State Department on six countries that receive security assistance. The inadequacies of the reports on Argentina, Haiti, Indonesia, Iran and the Philippines compel us to challenge both their content and their conclusions.

After careful scrutiny of these statements, we conclude that the State Department figures given for political prisoners are consistently underestimated and do not take into consideration higher estimates by international organizations. Responsible reports from international legal and human rights groups alleging widespread and routine torture by police and army personnel with the sanction of government leaders, are downgraded or disregarded entirely. (A detailed analysis is attached.)

The State Department's justifications for continuing security assistance to these countries is just one more indication of the Ford Administration's insensitivity to Human Rights. We do not believe that our national interest is served by the strengthening of dictatorial regimes through security assistance. The granting of such U.S. security assistance gives an appearance of legitimacy to repressive governments and their activities they otherwise would not enjoy.

The State Department's rationale for continued security assistance to these five governments is also simplistic. It asserts that this assistance promotes the stability and the goodwill of the recipient nation, enhancing our national security, regardless of their violations of human rights. In the short run, some stability may be achieved for individual leaders or groups. But clearly, over an

284

extended period of time, unpopular governments which use secret police, detention without charges and torture to maintain their power will fall.

We believe that our national security lies rather in the support of democratic governments. The new Administration and Congress must return our foreign policy to the principles of our Constitution and the Declaration of Independence. If they fail to do so, the confidence of the American people in our public institutions will continue to erode.

We, therefore, urge you and your new Administration to take these four immediate steps:

1. Declassify and release the entire reports prepared by the State Department under the Ford Administration.

2. Require the new Carter State Department to review these reports and submit new reports for public release giving greater detail on human rights violations and giving specific assessments of the impact of continued U.S. security assistance on human rights in these countries.

3. Redefine the criteria for allocating security assistance to reflect more adequately our national interest: human rights must not be sacrificed in order to promote the short term stability of repressive regimes.

4. Do not request any monies from Congress for security assistance to governments like these five which engage in a consistent pattern of gross violations of internationally recognized human rights.

Americans for Democratic Action
National Council of Churches
Jesuit Office of Social Ministries
Church of the Brethren, World Ministries Commission
Anti-Martial Law Coalition (Philippines)
Argentine Commission for Human Rights
Campaign for a Democratic Foreign Policy
Clergy and Laity Concerned
Friends and Committee on National Legislation and several others

Universal Declaration of Human Rights

PREAMBLE

Whereas recognition of the inherent dignity and of the equal and inalienable rights of all members of the human family is the foundation of freedom, justice and peace in the world,

Whereas disregard and contempt for human rights have resulted in barbarous acts which have outraged the conscience of mankind, and the advent of a world in which human beings shall enjoy freedom of speech and belief and freedom from fear and want has been proclaimed as the highest aspiration of the common people,

Whereas it is essential, if man is not to be compelled to have recourse, as a last resort, to rebellion against tyranny and oppression, that human rights should be protected by the rule of law,

Whereas it is essential to promote the development of friendly relations between nations,

Whereas the peoples of the United Nations have in the Charter reaffirmed their faith in fundamental human rights, in the dignity and worth of the human person and in the equal rights of men and women and have determined to promote social progress and better standards of life in larger freedom,

Whereas Member States have pledged themselves to achieve, in co-operation with the United Nations, the promotion of universal respect for the observance of human rights and fundamental freedoms,

Whereas a common understanding of these rights and freedoms is of the greatest importance for the full realization of this pledge,

Now, Therefore,

THE GENERAL ASSEMBLY
proclaims
THIS UNIVERSAL DECLARATION OF HUMAN RIGHTS as a common standard of achievement for all peoples and all nations, to the end that every individual and every organ of society, keeping this Declaration constantly in mind, shall strive by teaching and education to promote respect for these rights and freedoms and by progressive measures, national and international, to secure their universal and effective recognition and observance, both among the peoples of Member States themselves and among the peoples of territories under their jurisdiction.

Article 1. All human beings are born free and equal in dignity and rights. They are endowed with reason and conscience and should act towards one another in a spirit of brotherhood.

Article 2. Everyone is entitled to all the rights and freedoms set forth in this Declaration, without distinction of any kind, such as race, colour, sex, language, religion, political or other opinion, national or social origin, property, birth or other status.

Furthermore, no distinction shall be made on the basis of the political, jurisdictional or international status of the country or territory to which a person belongs, whether it be independent, trust, non-self-governing or under any other limitation of sovereignty.

Article 3. Everyone has the right to life, liberty and security of person.

Article 4. No one shall be held in slavery or servitude; slavery and the slave trade shall be prohibited in all their forms.

Article 5. No one shall be subjected to torture or to cruel, inhuman or degrading treatment or punishment.

Article 6. Everyone has the right to recognition everywhere as a person before the law.

Article 7. All are equal before the law and are entitled without any discrimination to equal protection of the law. All are entitled to equal protection against any discrimination in violation of this Declaration and against any incitement to such discrimination.

Article 8. Everyone has the right to an effective remedy by the competent national tribunals for acts violating the fundamental rights granted him by the constitution or by law.

Article 9. No one shall be subjected to arbitrary arrest, detention or exile.

Article 10. Everyone is entitled in full equality to a fair and public hearing by an independent and impartial tribunal, in the determination of his rights and obligations and of any criminal charge against him.

Article 11. (1) Everyone charged with a penal offence has the right to be presumed innocent until proved guilty according to law in a public trial at which he has had all the guarantees necessary for his defence.

(2) No one shall be held guilty of any penal offence on account of any act or omission which did not constitute a penal offence, under national or international law, at the time when it was committed. Nor shall a heavier penalty be imposed than the one that was applicable at the time the penal offence was committed.

Article 12. No one shall be subjected to arbitrary interference with his privacy, family, home or correspondence, nor to attacks upon his honour and reputation. Everyone has the right to the protection of the law against such interference or attacks.

Article 13. (1) Everyone has the right to freedom of movement and residence within the borders of each state.

(2) Everyone has the right to leave any country, including his own, and to return to his country.

Article 14. (1) Everyone has the right to seek and to enjoy in other countries asylum from persecution.

(2) This right may not be invoked in the case of prosecutions genuinely arising from non-political crimes or from acts contrary to the purposes and principles of the United Nations.

Article 15. (1) Everyone has the right to a nationality.

(2) No one shall be arbitrarily deprived of his nationality nor denied the right to change his nationality.

Article 16. (1) Men and women of full age, without any limitation due to race, nationality or religion, have the right to marry and to found a family. They are entitled to equal rights as to marriage, during marriage and at its dissolution.

(2) Marriage shall be entered into only with the free and full consent of the intending spouses.

(3) The family is the natural and fundamental group unit of society and is entitled to protection by society and the State.

Article 17. (1) Everyone has the right to own property alone as well as in association with others.

(2) No one shall be arbitrarily deprived of his property.

Article 18. Everyone has the right to freedom of thought, conscience and religion; this right includes freedom to change his religion or belief, and freedom, either alone or in community with others and in public or private, to manifest his religion or belief in teaching, practice, worship and observance.

Article 19. Everyone has the right to freedom of opinion and expression; this right includes freedom to hold opinions without interference and to seek, receive and impart information and ideas through any media and regardless of frontiers.

Article 20. (1) Everyone has the right to freedom of peaceful assembly and association.

(2) No one may be compelled to belong to an association.

Article 21. (1) Everyone has the right to take part in the government of his country, directly or through freely chosen representatives.

(2) Everyone has the right of equal access to public service in his country.

(3) The will of the people shall be the basis of the authority of government; this will shall be expressed in periodic and genuine elections which shall be by universal and equal suffrage and shall be held by secret vote or by equivalent free voting procedures.

Article 22. Everyone, as a member of society, has the right to social security and is entitled to realization, through national effort and international co-operation and in accordance with the organization and resources of each State, of the economic, social and cultural rights indispensable for his dignity and the free development of his personality.

Article 23. (1) Everyone has the right to work, to free choice of employment, to just and favourable conditions of work and to protection against unemployment.

(2) Everyone, without any discrimination, has the right to equal pay for equal work.

(3) Everyone who works has the right to just and favourable remuneration ensuring for himself and his family an existence worthy of human dignity, and supplemented, if necessary, by other means of social protection.

(4) Everyone has the right to form and to join trade unions for the protection of his interests.

Article 24. Everyone has the right to rest and leisure, including reasonable limitation of working hours and periodic holidays with pay.

Article 25. (1) Everyone has the right to a standard of living adequate for the health and well-being of himself and of his family, including food, clothing, housing and medical care and necessary social services, and the right to security in the event of unemployment, sickness, disability, widowhood, old age or other lack of livelihood in circumstances beyond his control.

(2) Motherhood and childhood are entitled to special care and assistance. All children, whether born in or out of wedlock, shall enjoy the same social protection.

Article 26. (1) Everyone has the right to education. Education shall be free, at least in the elementary and fundamental stages. Elementary education shall be compulsory. Technical and professional education shall be made generally available and higher education shall be equally accessible to all on the basis of merit.

(2) Education shall be directed to the full development of the human personality and to the strengthening of respect for human rights and fundamental freedoms. It shall promote understanding, tolerance and friendship among all nations, racial or religious groups, and shall further the activities of the United Nations for the maintenance of peace.

(3) Parents have a prior right to choose the kind of education that shall be given to their children.

Article 27. (1) Everyone has the right freely to participate in the cultural life of the community, to enjoy the arts and to share in scientific advancement and its benefits.

(2) Everyone has the right to the protection of the moral and material interests resulting from any scientific, literary or artistic production of which he is the author.

Article 28. Everyone is entitled to a social and international order in which the rights and freedoms set forth in this Declaration can be fully realized.

Article 29. (1) Everyone has duties to the community in which alone the free and full development of his personality is possible.

(2) In the exercise of his rights and freedoms, everyone shall be subject only to such limitations as are determined by law solely for the purpose of securing due recognition and respect for the rights and freedoms of others and of meeting the just requirements of morality, public order and the general welfare in a democratic society.

(3) These rights and freedoms may in no case be exercised contrary to the purposes and principles of the United Nations.

Article 30. Nothing in this Declaration may be interpreted as implying for any State, group or person any right to engage in any activity or to perform any act aimed at the destruction of any of the rights and freedoms set forth herein.

APPENDIX III

The Church and Modern Industry

Resolutions Unanimously Adopted by the Federal Council of the Churches of Christ
in America, December 4, 1908

The Committee on The Church and Modern Industry presents for the action of the Federal Council of the Churches of Christ in America, the following statement and recommendations:

1. This Federal Council places upon record its profound belief that the complex problems of modern industry can be interpreted and solved only by the teachings of the New Testament, and that Jesus Christ is final authority in the social as in the individual life. Under this authority and by application of this teaching the contribution to human welfare by the Church, whatever its lapses and its delays, has been incalculable. Out of the sacrifice and fervor of the centuries has come a fund of altruism which enriches to-day a thousand purposes for human betterment, some of which do not know the origin of their impulse. The interest of the Church in men is neither recent nor artificial. No challenge of newly posted sentries can exclude it from the ground where are struggle and privation and need. It has its credentials and knows the watchword.

2. Christian practice has not always harmonized with Christian principle. By the force of economic law and of social custom individual life has been, at times, swerved from the straight course, and the organized church has not always spoken when it should have borne witness, and its plea for righteousness has not always been uttered with boldness. Christianity has created both the opportunity and the principles of life. In the mighty task of putting conscience and justice and love into a "Christian" civilization, the Church, with all its splendid achievements, has sometimes faltered. But it has gone farther and suffered more, a thousand fold, to accomplish this end than any other organized force the world has ever known.

3. The Church now confronts the most significant crisis and the greatest opportunity in its long career. In part its ideals and principles have become the working basis of organizations for social and industrial betterment which do not accept its spiritual leadership and which have been estranged from its fellowship. We believe, not for its own sake but in the interest of the kingdom of God, the Church must not merely acquiesce in the movements outside of it which make for human welfare, but must demonstrate not by proclamation but by deeds its primacy among all the forces which seek to lift the plane and better the conditions of human life.

This Council, therefore, welcomes this first opportunity on behalf of the Churches of Christ in the United States officially represented, to emphasize convictions which have been in fragmentary ways already expressed.

4. We recognize the complex nature of industrial obligations, affecting employer and employee, society and government, rich and poor, and most earnestly counsel

tolerance, patience and mutual confidence; we do not defend or excuse wrong doing in high places or in low, nor purpose to adapt the ethical standards of the Gospel to the exigencies of commerce or the codes of a confused industrial system.

5. While we assert the natural right of men—capitalists and workingmen alike— to organize for common ends, we hold that the organization of capital or the organization of labor cannot make wrong right, or right wrong; that essential righteousness is not determined by numbers either of dollars or of men, that the Church must meet social bewilderment by ethical lucidity, and by gentle and resolute testimony to the truth must assert for the whole Gospel, its prerogative as the test of the rightness of both individual and collective conduct everywhere.

6. We regard with the greatest satisfaction the effort of those employers, individual and corporate, who have shown in the conduct of their business, a fraternal spirit and a disposition to deal justly and humanely with their employees as to wages, profit-sharing, welfare work, protection against accidents, sanitary conditions of toil, and readiness to submit differences to arbitration. We record our admiration for such labor organizations as have under wise leadership throughout many years, by patient cultivation of just feelings and temperate views among their members, raised the efficiency of service, set the example of calmness and self-restraint in conference with employers, and promoted the welfare not only of the men of their own craft but of the entire body of workingmen.

7. In such organizations is the proof that the fundamental purposes of the labor movement are ethical. In them great numbers of men of all nationalities and origins are being compacted in fellowship, trained in mutual respect, and disciplined in virtues which belong to right character and are at the basis of good citizenship. By them society at large is benefited in the securing of better conditions of work, in the Americanization of our immigrant population, and in the educational influence of the multitudes who in the labor unions find their chief, sometimes their only, intellectual stimulus.

8. We note as omens of industrial peace and goodwill, the growth of a spirit of conciliation, and of the practice of conference and arbitration in settling trade disputes. We trust profoundly that these methods may supplant those of the strike and the lockout, the boycott and the black-list. Lawlessness and violence on either side of labor controversies, are an invasion of the rights of the people and must be condemned and resisted. We believe no better opportunity could be afforded to Christian men, employers and wage-earners alike, to rebuke the superciliousness of power and the obstinacy of opinion, than by asserting and illustrating before their fellows in labor contests, the Gospel which deals with men as men and has for its basis of fraternity the Golden Rule.

We commend most heartily the societies and leagues in which employers and workingmen come together upon a common platform to consider the problems of each in the interest of both, and we urge Christian men more freely to participate in such movements of conciliation. We express our gratitude for the evidences that in ever widening circles the influence of the agencies established by some of the churches is distinctly modifying the attitude of the workingmen and the Church toward each other.

9. We deem it the duty of all Christian people to concern themselves directly with certain practical industrial problems. To us it seems that the churches must stand—

For equal rights and complete justice for all men in all stations of life.

For the right of all men to the opportunity for self-maintenance, a right ever to be wisely and strongly safeguarded against encroachments of every kind. For the right of workers to some protection against the hardships often resulting from the swift crises of industrial change.

For the principle of conciliation and arbitration in industrial dissensions.

For the protection of the workers from dangerous machinery, occupational disease, injuries and mortality.

For the abolition of child labor.

For such regulation of the conditions of toil for women as shall safeguard the physical and moral health of the community.

For the suppression of the "sweating system."

For the gradual and reasonable reduction of the hours of labor to the lowest practicable point, and for that degree of leisure for all which is a condition of the highest human life.

For a release from employment one day in seven.

For a living wage as a minimum in every industry, and for the highest wage that each industry can afford.

For the most equitable division of the products of industry that can ultimately be devised.

For suitable provision for the old age of the workers and for those incapacitated by injury.

For the abatement of poverty.

10. To the toilers of America and to those who by organized effort are seeking to lift the crushing burdens of the poor, and to reduce the hardships and uphold the dignity of labor, this Council sends the greeting of human brotherhood and the pledge of sympathy and of help in a cause which belongs to all who follow Christ.

RECOMMENDATIONS

To the several Christian bodies here represented the Council recommends:

I. That the churches more fully recognize, through their pulpits, press and public assemblies, the great work of social reconstruction which is now in progress, the character, extent and ethical value of the labor movement, the responsibilities of Christian men for the formation of social ideals, and the obligation of the churches to supply the spiritual motive and standards for all movements which aim to realize in the modern social order the fulfillment of the second great commandment, "Thou shalt love thy neighbor as thyself."

II. That the study of existing conditions in the industrial world, their origin and outcome, be more definitely enforced as an immediate Christian duty;

That to this end, in all theological seminaries, and, so far as practicable, in other schools and colleges, there be established, wherever they do not now exist, courses in economics, sociology and the social teachings of Jesus, supplemented, wherever possible, by investigation of concrete social facts, and

That study classes and reading courses on social questions, be instituted in connection with the churches and their societies, to foster an intelligent appreciation of existing conditions, and to create a public sentiment through which relief and reform may be more effectively secured.

III. That the churches with quickened zeal and keener appreciation, through their pastors, lay leaders and members, wherever possible, enter into sympathetic and fraternal relations with workingmen, by candid public discussion of the problems which especially concern them, by advocating their cause when just, by finding the neighborly community of interest and by welcoming them and their families to the uses and privileges of the local churches;

That the proper general authorities of the denominations endeavor by special bureau or department to collate facts and mold opinion in the interest of a better understanding between the Church and workingmen, and particularly to obtain a more accurate and general knowledge of the meaning of trade unionism, and especially

That all church members who, either as employers or as members of trade unions, are more specifically involved in the practical problems of industry, be urged to accept their unparalleled opportunity for serving the cause of Christ and humanity by acting, in His spirit, as mediators between opposing forces in our modern world of work.

IV. That the Church in general not only aim to socialize its message, to understand the forces which now dispute its supremacy, to stay by the people in the effort to solve with them their problems, but also modify its own equipment and procedure in the interest of more democratic administration and larger social activity;

That more generally in its buildings provision be made for the service of the community as well as for the public worship of God;

That in its councils of direction workingmen be welcomed and the wisdom of the poor be more freely recognized;

That in its assemblies artificial distinctions be rebuked and removed;

That in its financial management the commercial method, if it exist, be replaced by the principles of the Gospel as set forth in the Epistle of James, to the end that the workers and the poor, vastly in the majority in the United States, may ever find the church as homelike as the union hall, more attractive than the saloon, more tolerant of their aspirations than the political club, more significant of the best which in heart and life they seek than any other organization or institution which claims to open to them opportunity or ventures to offer them incentives to the better life.

V. That the Church fail not to emphasize its own relation, throughout the centuries and in the life of the world today, to the mighty movements which make for the betterment of social and industrial conditions;

That the attention of workingmen and of the churches alike be called to these facts:

That the institution of a day of rest secured for the toilers of Christendom by the very charter of the Church has been defended on their behalf by it through the centuries;

That the streams of philanthropy which supply a thousand needs have their springs, for the most part, in Christian devotion;

That the fundamental rights of man upon which rest the pillars of this mighty group of commonwealths are a heritage from the conscience and consecration of men who acknowledge Jesus Christ as Master;

That the free ministrations to the community on the part of tens of thousands of churches, attest the purpose of the followers of Christ;

That the Church, while it may not have accepted the task of announcing an industrial program, is at heart eager with the impulses of service and is more than ever ready to express the spirit of its Lord;

That in the quest for the forces by which the large hopes of the workingmen of America may be most speedily and fully realized, the leaders of the industrial world can better afford to lose all others than those which are today and have been for nearly two thousand years at work in the faith, the motive and the devotion of the Church of Jesus Christ.

Your Committee further recommends:

That this Federal Court instruct the Executive Committee to organize under such plan as it may in its discretion find expedient, a Commission on The Church and Social Service, representative of the churches allied in this Council, and of the various industrial interests, said Commission to cooperate with similar church organizations already in operation, to study social conditions and ascertain the essential facts, to act for the Council, under such restrictions as the Executive Committee, to which it shall from time to time report, may determine, and in general, to afford by its action and utterance an expression of the purpose of the Churches of Christ in the United States, to recognize the import of present social movements and industrial conditions, and to cooperate in all practicable ways to promote in the churches the development of the spirit and practice of Social Service and especially to secure a better understanding and a more natural relationship between workingmen and the Church.

We do not forget that the strength of the Church is not in a program but in a spirit. To it is not given the function of the school, of the legislature, of the court, but one deeper and broader, the revelation of the ethical and practical values of a spiritual faith. The Church does not lay the foundations of the social order; it discloses them. They are already laid. Ours is the blame if upon them we have allowed rubbish to gather, or let others build wood, hay, stubble, instead of ourselves lifting to the light the splendor of the gold, silver, precious stones. The Church must witness to the truths which should shape industrial relations, and strive to create the spirit of brotherhood in which alone those truths become operative. It must give itself fearlessly and passionately to the furtherance of all reforms by which it believes that the weak may be protected, the unscrupulous restrained, injustice abolished, equality of opportunity secured and wholesome conditions of life established. Nothing that concerns human life can be alien to the Church of Christ. Its privilege and its task are measured by the sympathy, the love, the sacrifice of its Lord. It is here to represent Jesus Christ. Let it speak out what is in its heart! Once again in the spirit of the Nazarene let it take from the hand of tradition the sacred roll and read so that everywhere the waiting millions may hear:

"The Spirit of the Lord is upon me, because he hath anointed me to preach the Gospel to the poor. He hath sent me to heal the broken-hearted, to preach deliverance to the captive, and recovering of sight to the blind, to set at liberty them that are bruised, to preach the acceptable year of the Lord."

May the Church dare to say to the multitude, "This day is this Scripture fulfilled in your ears."

The United Church Pronouncement on Human Rights

I. Human Rights are the gift and demand of God. They have their source in what God has done and is doing in creation, in Jesus Christ, and through the Holy Spirit. In every age God calls upon people to proclaim the righteousness and justice in the world. God creates, reconciles and redeems everything that is. Thus human rights are universal demands. No person, no group, no society is excused from recognizing the claim that other human beings must be treated justly and that societies must be ordered on the basis of freedom and equity.

When the Church of Jesus Christ has faltered in proclaiming and enacting God's righteousness, other advocates of human rights have stood up throughout the world. They have pointed to a universal moral law to be implemented in all civil orders. Different societies have understood human rights differently and have thus conferred civil rights in different ways. Universal moral law confers human rights that are diversely implemented in the civil orders. Thus, civil rights are subject to legislative acts or political fiat. Human rights, however, are God given and are not alterable by persons, groups or regimes. All persons and all civil orders are under moral obligation to develop policies, programs and politics which recognize basic human rights.

I. HUMAN RIGHTS TODAY

In recent years human rights have become a world-wide concern. The attention stems in large part from increased understanding and recognition of human rights and increased awareness of the widespread violation of human rights. We witness in many locations a growing division between declaration and implementation, recognition and realization, codification and enforcement, rhetoric and establishment of human rights. There is a growing awareness that human rights are decisive not only for the quality of human life but also for the very existence of human life.

We rejoice over what has been accomplished toward creating sound international legal standards since the signing of the Universal Declaration of Human Rights in 1948, but we realize that legal standards alone, however universally declared, are not enough. When we raise the questions of human rights today we are also raising the question of the power to realize them and of the powers that prevent their realization. To be committed to human rights means to be committed to the transformation of those values which shore up inhuman systems and the transformation of those systems which spawn inhuman values.

We further realize that standing up for human rights means becoming actively engaged in the struggle for human rights. We have to be willing to sense human misery in its various forms and to be able to suffer with the suffering of others. We have to refuse arguments which set out to rationalize or justify human misery, especially when these causes stem from our own interests and lifestyles. In this way we announce that we are ready to enter into solidarity with all those who struggle for human rights by working for the liberation of persons.

Today there are at least five dimensions of human life in which we hear the cries of those suffering from violations of human rights.

(1) In many parts of the world people are crying out from political oppression and yearning for the recognition of their right to determine their own future through participation in the decision-making of the community. They are demanding recognition of the right to the integrity of their person which involves the right to life, dissent and freedom from torture. Under the concept of human rights no civil order may deprive persons or groups of their rights to conscience, to speech, and to assembly by employing reasons of "national security," "true religion," or "political expediency."

(2) We hear the cries of those suffering from economic exploitation and pleas for the right of human existence in the face of hunger, unemployment and unjust economic systems. Human beings are demanding the right to the basic necessities of life; food, shelter, clothing, humanly satisfying work with just remuneration, health care and personal ownership of what is necessary to dignity and freedom. Both developed and developing societies are spawning economic values that determine the allocation of scarce resources in favor of the rich. While the right to property is essential to the well-being and the development of the human person, the principle of ownership can never justify accumulation of wealth by the few that produces poverty for the many.

(3) People are crying out from cultural alienation and yearning for the right to maintain and enjoy their cultural identity. Persons suffering from racism, sexism, age-ism and prejudice against the handicapped are demanding their right not to be humiliated by the cultural definition of others. In many societies today the most vulnerable people are prevented from claiming their names, their languages, their histories and their cultural identities by dominating cultural, political or social forms. People are calling out for a chance to contribute to the community and to develop their capacities for creativity. Human beings have a right to educational opportunity and to cultural forms which express their memories and their hopes. They have a right to the freedom to form and maintain families and to create meaningful relationships.

(4) People are crying out together with all creation against the misuses and/or ignorances of technology which are destructive of the relationships between humanity and habitat. The partial realization of our technical utopias has created unimagined possibilities for freeing human beings from disease, hunger and pain, but it has also created horrifying possibilities for the destruction of nature as well as the manipulation, repression and dehumanization of our own bodies. Because human beings are part of nature, a violation of the rights of nature is also a violation of human rights. Human rights entail a protection of natural resources and the environment for the sake of future generations.

(5) People are crying out from despair and lack of meaning in their lives and yearning for the right to be in open relationships with what they consider to be the source of life. Of primary importance in human rights is the freedom of religion. People have the right to the freedom of faith, the right to public worship and the expression of faith in teaching, criticism and practice. It is a human right to participate in communities of faith which are free to influence persons to righteousness and to exercise prophetic witness in society. The freedom to relate to what one believes to be the ultimate source of life should prevent the idolatry of society and self.

All of these dimensions of oppression and human rights are interrelated and interdependent. It is quite possible in specific actions to focus on one or another dimension. Under God's righteousness, however, it is impossible to be concerned about human rights without committing oneself to rights in all of these dimensions. At the same time we concentrate our efforts on specific problems, we must become engaged in relation to the total dimensionality and global context of human rights. There is today no single issue of human rights which is not ultimately global in character.

We acknowledge that there are diverse traditions of human rights which stem from different histories. For example, in the Western industrial nations where the struggle has been to limit the powers of rulers, individual freedom has been given primary stress. In the Eastern socialist countries, on the other hand, where the principal struggle has been against poverty, economic welfare rights have been central. These concepts of human rights are not mutually exclusive but are complementary. Both, however, can be used to exercise dominating political power to repress either individual or social rights. In some countries still dominated by hunger and poverty, the proper emphasis is on the right to existence itself. Because human rights questions are in fact global, the struggle for human rights must take all of the diverse perspectives into serious consideration.

As Christians in the United States we affirm our history of struggle for democratic and civil rights of the individual. We may not give up the gains which have been made in this history or the valid emphasis on the rights of the individual and the community over against the state. Our task is to use this democratic tradition to spread civil and individual rights into the economic, cultural and natural dimensions. We commit ourselves to the best in our tradition.

As Christians we also confess our own failures to achieve a society which fully protects the human rights of all of our citizens. We have been lacking in diligence and commitment to correct the systematic violations of human rights in some of our laws and institutions. We have been deaf to the anguished cries for help by those whose rights are violated because they hold unpopular views, pursue unconventional lifestyles, belong to powerless groups or are deprived of the resources with which to protect themselves. We confess that our lack of passion for human rights has led to economic crises, racial and sexual discrimination, food shortages, waste of resources, pollution of the environment, and inadequate care of and community with the handicapped and the aged. We confess that we have sometimes used the concept of individual rights as a false ideology of individualism to justify the unjust distribution of the necessities of life. Our freedom from the constant struggle for the basic necessities of life has degenerated into a compulsive dependence on exaggerated, destructive patterns of consumption. We have tried to bolster our own economic situation by an unbridled search for markets and raw materials overseas and by massive arms sales and investments in support of regimes which use them to enhance their own privileges and systematically and grossly violate the human rights of their own citizens.

II. BIBLICAL AND THEOLOGICAL FOUNDATIONS OF HUMAN RIGHTS

Human Rights are grounded in God's act of creating, reconciling and redeeming the creation. This act is called God's righteousness and power to make God's creatures alive against the power of death. As creator of everything God has a claim upon everyone and everything in creation. God comes to human beings in the person of Christ to judge, to forgive, to restore, and to justify us, in other words, to make us alive in the power of God's life or to make us righteous in God's sight. Human rights are promises and commands of God to make and keep God's creatures abundantly alive. Thus human rights are not grounded in static reality, in legal contracts, in the integrity of the individual or state, or in the nature of things. Rather they are grounded in God's faithfulness to man. This relationship of God to creation gives all human beings their inalienable human right.

This righteousness which God expresses in creation, reconciliation and redemption is the basis of God's covenant. Human rights are live and realizable in this covenant context. They are alive in actual historical relationships in which God accepts human beings and human beings accept, hope for and love each other. Rights must be not only declared and codified, but also must be cared for, nurtured and embodied in covenant relationships between persons, groups, nations and between human beings and nature.

All human beings have equal human rights by virtue of their being created in the image of God. Because of God's claim upon all God's creatures human rights have to do with the basic answerability or responsibility of being a human creature. To be created in the image of God means to be called to be God's representative to the creation. It means to be called to care for God's whole creation according to God's intention. Therefore the fundamental human right which gives the human being his or her dignity is also an obligation to serve and to help in the creation of the conditions for life in the whole creation. The fundamental human right is the right to be responsible to God. Human rights and human duties are two sides of the same coin. "My rights" is an abstraction and in reality nothing without the "rights of my neighbors," which constitute my duty. In view of God's claim upon God's human creatures, rights are given by God as the means for all human beings to fulfill their duties before God's righteousness.

Thus human rights are what people need in order to fulfill their fundamental task of becoming a human person, that is, fulfilling their calling as the image of God. No person, organization or state has the right to violate the right and dignity of being human in another human being. To do so is a sin against God: it is an attempt to frustrate God's will for the life of God's creation. As a function of God's righteousness human rights shape history. They give structure and form to human relationships that serve the systems of life as opposed to the systems of death. They are guides to and forms of the conditions of life. Where they are disregarded, there will be death.

The conditions of life which God is seeking to create through God's own suffering love are freedom, justice, equality, peace and recognition of God's glory. These are the conditions under which human rights are realized. Human sin, the reality of evil in the world and the power of death are constantly working against God's creation and producing human suffering. Thus our work for human rights is grounded in God's new creation. God the Holy Spirit is making present the liberating power of the messianic mission of Christ and the new creation of God's future. It is out of the righteousness which God is suffering to create in our midst that we struggle and work for the realization of human rights.

In the struggle for human rights there is no way to avoid conflict between groups, especially between the rich and the poor, the powerful and powerless. The message of reconciliation as the Word of the Cross does not remove these conflicts. It does, however, seek to bring into the midst of the conflicts the fundamental promise of the Gospel that the ultimate goal is the reconciled community within the one family of God.

In the midst of the struggles we will affirm that the power of freedom comes through the free grace of God. God's involvement in the midst of the historical struggle is the reality which prevents despair from failures and overwhelming frustrations in attempts at realizing human rights. At the same time the presence of God's grace keeps us from a compulsive slavery to our self-justification through works.

III. CALL TO STUDY AND ACTION

We have affirmed that our concern for human rights arises from God's grace and the call to be faithful participants in the care of creation and the realization of justice. In response we work in partnership with all persons and communities of good will to articulate, advocate and realize the rights of persons, particularly those without their own voice and power.

Responding then to God's call, the Twelfth General Synod commits itself to the struggle for human rights and

1. Calls upon all members of the United Church of Christ to study and reflect upon the biblical and theological basis for our commitment to human rights.

2. Calls further on the members of the United Church of Christ to advance the cause of human rights through the social and political processes available to them in their vocations as citizens at work in the world.

3. Urges that our churches, church-related agencies, associations, conferences and national agencies be sensitive to the human rights of persons within our own church institutions and their spheres of influence and, where there are violations, to seek to remedy them.

4. Calls upon churches, church-related agencies, associations, conferences and national agencies of the United Church to devote personnel and financial resources to denominational and ecumenical human rights programs that will enable the United Church of Christ to:

—seek ratification of the Covenant of Economic, Social and Cultural Rights, the Covenant on Civil and Political Rights and other Human Rights Conventions approved by the United Nations and submitted by the President of the United States to the U.S. Senate for ratification;

—affirm the protection of human life, condemn the needless loss of life, including murder and the judicial death penalty, and encourage the continuing study of the difficult ethical questions in any deliberate termination of life;

—participate in the corporate social responsibility movement to exert pressure on business corporations and government agencies, through a range of shareholder actions and recommendations to public officials, to end U.S. economic complicity in the human rights violations of repressive governments;

—be aware of new developments in the continuing struggle for human rights and to respond appropriately, with special attention given to the rights of future generations in relation to the government;

—participate in ecumenical bodies, coalitions, movements and other organizations which work in behalf of human rights through the world in terms consonant with this Pronouncement;

—bring strategically important aid to victims of human rights violations through its own services agencies and through various ecumenical assistance programs;

—request an agency of the Church to develop a course on human rights for congregations; and

—encourage the closely related seminaries to reflect this pronouncement in their total curricular endeavor.

5. Requests specifically that the United Church Board for Homeland Ministries, the United Church Board for World Ministries, the Commission for Racial Justice and the Office for Church in Society continue to give priority attention to human rights in their mission programming.

6. Commends to the churches, church-related agencies, associations, conferences and national agencies of the United Church of Christ, the study and consideration of the Petition of Human Rights Violations in the United States to the United Nations Commission on Human Rights and Sub-Commission on Prevention of Discrimination and Protection of Minorities, submitted by the Commission for Racial Justice of the UCC and others.

IV. CALL TO THE NATION

In accepting its own responsibility for participation in the struggle for human rights and recognizing the responsibility of the people of our nation to become concerned with these critical dimensions of the human rights efforts, the Twelfth General Synod:

1. Calls upon the people of our nation to press our governmental bodies—municipal, state and federal—to address more vigorously the continuing problems of

social, economic and judicial injustice in our own country, affirming the rights of all people to earn a living, correcting those conditions which prevent full equality of opportunity or deny the reality of equal treatment before the law.

2. Calls upon the people of our nation to insist that our federal government:

a) phase out systematically all existing involvements in the support of foreign governments that objective international investigations have found guilty of gross and systematic violation of the human rights of their own citizens;

b) assume its special responsibility for the defense of human rights in dictatorial countries deemed of strategic importance to our military and economic security;

c) end both military and economic assistance, and especially programs of intelligence and police training, wherever the regimes in power practice torture, arbitrary detention, and the systematic denial of freedom of religion, speech, press, assembly and of petition for the redress of grievances, including the right of workers to organize for collective bargaining and to resort when necessary to work stoppages in their quest for fair compensation and working conditions.

3. Calls upon the people of our nation to pursue the efforts to seek ratification of the multilateral United Nations human rights treaties which have been approved by the United Nations, signed by the President of the United States, and submitted to the U.S. Senate for ratification.

4. Calls upon the people of our nation to urge the President of the United States to sign the United Nations Optional Protocol on Civil and Political Rights (provides procedures for petition by individuals) and submit it to the U.S. Senate for ratification.

The Twelfth General Synod of the United Church of Christ requests the President of the Church to communicate this Pronouncement to the President and the Congress of the United States, the Secretary-General of the United Nations, and the National and World Councils of Churches and their respective member communions.

List of Works Cited

This list is a compilation of all the significant titles cited in this work. Some documents that are peripheral or are hard to obtain are not included here. In addition, certain standard works of which there are numerous editions and/or translations have been omitted—works by John Calvin, Thomas Hobbes, John Locke, Martin Luther, Jean Jacques Rousseau, Alexis de Tocqueville, Machiavelli, Hegel, Kant, Lenin, and Marx.

For current discussions of issues presented in this volume that are not cited in this work, see George R. Lucas, Jr., "Helsinki's Child: A Select Annotated Bibliography of Human Rights Publications Since 1975," *Philosophy Research Archives*, VII (March 1984).

BOOKS AND ESSAYS

Abell, Aaron. *The Urban Impact on American Protestantism, 1865–1900.* Cambridge, Mass.: Harvard University Press, 1943.

Achtemeier, Elizabeth. *The Committed Marriage.* Philadelphia: Westminster Press, 1976.

Adams, A. L., and Seward Hiltner, eds. *Pastoral Care in the Liberal Churches.* Nashville, Tenn.: Abingdon Press, 1970.

Adams, James Luther. *On Being Human Religiously.* Boston: Beacon Press, 1976.

Adjali, Mia, ed. *Of Life and Hope: Toward Effective Witness in Human Rights.* New York: Friendship Press, 1979.

Ahlstrom, S. E. *A Religious History of the American People.* New Haven, Conn.: Yale University Press, 1973.

Altholz, J. L. *The Churches in the Nineteenth Century.* New York: Bobbs-Merrill, 1967.

Althusius. *Politica Methodice Digesta.* Ed. C. J. Friedrich. Cambridge, Mass.: Harvard University Press, 1932.

Bainton, Roland. *Christendom.* Vol. I. New York: Harper & Row, 1966.

———. *The Travail of Religious Liberty.* Philadelphia: Westminster Press, 1961.

Baltzell, E. D. *Puritan Boston and Quaker Philadelphia.* New York: Macmillan, 1979.

Barnes, G. H. *The Anti-Slavery Impulse.* New York: Harcourt, Brace & World, 1933.

Barnet, R. J., and R. E. Muller. *Global Reach: The Power of the Multi-National Corporations.* New York: Simon & Schuster, 1971.

Barnsley, John H. *The Social Reality of Ethics: The Comparative Analysis of Moral Codes.* Boston: Routledge & Kegan Paul, 1972.

Basham, A. L. *The Wonder That Was India.* New York: Grove Press, 1954.

Beeson, T. "German Democratic Republic." In *Discretion and Valour: Religious Conditions in Russia and Eastern Europe.* Glasgow: Wm. Collins Sons, 1974.

Bellah, Robert. *The Broken Covenant.* New York: Seabury Press, 1975.

Bendix, Reinhard. *Kings or People.* Berkeley: University of California Press, 1978.

Berens, J. F. *Providence and Patriotism in Early America, 1640-1815.* Charlottesville, Va.: University Press of Virginia, 1978.

Berger, Peter. *The Heretical Imperative.* Garden City, N.Y.: Doubleday, 1979.

Berger, Peter, and Richard John Neuhaus. *To Empower People.* Washington, D.C.: American Enterprise Institute, 1977.

Billings, Peggy. *Paradox and Promise in Human Rights.* New York: Friendship Press, 1979.

Boehmer, Heinrich. *Martin Luther.* New York: Meridian, 1946.

Brauer, J. C. *The Impact of the Church upon its Culture.* Essays in Divinity Series, Vol. II. Chicago: University of Chicago Press, 1968.

Bultmann, Rudolf. *Primitive Christianity.* New York: Meridian Books, 1956.

Burrage, Champlin. *The Church Covenant Idea.* Philadelphia: American Baptist Society, 1904.

Buultjens, Ralph. "Human Rights in Indian Political Culture." In *The Moral Imperatives of Human Rights: A World Survey.* Ed. K. W. Thompson. Washington, D.C.: University Press of America, 1980, pp. 112–13.

Callihan, Daniel. *Abortion.* New York: Macmillan, 1970.

Carman, John. "Report from South India." In *The Religious Situation.* Ed. D. Cutler. Boston: Beacon Press, 1969, pp. 395ff.

Carstairs, G. M. *The Twice-Born.* London: Hogarth, 1957.

Clarke, J. H., et al., eds. *Black Titan.* Boston: Beacon Press, 1970.

Cochrane, C. M. *Christianity and Classical Culture.* New York: Oxford University Press, 1944.

Cohn, Norman. *The Pursuit of the Millennium: Revolutionary Messianism in Medieval and Reformation Europe and Its Bearing on Modern Totalitarian Movements.* New York: Harper & Row, 1961.

Cole, S. G. *A History of Fundamentalism.* New York: Harper & Row, 1931.

Cox, Harvey. *The Secular City.* New York: Macmillan, 1965.

Cross, Robert. *The Church and the City: 1865–1910.* Indianapolis: Bobbs-Merrill, 1967.

Daniélou, Alain. *Hindu Polytheism.* New York: Pantheon Books, 1964.

Dasgupta, Subhayu. *The Hindu Ethos and the Challenge of Change.* Calcutta: Minerva Associates, 1972.

Davis, John P. *Corporations.* New York: Revell, 1908.

Dawson, Christopher. *The Gods of Revolution.* New York: Minerva Press, 1975.

de Bary, William T., et al., eds. *Sources of Indian Tradition.* New York: Columbia University Press, 1958.

de Coulanges, Fustel. *The Ancient City.* Garden City, N.Y.: Doubleday, n.d.

Degler, C. N. *At Odds.* New York: Oxford University Press, 1980.

————. *Out of Our Past.* New York: Harper & Row, 1959.

DeJong, Peter. *The Covenant Idea in New England Theology.* Grand Rapids, Mich.: Eerdmans, 1945.

Devanandan, P. D., and M. M. Thomas, eds. *The Changing Pattern of Family in India.* Rev. ed. Bangalore: CISRS, 1966.

Dibble, V. K. *The Legacy of Albion Small.* Chicago: University of Chicago Press, 1975.

Dickens, A. G. *Martin Luther and the Reformation.* New York: Harper & Row, 1967.

Dombrowski, James. *The Early Days of Christian Socialism in America.* New York: Octagon, 1936.

Douglas, Ann. *The Feminization of America.* New York: Knopf, 1978.

Dube, S. C. *Indian Village.* Bombay: Allied Publishers, 1967.

Du Bois, A. J. *Hindu Manners, Customs and Ceremonies.* Ed. H. K. Beauchamp. 3rd ed. New York: Oxford University Press, 1905.

Dumont, Louis. *Homo Hierarchicus.* Chicago: University of Chicago Press, 1970.

Dworkin, Ronald. *Taking Rights Seriously.* Cambridge, Mass.: Harvard University Press, 1977.

Eisenstadt, S. N., ed. *The Protestant Ethic and Modernization.* New York: Basic Books, 1968.

Ellul, Jacques. *The Meaning of the City.* Grand Rapids, Mich.: Eerdmans, 1970.

Erikson, Erik. *Gandhi's Truth.* New York: Norton, 1969.

Fagen, P. W. "Bibliography on Human Rights..." Washington, D.C.: Library of Congress, 1980.

Figgis, J. N. *Studies of Political Thought from Gerson to Grotius, 1414–1625.* 1907; rpt. New York: Harper & Row, 1960.

Filer, J. H., et al. *Giving in America: Report of the Commission on Private Philanthropy and Public Needs.* Washington, D.C.: n.p., 1975.

Fisch, Harold. *Hamlet and the Word: Covenant Pattern in Shakespeare.* New York: Ungar, 1971.

Forell, George, and William H. Lazare. *Human Rights: Rhetoric or Reality.* Philadelphia: Fortress Press, 1978.

Frazier, E. F. *The Negro Church in America.* New York: Schocken, 1967.

Friedenberg, E. Z. *Coming of Age in America.* New York: Vintage, 1965.

Fürea-Haimendorf, C. von. "Caste and Politics in South Asia." In *Politics and Society in India.* Ed. C. H. Phillips. London: Allen & Unwin, 1963.

Gandhi, Mahatma. *Hind Swaraj: Collected Works of Mahatma Gandhi.* Vol. III. Delhi: Government of India, 1963.

Geertz, Clifford. *The Interpretation of Cultures.* New York: Basic Books, 1973.

Ghose, Sankar. *Socialism, Democracy and Nationalism in India.* Bombay: Allied Publishers, 1973.

Gibb, H. A. R. *Mohammedanism.* New York: New American Library, 1955.

Gossett, T. F. *Race: The History of an Idea in America.* New York: Schocken, 1965.

Gough, J. W. *The Social Contract.* 2nd ed. New York: Oxford University Press, 1957.

Greaves, Richard. *The Puritan Revolution and Educational Thought.* New Brunswick, N.J.: Rutgers University Press, 1969.

Green, Robert, ed. *The Protestant Ethic Thesis.* New York: Heath, 1960.

Green, Ronald. *Religious Reason.* New York: Oxford University Press, 1978.

Greene, Jack P., and W. G. McLoughlin. *Preachers and Politicians.* Worcester, Mass.: American Antiquarian Society, 1977.

Guillaume, Alfred. *Islam.* Baltimore: Penguin, 1954.

Hall, R. E., ed. *Abortion in a Changing World.* New York: Columbia University Press, 1970.

Hall, T. C. *The Religious Background of American Culture.* Boston: Little, Brown, 1930.

Haller, William. *The Rise of Puritanism.* New York: Columbia University Press, 1938.

Handlin, Oscar. *The Uprooted.* New York: Grosset & Dunlap, 1951.

Handy, Robert. *A Christian America.* New York: Oxford University Press, 1971.

Hansen, Marcus L. *The Immigrant in American History.* New York: Harper & Row, 1940.

Harrelson, Walter. *The Ten Commandments and Human Rights*. Philadelphia: Fortress Press, 1979.

Hauerwas, Stanley. *Vision and Virtue*. Notre Dame, Ind.: Fides Press, 1974.

Heilbroner, Robert. *The Worldly Philosophers*. 5th ed. New York: Touchstone Press, 1980.

Hennelly, Alfred, and John Langan, eds. *Human Rights in the Americas*. Washington, D.C.: Georgetown University Press, 1982.

Hertz, K. H. *Two Kingdoms and One World*. Minneapolis: Augsburg, 1976.

Hill, Christopher. *The Century of Revolution: 1603–1714*. Edinburgh: Nelson & Sons, 1961.

————. *Puritanism and Revolution*. London: Oxford, 1959.

Hindery, Roderick. *Comparative Ethics in Hindu and Buddhist Traditions*. Delhi: Motilal Banarsidass, 1978.

Hinrichs, C. *Preussentum und Pietismus*. Göttingen: Vandenhoeck und Ruprecht, 1971.

Hofstadter, Richard. *The Age of Reform*. New York: Knopf, 1956.

————. *The American Political Tradition*. New York: Knopf, 1948.

Hollenbach, David. *Claims in Conflict*. New York: Paulist Press, 1979.

Hopkins, C. H. *The Rise of the Social Gospel in America*. New Haven, Conn.: Yale University Press, 1940.

Hsu, F. L. K. *Caste, Club, and Clan*. Princeton, N.J.: Van Nostrand, 1963.

Huar, U. *Mensch und Politik in Geschichte und Gegenwart*. Berlin: UEB Deutscher Verlag, 1978.

Huizinga, Johan. *Homo Ludens*. London: Granada, 1949.

Hunter, Robert. *Poverty*. 1904; rpt. New York: Harper & Row, 1965.

Indian Social Institute: *The Indian Family*. New Delhi: Sterling Publishers, 1972.

Jacoby, Russell. *Social Amnesia*. Boston: Beacon Press, 1975.

Jellinek, Georg. *The Declaration of the Rights of Man and of Citizens*. Repr. ed. Westport, Conn.: Hyperion Press, 1979.

————. *Die Erklärung der Menschen und Bergerrechte*. 2nd ed. Leipzig: Dunsker und Humbolt, 1904.

Johnson, James T. *A Society Ordered by God*. Nashville, Tenn.: Abingdon Press, 1970.

Jung, C. G. "The Psychology of Eastern Mysticism." In Vol. 2 of *The Collected Works of C. G. Jung*. Ed. G. Adler et al. Trans. R. F. Hull. Princeton, N.J.: Princeton University Press, 1972.

Kamath, M. V. *The United States and India: 1776–1976*. Washington, D.C.: The Embassy of India, 1976.

Kamenka, Eugene. "Marxian Humanism." In *Socialist Humanism*. Ed. E. Fromm. Garden City, N.Y.: Doubleday, 1965, pp. 106ff.

————. *Marxism and Ethics*. London: Macmillan, 1969.

Kendall, R. T. *Calvin and English Calvinism to 1649*. London: Oxford University Press, 1980.

Kern, Fritz. *Kingship, Law and Constitution in the Middle Ages*. New York: Harper & Row, 1956.

Khare, R. S. *The Changing Brahmans*. Chicago: University of Chicago Press, 1970.

Klenner, H. *Studien über die Grundrechte*. Berlin: Staatsverlag, 1964.

Koch, H. W. *A History of Prussia*. London: Longman, 1978.

Koops, Hugh A. "Pressing the Claims, Interpreting the Cries." In *A Christian Declaration on Human Rights*. Ed. A. O. Miller. Grand Rapids, Mich.: Eerdmans, 1977.

Kopf, David. *British Orientalism and the Bengal Renaissance: The Dynamics of Indian Modernization*. Berkeley: University of California Press, 1969.

Kraditor, A. S. *The Ideas of the Women's Suffrage Movement.* New York: Columbus University Press, 1965.

Kuhrig, Herta, ed. *Familie in Geschichte und Gegenwart.* Berlin: Dietz Verlag, 1978.

Kuppuswamy, B. *Social Change in India.* Delhi: Vikas, 1972.

Kurien, C. T. *Poverty and Development.* CISRS Social Concerns Series, No. 17. Madras: CISRS, 1974.

Kuyper, Abraham. *Lectures on Calvinism.* Grand Rapids, Mich.: Eerdmans, 1931.

Lakoff, S. A. *Equality in Political Philosophy.* Boston: Beacon Press, 1964.

Latourette, K. S. *History of the Expansion of Christianity.* 7 vols. New York: Harper & Row, 1937–1945.

Levine, Andrew. *The Politics of Autonomy: A Kantian Reading of Rousseau's "Social Contract."* Amhurst, Mass.: University of Massachusetts Press, 1976.

Levitt, Theodore. *The Third Sector.* New York: Amacom, 1973.

Lewy, Guenter. *Religion and Revolution.* New York: Oxford University Press, 1974.

Ling, Trevor. *Karl Marx and Religion in Europe and India.* New York: Harper & Row, 1980.

Littell, F. *The German Phoenix.* Garden City, N.Y.: Doubleday, 1960.

Little, David. *Religious Conflict, Law and Order.* New York: Harper & Row, 1969.

Little, David, and Sumner B. Twiss. *Comparative Religious Ethics.* San Francisco: Harper & Row, 1978.

Loubser, Jan J. "Calvinism, Equality, and Inclusion: The Case of Afrikaner Calvinism." In *The Protestant Ethic and Modernization.* Ed. S. N. Eisenstadt. New York: Basic Books, 1968.

Lovejoy, Arthur. *The Great Chain of Being.* New York: Harper & Row, 1936.

Ludz, P. C. *The Changing Party Elite in East Germany.* Cambridge, Mass.: MIT Press, 1971.

McClelland, D. C. *The Achieving Society.* Princeton, N.J.: Van Nostrand, 1961.

McConica, James K. *English Humanists and Reformation Politics.* London: Oxford University Press, 1965.

McKelvey, Blake. *The Urbanization of America.* New Brunswick, N.J.: Rutgers University Press, 1963.

McLellan, David. *Karl Marx: His Life and Thought.* New York: Harper & Row, 1973.

McLoughlin, William G., ed. *The American Evangelicals.* New York: Harper & Row, 1968.

McNeill, John T. *The History and Character of Calvinism.* London: Oxford University Press, 1954.

————. *Modern Christian Movements.* Philadelphia: Westminster Press, 1954.

Macpherson, C. B. *The Political Theory of Possessive Individualism.* London: Oxford University Press, 1962.

Maddison, Angus. *Class Structure and Economic Growth: India and Pakistan Since the Moghuls.* London: Allen & Unwin, 1971.

Maitland, J. W. Intro. in *Political Theories of the Middle Ages* by Otto Gierke. Boston: Beacon Press, 1959.

Mandelbaum, D. G. *Change and Continuity.* Vol. II of *Society in India.* Berkeley: University of California Press, 1970.

Maritain, Jacques. *Man and the State.* Chicago: University of Chicago Press, 1951.

Marty, Martin. *Righteous Empire.* New York: Dial Press, 1970.

May, Henry F. *Protestant Churches and Industrial America.* New York: Harper & Row, 1949.

Mayer, A. C. *Caste and Kinship in Central India.* Berkeley: University of California Press, 1960.

Mayer, Hans E. *The Crusades.* London: Oxford University Press, 1972.

Mead, Sidney. *The Nation with the Soul of a Church.* New York: Harper & Row, 1975.

Meier, August. *Negro Thought in America.* Ann Arbor, Mich.: University of Michigan Press, 1963.

Merrill, F. E., and H. W. Eldredge. *Culture and Society.* Englewood Cliffs, N. J.: Prentice-Hall, 1952.

Merton, Robert. "Puritanism, Pietism and Science." In *Social Theory and Social Structure.* London: Collier, 1959, pp. 574ff.

Meyer, Donald. *The Positive Thinkers.* Garden City, N.Y.: Doubleday, 1965.

Michas, J., and G. Udke, eds. *Socialistisches Recht.* Berlin: Verlag die Wirtschaft, 1980.

Miller, Allen O., ed. *A Christian Declaration on Human Rights.* Grand Rapids, Mich.: Eerdmans, 1977.

Miller, P. "Revival." In *The Shaping of American Religion.* Ed. J. W. Smith and A. L. Jamison. Princeton, N. J.: Princeton University Press, 1961.

Miller, Perry. *The New England Mind: The 17th Century.* Boston: Beacon Press, 1961.

Miller, R. M. *American Protestantism and Social Issues.* Chapel Hill, N.C.: University of North Carolina Press, 1958.

Mollnau, Schoneburg, et al. *Macht und Recht: Enheit oder Gegensatz.* Berlin: Staatsverlag, 1976.

Moodie, T. Dunbar. *The Rise of Afrikanerdom.* Berkeley: University of California Press, 1975.

Morgan, Edmund S., ed. *The Puritan Family.* New York: Harper & Row, 1944.

————. *Puritan Political Ideas.* New York: Bobbs-Merrill, 1965.

Morgan, K. W. *Islam—The Straight Path.* New York: Ronald Press, 1968.

Morris, Colin. *The Discovery of the Individual, 1050–1200.* London: S.P.C.K., 1972.

Müeller, Alois, and Norbert Greimacher. *The Church and the Rights of Man: Concilium,* 124. New York: Seabury Press, 1979.

Müntzer, Thomas. "Sermon Before the Princess." In *Spiritual and Anabaptist Writers.* Ed. G. H. Williams. Philadelphia: Westminster Press, n.d., pp. 47ff.

Murdock, G. P., et al. *Outline of Cultural Materials.* New Haven, Conn.: Human Relations Area Files, Inc., 1942.

Myrdal, Gunnar. *An American Dilemma.* 2 vols. New York: Harper & Row, 1944.

————. *Asian Drama.* 3 vols. New York: Random House, 1968.

————. *The Challenge of World Poverty.* New York: Pantheon Books, 1970.

Naipaul, V. S. *India: A Wounded Civilization.* New York: Knopf, 1977.

Nehru, Jawaharlal. *An Autobiography.* London: John Lane, 1937.

Neill, Stephen. *The Story of the Christian Church in India and Pakistan.* Madras: C.L.S., 1972.

Nelson, B. "Max Weber." In *Beyond the Classics.* Ed. Glock, Hammond, et al. New York: Harper & Row, 1973.

Nelson, Benjamin. *The Idea of Usury: From Tribal Brotherhood to Universal Otherhood.* 2nd ed. Chicago: Chicago University Press, 1969.

Nichols, James Hastings. *Democracy and the Churches.* Philadelphia: Westminster Press, 1951.

Niebuhr, H. R. *The Kingdom of God in America.* New York: Harper & Row, 1937.

————. *The Social Sources of Denominationalism.* New York: Harper & Row, 1929.

Niebuhr, Reinhold. *Moral Man and Immoral Society.* New York: Scribner's, 1932.

————. *The Nature and Destiny of Man.* 2 vols. New York: Scribner's, 1939 and 1941.

Noonan, John T. *Contraception.* Cambridge, Mass.: Harvard University Press, 1965.

Organ, T. W. *The Hindu Quest for the Perfection of Man.* Athens, Ohio: Ohio University Press, 1970.

Ostrom, K. A., and D. W. Shriver, Jr. *Is There Hope for the City?* Philadelphia: Westminster Press, 1977.

Panikkar, K. M. *A Survey of Indian History.* 4th ed. Bombay: Asia Publishing House, 1971.

Parker, T. H. L. *John Calvin: A Biography.* Philadelphia: Westminster Press, 1975.

Parrinder, G. "Hinduism." In *Sex in the World's Religions.* London: Sheldon Press, 1980.

Paul, Robert. *The Lord Protector.* London: Oxford, 1955.

Perry, Ralph B. *Puritanism and Democracy.* New York: Vanguard Press, 1944.

Pope, Harrison, Jr. *The Road East.* Boston: Beacon Press, 1974

Poppe, E. *Menschenrechte—eine Klassefrage.* Berlin: Staatsverlag, 1971.

Powers, Edward, ed. *Christian Society and the Crusades.* Philadelphia: University of Pennsylvania Press, 1971.

Quinney, Richard. *Providence.* New York: Longman, 1980.

Raju, V. E., ed. *Religion and Politics in Medieval South India.* Hyderabad: Institute of Asian Studies, 1972.

Ramsey, Paul. *Nine Modern Moralists.* New York: Spectrum, 1962.

Rao, M. S. A. *Urbanization and Social Change.* New Delhi: Orient Longmans, 1970.

Rao, P. M. *Contemporary Indian Philosophy.* Bombay: Bharatiya Vidya Bhavan, 1970.

Rauschenbusch, Walter. *Christianizing the Social Order.* New York: Macmillan, 1912.

————. *A Theology for the Social Gospel.* 1917; rpt. Nashville, Tenn.: Abingdon Press, 1978.

Reeves, Marjorie. *Joachim of Fiore and the Prophetic Future.* New York: Harper & Row, 1976.

Richardson, Herbert, comp. *Deprogramming.* Toronto: Toronto School of Theology, 1977.

Riepe, Dale. *The Naturalistic Tradition in Indian Thought.* Seattle: University of Washington Press, 1961.

Robertson, A. H. *Human Rights in Europe.* Manchester, G.B.: Manchester University Press, 1977.

Robertson, D. B., ed. *Voluntary Association.* Richmond, Va.: John Knox Press, 1966.

Rosenstock-Huessy, Eugen. *Out of Revolution.* New York: Morrow, 1938.

Rudolph, L. I., and S. H. Rudolph. *The Modernity of Tradition.* Chicago: Chicago University Press, 1967.

Salisbury, John. *The Letters of John Salisbury.* Vol. II. London: Oxford University Press, 1979.

Saltmarsh, John. "Smoke in the Temple." In *Puritanism and Liberty.* Ed. A. S. P. Woodhouse. London: J. M. Dent, 1938.

Sandford, John. *The Sword and the Ploughshare: Autonomous Peace Initiatives in East Germany.* London: Merlin Press, 1983.

Savelle, Max. *Seeds of Liberty: The Genesis of the American Mind.* Seattle, Wash.: University of Washington Press, 1965.

Schmandt, H. J., and Warner Bloomberg, Jr., eds. *The Quality of Urban Life.* Beverly Hills, Calif.: Sage, 1969.

Schneider, Eberhard. *The G.D.R.: History, Economy and Society of East Germany.* New York: St. Martin's Press, 1978.

Schumacher, E. F. *Small Is Beautiful.* New York: Harper & Row, 1973.

Segal, Charles, and David Stineback. *Puritans, Indians, and Manifest Destiny.* New York: Capricorn Books, 1978.

Shah, A. B., and C. R. M. Rao, eds. *Tradition and Modernity in India.* Bombay: Manaktalas, 1965.

Sharpe, E. J. *Comparative Religion: A History.* New York: Scribner's, 1975.

Shinn, Roger, ed. *Faith and Science in an Unjust World.* Vol. I. Geneva: World Council of Churches, 1980.

Shirer, William. *Gandhi: A Memoir.* New York: Simon & Schuster, 1979.

Sider, Ron. *The Chicago Declaration.* Carol Stream, Ill.: Creation House, 1974.

Singer, Milton. *When a Great Tradition Modernizes.* Delhi: Vikas, 1972.

Smith, Donald E. *South Asian Politics and Religion.* Princeton, N.J.: Princeton University Press, 1966.

Smith, J. W., and A. L. Jamison, eds. *The Shaping of American Religion.* Princeton, N.J.: Princeton University Press, 1961.

Smith, Timothy L. *Revivalism and Social Reform.* New York: Harper & Row, 1957.

Smith, W. C. *Islam in Modern History.* Princeton, N.J.: Princeton University Press, 1957.

————. *Modern Islam in India.* Lahore: Minerva Books, 1947.

————. *The Modernization of a Traditional Society.* Bombay: Asia Publishing House, 1965.

Solberg, Richard. *God and Caesar in East Germany: The Conflicts of Church and State in East Germany Since 1945.* New York: Macmillan, 1961.

Somerville, Robert, and Kenneth Pennington, eds. *Law, Church, and Society.* Philadelphia: University of Pennsylvania Press, 1979.

Spiro, M. E. *Buddhism and Society.* New York: Harper & Row, 1970.

Spratt, P. *Hindu Culture and Personality.* Bombay: Manaktalas, 1966.

Srinivas, M. N. *Caste in Modern India.* Bombay: Asia Publishing House, 1962.

————. *Religion and Society Among the Coorgs of South India.* London: Oxford University Press, 1952.

————. *Social Change in Modern India.* Bombay: Orient Longmans, 1972, Indian edition.

Stackhouse, Max L. "Christianity and the New Exodus in Eastern Europe." In *The Religious Situation.* Ed. D. Cutler. Boston: Beacon Press, 1978, pp. 887ff.

————. *Ethics and the Urban Ethos.* Boston: Beacon Press, 1973.

————. *The Ethics of Necropolis.* Boston: Beacon Press, 1971.

————. Intro. in *The Righteousness of the Kingdom* by Walter Rauschenbusch. Nashville, Tenn.: Abingdon, 1968.

————, ed. *On Being Human Religiously.* Boston: Beacon Press, 1976.

————. "Social Ethics East and West." In *Man in Indian Society.* Madras: C.L.S., 1978.

————. "Social Ethics: Some Basic Elements East and West." In *A Vision for Man.* Ed. S. Amirtham. Madras: CSI Press, 1978, pp. 326–38.

Stammer, Otto, ed. *Max Weber and Sociology Today.* Trans. Kathleen Morris. New York: Harper & Row, 1971.

Steele, Jonathan. *Inside East Germany.* New York: Urizen Books, 1977.

Stevenson, S. *The Rites of the Twice-Born.* London: Oxford University Press, 1920.

Stoeffler, F. E. *The Rise of Evangelical Pietism.* Leiden: E. J. Brill, 1965.

Stone, Ronald. *Realism and Hope.* Washington, D.C.: University Press of America, 1977.

Strauss, Leo. *Natural Rights and History.* Chicago: University of Chicago Press, 1953.

Strauss, Leo, and Joseph Cropsey, eds. *History of Political Philosophy.* 2nd ed. Chicago: Rand McNally, 1972.

Stuber, Stanley. *Human Rights and Fundamental Freedoms in Your Community.* New York: Association Press, 1968.

Sutton, F. X., et al. *The American Business Creed.* New York: Schocken, 1962.

Szabo, Imre. *The Socialist Concept of Rights.* Budapest: Akademiai Kiado, 1966.

Tawney, R. H. *Religion and the Rise of Capitalism.* New York: Harcourt, Brace & Co., 1926.

LIST OF WORKS CITED

Taylor, J. F. A. *The Masks of Society: An Inquiry into the Covenants of Civilization.* New York: Appleton-Century-Crofts, 1966.

Thälmann, E. *Handbuch zur Jugendweihe.* Berlin: Volkseigener Verlag, 1974.

Tillich, Paul. *The End of the Protestant Era.* Chicago: University of Chicago Press, 1948.

Tiruvalluvar. *Tiruvacagam.* Trans. G. U. Pope. Oxford: Clarendon Press, 1960.

Troeltsch, Ernst. *The Social Teachings of the Christian Churches.* Trans. O. Wyon. New York: Harper & Row, 1931.

Tucker, Robert. *Philosophy and Myth in Karl Marx.* New York: Cambridge University Press, 1961.

Ullman, Walter. *A Short History of the Papacy in the Middle Ages.* London: Methuen, 1972.

Ullman, Wolfgang. "Das Geschichtsverständnis Thomas Müntzer." In *Thomas Müntzer.* Berlin: Evangelische Verlagsanstalt, 1977.

Unterkoefler, E. L., A. Harsanyi, et al. *Ethics and the Search for Christian Unity.* Washington, D.C.: U. S. Catholic Conference Publications Office, 1980.

Van der Vyer, J. D. *Seven Lectures on Human Rights.* Capetown: Juta & Co., 1976.

Van Leeuwen, Arend. *Prophecy in a Technocratic Era.* New York: Scribner's, 1968.

Venkataraman, S. *A Treatise on Hindu Law.* Madras: Orient Longmans, 1972.

Von Gierke, Otto. *Natural Law.* Boston: Beacon Press, 1967.

Walker, Mack. *German Home Towns.* Ithaca, N.Y.: Cornell University Press, 1971.

Walker, Williston. *Creeds and Platforms of Congregationalism.* Boston: Pilgrim Press, 1960.

Walzer, Michael. *The Revolution of the Saints.* New York: Atheneum, 1968.

Ward, Dudley A. *The Social Creed.* Nashville, Tenn.: Abingdon, 1961.

Washington, Joseph R. *Black Religion: The Negro and Christianity in the United States.* Boston: Beacon Press, 1964.

Watt, W. M. *The Influence of Islam on Medieval Europe.* Edinburgh: Edinburgh University Press, 1972.

_____. *Islam and the Integration of Society.* London: Routledge, 1961.

Weber, Max. "The City." In *Economy and Society.* Vol. III. Ed. G. Roth and C. Wittich. Trans. E. Fischoff et al. New York: Bedminster Press, 1968.

_____. *Economy and Society.* Vols. II, III. Ed. G. Roth and C. Wittich. Trans. E. Fischoff et al. New York: Bedminster Press, 1968.

_____. *The Protestant Ethic and the Spirit of Capitalism.* Trans. T. Parsons. New York: Harper & Row, 1958.

_____. *The Religion of India.* Trans. and ed. Hans Gerth and Don Martindale. Glencoe, Ill.: Free Press, 1958.

Weiner, Myron. *Modernization.* New York: Basic Books, 1966.

Weingärtner, E. *Human Rights on the Ecumenical Agenda.* Geneva: World Council of Churches, 1983.

Weinlick, J. R. *Count Zinzendorf.* Nashville, Tenn.: Abingdon, 1956.

Weinstein, James. *The Decline of Socialism in America, 1912–1925.* New York: Monthly Review Press, 1967.

Wielenga, Bastiaan. *Lenins Weg zur Revolution.* München: Kaiser Verlag, 1971.

_____. *Marxist Views on India.* Madras: C.L.S., 1976.

Wilkinson, T. W., and M. M. Thomas. *Ambedkar and the Neo-Buddhist Movement.* Madras: C.L.S., 1972.

Williams, G. H. *The Radical Reformation.* Philadelphia: Westminster Press, 1962.

Wilson, C. "Economic Conditions." In *Material Progress and World-Wide Problems.* Vol. XI of the *New Cambridge Modern History.* Ed. F. H. Hinsley. New York: Cambridge University Press, 1962, pp. 49ff.

Wilson, Edward O. *On Human Nature.* Cambridge, Mass.: Harvard University Press, 1978.

Wilson, John. *Religion in American Society.* Englewood Cliffs, N. J.: Prentice-Hall, 1978.

Winter, Gibson. *Love and Conflict.* Garden City, N.Y.: Doubleday, 1958.

————. *The New Creation as Metropolis.* New York: Macmillan, 1963.

Wiser, William and Charlotte. *Behind Mud Walls.* Rev. ed. Berkeley: University of California Press, 1970.

Wogaman, Philip. *The Great Economic Debate.* Philadelphia: Westminster Press, 1977.

Wolin, Sheldon. *Politics and Vision.* Boston: Little, Brown, 1960.

Woodhouse, A. S. P., ed. *Puritanism and Liberty.* London: J. M. Dent, 1938.

Woodson, C. G. *The History of the Negro Church.* Washington, D.C.: Associated Publishers, 1921.

ARTICLES

Allen, Joseph L. "A Theological Approach to Moral Rights." *Journal of Religious Ethics,* 2 (1974), 119ff.

Bancroft, N. "Does Marx Have an Ethical Theory?" *Soundings,* 62 (Summer 1980), 214ff.

Bathrich, D. "The Dialectics of Legitimation: Brecht in the G.D.R." *New German Critique,* 1 (Spring 1974), 90ff.

Baum, G. "Catholic Foundation of Human Rights." *The Ecumenist,* 18 (Nov.-Dec. 1979), 6ff.

Bellah, Robert. "American Civil Religion in the 1970s." *Anglican Theological Review,* Supplementary Series, No. 1 (July 1978).

————. "Civil Religion in America." *Daedalus* (Winter 1967).

Berman, Harold J. "What the Soviets Mean by Human Rights." *Worldview,* 22 (Nov. 1979), 15ff.

"Bibliography on Human Rights." New York: I.D.O.C., 1977.

The Committee on Church and Society and Secretariate of the V.E.L.K. in the G.D.R. "The Theological Relevance of Human Rights." Trans. J. Lissner and A. Sovik. *LWF Report,* 1 (Sept. 1978), 29–30.

Cort, John. "Can Socialism Be Distinguished from Marxism?" *Cross Currents* (Winter 1979–80), pp. 423ff.

Darnton, R. "What's New About the Old Regime." *New York Review of Books,* Apr. 3, 1980.

Das, S. "Contemporary Indian Understanding of Dharma." Diss. Boston University 1979.

Dawson, Christopher. "Religious Origins of European Disunity." *Dublin Review,* Oct. 1940, pp. 157ff.

Deats, Richard L. "Human Rights: An Historical and Theological Perspective." *Engage/ Social Action Forum,* No. 38 (March 1978), pp. 10–11.

Desai, I. P., ed. "Symposium on Caste and the Joint Family." *Sociological Bulletin,* 4 (Sept. 1955).

Eisler, Hans. "Letter to a Musician—and Others." *New German Critique,* 1 (Spring 1974), 63ff.

Elder, Joseph. "Industrialism in Hindu Society." Diss. Harvard 1959.

"European Responses to Human Rights." New York: I.D.O.C., 1978.

Fagen, P. W. "Bibliography on Human Rights . . ." Washington, D.C.: Library of Congress, 1980.

Gould, A., T. M. Madan, et al. *Contributions to Indian Sociology,* New Series, No. 5 (Dec. 1971).

Hertel, Bradley. "The 'Congregation' in Indian Religious Life." Paper delivered at the annual meeting of the American Academy of Religion, 1975.

Hollenbach, David. "Public Theology in America." *Theological Studies,* 37 (June 1976), 290–303.

Ikonitskii, V. "The Crisis of Bourgeois Democracy and Violations of Human Rights in the Capitalist World." *Soviet Studies in Philosophy,* 16 (Winter 1978–79), 69–77.

Interreligious Task Force on U. S. Food Policy. "Identifying a Food Policy Agenda for the 1980s." *Impact,* 1979.

Leites, Edmund. "Conscience, Leisure and Learning: Locke and the Levellers." *Sociological Analysis,* 39 (Spring 1978), 36ff.

————. "The Duty to Desire: Love, Friendship, and Sexuality in Some Puritan Theories of Marriage." *Comparative Civilizations Review,* No. 3 (Fall 1979), pp. 40ff.

Lissner, J., and A. Sovik. "A Lutheran Reader on Human Rights." *LWF Report,* 1 (Sept. 1978).

Lovin, Robin. "Natural Law and Popular Sovereignty." Paper delivered at the meeting of the American Society of Christian Ethics, 1979.

McNeill, J. T. "Natural Law in the Teaching of the Reformers." *Journal of Religion,* 26 (July 1946), 171–72.

"The Most Significant Minority." Washington, D.C.: Institute for the Development of Educational Activities, Charles Kettering Foundation, 1980.

Sellers, James. "Human Rights and the American Tradition of Justice." *Soundings,* 62 (Fall 1979), 226ff.

Shriver, P. "Theological and Other Rationales for Human Rights." National Council of Churches Background Paper, 1978.

Singh, K. "Godmen of India." Special Holi Issue of *The Illustrated Weekly,* Mar. 18, 1973.

Stackhouse, Max L. "Democracy and the World's Religions." *This World* (1982), pp. 108–20. Revised and expanded version in *Religion and Society* (Bangalore), XXIX (Dec. 1982), 19–49.

————. "Ethics: Social and Christian." *Andover Newton Quarterly,* 13 (Jan. 1973), 182–86.

————. "Gesellschaftstheorie und Sozialethik." *Zeitschrift für evangelische Ethik,* 32/4 (Oct. 1978), 275–95.

————. The Hindu Ethic and the Ethos of Development." *Religion and Society,* 20 (Dec. 1973), 5–33.

————. "The Location of the Holy." *Journal of Religious Ethics,* 4 (Spring 1976), 63–104.

————. "Reaffirmations." *Journal of Ecumenical Studies,* 15 (Fall 1978), 662ff.

————. "Technology and the 'Supra-natural.'" *Zygon,* 10 (March 1975), 59–85.

311

————— . "Theology, the Church and Human Rights." *Bangalore Theological Forum,* XIV (Sept.-Dec. 1982), 191–210.

————— . "Toward a Theology of Stewardship." *Andover Newton Quarterly,* 14 (March 1974), 245–66.

Stephan, A. "Johannes R. Becker and the Cultural Development of the G.D.R." *New German Critique,* 1 (Spring 1974), 72ff.

Sturm, D. "Corporations, Constitutions and Covenants." *Jounal of the American Academy of Religion,* 61 (Sept. 1973), 331ff.

Trickett, D. G. "Karl Marx and Ethical Theory." A.S.C.E., Jan. 1979.

Troeltsch, Ernst. "Stoic-Christian Natural Law and the Modern-Secular Natural Law." In *Gesammelte Schriften,* II, 515ff. Forthcoming.

Yost, John K. "The Traditional Western Concept of Marriage and the Family." *Andover Newton Quarterly,* 20 (March 1980), 169ff.

Index